DATE DUE

JAN 0 8 2015			

CONSTRUCTIVISM IN EDUCATION

Opinions and Second Opinions
on Controversial Issues

CONSTRUCTIVISM IN EDUCATION
Opinions and Second Opinions
on Controversial Issues

Ninety-ninth Yearbook of the
National Society for the Study of Education

PART I

Edited by
D. C. PHILLIPS

Editor for the Society
MARGARET EARLY

20 NSSE 00

Distributed by THE UNIVERSITY OF CHICAGO PRESS • CHICAGO, ILLINOIS

The National Society for the Study of Education

The National Society for the Study of Education was founded in 1901 as successor to the National Herbart Society. It publishes a two-volume Yearbook, each volume dealing with a separate topic of concern to educators. The Society's series of Yearbooks, now in its ninety-ninth year, contains chapters written by scholars and practitioners noted for their significant work on the topics about which they write.

The Society welcomes as members all individuals who wish to receive its publications. Current membership includes educators in the United States, Canada, and elsewhere throughout the world—professors, researchers, administrators, and graduate students in colleges and universities and teachers, administrators, supervisors, and curriculum specialists in elementary and secondary schools.

Members of the Society elect a Board of Directors. Its responsibilities include reviewing proposals for Yearbooks, authorizing the preparation of Yearbooks based on accepted proposals, and appointing an editor or editors to oversee the preparation of manuscripts.

Current dues (for the year 2000) are a modest $35 ($30 for retired members and for students in their first year of membership). Members whose dues are paid for the current calendar year receive the Society's Yearbook, are eligible for election to the Board of Directors, and are entitled to a 33 percent discount when purchasing past Yearbooks from the Society's distributor, the University of Chicago Press.

Each year the Society arranges for meetings to be held in conjunction with the annual conferences of one or more of the national educational organizations. At these meetings, the current Yearbook is presented and critiqued. All members are urged to attend these meetings. Members are encouraged to submit proposals for future Yearbooks.

Constructivism in Education is Part 1 of the 99th Yearbook. Part 2, published simultaneously, is entitled *American Education: Yesterday, Today, and Tomorrow*.

For further information, write to the Secretary, NSSE, 5835 Kimbark Ave., Chicago, Illinois 60637.

ISSN: 0077-5762

Published 2000 by
THE NATIONAL SOCIETY FOR THE STUDY OF EDUCATION

5835 Kimbark Avenue, Chicago, Illinois 60637
© 2000 by the National Society for the Study of Education

First Printing

Printed in the United States of America

Acknowledgments

During a decade in which school faculties describe themselves as pursuing a constructivist philosophy and teacher educators declare they are preparing constructivist teachers, and these phrases mean many different things to different people, the Board of Directors of the National Society for the Study of Education was pleased to receive a proposal from a philosopher of education who promised to engage colleagues in a lively discussion of the varied meanings that adhere to this currently overworked concept. At the request of the Board, Denis C. Phillips recruited a team of authors from around the world, asking pairs of scholars to contribute opinions, often divergent opinions, on social constructionism and radical constructivism and the relevance of these philosophies to teachers and administrators in the schools, to teacher educators, and to researchers. For more than a year Professor Phillips worked with a baker's dozen of authors who responded appropriately to his request for "lively opinions," and manuscripts flowed via e-mail and computer disks to and from his office at Stanford University, arriving eventually on my desk on their way to the printer in Bloomington, Illinois.

And from my desk queries on manuscripts and galleys went out to far-flung authors, and I am grateful to all of them for their patient and prompt responses to what must often have seemed to them niggling questions and curious doubts. I especially appreciate the patience with which the authors from Australia and the United Kingdom put up with my preference for American spellings and NSSE's loyalty to *The Chicago Manual of Style*.

Though Kenneth Rehage has relinquished the role of editor while keeping on with all the other tasks of the Executive Secretary, he continued this year to give freely of his time and expertise whenever I called upon him, and I did so frequently, as we prepared the ninety-ninth volumes of the Society for publication in the year 2000.

MARGARET EARLY
Editor for the Society

Editor's Preface

For about a decade I was the main lecturer in the Philosophy Department's spring quarter offering in Stanford's compulsory freshman program "Cultures, Ideas and Values." The students had spent two quarters investigating the ancient world, the age of faith, and the age of Enlightenment; my quarter focused upon the nineteenth and twentieth centuries. In my opening lecture I reminded them of the path they had traversed, and then sprang the following question on them: "In a century's time, intellectual historians will look back at us, as we have looked back on the centuries before us. What will they see? What will they label our age as, for label it they will!"

As might be expected, my question drew a muted response. Each year I chided the two hundred or so freshmen for supposing that history stopped when they were born, and I exhorted them that they were living in exciting times. Scholars in later ages might well look back and "think themselves accurs'd they were not here, and hold their manhoods cheap," just as Henry V chided the men who were back in England, asleep when momentous events were unfolding far away at Agincourt.

This yearbook is a child of some of the momentous events that have taken place around us as the millennium has drawn to a close, although its lineage goes back much farther. Perhaps I can make matters graphic by using another personal reminiscence. For many years I occupied an office at Stanford that looked out onto Rodin's famous statue, the Thinker. It is a brilliant depiction of the world view of the Enlightenment—of thinkers like Descartes and Kant—for the Thinker is a solitary figure, deeply engrossed in cogitating about the world's problems, using nothing but the power of his rational intellect. Descartes himself must have cut a rather similar figure as he sat locked away in a small room with only a fire for company during one winter while on military service. There he reexamined all of his beliefs to determine which ones it was rational for him not to doubt—and thus he arrived at his famous "cogito ergo sum," the indubitable foundation upon which he erected all the rest of his beliefs. One of the features of the age in which we live has been the challenging, if not the overthrow, of this traditional view about the origin of knowledge—the view that knowledge can be produced by the rational individual thinking alone.

Descartes and Kant also lived in times when empirical science was undergoing a miraculous early adolescent growth spurt; but scientists, too, seemed to be thought of as mainly solitary workers, who might correspond with like-minded colleagues or who might occasionally venture forth from their laboratories to perform demonstrations for small groups of the cognoscenti. This view, too, thanks to the influence of Thomas Kuhn and others, is now widely regarded as deficient.

The overwhelming consensus as the twentieth century closed has been that knowledge is constructed. Furthermore, the knower is not a passive Rodin-like thinker, but is both physically and mentally active. Rather than being alone on a pedestal, the constructor of knowledge is a member of a sociocultural group from which he or she draws innumerable resources and obtains invaluable direction. We have Piaget and Vygotsky, Dewey and Kuhn, Marx and Geertz, and many others to thank for this important intellectual revolution. Whether it is actually *one* revolution or *many* remains to be seen, although some contributors to this book think that there are many different and often conflicting themes that need to be disentangled in contemporary constructivism.

There are some, such as the postmodernists and radical social constructivists, who go further in a radical direction and assert that we live in an age when the entire Enlightenment edifice is lying in ruins, including belief in "truth," "objectivity," and "rational warrants for belief." There are others who, while acknowledging the importance of the new insights, despair that the intellectual baby is in danger of being thrown out with the Enlightenment bath water, and they want to salvage some at least of the old attitudes toward knowledge. There are some moderates who want to add new insights about the social nature of knowledge construction to traditional notions of rational warrant. The radicals tend to see this as a "wishy-washy" position.

These disparate forces will be relatively easily detected in the pages of this book. We live in a time of (to adopt an expression from William James) "blooming buzzing confusion," and this yearbook also captures this rather nicely. The authors do not mince words, and they do not oversimplify; it is clear that they all regard themselves as being engaged with issues of great import. And they are right.

There are hosts of important educational issues that emerge in these debates about knowledge construction. Is the way experts construct knowledge parallel to the way that students construct their own understandings? Should the fact that scientific and mathematical knowledge-construction takes place in communities be reflected in the way that science and mathematics are taught in elementary and secondary schools?

Or should we make a distinction between the way individuals learn and the way that the great public disciplines of mathematics and science develop and progress? Can we even talk of progress, for isn't such talk based upon the outmoded view that knowledge is in some sense a *copy* of a preexisting realm that is apart from, or outside of, human "knowers"? Is, in fact, the philosophical position known as realism (a metaphysical position that seems to be adopted without question by many scientists and teachers) also a major victim of the fall of Enlightenment philosophy?

These are heady, difficult, vitally important, and as yet *unresolved* issues that enliven intellectual debate at the dawn of the new millennium, and these same issues enliven the pages of this yearbook.

D. C. PHILLIPS

Table of Contents

CHAPTER I

An Opinionated Account of the Constructivist Landscape

D. C. PHILLIPS

Overview of the Volume

Slogans and "magic words" (such as "democracy," "freedom fighter," "natural," "liberal" and "conservative," "positivist," "modernist" and "postmodernist") undoubtedly serve useful psychosocial purposes. They give their users a sense of certainty, of being sure-footed when traversing difficult or slippery terrain; they also promote a sense of fellow-feeling with like-minded others, and they help to identify as the enemy those who use different slogans or key words. But they rarely stimulate their adherents to probe deeply into the underlying ideas and assumptions—indeed, the function of such labels is often to *discourage* this type of inquiry. (All this was brilliantly parodied by George Orwell in *Animal Farm*, where the reigning slogan was "all animals are equal," except that pigs were more equal than others!) Worse still, those who have become possessed by a slogan or by a magic word can become irritable when faced with a recalcitrant individual who *wants* to expose and examine assumptions and underlying issues.

All this is by way of a warning to the reader. "Constructivism" is a currently fashionable magic word in the Western intellectual firmament, one which has beguiled a great many educational researchers, curriculum developers, trainers of teachers and teachers themselves, school administrators, sociologists, philosophers, and anti-philosophers who regard themselves as being of postmodern disposition. The philosopher Michael Devitt nominates constructivism as a candidate for "*the* most dangerous contemporary intellectual tendency,"[1] while the Continental educational researcher, Reinders Duit, regards it as a

D. C. Phillips is Professor of Education and, by courtesy, of Philosophy, at Stanford University, where he is also Associate Dean for Academic Affairs in the School of Education. His main interest is examining educational research from the perspective of philosophy of science.

"fashionable and fruitful paradigm" for guiding educational research and practice.[2] The authors represented in this volume are spread out along this continuum of opinion, but they have refused to allow themselves to be diverted from examining the deep underlying issues; some, indeed, are aptly called "constructivists," while others are not; but what they all have in common is their willingness to probe beneath the surface, to attempt to tease out what is important and good, what is important but mistaken, and what is not important at all in the various schools of thought that have appropriated the constructivist label in one or other of its various manifestations.

No doubt some readers will become irritable, and there are many who will be surprised at the detail into which some of the chapters go in this quest for clarity and resolution. Several decades ago, Donald Campbell and Julian Stanley, in their classic work on experimental design, wrote that "insofar as the designs discussed [in this book] . . . become complex, it is because of the intransigency of the environment."[3] The same might be said by most of the authors represented in this volume; their work is detailed and nuanced because the environment in which the term "constructivism" is very widely and very confusingly used is complex and often intransigent. For example, the writings of Ernst von Glasersfeld and Kenneth Gergen—giants in the field—which are discussed in a number of chapters in this volume, range over the last several centuries of epistemology and ontology, psychology, the relation between language and thought, and other complex topics. Essays which aim to engage fairly with the thought of these men cannot be simple and cannot avoid dealing with some complexities. Too often the discussions in the educational literature have verged upon the superficial.

But although the following chapters are nuanced, they also are quite lively and, given the complexity of the topics dealt with, clear. The readers who persist will be both pleasantly surprised and well informed by the time they reach the last page. And to avoid the reasonable suspicion that an editor who puts a toe into such troubled waters might have an intransigent viewpoint of his own that colors the whole volume, two different authors (or teams of authors) were invited to present their considered opinions about a number of aspects of constructivism; sometimes these opinions and second opinions agree with each other, but often they do not. Indeed, where the authors came out on the issues was in each case something of a surprise to the editor! On a number of occasions an author in one pairing disagrees with one or another author in a different pairing. Thus, while Kenneth Tobin, Michael Matthews, and Richard Gunstone agree on some matters, they strongly disagree over others, as do Joan Solomon and Matthews. In some cases the contributors were deliberately chosen because I had an inkling that they disagreed with my own opinions on the relevant topics; and some were chosen because, while I was an admirer of their acumen, I had no clear sense of where they stood on the controversial issues concerning constructivism. The result is a stimulating set of assessments of the constructivist landscape as it exists at the end of the millenium. To help bring the overall structure of the volume into focus, I have added a brief introduction to each of the pairs of essays, to highlight the issues that they tackle and to place the chapters in broader context.

I also need to enter a disclaimer at the outset: Although I am of skeptical disposition, personally I am not entirely ill disposed to the various types of constructivism that are discussed in the following chapters. On the contrary, I find much that is of great interest in the writings of the constructivists; but I also find much in this corpus that leaves me unsettled and crying out for the sort of detailed critical (but not necessarily unfriendly) examination that the following chapters provide. I have even acknowledged that, in what some would regard as a weak or "wishy-washy" sense to be explained later, I am clearly a constructivist myself.[4] More of this will emerge in the last portions of this opening chapter. But first there are some other preliminary matters about the volume as a whole that need to be discussed.

Why Are Science and Mathematics So Central?

Several, but by no means all, of the following chapters discuss constructivism in the context of mathematics and science education; several also deal with the question of to what degree the disciplines of science and mathematics (but particularly the former) are "socially constructed." All of these discussions have wide significance and raise intellectual issues that are of relevance to educators who have no professional dealings with these specific fields. But still the question arises: Why this emphasis on science, both in this volume and in the enormous constructivist literature? Discussion of this will serve to open up some core issues surrounding constructivism.

It is not particularly controversial to say that when readers grapple with a work of literature, they individually construct (or interpret) the text's meaning for themselves. This is so even if the individuals concerned discuss the work with each other, in a book club or in a literature class in high school or college. What is made of the work is likely to vary from person to person; my interpretation of Hamlet's soliloquy is likely to differ slightly, if not markedly, from yours. Stanley Fish developed an extreme version of this position. He tells the story that when students asked him at the start of a semester what the text would be in his class, he replied that there was "no text in this class" even though all the students were expected to purchase the same book—the point being that each reader of the book would construct a different text, a different set of meanings.[5]

Furthermore, although the various interpretations are undergirded by a common language that has been socioculturally constructed (I am supposing for the sake of simplicity that the readers are all operating in the same language), they may differ with respect to their understandings of individual words, the range and subtlety of their vocabularies, and the associations that various words have for them. In a sense, then, while language is a human construct, different individuals may construct slightly different things with it, even when they use the same words.

Finally, it is not particularly controversial to assert that the literary canon—the set of works that are regarded as exemplary or groundbreaking or standard-setting—has been socially constructed. How else could it have been produced? It is also evident that the content of this canon has varied across generations (works rated very highly by one generation of experts may not be so regarded by others), and this underscores the canon's origin in human tastes and values and also in the theories that are held about the nature and purpose of literature.

In saying that the various views outlined above are not particularly controversial, I do not wish to imply that they are entirely unproblematic. But if important subtleties are overlooked, there clearly seems to be *something* in them; they are not outrageous positions for people to adopt. So dealing with the social construction of texts, or of language, does not seem to have the same potential for provoking deep controversy that exists if we move to other domains, such as science and mathematics that seem at first blush to be far less fertile soil for the blossoming of constructivism. For centuries these disciplines have been held up as prime examples of objective knowledge. Although it has relatively recently been recognized that scientists and mathematicians work as members of communities of inquirers, nevertheless the knowledge that these communities construct is determined (or severely constrained) by the realities that lie outside the community itself.

According to this traditional view, scientific knowledge is constrained by, and largely shaped by, those aspects of the natural world that are the subject of study (thus, for example, the discipline of physics in essence has been shaped by the nature of the physical universe, rather than by the characteristics of physicists or their communities; and mathematics is shaped by the objective properties of number systems and the requirements of deductive logic.) If constructivism can take root in these disciplines, it can succeed anywhere, and this is one reason why the academic world has paid so much attention to mathematics and science, and why the disputes known collectively as the "science wars" have been waged so bitterly. This intellectual centrality of mathematics and science is necessarily reflected in this volume.

I shall say a little more about the controversies surrounding the social construction of scientific knowledge shortly, but the following passage from a well-known participant in the "science wars," the sociologist of science Steve Woolgar, brings out clearly the important place that discussion of the nature of scientific knowledge has had in recent intellectual life:

> Challenges to the idea of science as a privileged way of producing reliable knowledge can be found in different forms in several disciplines: literary theory, philosophy, history, anthropology and sociology. In addition, several significant intellectual movements cut across these traditionally defined boundaries and provide the basis for an interdisciplinary critique: deconstruction, the critique of representation, structuralism and post-structuralism, relativism, post-modernism. Not surprisingly, criticisms of science evolved by these developments have radical and far-reaching consequences. . . . the same critique affects fundamental preconceptions about science, especially as these underpin most bodies of modern scholarship.[6]

The philosopher David Hull, writing in a recent book review, brings into stark focus the radical position that this critique of science has led many constructivists to adopt:

> The most extreme constructivists seem to hold that all of us, scientists included, are helpless victims in the maws of our societies. We all believe what our societies force us to believe. On this extreme view, the appeals that scientists make to reason, argument, and evidence are merely so much show to cover the social origins of our beliefs.[7]

There is a second reason, however, for the focus upon science and mathematics in a great deal of the constructivist literature in education. Much—although clearly not all—of the cutting-edge research in the domains of the cognitive-psychological approach to learning theory, classroom learning, and the improvement of teaching has been based on the learning and teaching of science and mathematics. (Those who research learning and teaching obviously have to study the learning and teaching of *something*, and an important fashion in recent years has been that this "something" is mathematics or science.) This is reflected in the large and comprehensive collection on constructivism edited by Leslie Steffe and Jerry Gale in 1995, where somewhat more than half the chapters deal with these two fields, or were written by researchers who chiefly work in these fields; most of the other chapters were not subject-specific.[8]

The Constructivist Landscape

The foregoing discussion leads to another issue: It is apparent already that the term "constructivism" refers to at least two quite different things. A great deal of confusion can result if these two major senses of constructivism are not distinguished from each other. There are extreme and more moderate variants of each of these two, so that a score or so of different "constructivisms" have been described in the literature. Matthews, in particular, gives references to most of these variants in Chapter VI. It seems wise to start our mapping of the terrain with a description of the two radically different poles that serve to delineate the whole domain.

In the first case, "constructivism" embodies a thesis about the disciplines or bodies of knowledge that have been built up during the course of human history. I have described this thesis as, roughly, that these disciplines (or public bodies of knowledge) are human constructs, and that the form that knowledge has taken in these fields has been determined by such things as politics, ideologies, values, the exertion of power and the preservation of status, religious beliefs, and economic self-interest. This thesis denies that the disciplines are objective reflections of an "external world." A consequence of this general position for many theorists has been that the origin of human knowledge, and its standing *as* knowledge, are to be explicated using sociological tools rather than epistemological ones; hence Hull's remark that this version of constructivism regards evidence, reason, and disciplinary argument as "so much show." (This consequence follows because sociology is the discipline that studies, among other things, the influence of social forces and ideologies on human beliefs and actions.) This broad area of constructivism is often called *social constructivism* or sometimes *social constructionism*.

In the second case, "constructivism" refers to a set of views about how individuals learn (and about how those who help them to learn ought to teach). Roughly, this second type of constructivist view is that learners actively construct their own ("internal," some would say) sets of meanings or understandings; knowledge is not a mere *copy* of the external world, nor is knowledge acquired by passive absorption or by simple transference from one person (a teacher) to another (a learner or knower). In sum, knowledge is *made*, not *acquired*. Some constructivists of this broad type go on to stress that we cannot be certain that any two individuals will construct the same understandings; even if they use the same linguistic formulations to express what they have learned, their deep understandings might be quite different. There is no absolutely perfect label for this broad constructivist domain. In previous papers I have used the expression *psychological constructivism*, because the center of interest is the *psychological understandings of individual learners*, and several of the contributors to the present volume have adopted this terminology.[9] (One reason, however, that it is not perfect is that it can lead to a misunderstanding: not all psychological constructivists are psychologists!)

This is the beginning of a trip into a nightmarish landscape: Does labeling a researcher as a "constructivist" tell us anything clearcut about his or her position? How many forms of constructivism are there? Do the forms have common elements? What sort of arguments or evidence do supporters of one or another form of constructivism offer to support their position? What are the underlying issues that divide—and often so upset—the theorists and researchers whose daily lives take them into this landscape? It is to these and other related matters that we now must turn. I shall set out my description of the terrain in the form of a series of points; most of the issues I raise will be dealt with in greater depth by one or more of the contributors to this present volume.

I

Although debates over one or other of the forms of constructivism have become very common over the past two decades or so, the issues were not invented in the late twentieth century, but have a venerable history. Only a random sample from this rich past can be mentioned here, by way of illustration. John Locke, a key figure in the development of the empiricist school of epistemology, believed that individuals rather mechanically built up bodies of knowledge from a foundation of simple ideas that were passively derived from their experience (he used the example of a wax tablet being marked from outside); and he stressed that if you had not experienced the color blue, for example, you could not have knowledge of blueness. In the key initial phases of knowledge production, then, the individual was a passive absorber, and thus Locke's view was a non-constructivist one. (A few details of Locke's model appear more constructivist, as I have discussed elsewhere.[10]) On the other hand, Rene Descartes, an important rationalist epistemologist, was somewhat more constructivist; he is famous for claiming that he had examined all of his beliefs and had discarded those which did not appear indubitable to his "light of reason," and, having arrived at a foundation in "cogito, ergo sum," in a paroxysm of constructivist activity he then rebuilt his stocks of knowledge! Immanuel Kant (and later Jean Piaget, who was greatly influenced by him) argued that certain aspects of our knowledge of the physical universe (time and space, for example) were the products of our own cognitive apparatus—we "construct" the universe to have certain properties, or rather, our faculty of understanding imposes these temporal and spatial properties on our experience. Thus Kant and Piaget are ancestors of modern psychological constructivism (this is made abundantly clear in the title of one of Piaget's books: *The Child's Construction of Reality*). Karl Marx, in holding that the ruling ideas of a society in a given age were the ideas of the ruling class (or were ideas that fostered that class's interests), was an ancestor of twentieth-century social constructivism.

II

Both social constructivism and psychological constructivism have important implications for, or applications in, education. While the latter has been the one most debated in the educational literature, it is the former that has been of wider intellectual interest, particularly, as noted earlier, in the so-called "science wars."

The most extreme version of social constructivism was developed initially by a group known as the "Edinburgh School" of sociologists of knowledge (although arguably its roots go back to Marx and Emile Durkheim). Foundational contemporary figures are David Bloor and Barry Barnes, but "fellow travelers" include Steven Shapin, Steve Woolgar, and Bruno Latour. The classic position of Bloor and Barnes has also been labeled "the Strong Program in sociology of knowledge." This school holds that the form that knowledge takes in a discipline can be *fully explained*, or *entirely accounted for*, in sociological terms. That is, on this view what is taken to be knowledge in any field has been determined by sociological forces including the influence of ideologies, religion, human interests, group dynamics, and so forth. To repeat the point made earlier, this group of thinkers wishes to deny that so-called knowledge is in any sense a reflection or copy of the "external reality" that the community in question is investigating.

A bizarre (and unsophisticated) example of social construction is the decision taken by the General Assembly of the State of Indiana in 1897 to define the geometrical constant pi (the ratio of the circumference of a circle to its diameter) as being 4 (instead of its actual value of 3.14159 . . .). A non-constructivist, of course, would claim that the value of pi is determined by the geometrical realities that pertain. A more sophisticated case—still of "strong" social constructivism—would be the claim that Darwin's theory of evolution was a reflection of the ideas of individualism and competition that were dominant in the Victorian culture in which he lived, rather than being shaped by anything that was occurring in biological nature.[11] Perhaps the most famous example of social constructivism in recent years is not a genuine example at all, but a hoax. The physicist Alan Sokal wrote a spoof paper giving a constructivist (and postmodernist) account of the field of quantum gravity, giving rise to extremely heated exchanges when the paper was judged mistakenly to be genuine.[12]

I should point to an important distinction here: There is a difference between the social construction of the natural world, about which the above controversies rage, and the *social construction of the social world*. To my knowledge there is no dispute at all that social worlds, and the regularities within them, are socially constructed. A Martian would notice that people in the United States drive on the right side of the road while those in Australia drive on the left; and this extraterrestrial visitor would notice a great number of other sociocultural regularities or realities. But the visitor would not be able to find any extrahuman natural laws or forces that produce these regularities. Rather, they are produced by rules or mores that in many cases could be changed by legislation or mutual consent, just as some decades ago Australia changed from imperial measures to the metric system.[13]

Not all social constructivists are as radical as the adherents of the Strong Program, although many contemporary scholars who study the sociology of scientific knowledge (SSK) and have participated in the science wars that have enlivened intellectual life in the past few years seem to be tarred with the same brush. The social constructivist Bruno Latour described as follows the various schools of thought that can be found in this domain:

"Radical," "progressivist," "conservative," "reactionary," "golden mean". . . . A radical is someone who claims that knowledge is entirely constructed "out of" social relations; a progressivist is someone who would say that it is "partially" constructed out of social relations but that nature somehow "leaks in" at the end. At the other side of this tug-of-war, a reactionary is someone who would claim science becomes really scientific only when it sheds any trace of social construction; while a conservative would say that although science escapes from society there are still factors from society that "leak in" and influence its development. In the middle, would be the marsh of wishy-washy scholars who add a little bit of nature to a little bit of society and shun the two extremes.[14]

In this volume, Peter Slezak represents the views of many scholars from the conservative/reactionary end of Latour's spectrum who find the radical position of the Edinburgh Strong Program and its fellow-travelers, including the work of Latour himself, to be of very little merit and to have serious negative educational ramifications. Eric Bredo presents (from a progressivist or wishy-washy position) a more moderate form of social constructivism which he has based on the work of the important early pragmatist and social psychologist George Herbert Mead, a close friend and intellectual ally of John Dewey. Michael Matthews tends to agree with Slezak. I identified myself above as a wishy-washy person, although I tend to drift towards conservatism.

III

It is necessary to return briefly to psychological constructivism and to stress again that labels can be quite misleading. For, despite the appellation that has been given to them, not all psychological constructivists are psychologists—the crucial thing is that their focus is on the way in which individuals construct their own (psychological) understandings. Thus, Ernst von Glasersfeld, who writes chiefly under the spell of epistemological ideas (but also, to be sure, under the influence of Piaget and others), describes his own radically individualistic version of psychological constructivism in the following terms; it is no accident that he labels his own position as *radical constructivism*:

What is radical constructivism? It is an unconventional approach to the problems of knowledge and knowing. It starts from the assumption that knowledge, no matter how it is defined, is in the heads of persons, and that the thinking subject has no alternative but to construct what he or she knows on the basis of his or her own experience. What we can make of experience constitutes the only world we consciously live in . . . all kinds of experience are essentially subjective, and though I may find reasons to believe that my experience may not be unlike yours, I have no way of knowing that it is the same . . . Taken seriously, this is a profoundly shocking view.[15]

His own judgment in this last sentence is shared by several of our contributors, although not always in quite the way von Glasersfeld would hope. His work is discussed in some depth in chapters by Kenneth Howe and Jason Berv, Luise McCarty and Thomas Schwandt, and Matthews (and it is mentioned in several other chapters).

There is one further complexity. Although their focus is on individual learning or construction, not all of the so-called psychological constructivists posit individual mechanisms to explain learning; some bring *social influences* into the story to account for how it is that individuals construct the knowledge that they do. (It should be noted that there is ample room here for further terminological confusion, as some scholars refer to these socially oriented psychological constructivists as "social constructivists," although it should be clear they are quite different from the group I identified with the same label earlier.) Thus, for example, the Russian social and developmental psychologist Lev Vygotsky and the contemporary social psychologist Kenneth Gergen have stressed the role played by language in shaping the individual's construction of knowledge. Language, of course, is the social phenomenon *par excellence*, and it is the medium through which parents, teachers, and peers can influence the way in which the individual comes to understand. Vygotsky and many others also point to the often underappreciated role played by the vast cultural repertoire of artifacts, ideas, assumptions, concepts, and practices which the individual inherits or is "born into." The important roles of language and of culture are touched upon in the chapters by Bredo and by McCarty and Schwandt, who also go to some depth in analyzing Gergen's work.

IV

As might be expected, there are many complex issues that arise from these various types of constructivism; I will have more to say about some of them later when I introduce each of the pairs of chapters. However, a preliminary and very cursory survey of the terrain seems appropriate before we move to see what the contributors have to say. I find it useful to categorize these issues as follows:

Interpretive Issues. There are many issues about what, precisely, the chief exponents of one or other form of constructivism actually want

to assert. Ernst von Glasersfeld, for example, has written quite volu-
minously, and some of his views are "shocking" (to use his own
description). A scholar wishing to discuss his work, then, has to take
pains that he or she has understood precisely what it is that is being
claimed (for shocking views are too often easy to misunderstand simply because they are so shocking). This also explains why it is that
some of the chapters that follow have so many references and quotations. I know from personal experience that if one paraphrases a
"shocking" position (rather than quoting from it quite precisely and in
detail), one's audience is tempted to say that "no one could ever say
such a thing!" (The same considerations arise in the case of the social
constructivists.) Readers will find that many of the contributors have
truly encyclopedic knowledge of the constructivist literature in the
domains they are discussing, as they marshal evidence for the interpretations and cases that they wish to make.

There is a related interpretive issue: Sometimes a writer is inconsistent, or seems to be saying in one place something that, taken literally, contradicts what he or she has said somewhere else. Judgment is
required to determine if this is a genuine contradiction or confusion,
or whether there is some reading that would dissolve the apparent
problem. I have personally struggled with this phenomenon in discussing the writings of David Bloor.[16] He stresses the core idea of the
Strong Program, namely, that sociology can fully account for the content of the knowledge that is built up by scientists; yet later in the
same book he claims that of course he is not asserting that scientists
can say anything they please about the realms of nature they are
(apparently) studying, for there are natural constraints on the views
that can be advanced. It appears that the latter view contradicts the
former, a serious issue that Bloor does not resolve.

Philosophical Issues. There are many fascinating issues, but I shall
give only a brief description of two of them that will be taken up in
later chapters. (1) Radical constructivists insist that each of us is "in
contact" only with our individual "experience"; we do not have "contact" with an "external world," which is simply a construction of ours.
Animals, plants, physical objects, and even other people are constructions that (presumably) each of us makes in order to be able to deal
adequately with our experience. This position seems to isolate each of
us in a universe of our own construction, a shocking view indeed, and
one that has appeared in the earlier history of Western philosophy and
which has been subject to strong criticism. (I have broken my own
rule here, and have not documented the above account of what the

radical constructivists believe or assert, for I do not want to needlessly repeat what can be found in the later chapters. But if the reader finds my account hard to believe in the absence of documentation, then my case is made!)

(2) The work of Bloor, outlined above, also raises core philosophical issues. Certainly a sociological account can be given of what led to an item of knowledge being formulated and then led to its gaining wide acceptance (after all, people were involved at every stage, and the degree and kind of their involvements certainly can be studied). But does this need to be distinguished from an account of the *logical or theoretical or empirical warrants* that were adduced in order to show that the item was, indeed, epistemically justified? Does the Strong Program mistakenly cast aside the need for our beliefs to be warranted, by regarding this need as being satisfied by—or as being superseded by—the sociological account? Or is it scientists and philosophers who are mistaken when they think that "epistemic warrant" is a non-vacuous and rather central notion? If one regards the two endeavors—epistemological and sociological—as being different, and not as *alternatives* but as *complementary* (the wishy-washy position that I personally favor), how can the details be worked out?[17]

Educational Issues. There are many examples of these that arise in the constructivist literature—too many to list here, but the chapters that follow certainly do an excellent job of exposing and discussing the pros and cons of many of them. Again I shall only mention a few here to whet the reader's appetite.

(1) Research on student learning and classroom teaching methods long antedates the rise to popularity of the recent wave of psychological constructivism and particularly the widely cited writings of Ernst von Glasersfeld. (This is not to deny that the work of Piaget, Dewey, and others was a significant prior influence on the research community, and of course these men were constructivists.) And yet, constructivist terminology probably dominates the recent literature. The conventional wisdom, therefore, is that the ideas of von Glasersfeld and others have had a major impact in shaping the nature of recent research in these fields. But how, precisely, did these ideas change the nature of educational research? Several of the contributors to this volume touch on this issue (see the chapters by Michael Matthews, Richard Gunstone, Kenneth Tobin, Deborah Lowenberg Ball and Hyman Bass, and Joan Solomon); several see von Glasersfeld as being an important stimulus to contemporary research. Gunstone, however, argues that some important research groups had agendas that were basically unaffected

by radical constructivism; these groups simply adopted (wisely or not) the currently modish constructivist terminology when *discussing* their work.

(2) Constructivists, from the time of John Dewey and Jean Piaget on down to the present, have stressed the importance of students being *active inquirers*. Is this simply a more modern version of the older idea of discovery learning? Some constructivists, and others, argue that there is a difference between these two ideas.

(3) In teaching a subject such as science, it seems important that students come to learn the bodies of knowledge that the scientific community regards as currently warranted; many of us would not want to say that a student was scientifically educated if he or she did not know such things as Newton's laws of motion or theory of gravitation, or Einstein's formula, or Mendelian genetics. According to this view, teachers cannot be satisfied with students constructing their own "scientific theories"—they have to learn what the broader intellectual community regards as "science." Various forms of psychological constructivism have different positions on this important issue, and it poses a special problem for the radical constructivists if they wish to remain consistent. (Gunstone and Matthews are particularly concerned about all this, as are Ball and Bass.)

(4) Finally in this brief survey, it seems that there is a close resemblance between the educational views of many of the psychological constructivists (across the many forms of this major type of constructivism) and the classic progressive educators. Is constructivism best seen in historical perspective as being the most recent form of progressivism? Consider the work of that quintessential progressive educational theorist, John Dewey. He was also a constructivist of sorts. He stressed that learners must be active, he advocated the use of projects and inquiry methods, he attacked the acquisition by students of "cold storage knowledge" (knowledge that was acquired passively or by rote and that students did not know how to use), he regarded learning as best proceeding in social contexts, and he wanted the classroom to be seen as an interactive community. He was also aware of the issue outlined above, namely, that students have to learn the bodies of knowledge that are represented in the curriculum. He would not regard a student as being scientifically educated if he or she did not know the "funded wisdom" that is represented in the discipline publicly recognized as science.

Dewey's account of the typical schoolroom of the early twentieth century, written with horror at the passivity it enforces on students, clearly displays his constructivist sympathies:

Just as the biologist can take a bone or two and reconstruct the whole animal, so, if we put before the mind's eye the ordinary schoolroom, with its rows of ugly desks placed in geometrical order, crowded together so that there shall be as little moving room as possible. . . . and add a table, some chairs, the bare walls, and a few pictures, we can reconstruct the only educational activity that can possibly go on in such a place. It is all made "for listening."[18]

It is clear to me, and by the time readers have finished this volume it should be clear to them, that there are close similarities, but also some differences, between the ideas of Dewey and those of Tobin, Gunstone, Ball, and Solomon, and even—surprisingly—von Glasersfeld, Piaget, Vygotsky, and Gergen.

NOTES

1. Michael Devitt, *Realism and Truth* (Oxford: Blackwell, 1991), p. ix.

2. Reinders Duit, "The Constructivist View: A Fashionable and Fruitful Paradigm for Science Education and Practice," in *Epistemological Foundations of Mathematical Experience*, ed. Leslie Steffe (New York: Springer-Verlag, 1993).

3. Donald Campbell and Julian Stanley, *Experimental and Quasi-Experimental Designs for Research* (Chicago: Rand McNally, 1966), p. 1.

4. See Denis C. Phillips, "The Good, the Bad, and the Ugly," *Educational Researcher* 24, no. 7 (1995): 5-12; "Coming to Grips with Radical Social Constructivisms," *Science and Education* 6, nos. 1-2 (1997): 85-104; "How, Why, What, When, and Where," *Issues in Education* 3, no. 2 (1997): 151-194.

5. Stanley Fish, *Is There a Text in This Class?* (Cambridge, MA: Harvard University Press, 1980).

6. Steve Woolgar, *Science: The Very Idea* (London: Routledge, 1993), p. 9.

7. David Hull, "Uncle Sam Wants You," *Science*, 284, 14 May (1999): 1131.

8. Leslie Steffe and Jerry Gale, eds., *Constructivism in Education* (Hillsdale, NJ: Lawrence Erlbaum, 1995).

9. Kenneth Gergen makes the same distinctions as I do, but uses slightly different labels; see his *Realities and Relations: Soundings in Social Construction* (Cambridge, MA: Harvard University Press, 1994).

10. Phillips, "How, Why, What, When, and Where."

11. This is discussed in Michael Ruse, *Mystery of Mysteries: Is Evolution a Social Construction?* (Cambridge, MA: Harvard University Press, 1999).

12. For further discussion and references, see Phillips, "How, Why, What, When, and Where."

13. See John Searle, *The Construction of Social Reality* (New York: Free Press, 1995).

14. Bruno Latour, "One More Turn After the Social Turn," in *The Social Dimensions of Science*, ed. Ernan McMullin (Notre Dame, IN: University of Notre Dame Press, 1992), p. 276.

15. Ernst von Glasersfeld, *Radical Constructivism: A Way of Knowing and Learning* (London: Falmer Press, 1995), p. 1.

16. Phillips, "Coming to Grips With Radical Social Constructivisms": 92-95.

17. Two important recent attempts to do this—not discussed by the contributors to this volume—have been made by Catherine Elgin, *Between the Absolute and the Arbitrary*

(Ithaca, NY: Cornell University Press, 1997), esp. Chapter 10, and Ian Hacking, *The Social Construction of What?* (Cambridge, MA: Harvard University Press, 1999).

18. John Dewey, *The School and Society* (joint edition with *The Child and the Curriculum*) (Chicago: University of Chicago Press, 1956), p. 31.

Section One

Constructivism as an Epistemology and Philosophy of Education

Editor's Introduction

Both of the major types of constructivism have important educational implications. If the public bodies of knowledge—the disciplines—are socially constructed, or if social processes play an important part in determining the form that they take, then the curriculum, especially in high schools and colleges, will need some degree of reformulation. For it is often held that one of the aims in teaching natural science, mathematics, psychology, history, literature, and other subjects is to give students an understanding of how these fields developed—what the "logic of inquiry" is within each of them. (This is the domain that the curriculum theorist Joseph Schwab termed the "syntactical structure" of a discipline.) If something like the Strong Program in sociology of knowledge is correct, then traditional accounts of the methodologies of the disciplines probably need to be thoroughly recast.

Educational philosophers and theorists, however, have paid more attention to the work of the constructivists who focus on individual learning—the so-called psychological constructivists. This is largely because of the great influence of the radical constructivist Ernst von Glasersfeld (influence as judged by the frequency of citations that he has received), and because of the truly radical nature of his position. In the pair of chapters that follow, the authors (philosophers of education who also have more than a toe in various areas of educational research and have a special interest in educational research methodologies) have as their focus the considerable body of important philosophical issues that arise in the work of von Glasersfeld and other psychological constructivists.

Kenneth Howe and Jason Berv point out that the term "constructivism" is not commonly found in the philosophical lexicon, although philosophers outside education have been actively concerned with *issues* relevant to constructivism. They provide some much needed history (albeit briefly) of constructivist ideas in the branch of philosophy—epistemology—that deals with theory of knowledge, and in effect they locate the epistemology of the radical constructivists in this historical panoply where some of its defects become apparent. (It is interesting to note that in various of his writings von Glasersfeld gives his own version of this same history.) They also raise the issue of the "looseness of fit" between constructivist epistemology and constructivism as practiced in contemporary classrooms—this practice usually taking the form of some kind of active inquiry on the part of the students. The point is that it seems possible for a person who accepts constructivism as a philosophy to adopt any of a variety of educational practices (or for a teacher who uses constructivist classroom practices to justify doing so in a variety of ways, some of which might not philosophically be constructivist at all). The key, as Howe and Berv see it, is that teachers must challenge students to examine thoroughly their own constructions, and this challenge can be made in a variety of philosophically acceptable ways.

McCarty and Schwandt give a detailed analysis of the views of von Glasersfeld and of Kenneth Gergen, who interestingly define the opposite poles of the broad psychological constructivist domain. The first of these thinkers is radically individualistic and seems to entrap individuals in worlds of their own making, which leaves little room for the influence of parents, teachers and peers (who are part of the world that the individual knower has personally constructed). Thus von Glasersfeld's radical individualism seems to lead to a strong form of relativism or even idealism (the view that the only reality is the subjective experience or ideas of the individual); in a sense he problematizes the existence of—or the usefulness of referring to—an external reality. The influential social psychologist Kenneth Gergen, on the other hand, is radically social, while largely (but not exclusively) remaining interested in the issue of how individuals gain their knowledge. His view is that each of us is born into a culture in which there is *already* a language and a stock of concepts and other cultural artifacts, which we acquire to differing degrees more or less as a matter of course. He argues that the traditional view that takes the individual knower as the "unit of analysis" in epistemology is entirely mistaken; the correct unit is the social group or culture, a position that makes him diametrically opposed to von Glasersfeld. In a sense, then, Gergen is a social relativist, a position that also leads to interesting problems that McCarty and Schwandt discuss.

CHAPTER II

Constructing Constructivism, Epistemological and Pedagogical

KENNETH R. HOWE AND JASON BERV

The idea of "constructivism" now pervades the educational literature. Indeed, so much has been written on the topic that we are reluctant to claim that we make any points in this chapter that haven't been made in one form or another before. Nonetheless, we believe that a considerable amount of fog continues to obscure the landscape, particularly its epistemological contours. We hope to disperse much of it and provide a clearer view.

The chapter is divided into two major parts. In the first, we provide a characterization—*our construction*—of constructivism as an epistemological view. This endeavor is worth undertaking for two general reasons. First, "epistemology" is a much overworked term these days, so much so that it is often difficult to discern the difference between embracing a different epistemology—something quite fundamental and far reaching—and merely embracing different beliefs. Clarity is to be gained by examining constructivism in terms of the traditional philosophical sense of epistemology, as a general theory of knowledge.

A second reason is that "constructivism" is not prominent in the lexicon of philosophy. Though some contemporary philosophers explicitly employ the label,[1] much more often constructivist-type epistemology is associated with labels such as Kantianism, post-Kantianism, pragmatism, and naturalism. Getting clear on what might plausibly count as constructivist epistemology requires understanding the basic contours of several important epistemological views in the history of Western philosophy, as well as certain problems these views encountered.

In the second major part of the chapter, we take up constructivism as a pedagogy, focusing on the relationship it bears to constructivism as an epistemology. We explore a certain "looseness of fit" between the

Kenneth R. Howe is a professor who specializes in philosophy of education and educational policy. Jason Berv has been a high school teacher and administrator and is currently a doctoral student in social foundations and educational policy. Both are at the School of Education, University of Colorado, at Boulder.

two kinds or levels of constructivism. Our aim here is to illustrate how constructivist pedagogical techniques may be undergirded by a decidedly non-constructivist epistemology, and vice versa. We next provide a brief critique of "radical constructivism,"[2] distinguishing it from epistemological constructivism as we conceive it and showing how it founders on radical subjectivism/relativism. We end this section with a characterization of a "thoroughgoing constructivism" that weds constructivist epistemology with constructivist pedagogy. This is *our construction* of constructivist pedagogy, if you will, in which we advocate extending constructivism to include moral and political education.

Constructivism as Epistemology

In the sense that the mind is implicated in some way in what the world is, all epistemological views are constructivist, a point made well by Denis Phillips.[3] So "constructivism" must pick out something deeper than this, something deep enough to distinguish among epistemological views. Otherwise, it may as well be dropped as superfluous.

Two non- (or half-way) constructivist epistemologies have dominated in the history of Western philosophy: empiricism and rationalism. In empiricism, all knowledge is grounded in experience. The mind passively receives experience and is active in knowledge construction only *post hoc*, as it were, only in the sense of ordering what is already *given* in experience. In rationalism, by contrast, the mind contributes to the construction of knowledge at each level. Consider Descartes' famous wax example. How is it, asks Descartes, that a melting piece of wax can undergo changes in shape, color, and other sensible qualities and yet remain the same piece of wax? His answer is that the mind detects the non-experiential "substance" that makes the piece of wax the same thing through its sensible changes. The mind is always active in experience insofar as it contributes more than merely ordering what is already *given*.

Empiricism and rationalism faced different kinds of problems. Empiricists were faced with the difficulty of making sense of experience as totally detached from the workings of the mind. For if the mind were altogether passive in experience, how could experience organize *itself* into the chairs, the sky, the electrons, the persons, and so forth, that minds experience? Related to this, if a mind were not something distinct from a mere bundle of experiences, how could it persist as a thing over time that *has* experiences? Wouldn't it be nothing but a sequence of ever-changing minds as it (whatever *it* refers to) received new experiences over time? Wouldn't it be like a piece of wax that became apparently different each time its experiential contents changed?

Rationalists had an answer. Descartes proposed that the mind is a special kind of "substance" that exists independent of its experiential contents. But this engenders a different problem: If the mind operates autonomously, guided only by its own rules, how is a coherent connection established between reason and experience? Consider Zeno's famous paradoxes. Reason tells us that Achilles cannot cross the stadium. He must first traverse half the distance, then half the remaining distance, then half the remaining distance, and so on, ad infinitum, such that there will always be some remainder. Viewed from the other end of the sequence, Achilles not only cannot cross the stadium, he cannot move at all! Zeno, the rationalist, took this to be a victory. For, in his view, it shows that motion is an illusion and experience cannot be trusted. The alternative conclusion is that it is the reasoning here that cannot be trusted. Why? Because it conflicts with common experience. On this alternative view, if reason is to be more than just a set of formal rules that have nothing to do with experience, then reason and experience have to somehow be brought in line with one another.

KANTIAN CONSTRUCTIVISM

Enter Kant's attempted synthesis of empiricism and rationalism. To paraphrase one of Kant's leading ideas: A conceptual scheme without sensory data is empty, sensory data without a conceptual scheme are blind. This idea has to rank among the most influential and prescient in the history of Western philosophy, and, in our estimation, it ushered in the true sense of constructivist epistemology. Kant's view exemplifies a true constructivist view because it is more thoroughgoing than the half-way variants of empiricism and rationalism: It denies that there can be any *raw* sensory experience that the mind takes as given and then performs its formal operations on (empiricism). Alternatively, conceptual schemes are not *pure* (rationalism), but have meaning only as as they *construct* experience. This mixing of the empirical and the conceptual, as it were, was not individual/subjective for Kant. Rather, the mental categories of space, time, causation, and enduring objects ("substance"), among others, were the preconditions of experience, the furniture of *all* minds. His "transcendental deduction" aimed to show that such categories were required to account for the character of the experience of the world we all share.

In the twentieth century, language has supplanted the role played by Kant's transcendental (and somewhat mysterious) categories. Ludwig

Wittgenstein, whom we consider extensively in the next section, exemplifies the parallel. The important historical point to note about Kant's view is that constructivism was born in reaction to the two half-way constructivisms of empiricism and rationalism—and also born intersubjectivist.

CONSTRUCTIVIST EPISTEMOLOGY AND THE "LINGUISTIC TURN"

Twentieth-century constructivist epistemology (so-called) may be approached from two general directions: post-Kantianism and the related assault on positivism. The first pertains to epistemology generally, whereas the second focuses more on the epistemology of science. The two are intimately related insofar as each *naturalizes* epistemology by detaching knowledge from a transcendent realm and locating it instead in the natural phenomenon of language.

Twentieth Century Post-Kantianism. Arguably, Wittgenstein was one of the twentieth century's greatest philosophers. He had his most profound influence on Anglo-American philosophy. But his influence was wide ranging, extending as far as to French postmodernists such as Jean-Francois Lyotard.

Unfortunately, Wittgenstein's aphoristic style, which was also cryptic because of its frequent failure to identify the philosophical figures and positions targeted for criticism, prevented his work from gaining anywhere near as much attention outside of academic philosophy as the work of other post-Kantians such as Thomas Kuhn. But because we are compelled by Wittgenstein's insights, believe them to be of seminal importance, and find the parallels with Kant very illuminating, his work looms large in this section. We hope to render it transparent.

Kant asked: "How is experience possible?" He then deduced categories like (Euclidean) space, cause and effect, enduring object ("substance") and the like. These categories are not themselves experienced because they "condition" experience and are presupposed by it from the start.

Wittgenstein asked a similar question: How is language use and learning possible? Like Kant, he didn't start from a "given" in the traditional sense—some self-certifying sense data or revelations of reason—but with a familiar fact about the world that must be accounted for. Also like Kant, he was neither an empiricist nor a rationalist in the classical senses described above. Finally, insofar as he may be attributed with having advanced an epistemological thesis,[4] it was constructivist, once again like Kant's.

Individuals are born, or "thrown,"[5] into linguistic communities. The linguistic resources and practices available, which they have no choice about whether or not to learn, are saturated with cultural, historical, and social dimensions. And in order for someone to learn a language, both through instruction and more informally, the practices and concepts they encounter must exhibit consistency. Imagine the parent of a toddler pointing to a ball on one occasion and calling it a peach, then pointing to it on another occasion and calling it a parrot, then on a third occasion calling it a rhinoceros, then a glacier, and so forth. Imagine that this parent spanks the child, while saying in reassuring tones, "Good girl," and then, while saying in harsh tones, "No, bad girl," gently strokes the child's head. In the first case, the child is never going to learn what objects count as balls (or, incidentally, to learn what pointing means); in the second case (assuming this parent is consistent in this odd behavior) the child is going to be introduced into a very different "form of life" than we know.

This all seems obvious enough, but Wittgenstein drew some profound conclusions from the starting point of humdrum linguistic practice. Against empiricism especially, he criticized the idea that linguistic constructions correspond to raw "private" experiences out of which knowledge is then built up. For Wittgenstein, there are no raw sensory experiences—"experiencing spherical object now," "experiencing happy feeling now"—that exist prior to linguistic constructions and to which linguistic constructions are only later attached. Rather, the meanings of "ball" and "being happy" are inherent in language learning and use. Wittgenstein coined the term "language game" as a way of pointing to the rule-governed nature of linguistic practices and to the manner in which people catch on to these rules by actively engaging in such practices. Analogous to Kant's categories, language games are *presupposed* by the experiences individuals have, *not the results* of them. And for this reason, they are also intersubjective through and through.

As we observed before, "constructivism" is not prominent in the philosophical lexicon. One place it is used specifically, however, is in reference to Wittgenstein's philosophy of mathematics. His view is that mathematical truth grows out of and cannot be separated from human activity. This is *constructivism* in the broad sense that goes just as easily (perhaps better) under the name of *naturalism*. Naturalism denies any non- or super-natural criterion of truth, in contrast with the rationalist and non-constructivist view (e.g., Plato's) that mathematical knowledge is about a universal and timeless reality that is revealed by reason alone and whose features are totally independent of human experiences and activities.

Wittgenstein applies his brand of *naturalized* constructivism across the board, to also include epistemologically central concepts such as knowledge, doubt, and justification. He warns against "subliming" these concepts and turning them into "super concepts." Their meanings, no less than the meanings of more work-a-day concepts, are to be found in how they function in their "natural homes," that is, existing linguistic practices or "language games." So, for example, when Descartes wants to begin the epistemological enterprise by doubting everything, including his own existence, Wittgenstein demands to know what the grounds for such a doubt could be. Wittgenstein's point is that certain rules govern how doubt functions as a concept, including having some grounds for doubt. If one doubts everything, including that one doubts, then the whole "game" falls apart.

To reiterate, Wittgenstein's naturalized constructivism eschews a "given" in the traditional sense. The ultimate justification for knowledge claims is what we say and do, our "form of life." Wittgenstein famously remarked on the logic of justification that it ". . . comes to an end. If it did not, it would not be justification."⁶ And he added, "If I have exhausted the justifications I have reached bedrock . . . Then I am inclined to say: 'This is simply what I do.'"⁷

The general epistemological position of Wittgenstein holds that it is fruitless, or worse, to seek any points of reference—"foundations"— for knowledge wholly outside the natural world, of which humankind is a part. "The world as we know it bears the stamp of our own conceptual activity," as Hilary Putnam says.⁸ Such a view—"anti-foundationalism" as it is often called—is by no means confined to Wittgenstein and his close followers. The general contours of this view have come to dominate in the latter half of the twentieth century.

We should be clear that our primary focus in this chapter is on explicating constructivist epistemology, not defending it. Nonetheless, a few observations are in order about the *conventionalism* that constructivist epistemology is allegedly committed to and the problem of relativism that goes with it. What we have to say in this connection will be pertinent to our subsequent remarks on constructivist pedagogy. It will also help set the stage for the next section.

Opponents of epistemological constructivism find it worrisome (if not disastrous) that it allegedly renders truth contingent on the ultimately ungrounded conventions of linguistic communities. The criterion of truth on such a view, or so it is argued, amounts to nothing more than agreement (if only tacit) among the members of such communities. But what if the members of such communities disagree amongst themselves? Can't the minority be right? Are there then no truths to be found? Are there many truths, each relative to those who hold them? And what if the members of a given community agree amongst themselves but disagree with the members of a different community?

This is a challenge that epistemological constructivists can ill afford to be sanguine about. In our view, they can ill afford to simply capitulate, to say, "Yes, truths are *merely* matters of agreement," or "Yes, they're *merely* constructions." For this dooms epistemological constructivists to a radical and untenable form of relativism—so radical that it leads to a position (solipsism) in which each individual constructs his or her own world.

One stratagem for epistemological constructivists is to flat out deny that it makes sense to claim truth merely amounts to convention. For when someone makes a claim of the general form "X is true," *by convention*, they are not claiming that this is something everyone in fact agrees to. That people agreed to X would be a separate claim, the truth of which would not necessarily affect whether X is indeed true. For example, when Copernicus claimed the earth revolves around the sun, not vice versa, he was not appealing to conventional belief. On the contrary, he was trying to change it. The convention governing truth is that truth is not a matter of convention! This point harkens back to Wittgenstein's advice about not subliming epistemological concepts, in this case "truth," ignoring how they function in their "natural home" of human practices. A similar stance toward the concept of truth is to be found in pragmatists and neo-pragmatists such as William James, John Dewey, Hilary Putnam, and Richard Rorty.

But isn't this just sleight of hand? "The *real* problem," critics are likely to rejoin, "is that epistemological constructivism has no criteria outside of what people say and do to determine the truth. *This* is the sense of conventionalism that leads to a disastrous relativism." Invoked implicitly here is a fundamental Either-Or: *Either* there exists some wholly external, extra-human world by which to verify knowledge claims, *or* truth resides solely in what individuals or groups construct, i.e., in their conventions. It is the latter disjunct that epistemological constructivists are attributed with embracing, and it is because these constructions/conventions don't have to hook up with the world that relativism is the ineluctable result.

The response of epistemological constructivists is not to provide a *solution* to the question of how the world hooks up with mind/language. Rather, they reject this question as fruitless and misguided because based on an untenable dualism between the world and humans' construction of it. If there is no rigid demarcation between the world and humans' construction of it, then there is no sense worrying about whether and how the two hook up. This is essentially the position taken by Kant in his synthesis of mental categories and experience. The parallel stance of post-Kantian, naturalized constructivists is exemplified well by Putnam:

[E]lements of what we call "language" or "mind" *penetrate so deeply into what we call reality that the very project of representing ourselves as "mappers" of something "language-independent" is fatally compromised from the very start.* . . . In this situation it is a temptation to say, "So we make the world," or "our language makes up the world," or "our culture makes up the world"; but this is just another form of the same mistake.[9]

THE CONSTRUCTIVIST ASSAULT ON POSITIVISM

In philosophy of science, the twentieth-century "linguistic turn" saw classical empiricism rejuvenated as logical positivism. Once again a wedge was driven between the empirical and the conceptual—the world and our constructions of it—just as in classical empiricism. On the other hand, logical positivism relativized the distinction to language. Rather than setting minds and their ideas over and against experiences, the logical positivists set formal logic over and against what they called observation sentences (that is, sentences of the form "this chemical compound is red"). Observation sentences served as conceptually neutral building blocks that logic organized, established connections among, and deduced predictions and explanations from. Like its forerunner, classical empiricism, logical positivism was a non- (or half-way) constructivist view.

The twentieth-century linguistic turn also saw constructivism rejuvenated. At least as important as the developments described in the previous section (and not unrelated to them) were important developments in philosophy of science. Paralleling the place Wittgensteinian "language games" occupied in the analysis of knowledge in general, W.V.O. Quine's "conceptual schemes" and Thomas Kuhn's "paradigms" assumed a prominent place in the analysis of scientific knowledge in particular.

Notions such as conceptual schemes and paradigms exemplify a constructivist view because they are characterized in a way that precludes abstracting the purely linguistic from the purely empirical and setting the two over and against one another. Contrary to logical positivism, observation is always "theory-laden"—the basic empirical building blocks of knowledge are laden with conceptual content at birth. And, once again, as in the case of Kant and Wittgenstein, knowledge is conceived as intersubjective.

To be sure, the Quinean-Kuhnian account is threatened by a certain form of the relativity of knowledge, namely, relativity to conceptual schemes or paradigms. Insofar as it is based on the same dualism between language-mind (conceptual scheme, in this case) and the world discussed in the previous section, it may be dismissed in the same way. Indeed, the denial of this dualism is central to Quine's seminal critique of positivism.[10] In any case, the kind of relativism associated with Quine and Kuhn is a far cry from the radical, individualistic version found in "radical constructivism." For there remains a good deal of room for truth, objectivity, and rationality within communities that share conceptual schemes and paradigms because such communities inherently incorporate standards that serve as the basis for their identities and for intersubjective judgments among their members. Indeed, one of Kuhn's major points is the social and socializing character of scientific paradigms.

Furthermore, although moves from one conceptual scheme or paradigm to another cannot be characterized in terms of a set of mechanically applied rules and are not straightforwardly cumulative, such scientific "revolutions" or "paradigm shifts," as Kuhn calls them, are not therefore based on private, subjective beliefs. The shared problems, vocabulary, and methodological canons specific to a given area of scientific endeavor loom large in dealing with anomalous findings. Even where major theoretical upheaval—scientific revolution—is on the horizon, the old paradigm, although not straightforwardly subsumable under the new, nonetheless overlaps significantly.[11] In general, whether revolutionary or more modest theory revision is at issue, overarching "values" (as Kuhn calls them) or "pragmatic criteria" (as Quine calls them) apply intersubjectively so as to markedly circumscribe what theories ("constructions") are viable candidates and to determine which among them wins out. Among these values or criteria are consistency, coherence, scope, simplicity, and explanatory power.[12]

The Quinean-Kuhnian alternative to positivism, then, does not go so far in repudiating positivism as to jettison truth, scientific rationality, and objectivity. On the contrary, it reinterprets these concepts in a way that dispenses with the kind of pristine observational basis for science associated with positivism and, especially in Kuhn's work, seeks to bring them into line with the history of theoretical advances. On this account, scientific progress proceeds by a kind of bootstrapping that Kuhn likens to Darwinian evolution: new theories are compared to those they seek to displace in terms of their fitness vis-à-vis the existing problem situation and the kinds of general pragmatic criteria described above, rather than to some criterion to which science must inexorably move.[13] Importantly, however, rationality, objectivity, and truth-seeking remain hallmarks of the scientific enterprise. These are inherently intersubjective concepts. As such, they constrain what individual "constructors" can come up with, as well as how what they come up with is to be judged.

In addition to natural science, twentieth-century philosophy of social science, too, moved toward a naturalized constructivism. Logical positivism had also gained a strong foothold in social science, and it also came in for intense criticism there.

The "interpretive turn"[14] describes well the focal point of the assault on positivism in the social sciences. Positivism's commitment to a neutral observation language was doubly problematic when it came to investigating human behavior. The vocabulary of social science is conceptually laden in the same way that it is in natural science. But in addition, the objects (subjects) it attempts to conceptualize are themselves conceptualizers who have to be understood (partly, at least) on their own terms, cultural and otherwise.[15] Understanding human behavior requires that various perspectives be included in a "critical knowledge-constructive dialogue," as Helen Longino puts it.[16] Understanding the behavior of sub-atomic particles requires no similar kind of dialogue.

Thus, constructivism comes closer to being a literal description of the currently ascendant epistemology of social science than of the philosophy of natural science or of epistemology generally. For example, in his suggestively titled *The Construction of Social Reality*, John Searle contends that human behavior must be understood against a "background of intentionality."[17] The basic idea here is that the description and explanation of human behavior, unlike that of physical objects, requires appeal to human purposes that, in turn, can only be interpreted within a consensus on norms that determines what counts as what. For example, saying certain things, with certain purposes, under certain conditions constitutes getting married. By contrast, merely moving in certain ways and emitting certain noises—a physical description of events—does not by itself suggest that a marriage has occurred. Neither does doing all the typically right things, except in the context of performing a play. In both cases the movements, noises, and situation must be interpreted against a background of shared meanings. And what distinguishes *these* meanings from those in the natural sciences is that they have to be known from the inside, from the interpretive point of view of the actors themselves.

Still, even in the case of social reality, constructivism shouldn't be taken too literally. As a rule, individuals do not reflect on and actively construct the social meanings that govern their lives. As we observed before, they are "thrown" into a network of such meanings—a network that for the most part has itself not been deliberately constructed. Through their on-going participation in social activities, individuals master the typically unarticulated and tacitly conveyed "know hows"[18] of social life. Only against such a large and complex background of *shared social constructions* can they consciously reflect and evaluate social life; that is, only thus can they put together their *individual constructions*.

Once again the challenge of relativism raises its head, and it appears more acute in the case of social reality than in the case of physical reality. For constructions of social reality, even though unavoidably shared to a large degree *within* groups, are nonetheless relative to the norms and purposes that comprise this or that social/cultural group's "background of intentionality," norms and purposes that vary *among* groups and that can only be properly understood with some reference to the insider's perspective. Furthermore, because shared norms and purposes may be judged good or bad, an additional kind of relativism arises, namely, moral relativism.

Once again, the challenge of relativism has to be taken seriously, and the kind of responses that naturalized constructivism can provide to relativism parallels the ones offered before. First, it won't do to say, "Yes, morality is merely a matter of agreement," or "Yes, morality is merely a construction." For "X is right (or wrong)" is no more a claim about what people in fact agree to than is "X is true." Both are general claims for which argument and evidence has to be marshalled and, to hold up, such claims must withstand counter arguments and evidence. In this vein, Sandra Harding distinguishes between "descriptive relativism"—group X believes thus and so, group Y believes this and that, group Z believes, etc.—and "judgmental relativism"—groups X, Y, and Z are each right; and she denies that the first kind of relativism implies the second.[19]

Second, just as epistemological constructivism denies the dualism between mind/language and the world, it denies the dualism between values and the world. As Putnam says, "without *values* we would not have a *world*."[20] Epistemological constructivism puts ethical values—justice, goodness, rightness—on the same footing with cognitive values—coherence, scope, explanatory power—such that both "penetrate" the world. Disagreement about interpretation, application, and relative importance cannot be eliminated in either case. Putnam concludes from this, "if . . . ethical values are totally subjective, then cognitive values are totally subjective as well."[21] Though certain postmodernists may be prepared to draw the conclusion that *both* morality and science are completely subjective, epistemological constructivism (as we conceive it) draws the conclusion that *neither* are.

In epistemological constructivism, truth and knowledge are established holistically and tentatively, and are not compartmentalized into language/mind, the world, and values. There is no such thing as knowledge *uncontaminated* by any particular system of human purposes, beliefs, values, and activities. Lorraine Code sums up this conception of knowledge well: "It has no ultimate foundation, but neither does it float free, because it is grounded in experiences and practices, in the efficacy of dialogic negotiation and of action."[22]

Constructivist Pedagogy

Unlike in the field of philosophy, constructivism is prominent— very prominent—in the field of education. It is also applied to different things. In addition to characterizing epistemological views, it may also be used to characterize learning theory, teaching techniques, and a general pedagogical approach.

We begin this section by exploring the relationships among these three. We reveal a certain "looseness of fit" among them, as well as between them and constructivist epistemology. We then endeavor to tighten things up by exploring what characterization of constructivist epistemology best supports constructivism as a general pedagogical approach. Here we bring to bear the *naturalized* constructivist epistemology worked out previously. In the process, we first dispose of its major competitor, radical constructivism.

THE LOOSENESS OF FIT AMONG ELEMENTS OF A
CONSTRUCTIVIST PEDAGOGY

Constructivist learning theory has its primary roots in the work of Jean Piaget and Lev Vygotsky. It is by no means a stretch to claim that John Dewey also held a constructivist theory of learning, indeed in a rather carefully developed form.

Constructivist learning theory has two basic premises: (1) learning takes as its starting point the knowledge, attitudes, and interests students bring to the learning situation, and (2) learning results from the interaction between these characteristics and experience in such a way that learners *construct* their own understanding, from the inside, as it were. Constructivist pedagogy is broader in ways we describe later but incorporates two premises that parallel those of constructivist learning theory: (1) instruction must take as its starting point the knowledge, attitudes, and interests students bring to the learning situation, and (2) instruction must be designed so as to provide experiences that effectively interact with these characteristics of students so that they may *construct* their own understanding.

As Dewey observed, although simple in principle, constructivist learning theory is by no means simple to apply in instructional practice.[23] On the contrary, because it requires knowing a good deal about students' starting points, it is much more demanding than subject-centered, authoritarian approaches to teaching. To further complicate matters, specific teaching techniques—for example, lecture versus Socratic dialogue versus collaborative learning—are not necessarily constructivist or not in relation to a more general pedagogical approach and epistemology.

Paul Ernest has noted in this vein that "a lack of clarity in representing constructivism may allow its appropriation by the most authoritarian of pedagogies."[24] An episode in Plato's *Meno* provides a case in point. Socrates (representing Plato's views) painstakingly leads a slave boy to embrace the truth of the Pythagorean theorem. Socrates insists that he never tells the boy what must be so, but rather that through the skillful application of questioning the boy comes to see for himself what was never in doubt for Socrates.

The teaching technique here is a paradigm case of constructivism. But it is part of a largely non-constructivist learning theory and more general pedagogy. In his overall education theory, Plato advocated reserving this method of posing questions for a talented few and for relatively advanced subject matter. The predominant mode of learning and instruction, for the vast majority of people, was acquiring "right opinion" as dispensed by authorities. The teaching technique used with the slave boy is also part of a non-constructivist epistemology. The knowledge to which it is supposed to lead is grounded in a transcendent and unchanging reality, existing in another world totally independent of and unsullied by the perceptions, interests, and practices of this one.

Viewed from the other direction, ostensibly *non*-constructivist teaching techniques don't necessarily imply a *non*-constructivist learning theory, general pedagogy, or epistemology either. It is easy to think of ways in which direct, didactic techniques of instruction may be combined with an overall constructivist view. Often one wants to convey to students what the currently accepted truth is (however fallible in certain cases), to serve as the starting point and as grist for critical analysis. Indeed, it is difficult—impossible—to see how to avoid direct instruction a good deal of the time, especially with young children. Should teachers use Socratic dialogue or collaborative learning, for instance, to teach the sounds represented by the letter "A"? who the first president of the United States was? that 2 plus 2 equals 4? that the earth is spherical? This last example, no doubt, is the one most open to question. Still, we trust, educators would want to ultimately undermine false beliefs. Part of reaching this goal might very well involve pursuing how students had come to "construct" such a world, and it might very well involve acknowledging how this could make sense. But at the end of the day (or unit, or week, or what have you) students who hold false beliefs such as the earth is flat should be disabused of them.

Furthermore, it is surely impracticable to always rely on constructivist teaching techniques. Michael Matthews asks, "if knowledge cannot be imparted . . . then how can children come to knowledge of complex conceptual schemes that have taken the best minds hundreds of years to build up?"[25] There is no uniform answer to the question of what should be straightforwardly imparted by teachers and what should be made the topic of critical analysis and questioning. But not everything can be put up for grabs all of the time, and curriculum and instruction ought not be formulated—*constructed*—willy-nilly.

So a general constructivist pedagogy includes (1) embracing a constructivist learning theory and (2) mixing ostensibly constructivist and non-constructivist teaching techniques as appropriate. Where constructivist epistemology fits in admittedly still remains pretty much up in the air. One answer to this question is provided by "radical constructivism."[26] It is an answer we fundamentally reject.

THE FOUNDERING OF RADICAL CONSTRUCTIVISM

Radical constructivism holds that individuals can only really know their own private constructions of reality. Everything else must be built up from there. This thesis (interestingly reminiscent of classical empiricism) has invited much criticism. The primary charge leveled by "social constructivists," as well as other observers of the debate not easily classified, is that radical constructivists fall victim to a hopeless relativism.[27] The implications of radical relativism are that individual knowers can construct truth that needs no corroboration from outside of the knower, making possible any number of "truths." Consider the pedagogical puzzles this creates. What is the teacher trying to teach students if they are all busy constructing their own private worlds? What are the grounds for getting the world right? Why even care whether these worlds agree?

It seems that the only way to adequately address these questions is in terms of a shared world, made up of shared meanings. Yet radical constructivists like Ernst von Glasersfeld want to challenge the notion of shared meanings. According to him, no grounds exist for believing the conceptual structures that constitute meanings or knowledge are held in common among different individuals. Rather, each individual builds up conceptual structures for himself or herself, and one can never say whether or not two people have produced the same construct. At best one may observe that in a given number of situations individual constructs seem to function in the same way; that is, they seem compatible. Borrowing an expression from Paul Cobb, von Glasersfeld contends that shared meanings are really only "taken-as-shared."[28]

For von Glasersfeld, belief in shared meanings may have more or less "viability." He writes:

Where knowledge is concerned, the concepts, theories, beliefs, and other abstract structures which the individual subject has found to be viable gain a higher degree of viability when successful predictions can be made by imputing the use of this knowledge to others. The additional viability can be interpreted as indicating intersubjectivity and constitutes the constructivist substitute for objectivity.[29]

The bridge between the subjective and the intersubjective is built by "imputing" shared meanings. The private worlds of the teacher and her students are "taken-as-shared." In answer to the above pedagogical puzzles, then, the teacher proceeds *as if* there were a world about which meanings were shared.

This is a shaky bridge indeed, in serious danger of collapsing at several points. For doesn't replacing "shared meanings" with meanings that are "taken as shared" just push the question back a step? Do we share a meaning for "taken as shared" or is the meaning of "taken as shared" merely "taken as shared?" If the latter, is *that* merely "taken as shared?" How can radical constructivists talk to one another? Worse, how can they talk to themselves? Are von Glasersfeld's meanings on Monday the same as his meanings on Friday, or does he merely take them to be the same? How could he know?

The earlier discussion of Wittgenstein's views on the preconditions of language learning are pertinent here, and may be expanded somewhat to further undermine using the notion of "taken as shared" as the bridge between private worlds and a shared one. For individuals *construct* meanings within a community into which they have been "thrown" in the way described previously. The meanings they construct—master and learn to employ—come to them as saturated with what the community shares as a community. Recall the example of the child learning the meaning of "ball." Does this child merely take it as shared, assume that her parent means the same thing by pointing that she does? Is this assumption one the child consciously makes ("I assume when Mommy takes that position she's pointing, not hailing a cab.")? This is pretty far fetched, particularly for a child at the rudimentary stage of language learning, who has not mastered the "language game" of assuming.

To be sure, there is a sense in which accomplished language users assume that people share meanings with them. However—and this is the crux—public, intersubjective criteria are required to show when this assumption is violated. If not, if each individual lived in a privately constructed world accessible only to him, what grounds could there ever be for *not* taking meanings as shared? For example, if Susan mistakes a tiger for a lion and Johnny contends the square root of 9 is 4½, why shouldn't I continue to take their meanings as shared with mine? Why isn't this just as warranted as the conclusion that we don't share meanings? After all, I have no access to their private worlds. Maybe Susan's meaning for "tiger" is my meaning for "lion," and Johnny's meaning for "4½" is mine for "3." But there is a public world, and in it there is a correct class of referents for "tiger" and a correct answer to the question, "What's the square root of 9?" and Susan's and Johnny's behavior tell me that they don't know what these are. And the response to Susan and Johnny, particularly if I'm their teacher, is to correct their mistaken beliefs. "No, Susan, I can see why you might think that's a tiger, but it's a lion. Tigers have stripes." "No, Johnny, but good try,—4½ is what you get when you divide 9 by 2. The square root of 9 is the number that gives you 9 when you multiply it by itself, which is 3. Do you see? So, what's the square root of 25?"

A big part of the problem here is that radical constructivists presuppose a dubious view of the *meaning of meaning*. Consider the meaning of Grant Park. In one sense, it means a large park in Chicago, on the shore of Lake Michigan, the site where protesters at the 1968 Democratic convention were beaten and teargassed. In another sense—in the sense of what a teacher might assign as an essay entitled "What Grant Park Means to Me"—the *meaning* of Grant Park is associated with personal experiences. In this sense, Grant Park *means* something very different to a person who was beaten and arrested than to someone who spent a lovely spring afternoon there. The important point is that we don't have to—and don't in fact—take this latter sense of meaning as shared. By contrast, the first sense isn't merely "taken as shared," but *has to be* shared for communication to be possible. Also, it is presupposed by the second kind of meaning. For example, if a student proceeded to write his essay "What Grant Park Means to Me" about some other park, he would have to be corrected, taught what the referent of Grant Park is.

These observations about shared meanings can be extended beyond the simple case of naming. Consider Charles Taylor's discussion of "constitutive meanings," as distinct from "common meanings."[30] The latter refer to beliefs we largely share but that are not definitive of social life and activity; for example, in chess it is bad strategy to move the Queen early. "Constitutive meanings" go deeper, however. The rules governing how the Queen may move provide a case in point. If one violates or ignores these rules such that the Queen is moved willy-nilly, or moved like a Knight, then there would still be the activity of pushing pieces around on a board made of squares but it wouldn't be chess. In the case of constitutive meanings, without all parties having a shared concept, meaning dissolves.[31]

Similarly, suppose a student writes "10)(=+4, 6" on his paper. Is this an idiosyncratic "construction?" Perhaps it is a novel way of adding 4 and 6. Further investigation could reveal whether this is true. But its truth would turn on whether there was some way to translate this string of symbols into the more conventional "(4+6)=10." Otherwise, we couldn't make sense of it as arithmetic and would have no grounds for taking meanings to be shared. Furthermore, it would be a disservice to the student not to teach him the proper rules of the game.

THOROUGHGOING CONSTRUCTIVISM

In her characterization of constructivist pedagogy, Catherine Fosnot writes:

[N]ew experiences sometimes foster contradictions to our present understandings, making them insufficient and thus perturbing and disequilibrating the structure, causing us to accommodate. Accommodation is comprised of reflective, integrative behavior that serves to change one's own self and explicate the object in order for us to function with cognitive equilibrium in relation to it.[32]

Echoing Piaget, Fosnot says cognitive "disequilibrium facilitates learning."[33]

She continues, "Dialogue within a community engenders further thinking. The classroom needs to be seen as a 'community of discourse engaged in activity, reflection, and conversation.'"[34] Taking the necessity of dialogue in genuinely constructivist pedagogy as our guide, one may begin to evaluate practical efforts in the classroom by posing the question, "Are these efforts essentially monological or dialogical?"

One such criterion can be found in consideration of the "directionality" of the instructional effort. Is an activity "unidirectional, such that students are simply led to a mastery of pre-existing cultural tools, or [is it] bi-directional creative space, in which both participants learn and cultural tools can be reconstructed[?]"[35] On this score, the non-constructivist premise of Plato's rationalism comes into sharper focus. Plato sought to lead us to once-and-for-all true answers. Unlike epistemological constructivists, he provided no room for the fallibility of knowledge or for its dynamism.

Yet, as we observed before, constructivist practitioners are not precluded from using more direct methods of instruction. Using such methods does not imply that there is some transcendental or ahistorical perspective from which we can evaluate competing claims to truth. Instead, one can present complex conceptual schemes to students; one can "lecture" on them, as part of the dialogue, while avoiding the presupposition that these conceptual schemes are independent of history or culture, or are impervious to challenge. The constructivist educator must actively promote a fallible view of knowledge by inviting critical perspectives to be brought to bear on these conceptual schemes. But this activity must occur against a background of shared meanings, only a few of which can be up for grabs at a given time. Otherwise, dialogue and the construction of knowledge spin their wheels, unable to get any traction.

Dewey anticipated, if he did not explicitly articulate, most of what is important and interesting about constructivist pedagogy. He also provided it with a foundation in constructivist epistemology though his view was variously referred to as "instrumentalism," "experimentalism," and "pragmatism." This is not the place for yet another rediscovery and celebration of the insights of Dewey. Still, we want to say enough to reinforce one of his themes that has received little attention on the contemporary scene: constructivism as it applies to moral and political education.

Dewey advocated a holistic approach to curriculum and instruction, in which all subjects in the curriculum were to be integrated and subsumed under the overarching goal of promoting a truly democratic community. To be sure, Dewey's abiding commitment to democracy looms large here, but this commitment is by no means an isolated feature of his view. For it is also undergirded by a constructivist epistemology that is fallibilistic and dynamic, and that significantly blurs the boundaries between facts and science, on the one hand, and morals and politics, on the other. Complementing Dewey's constructivist epistemology is a constructivist pedagogy that spans the curriculum and that *begins* with what students value, understand, and have an interest in. If successful, it *ends* with having initiated students into the shared meanings—"experience *funded*," as William James put it[36]—of a community, however subject to test some of these may be.

A general constructivist pedagogy along these Deweyan lines, then, requires fostering the moral and intellectual dispositions required of democratic citizenship, as well as other skills and knowledge (in natural science, mathematics, history, geography, anthropology, etc.) needed to be in control of one's life and to engage in fruitful and respectful dialogue with other members of the community. Such a pedagogical approach, it should be noted, is congenial to the burgeoning contemporary interest and scholarship in moral and political education exemplified by a diverse group of radical pedagogues, feminists, and contemporary liberals.

Conclusion

History could be in the process of repeating itself—albeit donned in a new set of clothes. For the constructivist movement is strikingly reminiscent of the progressive movement. Like constructivists, progressives set themselves in opposition to the prevailing authoritarian tradition in education. But certain progressives went too far. Reacting against the manner in which traditional educational arrangements invested authority almost exclusively in teachers and subject matter, they invested authority almost exclusively in students. Dewey was often associated with this so-called "child-centered" approach, but he actually disdained it as Either-Or thinking, and likened it to jumping "out of the frying pan into the fire."[37] No matter, the progressive movement as a whole, including Dewey's version, suffered its own kind of "back to basics" backlash, and was eventually relegated to the margins.

Certain constructivists are also in danger of going too far (if they haven't already). An epistemological stance that leaves knowledge ultimately stranded on private constructions encourages teachers to become overly cautious about what they can confidently claim to know. This, in turn, encourages them to be overly timid about challenging students' personal constructions of the world, for fear of imposing their own personal view of things. (In this vein, we've had accomplished teachers report to us that preservice teachers, avowing constructivism, aren't good at asking challenging questions of their students.) But having learning goals clearly specified ahead of time and challenging students to meet them doesn't mean the system of beliefs they encompass is necessarily final and unimpeachable, that teachers should always and only engage in "teaching by telling," or that teachers should not take care in dealing with students' mistakes. It is clearly wrong for teachers to simply assert their authority and to use humiliating tactics with a student who gives a mistaken answer to "What's the square root of 9?" And it's pedagogically ineffective not to explore why the student got the answer he did. But it's also wrong not to correct judiciously but unequivocally the student's error.

To be sure, things get considerably more dicey when teachers leave the relatively safe havens of mathematical and scientific truth for the more treacherous territory of moral and political education, though even here there are things that teachers may safely insist are mistaken; for example, "Racism is okay." Certain issues clearly require a more noncommittal stance on the part of the teacher; for example, "Wearing fur coats is morally wrong." But controversy exists in mathematics and science as well, especially at their frontiers. The primary thing that thoroughgoing constructivism should embody and foster *across the curriculum* is the ability to effectively deal with uncertainty and the controversy that may attend it. And that requires judging when uncertainty and controversy are appropriate to the context and issue at hand. Lest educational reformers once again jump from the frying pan into the fire, it also requires judging when they are not.

We thank Nick Peresinni and Lorrie Shepard for their instructive comments.

Notes

1. See, for example, Catherine Z. Elgin, *Between the Absolute and the Arbitrary* (Ithaca and London: Cornell University Press, 1997).

2. The leading proponent of this view is Ernst von Glasersfeld. His most extended treatment is *Radical Constructivism: A Way of Knowing and Learning* (London: The Falmer Press, 1995).

3. Denis C. Phillips, "The Good, the Bad, and the Ugly: The Many Faces of Constructivism," *Educational Researcher* 24, no. 7 (1995): 5-12.

4. In an important sense Wittgenstein swears off the enterprise of epistemology as misguided.

5. Iris M. Young employs this term in "Polity and Group Difference: A Critique of the Ideal of Universal Citizenship," in *Feminism and Political Theory*, ed. Cass R. Sunstein (Chicago and London, The University of Chicago Press, 1990). She attributes its origin to Heideggar.

6. Ludwig Wittgenstein, *The Philosophical Investigations*, 3rd edition (New York: The Macmillan Company, 1953), p. 132e.

7. Wittgenstein, *The Philosophical Investigations*, p. 85e.

8. Hilary Putnam, *Realism with a Human Face* (Harvard University Press: Cambridge, MA, and London, 1990), p. 261.

9. Putnam, *Realism with a Human Face*, p. 28.

10. Willard V. O. Quine, "Two Dogmas of Empiricism," in *From a Logical Point of View* (New York: Harper Torchbooks, 1961).

11. Thomas S. Kuhn, *The Essential Tension: Selected Studies in Scientific Tradition and Change* (Chicago: University of Chicago Press, 1977).

12. See Willard V. O. Quine, "The Basis of Conceptual Schemes," in *The Foundations of Knowledge*, ed. Charles Landesman (Englewood Cliffs, N.J.: Prentice-Hall, 1970); and Kuhn, *The Essential Tension*.

13. Thomas S. Kuhn, *The Structure of Scientific Revolutions* (Chicago: University of Chicago Press, 1962).

14. This description owes to Paul Rabinow and William Sullivan, "The Interpretive Turn: Emergence of an Approach," in *Interpretive Social Science*, eds. Paul Rabinow and William Sullivan (Los Angeles: University of California Press, 1977).

15. See Charles Taylor, "Interpretation and the Sciences of Man," in *Interpretive Social Science*, eds. Rabinow and Sullivan.

16. Helen Longino, "Subjects, Power and Knowledge: Description and Prescription in Feminist Philosophies of Science," in *Feminist Epistemologies*, eds. Linda Alcoff and Elizabeth Potter (New York: Routledge, 1993).

17. John Searle, *The Construction of Social Reality* (New York: The Free Press, 1995).

18. Searle, *The Construction of Social Reality*.

19. Sandra Harding (1993). "Rethinking Standpoint Epistemology: What is "Strong Objectivity"? in *Feminist Epistemologies*, eds. Linda Alcoff and Elizabeth Potter (New York: Routledge, 1993).

20. Putnam, *Realism with a Human Face*, p. 141.

21. Ibid., p. 140.

22. Lorraine Code, "Taking Subjectivity into Account," in *Feminist Epistemologies*, eds. Linda Alcoff and Elizabeth Potter (New York: Routledge, 1993).

23. John Dewey, *Experience and Education* (New York, Macmillan Publishing Company, 1938), p. 64.

24. Paul Ernest, "The One and the Many," in *Constructivism in Education*, eds. Leslie P. Steffe and Jerry Gale (Hillsdale, N.J.: Lawrence Erlbaum Associates, 1995), p. 459.

25. Michael Matthews, "Introductory Comments on Philosophy and Constructivism in Science Education," *Science and Education* 6 (1997): 5-14, p. 12.

26. von Glasersfeld, *Radical Constructivism: A Way of Knowing and Learning*.

27. See, for example, Phillips, "The Good, the Bad, and the Ugly: The Many Faces of Constructivism"; James Garrison, "Realism, Deweyan Pragmatism, and Educational Research," *Education Researcher* 23, no. 1 (1994): 5-14; and David C. Gruender, "Constructivism and Learning: A Philosophical Appraisal," *Educational Technology* (May-June, 1996): 21-29.

28. Ernst von Glasersfeld, "Introduction: Aspects of Constructivism," in *Constructivism: Theory, Perspectives, and Practice*, ed. Catharine T. Fosnot (New York:Teachers College Press, 1996), p. 4.

29. von Glasersfeld, *Radical Constructivism: A Way of Knowing and Learning*.

30. Taylor, "Interpretation and the Sciences of Man."

31. This observation is also in Gruender, "Constructivism and Learning: A Philosophical Appraisal."

32. Catherine T. Fosnot, "Constructivism: A Psychological Theory of Learning," in *Constructivism: Theory, Perspectives, and Practice*, ed. Fosnot (New York: Teachers College Press, 1996), p. 13.

33. Fosnot, *Constructivism: Theory, Perspectives, and Practice*, p. 29; see also Jacqueline G. Brooks and Martin Brooks, *The Case for Constructivist Classrooms* (Alexandria, Virginia: Association for Supervision and Curriculum Development, 1993).

34. Fosnot, *Constructivism: Theory, Perspectives, and Practice*, pp. 29-30.

35. James Garrison, "Deweyan Pragmatism and the Epistemology of Contemporary Social Constructivism," *American Educational Research Journal* 32, no. 4 (Winter 1995), p. 726.

36. William James, "Pragmatism's Conception of the Truth," in *Essays in Pragmatism* (New York: Hafner Publishing Company, 1968), p. 171.

37. Dewey, *Experience and Education*, p. 64.

CHAPTER III

Seductive Illusions: Von Glasersfeld and Gergen on Epistemology and Education

LUISE PRIOR McCARTY AND THOMAS A. SCHWANDT

Introduction

Constructivism in its various guises is incredibly attractive to many educators. In her introduction to an issue of the *Journal of Teacher Education* devoted solely to constructivism, the editor wrote:

Constructivism is the new rallying theme in education. Its popularity derives from its origins in a variety of disciplines, notably philosophy of science, psychology, and sociology. The implications of a constructivist perspective for education differ depending on its disciplinary foundation, but professional education groups as diverse as the National Association for the Education of Young Children and the National Council of Teachers of Mathematics have based revisions of their standards for practice on the constructivist assumption that learners do not passively absorb knowledge but rather construct it from their experiences.[1]

Jacqueline and Martin Brooks, in their *In Search of Understanding: The Case for Constructivist Classrooms*, spell out presumed advantages for constructivistic pedagogy, with chapters entitled "Honoring the learning process," "Adapting curriculum to address students' suppositions," "Seeking and valuing students' point of view." They write:

Most teachers agree with the quests and goals of the constructivist orientation: teachers want students to take responsibility for their own learning, to be autonomous thinkers, to develop integrated understandings of concepts, and to pose—and seek to answer—important questions.[2]

Designing curriculum in such a way that it reflects careful thought about the teacher-student relationship, is relevant to students' interests, addresses real-world problems, values students' efforts to come to

Luise Prior McCarty is Associate Professor of Education and Thomas A. Schwandt is Professor of Education and Associate Dean for Graduate Studies in Education at Indiana University, Bloomington.

terms with ideas and arguments, and encourages their full participation in acts of knowing is, of course, a laudable goal. But we find it incredible that these classroom practices require justification from various philosophies of constructivism and constructionism that promise bold new solutions to contemporary pedagogical problems, when in fact these philosophies are shown to be, on closer examination, little more than a garage sale of outdated philosophical falsisms.

Constructivism has lately become the modish descriptor of choice for a range of hazily imagined mental activities, among them gender construction and social construction. The term has achieved currency within a number of the human sciences and pseudosciences—gender studies, literary theory and postmodernist philosophy—as well as among those committed to qualitative research methods in anthropology and sociology. Many educational practitioners nowadays call themselves constructivists without much awareness of fundamental differences among the varieties of constructivism. Nor are they always absolutely clear about the epistemological, ontological, metaphysical, and moral assumptions, concepts, and values that undergird constructivistic beliefs. Our contention is that pedagogical and ideological convictions feed this identification with a movement that, as Denis Phillips points out, has recently achieved the status of political correctness.[3]

In this chapter we focus exclusively on the works of Ernst von Glasersfeld and Kenneth Gergen as exemplary representatives of psychological and social versions of constructivist epistemology, respectively (or, more commonly, radical constructivism and social constructionism). Radical constructivism and social constructionism represent two of the most influential and well-articulated versions of constructivist thinking in the current educational literature. In selecting von Glasersfeld's and Gergen's writings as the foci of our critical analysis and assessment, we are extending the descriptive and clarificatory tasks initiated by a number of authors who have cast von Glasersfeld and Gergen as representative of two extremes on a spectrum of constructivisms.[4] Although these two views share some crucial assumptions, they are logically contraries. The two authors converge in their critical stance toward traditional epistemology and both perceive their contributions as post-epistemological challenges to conceptions of how we come to know. However, von Glasersfeld concentrates on individual, cognitive, private constructions of knowledge whereas Gergen's analysis of knowledge construction is set in a social realm of public discourse.[5]

In what follows we rehearse the basic epistemological conceptions of both positions as well as their criticisms of traditional epistemology.

More importantly, we frame such epistemological work within a larger analysis of ontological, metaphysical, and ethical questions that are often overlooked and desperately need to be addressed. Our targets are the solipsisms of von Glasersfeld (both epistemological and semantical) and Gergen's sociolinguistic idealism.[6] Our analysis and criticism reveals that an influential educational approach cannot stay ontologically "mute" (Gergen)—that is, silent on questions of the nature, constitution, and structure of reality—or metaphysically "agnostic" (von Glasersfeld)—refusing to either deny or affirm the existence of reality—even if ontology and metaphysics are thrown by the wayside as part of a postmodern call for the "end of philosophy." Far more troublesome ethically are the barely hidden moral commitments of both perspectives, commitments which raise in a serious way the question of their suitability as educational approaches. As Gergen himself has pointed out, relativism in all its forms (cultural, moral, conceptual) represents a major critical charge against constructivism in all its guises.

The discussion that follows is structured in three parts. The first part offers a largely expository account of the central features of von Glasersfeld's philosophy of radical constructivism. The second part is an exposition of Gergen's social constructionism. The third part compares and criticizes both philosophies along several important dimensions.

Von Glasersfeld's Radical Constructivism

The philosophical mainspring of radical constructivism is the insistence that human knowledge cannot consist in accurate representation or faithful copying of an external reality, that is, of a reality which is nonphenomenal, existing apart from the subject's experiences. While rejecting the idea of cognitive representation whole cloth, von Glasersfeld spurns all correspondence accounts of truth. In place of these time-honored visions of knowledge and truth, the radical constructivist prefers to reconstrue knowledge procedurally: as an unending series of processes of inner construction. He or she also wants to assess the reliability of knowledge instrumentally in terms of the evolutionary viability of constructions. From this combination of metaphysics and epistemology, von Glasersfeld claims to derive a detailed theory of acceptable pedagogy and a less detailed theory of moral concepts and actions.

RADICAL CONSTRUCTIVIST EPISTEMOLOGY

Key to a full exposition of the epistemology and metaphysics of radical constructivism are four ideas: skepticism, subjectivism about truth, mental construction and self-versus-other. The philosophical jumping-off point for von Glasersfeld and the primary target of his critique is a classical concept of representation:

Radical Constructivism was conceived as an attempt to circumvent the paradox of traditional epistemology . . . the assumption that knowledge may be called 'true' only if it can be considered a more or less accurate *representation* of a world that exists 'in itself,' prior to and independent of the knower's experience of it.[7]

In accusing traditional epistemology of paradox, von Glasersfeld marks himself as a traditional epistemologist, but of another stripe. He joins a long and distinguished line of skeptical mavericks, among them Bishop Berkeley and David Hume, who pressed the question, "If our knowledge of the extra-mental world is thoroughly mediated by representations, then why isn't our knowledge, in the fullest sense, limited to representations alone? Can I know anything other than my own sense data?" These old-time epistemologists parted company with realism, the idea that we have objective knowledge of an extra-mental reality in virtue of a happy correspondence between our mental contents and the reality they intend. The radical constructivist remains faithful to another traditional notion, philosophical idealism, which was skeptical of prospects for substantiating the existence of objective knowledge conceived as the proper mapping of a non-phenomenal realm, "outside the mind."

Von Glasersfeld does not deny extra-mental existence outright (and, on this point, joins forces with Kant against Berkeley and Hume), but prefers to insist that external reality cannot be known. What remains of knowledge for the constructivist extends no further than the edges of the individual mind. Should one hanker after some wisp of reality, the constructivist offers an experiential reality, a subjective realm constructed by the individual mind. In these views, the radical constructivist stands in full concord with his idealist ancestors. (Von Glasersfeld himself treats his epistemology as part of the current pop scene in antifoundationalism, wherein Rortyans and kindred postmodernists wrestle for the limelight.)

Von Glasersfeld supposes that an extreme subjectivism follows from his brand of skepticism, a subjectivism on which scientific and, one supposes, ordinary, well-founded truth cannot be objective, since it cannot consist in a correspondence between representation and reality. What remains of truth becomes a thoroughly subjective means for organizing an individual's own experiential reality. There are to be no standards external to the individual which subjective truth has to satisfy if it is to count as truth. The remaining standards are entirely inner. The criteria of fit and viability which von Glasersfeld enlists as replacements for truth are relations of internal coherence among one or more aspects of the subject's constructed reality.

According to the constructivist, each organism constructs its own experiential reality out of phenomenal elements. Hence, the "reality" just referred to is also wholly mental or inner. In this reality, suitable processes of world construction are to reflect, on an abstract level, evolutionary theories in biology, according to which relations of variation, adaptation, and selection allow organisms to survive. A particular construction counts as knowledge insofar as it works along with the battery of constructions already accomplished, that is, its mental gears fit the available cogs, or it is a useful way of organizing experiences and attaining desired goals (also constructed).[8] The constructivist knower does not peer out to catch a clear view of a non-constructed world, but is always looking over his shoulder at what has been constructed to date.

CONSTRUCTING CONSTRUCTIONS

As for constructions themselves, von Glasersfeld conceives them procedurally. Radical constructivists prefer the verb "knowing" to the noun "knowledge" to underscore the procedural vision, the view of individual organisms knowing by acting and choosing in a continuous and unending process of creating more viable constructions: "Applied to cognition, this means that 'to know' is not to possess true 'representations' of reality, but rather to *possess ways and means of acting and thinking that allow one to attain the goals one happens to have chosen.*"[9] Von Glasersfeld's views on the fine details of constructing derive from a reading of Piagetian developmental theory on which a child builds up concepts and cognitive schemes by isolating different experiences and treating them as equal or near equal. For example, a child has, over time, different experiences with a rattle. In order to forge a unitary concept of rattle, the child must compare these repeated experiences and recognize the similarities among them, while ignoring irrelevant differences, such as the slightly different sounds produced each time it shakes the rattle.[10]

The concept is something the child constructs from sensory raw materials by abstracting out the similar features. It is not, as on some classical accounts, a fixed piece of knowledge, but is viewed as a relatively stable cognitive scheme for guiding constructive processes. As construction proceeds, new experiences are modified to fit schemes previously developed. Piaget calls this process of imposing schemes on experience "assimilation." Objects acquire permanence or come to fit the scheme of permanence once a constructed object, say a child's rattle, can be imagined apart from any immediate experience of it. This fit is a cognitive accomplishment stored in memory so that it can later be called up. Further abstraction is to take place as the child goes from initial operations to higher cognitive functions which no longer demand immediate sensory input. These functions are themselves higher-level schemes, patterns that acquire a kind of permanence needed to construct (but not to constitute) the impression of separation between the individual and perceptual reality. Von Glasersfeld maintains that, in contrast to Piaget's view, there is here no construction independent of or outside the constructor's mind.

Important to von Glasersfeld's treatment of learning and motivation is the notion of perturbations. These enter into the constructive business to allow for another Piagetian force, accommodation. Obviously, if there can be success in construction (viability), there can also be failure: certain constructions are supposed to lack viability. Some of these serve to create situations of inner perturbation or even crisis— Kuhnian revolutions confined to the knowing mind. These von Glasersfeld considers not cognitive disasters but positive spurs to the constructing mind. The idea is that only through perturbation is the organism motivated to develop adaptive processes and to achieve equilibrium: "Cognitive organisms operate in a world of constraining conditions. They can learn what they are *not* permitted to do."[11] Lastly, von Glasersfeld also allows criteria of personal preference to constrain construction: the individual may simply prefer one construction to another or may wish to change a manner of constructing. These preferences are brute, for the individual wishes to so construct and that is all there is to it.

One way of illustrating constraints is to look at the way language and communication are construed in radical constructivism. In keeping with the procedural overtones, language is viewed as a tool whose use is revealed in the creation of high-level abstractions, among them the kinds of abstractions that play a role in teaching. Here, linguistic meaning is not socially or intersubjectively constructed but only individually. Von Glasersfeld writes, "Once we come to see this essential and inescapable subjectivity of linguistic meaning, we can no longer maintain the preconceived notion that words convey ideas or knowledge."[12] As we shall see, the relativistic view that only each individual speaker knows what his or her words and thoughts mean holds extreme consequences for teaching and learning.

Accommodation occurs when new and viable patterns are constructed as a result of perturbations that serve, in turn, future assimilative processes. Assimilation and accommodation are viewed as forces that constantly neutralize each other. With Piaget, von Glasersfeld calls this neutralization "equilibrium," considered not as a steady state but dynamically, as the "regularity of recursive processes."[13] Each action or operation of the organism is effective and viable insofar as it reinstates the equilibrium of the actor. In constructivism as in elementary physics, equilibrium is the goal state to which the system tends. On this picture, we construct in order to reach ever more satisfactory states of cognitive equilibrium.

SELF-OTHER/SELF-WORLD RELATIONS

For assessing the pedagogy of radical constructivism, one further point is of great importance, namely, the constructivistic reworking of the distinction between self and environment, or self, other, and world. As we have seen, von Glasersfeld conceives of the individual as an organism in systems-theoretic terms, as a closed evolutionary system. Among other things, this means that there can be no strict distinction between the organism and its constructions or between the organism and its environment. For there is to be nothing "outside" the experiential reality constructed by the organism, nothing external to which the organism is responsible in knowledge. To deploy one of von Glasersfeld's own examples, when we recognize a book before us, this book cannot exist as an object separate from us. "All it means is that in some part of our present experiential field there is the kind of raw material which, if coordinated in a particular way, is sufficiently close to what our concept of book demands, so that we accept it as an instantiation of that concept."[14] The constructing organism and its constructed object (in this case, a book) are both viewed as constructed aspects of the same experiential field. One perceives and knows books only insofar as the private experiential reality provides a viable construction that confirms or disconfirms previous constructions, schematized as a concept of book. Everything, therefore, is constructed, assembled from the experiential field—from the self that constructs, to the objects that populate the constructed world. Any remaining distinctions between self and object are relative or phenomenal only and not absolute; they are instrumental distinctions drawn, perhaps temporarily, entirely for the purposes of the organism, exhausted in affording more viability.

Hence, radical constructivism is a form of philosophical solipsism, the view that only one being, the individual mind, exists substantially. All else is construction. The validity of an individual's knowledge, therefore, ends at the limits of his or her own consciousness. Consistent with this, von Glasersfeld will draw no distinction in principle between self and other. Other people are to be my constructions in just the way that books or trees or cars are and so are metaphysically inseparable from the self. In constructing knowledge, then, I owe nothing to others conceived as independent beings.

Von Glasersfeld, therefore, must view social construction as a metaphysical impossibility and the words "social knowledge" as a contradiction in terms. How then does this solipsistic picture come to include any recognizable idea of other persons and of society? Von Glasersfeld describes the conceptual construction of the other in Piagetian developmental terms. In the process of assimilation and accommodation in inner experience, a child encounters unruly "entities" that cause particularly severe perturbations. They lead a child to experience these entities as radically different from, say, dolls or puppies. They cannot be avoided, for these unruly entities are constructions of other human individuals. Children first ascribe to these strictly perceptual properties. Only later do constructed others receive cognitive properties, since they are viewed as self-moving and relatively unpredictable in their behavior. On the construction of others, von Glasersfeld cites Kant: "It is manifest that, if one wants to imagine a thinking being, one would have to put oneself in its place and to impute one's own subject to the object one intended to consider."[15]

Through assimilation and accommodation, then, the individual subject comes to consider others as essentially like itself and to construct an idea of others in parallel to his or her idea of self. Should these ideas prove to be viable, they are deemed to be (constructed as) viable intersubjectively. This is also an old idea in philosophy: that one ascribes mental states to others only on the basis of an analogy with the self.

Clearly, other humans can serve in the creation of knowledge merely corroborative functions, as do any constructions. As such, they are conceived instrumentally by von Glasersfeld. To repeat, others cannot be real subjects, existing independently of the subject, but are constructions whose usefulness is exhausted in achieving a confirmation of viability. These sorts of confirmations von Glasersfeld treats as a mentalistic analogue of objectivity.[16] There is a sense, therefore, that a constructed, interiorized version of social context is involved in viability. In sum, for von Glasersfeld, the other serves no real ethical need (and in this regard constructivism appears committed to a severe form of ethical relativism) but merely an epistemic need arising relatively late in the Piagetian developmental story.

From this perspective, the concern for others can be grounded in the individual subject's *need* for other people in order to establish an intersubjective viability of ways of thinking and acting. Others have to be considered because they are irreplaceable in the construction of a more solid experiential reality. This in itself does not constitute an ethical precept, but it may supply a basis for the development of ethics.[17] Von Glasersfeld goes on to suggest that responsibility for others and "greater tolerance in social interactions" follow from the basic constructivistic vision but offers no more detailed treatment of ethics, since he explicitly refuses to make ontological and ethical claims about the nature of people and how they ought to act, apart from a few minimal ethical considerations.[18]

CONSTRUCTIVISM AND EDUCATION

Now we turn to issues specifically educational. Von Glasersfeld accuses educators of creating educational crises through their determined efforts to impart value-free objective knowledge to students and their focus on a didactic teaching method that Paulo Freire has derided as "the banking method of teaching." Of such methods, radical constructivism is to be free. In their stead, von Glasersfeld proposes teaching and learning methods he thinks to be direct licensees of constructivism's procedural and instrumental conception of knowledge.

From a constructivistic perspective, learning is primarily a process of assimilation and accommodation to disturbances in the subject's experiential environment. The disturbances or perturbations alert the subject to the need to check cognitive patterns previously established and to recognize those problems that call for new and equilibrating solutions. Comparing, recognizing similarities and differences, and constructing solutions are, then, among the most important cognitive abilities a constructivist teacher would hope to foster. Because von Glasersfeld has replaced truth with viability, students' constructions need not be true in order to be viable solutions to problems; indeed, there is to be no notion of correct solution, no external standard of right or wrong. As long as a student's solution to a problem achieves a viable goal, it has to be credited. Nor can relevant educational goals be set externally; they are only to be encountered by the student as perturbations. Therefore, class objectives and curricular targets cannot be devised *a priori* by a teacher; they should be reconceived as problems geared to the cognitive array which each individual brings to the learning situation. This underscores the supposed need for constructivist teachers to model, as closely as possible, each student's cognitive capacities. Von Glasersfeld adds that learning how to think, and how to do so independently, are also goals to be adopted. By his lights, students are better motivated when they encounter the satisfaction of thinking out viable solutions for themselves. They do not need external rewards, as the behaviorists would have it.

In addition to taking a general cognizance of the active character of construction and the individualistic nature of knowledge, a constructivist teacher has two specific tasks: to establish a learning environment suited to providing perturbations for the student's mental constructive processes and to project a model of each individual student's stage in mental development and constructions, one that will allow the teacher to understand the student's notion of a viable solution. For von Glasersfeld, teaching cannot be a matter of conveying knowledge from teacher to student. Not only is there no objective or interpersonal knowledge but words are also barred from carrying shared linguistic meaning. For the teaching process this means that when teacher speaks to student the teacher sends an encoded signal which the student has to decode and to construct with a meaning. There can be no true or correct match between teacher's meaning and student's; there is, at best, a viable fit that can be constructed between them. This linguistic fit serves von Glasersfeld as an analogue for understanding as well as a preferred goal for successful teaching:

Instead, we come to realize that 'understanding' is a matter of fit rather than match. Put in the simplest way, to understand what someone has said or written means no less but also no more than to have built up a conceptual structure that, in the given context, appears to be *compatible* with the structure the speaker had in mind—and this compatibility, as a rule, manifests itself in no other way than that the receiver says and does nothing that contravenes the speaker's expectations.[19]

Understanding is deemed more desirable than the imparting of knowledge since students are thereby enabled to demonstrate their constructive efforts and to aid their teachers in modeling their stage in learning. In consequence, external criteria such as test results ought not to set demands on students' understanding. Radical constructivists refuse in fact to allow that tests demonstrate student understanding. For them, instead of teaching to the test or to shared curricular goals, that is, to the results of construction, teachers ought to pay close attention to the processes of individual student learning. For there can be no correct results in radical constructivism.

Pertinent to constructivism's picture of education are a number of questions. The first concerns solipsism in epistemology and the second, abstraction as a model of concept formation. Solipsism is the metaphysical view that only one individual mind exists; there are to be no other minds, no external world. An obvious point is that if one is a solipsist then why worry about educating others—they don't exist! We can also note the ethical issue attendant to solipsism in education, the question of instructing small children that each one of them is nothing but a mind, alone in a world each must construct for himself or herself. Most philosophers charge that solipsism fails as an epistemology, since no one has been able to explain adequately how the vast amount that we know on the basis of interpersonal contact (from books, newspapers, teachers and so on) and interaction with a world which is outside our control (through scientific experiments and experience with eating, building, or sport, for example) could be reconstructed on a strictly individualistic basis, on the basis of the idea that there is only one creature who makes it all. To this charge, leveled by a number of scholars, among them Gergen, von Glasersfeld has yet to provide a fully adequate defense.[20]

He has responded that, in radical constructivism, there is a need for the individual to construct others, for there have to be (constructed) others to corroborate individual construction. Hence, argues von Glasersfeld, his view is not solipsistic. Unfortunately, this response remains unconvincing. Since the other is constructed and is not independent of the individual mind, it is hard to see what could be meant by "corroboration" here. If the only corroboration I ever get for my ideas is the agreement of creatures who owe their very existence to me, then my ideas are never truly and independently corroborated. After all, I may find the construction of leagues of "Yes men" who corroborate what I do regardless of the consequences a perfectly viable circumstance. The "others" of which von Glasersfeld speaks are cognitive abstractions made to play an ancillary epistemic role at best, images or models of real persons. It remains to be seen that these intellectual schemes for organizing experience can go proxy in full-scale manner for real persons, individuals whose entire being is independent of and external to my constructions and to whom I stand (from the first day of my life) in objective ethical and moral relations of mutual responsibility which I do not seem to construct. Barring further clarification from von Glasersfeld, one can only conclude that he is a solipsist in the objectionable sense.

The idea that concepts are first acquired by abstracting from experience is an old story in philosophy. John Locke, Berkeley, and Hume were hardly the first to argue along these lines. Tradition notwithstanding, the idea is a nonstarter, because it begs the question of concept acquisition. Remember that, on the constructivist view, concepts are nothing more than means to organize and classify similar experiences. If a child lacks the concept of "rattle," that is, lacks the means to pick out and organize similar experiences and to classify them all as "rattle," he needs to abstract that concept from his own experiences, or so the story goes. When he abstracts, he sifts through similarities and differences in experience, picking out those relevantly similar to previous experiences of a rattle. But how, without having the concept of "rattle" already, is he to determine which is a relevant difference and which a relevant similarity? Will it matter if the experience is had on a Thursday, or on a cloudy day, or with a rattle held in the hand or lying on the floor? To select out of the booming, buzzing confusion of experience those features relevantly similar, those to be organized under the concept "rattle," the child must already be in possession of the concept. Without having a concept of rattle as an enduring physical object, that is, without a full battery of concepts for sorting and comparing experiences, it is difficult, to put it mildly, to see how the experiential sorting required for abstraction is to take place. Therefore, in order to abstract a concept, one already needs to have that concept and the old idea is shown to be empty.

Lastly, we wish to raise an issue arising from radical constructivists' efforts to bring their views of knowledge and education into the classroom, in particular into those classrooms where constructivism has, to date, had most impact: the teaching of science and mathematics. Remember that the constructivistic teacher is to make do without any concept of objective truth or falsehood. Radical constructivism provides no basis to identify a proposed theory as incorrect or mistaken. Instead of speaking of objective error, the teacher is to make use of each student's propensity to build viable constructions. It is difficult to see, however, how talk of propensity to viability can replace truth and error in practical cases, especially when we realize that many of the scientific theories currently accepted are deeply counterintuitive and go against a great deal of everyday experience. To take a simple example, students may reasonably prefer a geocentric theory of the solar system (on which the sun rotates around the earth) to any heliocentric theory. After all, the hypothesis that the sun actually moves across the sky each day is certainly far more consonant with their previous experiences, as it was for millions of humans before Copernicus. When we look further into the corpus of science currently accepted, we find talk of the bending of light and of space itself in the neighborhood of large bodies, of time slowing as speeds increase, of diseases spread by the invasion of our bodies by millions of invisible agents. Without the leverage provided by traditions of truth, error, and error correction, it remains wholly unclear how a teacher is to convey to students on the basis of their previous experiences alone what any of these "wild" ideas mean, let alone the fact that they are, in terms of scientific theorizing, the very best we can come up with today. Researchers on constructivistic teaching themselves seem to concur in this judgment. Rosalind Driver and colleagues encouraged students to construct their own accounts of the oxidation that causes nails to rust. They wrote, "The theory that rusting is a chemical reaction between iron, oxygen and matter, resulting in the formation of a new substance is not one that students are likely to generate for themselves. . . . The process of investigating personal ideas and theories may lead students to reflect upon and question them [viz., those ideas and theories]. At the same time, it is unlikely to lead to the scientific view."[21]

Gergen's Social Constructionism

Kenneth Gergen's version of social constructionism has its roots in the Diltheyan conviction, as Charles Taylor once put it, that being illuminating and insightful about human beings involves something rather different from being illuminating and insightful about stars and amoebas.[22] Gergen began to stake out what that difference consists of in a comprehensive way in *Toward Transformation in Social Knowledge*. However, as he explained in the preface to the second edition, that work was given largely to deconstructing and criticizing the mix of logical positivism, empiricism, and naturalism that characterized the epistemology and methodology of the sociobehavioral sciences. A full-blown effort to develop a successor project awaited the appearance of his *Realities and Relationships*.[23]

In Gergen's view, social constructionism is a valuable post-empiricist framework for the human sciences for at least two reasons. First, it offers a synthesis of three kinds of scholarly work that characterize much of the contemporary dissatisfaction with the aims and methods of the human sciences. Marxist criticism and ideological critiques inspired by critical theory, poststructural and literary-rhetorical criticism, and criticisms that elevate social factors in knowledge production to a place of prominence are, in Gergen's view, wedded in social constructionism, which he defines as "a form of intelligibility—an array of propositions, arguments, metaphors, narratives, and the like—that invite habitation."[24] Second, Gergen views "doing" social construction as kind of "discursive positioning" in a multiplicity of language games whereby it is possible to realize the promise of a project of "reconstruction" and "democratization" of the human sciences "wherein new realities and practices are fashioned for cultural transformation" and the "range of voices participating in the consequential dialogues of science is expanded."[25] Thus, undeniably, Gergen's vision of social constructionism is wedded both to epistemological and moral-political agendas. It is both a successor to post-empiricist "social epistemology" and a call to action.

Constructionism's main bugbear is the modern epistemological project—the development and consequences of empiricist and rationalist theories of knowledge (which Gergen labels the "exogenic" and "endogenic" views, respectively).[26] The particular target of social constructionism is the foundational ambitions of these epistemologies, associated theories of the mechanistic self, and a designative view of the significance of language.[27] Given that Gergen offers social constructionism as a successor project to foundationalism, we have organized the discussion that follows by first explaining what social constructionism rejects and then what it affirms in ontology, epistemology, ethics, and education.

ONTOLOGICAL AND EPISTEMOLOGICAL MATTERS

Gergen rejects all manner of what might be generally called foundationalist thinking, or what Richard Bernstein calls objectivism, in matters metaphysical, empirical, and moral.[28] He is radically skeptical toward all efforts to establish foundational descriptions, first principles, or certain truths about the world. Gergen finds that all efforts to distinguish mind and world, mental and material, are faced with intractable and insoluble problems centering on familiar concerns such as the problem of other minds and the difficulties of establishing with clarity and certainty how it is that the external world is made manifest to the mind. Accordingly, constructionism grants neither mind nor world ontological status. In a phrase, constructionism is "ontologically agnostic":

Constructionism makes no denial concerning explosions, poverty, death or the "world out there" more generally. Neither does it make any affirmation. . . . [C]onstructionism is ontologically mute. Whatever is, simply is. There is no foundational description to be made about an "out there" as opposed to an "in here," about experience or material.[29]

Not only does Gergen reject all efforts to "ontologize," but he aims to render all links between observation and perception, between mind and world, between language and reality as at best contingent, and, at worst, non-existent. As he explains in *Toward Transformation in Social Knowledge*, such conventional epistemological notions as "what are the facts of the matter?" and "what is the case?" provide neither "the source nor the sanction" for our descriptions and explanations of the world: "The extent to which any given datum corroborates or falsifies a given theoretical statement is fundamentally ambiguous and open to continuous negotiation."[30]

Gergen claims that what we would commonly consider to be "observations" of real-world phenomena are in fact a product of our use of language: "language create[s] independent and enduring entities in an experienced world of prevailing fluctuation;" "empirical research in the sociobehavioral sciences does not furnish observations. . . . Rather, the chief product of research is language."[31] Thus, the very notions of representation and reference, of some kind of understanding (albeit imperfect) of the fit between our claims about the world and the world itself, are rendered suspect.

Gergen also rejects the picture of human agency that he argues accompanies all dualistic thinking: the idea of an individual mind striving to ground its knowledge claims about objects in the world in some kind of privileged representation. For Gergen, a satisfactory account of what constitutes knowledge or meaning cannot be had by placing individual mental processing at center stage. He claims that:

There is broad agreement now emerging within poststructural, postempiricist, and postmodernist domains of scholarship that the Western conception of the individual self has run its course. The view of the private self as the source of art and literature, practical decisions, moral deliberation, emotional activity and the like is no longer viable—not only on conceptual grounds but in terms of the societal patterns which it invites.[32]

In place of a disengaged, autonomous self (mind) standing over against the world making pronouncements *about* it, social constructionism affirms sociality and community at the heart of things and reconceives knowledge and meaning as forms of participation in language games. On any occasion in which we attempt to talk of a "self," of "what there is," of minds and families, cabbages and kings, and so on, we inevitably "enter the world of discourse." So it is that social constructionism starts with neither mind nor world but with language and

places the locus of knowledge not in the minds of single individuals but in the collectivity. It is not the internal processes of the individual that generate knowledge, but a social process of communication. It is within the process of social interchange that rationality is generated. Truth is the product of the collectivity of truth makers.[33]

This linguistic relativism arises from a particular reading of Wittgenstein's notion of language games (as elaborated by Peter Winch). Gergen's radical social constructionism begins with the premise that language is embedded in social practices or forms of life. Moreover, it assumes that the rules that govern a form of life circumscribe and close off that form of life to others. Hence, it is only within and with reference to a particular form of life that the meaning of an action can be described and deciphered. Gergen is keen to point out that any standards for rationally evaluating beliefs are completely dependent on the language game or form of life in which those beliefs arise. Hence, the meanings of different language games or different forms of life are incommensurable. When this view is coupled with an insistence on radical conceptual difference, as it is in Gergen's account of, for example, the cultural meanings of psychological terms, it readily leads to epistemological relativism. As Brian Fay explains, in epistemological relativism "no cross-framework judgments are permissible [for] the content, meaning, truth, rightness, and reasonableness of cognitive, ethical, or aesthetic beliefs, claims, experiences or actions can only be determined from within a particular conceptual scheme."[34] It is, of course, but a short step from epistemological relativism to ontological relativism: if all we can know about reality depends on our particular conceptual scheme, is it not the case that reality itself can only be how it seems in our conceptual scheme?[35]

MORAL AND POLITICAL MATTERS

It is perhaps not surprising that the conceptual relativism that governs matters of what can be known also extends to matters of how we should be. In social constructionism, morality is properly understood as "an action that possesses its moral meaning only within a particular arena of cultural intelligibility. . . . A moral life, then, is not an issue of individual sentiment or rationality but a form of communal participation."[36] Hence, the rejection of theories of the atomistic self which is evident in the previous discussion is also reiterated here. Echoing the well-known work of Robert Bellah and colleagues, Gergen is highly critical of the ideology of individualism for it creates a sense of fundamental independence or isolation, not simply with respect to what we can know, but with respect to our sense of obligation toward and responsibility for one another. Here, there is at least an implicit endorsement of a communitarian view of ethics and morality. And, of course, this raises the complicated issue of whether, as Nel Noddings recently expressed it, there is a way "to avoid the dark side of community—its tendencies toward parochialism, conformity, exclusion, assimilation, distrust (or hatred) of outsiders, and coercion."[37]

Gergen insists that there is no explicitly moral-political vision that accompanies social constructionism and that a variety of contradictory moral visions are in fact compatible with it.[38] Yet he claims that this is not equivalent to a stance of moral relativism. First, he argues that this is so because social constructionism does not traffic in the "problem of moral principles" or the issue of grounding an ethical code in either psychological or philosophical foundations. Rather, this problem is "bracketed" in favor of an exploration of communal or "relational practices that enable people to achieve what they take to be a 'moral life.' "[39] In sum, says Gergen, the issue of morality in social constructionism is not about answering the question, "what is the good?" Rather, given the heterogeneity of cultural and group views on morality, the proper question for the social constructionist is, "What are the relational means by which [these cultures and groups] can move toward mutually satisfactory conditions?"[40] Gergen claims that social constructionism thus shifts our examination from traditional axiological concerns with the nature of value and value judgments to "the practicalities of morality as a social achievement."[41]

Second, Gergen argues that moral relativism is not a reasonable charge against social constructionism, because, again, the "real" problem isn't about cultural moral relativism. The "problem of morality" is a political problem: any commitment to an ethically superior standpoint inevitably "sets the stage for the kind of separatism, name-calling, and defamation that breeds civil strife."[42] Hence, the real virtue of social constructionism, in Gergen's view, is that it is mute on matters of justifying a moral theory or set of ethical principles, and redirects our attention away from a pointless quarrel with moral principles and toward examining the enactment or practices of communal moral life.

So it is that Gergen claims that a primary characteristic of the practice of social constructionism is its emancipatory, transformative function. It serves as a "scholarship of dislodgment" because it is not committed to any particular value position and is concerned only with the "general disruption of the conventional." In this way, social constructionism places a premium on the critical deconstruction of various "intelligibilities"—various discourses and practices that seem to have a "clear, elegant, and compelling" rationale for our lives. The aim is not simply to destabilize and unravel "all presumptions of the true, the rational, and the good," but thereby to make it possible to expand the range of participants and voices in "consequential dialogues" of human life, which in turn enables the "reconstruction, wherein new realities and practices are fashioned for cultural transformation."[43]

EDUCATIONAL MATTERS

Not surprisingly, linguistic or semantical idealism underlies social constructionist thought about education. What we might commonly take to be a culture's fund of knowledge built around the content and syntax of various disciplines is, in social constructionism, primarily "a repository of linguistic artifacts."[44] The notion that what knowledge claims about self, world, or other might be true or false is nonsensical within social constructionism because the very concepts "true" and "false" are themselves regarded as linguistic artifacts. Hence, what counts as knowledge in a classroom is nothing more or less than a "temporary location in dialogic space—samples of discourse that are accorded status as 'knowledgeable tellings' on given occasions."[45] Whether, on any given occasion, one is considered knowledgeable depends strictly on how one is positioned within the dialogue where the "telling" takes place. The fact that others might say of me as a teacher "he knows that p" is not a statement about my ability to warrant my claim in evidence and reason. Rather, if others say "he knows that p," what they are telling me is that they recognize that I occupy some privileged position within the community of discourse, and that I know how to produce language that is accorded status in that discourse. Similarly, if classroom members consider one of their company to be "knowledgeable" on some specific occasion, they are simply claiming that that individual happens "to occupy a given position at a given time within an ongoing relationship." "For the purposes of the conversation, 'I know' when I speak in ways that enable you to treat me as if I know, and vice versa. We successfully generate dialogue because we are mutually accorded the status of knowledgeables across time."[46]

Gergen is thus keen to reject any pedagogical approach that appears to locate authority in the person of the teacher (or, we imagine, in *any* member of the classroom for that matter). The traditional lecture format is particularly troublesome here because it is based either on an unwarranted "banking model" of knowledge transmission or on the Socratic ideal of challenging the capacity of students to reason well. Either way, in Gergen's view, the lecture format is an exercise of unfounded authority; in reality what lecturers are doing is "primarily demonstrating their own skills in occupying discursive positions."[47] A similar kind of alleged unfounded authority is evident when a teacher decides what should be taught. This action too is based on the false assumption that it is the teacher "who possesses knowledge and is thus positioned to determine how it should be acquired by the unknowing student."[48]

The social constructionist educator is advised to reject all models of teaching and learning that stem from the false notion that knowledge resides within individual minds. These models, Gergen claims, all favor a sharp distinction between teacher and student—one who knows and the other who doesn't. Moreover, the "unknowing" student is treated simply as a "mind to be filled with contents or rationalities."[49] Because neither teacher nor student is "the possessor of contents or rationalities, but rather participates in them," pedagogy must be designed so as to enable students to participate in a range of conversations and to acquire the kinds of rhetorical skills that allow them to take persuasive positions within these conversations. Collaborative and student-centered learning are to be highly prized. Finally, the social constructionist educator is committed to "pragmatically contextualized education"—structuring the learning experience around practical issues and problems.[50]

ADDITIONAL CONCERNS

The fundamental question for readers is whether social constructionism is in fact illuminating and insightful about human beings. Does this particular "form of intelligibility" represent a gain in our self-understanding? We are hard pressed, for several reasons, to answer in the affirmative.

Severing sociality from world. Gergen is keen to claim that social constructionism offers a gain in understanding when viewed against other social theories that likewise argue for the importance of sociality in knowledge. But does it? It is well known that the symbolic interactionist theory of society, with its roots in the work of George Mead and Herbert Blumer, is premised on the primacy of social interaction. In other words, the very ideas of reflective consciousness and self imply a social situation as their precondition.[51] Symbolic interactionism rests on four premises: (1) that human worlds are symbolic, material, and objective, and hence the primary aim is to understand how human beings go about the task of assembling meaning through interaction with others; (2) that process characterizes lives, situations, and societies—these things are always "evolving, adjusting, emerging, becoming"; hence there is great interest in "strategies for acquiring a sense of self, developing a biography, adjusting to others, organizing a sense of time, negotiating order, constructing civilizations"; (3) that neither the individual nor society is primary in understanding meaning; rather the starting point is the joint act of people doing things together; (4) that interaction means engagement with the empirical world, and "only in the grounded empirical world open to observation can self, encounter, social object, meaning be investigated."[52]

Each of the first three premises could well describe the assumptions of social constructionism, and Gergen admits as much. But social constructionism denies the fourth premise. It refuses to talk about a world of observations that furnish us with the stuff out of which meaning is fashioned and in which the struggle to make justified interpretations make sense. Gergen claims:

The degree to which a given account of world or self is sustained across time is not dependent on the objective validity of the account but on the vicissitudes of social process.[53]

[T]he achievement of objectivity [is] found to be textual—inhering in historically and culturally situated practices of writing and speaking.[54]

By reducing any talk of objective reference to simple word play, social constructionism thus undermines all interest in how and why we form accounts to explain our actions, and how and why meanings are modified, transformed, and evolve through encounters. Cut off from the world to which our accounts of what we know and how we should act are inevitably bound, we are alienated. What we once thought were strong commitments to making sense of our lives are revealed to be nothing but a play of words.

Stealth ontology? Simply stating that social constructionism is mute on ontological issues (on matters relating to what really exists) does not make it so. Clearly what Gergen is about is replacing an ontology of mental and material substance with a "communal or relational ontology," or stated somewhat differently, substituting the metaphysical category of relation for the metaphysical category of substance.[55] *Realities and Relationships* bristles with explicit and implicit references to this "ground" for questions of knowing and being. More troubling is the fact that social constructionism's sub rosa ontology of relations—its efforts to replace the individual knower with the metaphor of "a culturally and historically contexted dialogue"—turns out to be an empty metaphor.[56] It is empty because social constructionism is unable to flesh out an account of humans as practical agents divorced from a representationalist epistemology. There is such strong objection to the self-other, mind-world dualisms on which representationalist models rest that the social constructionist cannot imagine a way of justifying being and knowing in the world apart from an ontology of self-other. For the social constructionist, to reject representationalism as an epistemology is to reject all attempts to establish a way of understanding our being in the world that is other than the verbal exchange of notions.

The best that social constructionism can do is replace the idea of relation to world with a metaphor of textualism—Richard Rorty's term for the view "that all problems, topics, and distinctions are language-relative—the results of our having chosen to use a certain vocabulary, to play a certain language game."[57] Accompanying textualism is the claim that all foundational talk of traditional philosophical matters about knowledge and being is pointless and such talk only has meaning if it can be translated "into an idiom that refers solely to features of our social practices."[58] Talk of what is "in our nature" or having "reasons" or "being rational" can be made sense of only in terms of some group's point of view. Thus, "opinion" becomes a term for belief which signals acceptance within a community of deviance of point of view; "knowledge" is a term for belief wherein deviance is not permitted; "truth" is a term for commendable beliefs within some community, and so forth. For Rorty, and for Gergen's version of social constructionism, our beliefs and practices have no deeper grounding than our participation in a community where these things are generally accepted. We simply start within our own community—our own language game—and "play" with various games to invent new ways of talking about ourselves.

The irony here is that the turn to the *lebenswelt* in social constructionism—to practice, dialogue, and language—is salutary (and, of course, quite contrary to von Glasersfeld's views). The dialogue in which we participate is about the meaning of human action and meanings are expressed in language. That language is not private but shared, and hence meaning is not subjective but intersubjective. Moreover, the significance of our language use does not reside solely in its capacity to designate, discover, refer, or depict actual states of affairs. Rather, language is used to carry out or perform actions and to disclose how things are present to us as we deal with them.[59] So far, so good: these are insights shared by a variety of critics of a strict realist or designative account of language. But social constructionism draws from these premises the unwarranted conclusion that our practices and our knowledge claims are nothing more or less than communally shaped linguistic constructions. It is necessarily driven to this conclusion because it cannot accept a real world of everyday practice. What social constructionism ignores is that:

[A]lthough our practices preshape how things show up in our lives, we are nevertheless dependent on the world around us in order to *be* practical agents. There is no way to sever ourselves from our ties to the world without undercutting our ability to be human at all. In Heidegger's vocabulary, our being-in-the-world—our involvement in contexts of significance—is the bedrock of all theorizing. And to the extent that there is no external vantage point from which we can describe this all-pervasive background of everydayness, there is no way to make it explicit once and for all. But the fact that our quest for insight into our being as situated agents is open ended does not imply that everything is up in the air, a matter of mere "play." This seems to be Wittgenstein's point when he says, "The difficult thing is not to dig down to the ground; no, it is to recognize the ground that lies before us as ground."[60]

On the impossibility of evaluation without criteria. Why should any given group care about the question of being rational or forming true beliefs among their compatriots, and why should any group care to "play" with the views of any other? *Some* justification for our efforts to be reasonable and rational, to criticize our own and others' views, and to convince others of our point of view is required. Without some such justification, it is hard to imagine that an individual (or group) will engage in the kind of project of reconstruction or reinvention that social construction claims is its *raison d'être*. The ambitious normative agenda of social constructionism is not sustainable for it is impossible to mount a critical evaluation (not simply a description) of various "intelligibilities" absent any clear ties to a world and any clear ties to notions of epistemological and moral justification.

In general, one reason for the impossibility of the social constructionist project is the fact that it adopts a kind of "all or nothing" approach to matters of metaphysics, epistemology, and axiology: "Constructionist writings . . . challenge any attempt to establish first principles, a grounding ontology, or an epistemological basis for the universal prioritizing of any given reality posit."[61] But from the failure of both rationalism and empiricism to generate sure foundations for knowledge, values, and identity it does not necessarily follow that normative concerns about these matters disappear. As Gergen's explication of social constructionism makes completely clear, we continue to seek *better* (not simply "different") answers to questions regarding who we are, what we can know, and how we should act. Unless it is random, the "transformation" that Gergen seeks is some kind of progress, betterment, increased perspicuity, development, and so on. These are all normative notions.

A second related reason is that there is no room in social constructionism for a world filled with actions, meanings, and language that we must constantly interpret and appraise. All talk of a world "out there" is to ontologize, and such talk is strictly forbidden in social constructionism. The world may be there or it may not be there, but social constructionism has nothing to say about it. It is impossible to argue that somehow relations matter in a world that may or may not be there.

A third reason is that there is no possibility for social constructionism to embrace a non-foundationalist conception of notions such as "validity in interpretation" or "justification." Gergen claims that we have "no viable account of validity in interpretation" and "little reason to suppose that such an account will be forthcoming."[62] Social constructionism trades, more or less explicitly on two premises that have received considerable support in current epistemology: (1) the replacement of a philosophy of consciousness by the primacy of social interaction and a theory of action; (2) the replacement of foundationalist ambitions in epistemology with fallibilism. But accepting these premises does not entail rejecting all accounts of justification in interpretation. Social constructionism in the main is guilty of what Susan Haack describes as "the fallacious inference from the true premise [that] what has passed for relevant evidence, known fact, objective truth, and so forth, sometimes turns out to be no such thing, to the false conclusion that the notions of relevant evidence, known fact, established truth, etc., are revealed to be ideological humbug."[63]

Commonalities, Differences, Educational Problems

We know from the outset that, unless restricted, radical constructivism and social constructivism could not both be correct accounts of education and knowledge: radical constructivism denies that society plays an intrinsic role in every successful construction of knowledge, while the intrinsic role of society in construction is the very mainspring of social constructionism.

REJECTION OF "TRADITIONAL" EPISTEMOLOGY

Nonetheless, from a philosophical perspective, radical constructivism and social constructionism share a launching pad: lengthy criticisms of epistemological traditions in which knowledge is held to represent an extra-mental world. Their main joint complaint seems to be the very idea of representation, since from both standpoints no representation can be certified as true. This attempted attack on one wing of old-time epistemology is not entirely negative. It purports equally to announce the birth and to christen (what its proponents take to be) new theories of knowledge, based upon (once again, what are taken to be) new conceptions of knowledge. This new conception is strung between two poles: the image of procedure and the image of instrument. Knowledge, when viewed as procedure, is no longer to be treated as a truth-bearing encapsulation of objective features plucked from a mind-independent world. A procedural reconception of knowledge is put in its place: knowledge as a matter of process, a matter of "getting on with something," a business of continuous unfolding without a goal (truth or verification) fixed *a priori*. The value of procedural knowledge is to be assessed according to the second image, that of instrument. When anything—steak knife, automobile, skyscraper—is conceived as a pure instrument, we think of its value as exhausted in the serving of one or another goal. If the thing is an automobile, that goal is taking us from place to place. In the case of knowledge-under-the-guise-of-procedure, the goal may be social survival (for Gergen) or evolutionary fit (for von Glasersfeld). One or another business of knowing is to be evaluated according to the extent to which it achieves the relevant goal.

EPISTEMOLOGICAL SKEPTICISM

Terminological quibbles notwithstanding, von Glasersfeld and Gergen truly count as epistemological skeptics.[64] Both deny outright the knowability of mind-independent objects, but not always for reasons associated conventionally with skepticism, viz., arguments from illusion or worries that "the senses cannot be trusted." Von Glasersfeld and Gergen question the very intelligibility of subject-object and representation-represented distinctions. At times, they seem to dismiss all prospects for empirical knowledge: von Glasersfeld maintaining that the concept of empirical knowledge itself commits one to the objectionable existence of a mind-independent but experienced environment from which the knower derives sensory input, Gergen insisting that there is no such thing as non-socially-mediated (or non-socially-saturated) human experience.

Radical constructivism and social constructionism are characterized by anti-metaphysical attitudes, by strivings to cut loose from what their proponents view as traditional metaphysical baggage. Constructivists and constructionists wish, in effect, to join ranks with Rorty and kindred postmodernists in forms of thinking ungoverned by familiar concepts like "reality," "in principle difference," and "existence." Notions of reality afford a major common target. Von Glasersfeld deems any serious, affirmative talk of reality completely antithetical to the idea of constructive process; he treats reality as a fiction, a philosopher's fantasy.[65] Gergen denies the external world altogether, refusing to countenance any objective distinction between, to use his examples, desks and cheeses.[66]

As far as the metaphysics of humans (selves and others) is concerned, differences between von Glasersfeld and Gergen far outweigh the similarities. This is no surprise, given that constructionism relies upon an analysis of the social and cultural world, while von Glasersfeld's idea of construction is that of cybernetic interactions between creatures that need not be human. One can say with Gergen that persons are in the foreground and hold an epistemically privileged position. Yet on Gergen's view we cannot be individuals of any very ordinary sort. This is so because for Gergen persons cannot be conceived as individuals. They are to be imagined relationally and linguistically. This means, at least, that traditional pictures of the substantial individual are jettisoned in favor of an idea of the individual self (if that is an appropriate expression) existing only in strikingly reduced form, that is, only within a nexus of sociolinguistic activities. Through these activities are all entities to be constructed. If there is to be social construction at all, others, although in the reduced form, have to exist and do not await constructional ratification by any one person. To put it another way, there is here no significant epistemological or ontological difference between "me" and "other people," as far as Gergen is concerned. One constructive size fits all.

By comparison, the attitude of radical constructivists toward matters of people and persons could not be more different. Here, there is to be a vast metaphysical gulf between self and other, with all epistemic and ontological privileges belonging to the self and very few, if any, to the other. As far as von Glasersfeld is concerned, knowledge and its construction depend upon no mental features not constitutive

of individual minds: as a mind, I exist in splendid and isolated independence of other minds and carry out my constructive activities
wholly untroubled by them. No process of knowledge intrinsically
requires that there exist any beings beyond the individual. In addition,
there is to be no large difference between others thought of as objects
of construction and others thought of as people. Trees, frogs and fellow humans are all set on a metaphysical and epistemological par, all
constructed by the mind.

LANGUAGE AND MEANING

Language plays a role far more constitutive of knowledge within
social constructionism than within von Glasersfeld's individual constructivism. For the latter, meaning is a subjective abstraction in the
head of a subject; for Gergen, meaning is a product of assent and
coordination among two or more people engaged in social relationships. Yet, in both views, there is no fixed or prior agreement on word
meaning before constructive processes take off. Moreover, both theorists think of the effectiveness of language as strictly local, extending
in no way beyond the tight confines of the particular actions, mental
or social, that they believe to foster meanings. As such, both von
Glasersfeld and Gergen seem committed to semantic relativism—the
view that meanings can be constructed and preserved only within contextual limits narrow in time as well as in space. "My" meanings today
and now are supposed not to carry over into other contexts; they have
to be constructed anew each time, each place.

ETHICAL AND POLITICAL STANCES

When it comes to ethics and politics, one can say that neither von
Glasersfeld nor Gergen sees the need or justifiability for a moral code
anchored in objective principles or exerting objective authority over
individual and/or social action. Authority, whether epistemological or
moral, can rest either in the individual mind only (as in the case of
radical constructivism) or in social dialogue alone (in Gergen's constructionism). In addition, both authors seem committed to moral
localism and relativism, namely, the position that the ethical standards
by which the behavior of one person or group is to be assessed extend
no further than the life of that person or that group (localism). Moreover, there is no principled means for adjudicating moral disagreements between the codes constructed by one person or group and
those of another (relativism).

Paradoxically, both forms of constructivism advocate equilibrium and order, variously described as objective moral virtues or constructivized forms of Aristotle's "the final good for mankind." We say "objective," because they are only intelligible as requirements set upon the adequacy of individual or social construction *a priori*, that is, in advance of any instance of constructing. For both groups, the constructive process aims ultimately at a state of stability or order. For von Glasersfeld the order is epistemic and for Gergen it is dialogic. These stable states are to be achieved through the application of suitably constructed rules, norms, conventions and constraints. Constructivistically conceived, life—whether mental or social—seems circumscribed by rules. Consider, for example, how one achieves equilibrium in von Glasersfeld's picture. Comparisons between what has worked in the past are to be captured in conceptual schemes and then used for testing hypotheses for future prediction. All this comparing and testing requires mental operations that aim at regularity as well as the recognition of constraining conditions in the environment.

Gergen's picture is similar. Knowledge, being socially constructed, is to be understood and evaluated solely along instrumental lines. One of these lines is generative capacity—the ability to generate more open possibilities for dialogue and so to further the business of social construction. Another is transformative force, presumably the potential of a conversational norm for creating positive changes within society. According to Gergen, contributions to the dialogue and social efforts generally can be judged according to these standards, to the extent to which they are generative and transformative. Therefore, it would appear that this call to proceed generatively and transformatively amounts to setting fixed moral requirements on the ongoing dialogue. Thus, a form of stable subsistence serves as an ultimate goal: the constructor or constructing society ought to strive to attain such ends.

As far as politics is concerned, both radical constructivism and social constructionism are officially apolitical, even politically agnostic. Apart from the very general commitments just outlined, both appear to foreswear allegiance to principles for proper political arrangements or specific visions of the good life. For instance, neither picture stands in any unambiguous logical or thematic relation to democracy or liberalism.

EDUCATIONAL CONCERNS

Both Gergen and von Glasersfeld reject behaviorism as an approach to education, declaring behaviorism a source of faulty conceptions of mental functioning that emerge in education, such as wrong assessments of learning motivation and misguided achievement tests. Further, teaching and learning based on behaviorist principles aim, according to both authors, at students acquiring correct knowledge. Since the very idea of correct knowledge is put into serious doubt by their philosophical approaches, correct knowledge is deemed an undesirable educational goal to be replaced by a goal considered more appropriate, namely, understanding.

Both Gergen and von Glasersfeld oppose a picture of education in which the accumulation of knowledge is a primary educational aim. In contrast to knowledge acquisition, which they associate with unacceptably passive learning, both authors favor a learning for understanding which demands and fosters an active learner. Learners are intrinsically motivated to learn because they wish to make sense of their context through a constructive process. The active learner is a participant in learning processes whose mental or social activities generate new engagements with an environment, whether intramental or social. Since the active learner is thought to shape understanding itself and active learning is adopted as a goal, both authors conclude that no predetermined curricula ought to be imposed on a student. Nor should teachers be concerned to convey a body of knowledge to students via direct instruction.

Beyond these similarities, the differences between von Glasersfeld and Gergen on apposite characteristics of teachers and students are well captured in the general contrast between the views as "individual mind versus dialogue." For students, von Glasersfeld favors curricula based on individual problem solving, where problems arise as perturbations in the environment, situations in which "something doesn't fit." Solutions are constructed through an adaptive process as situations wherein perturbation is resolved and equilibrium restored. Gergen thinks of appropriate education as a conversation in which students construct meanings by participating in ongoing social practices.

Not surprisingly, appropriate roles for teachers are also conceived differently. Von Glasersfeld expects a teacher to get to know each student's mental constructions by establishing an environment in which experiential and conceptual differences emerge as points of learning. Gergen expects the teacher to be a "coordinator, facilitator, or resource advisor, . . . tutor or coach."[67] Such a teacher prepares students to become effective and knowledgeable authorities, to learn to take up various social positions in ongoing conversations.

Critical Discussion: Old Wine and Old Bottles

Michael Matthews was more right than he knew when he described constructivism as "old wine in new bottles." For, as Martin Heidegger reminded us, philosophical problems, issues and positions, once discovered, never go away. They are never permanently answered, solved, resolved, refuted, shown to be pseudo-problems, deconstructed, or "Wittgensteined." In this very real sense, there can be neither post-philosophy nor post-epistemology. Hence, given that von Glasersfeld and Gergen conceive themselves as postmoderns with final solutions to philosophical problems, we already know that they fail to disentangle themselves from metaphysical and epistemological questions they think to have answered and from positions they think to have discarded. In comparison with Enlightenment epistemology, constructivism and constructionism are old wine in old bottles; only the labels, only the puff and the fluff of the packaging, are new.

WELCOME BACK, OBJECTIVITY

Despite the suggestion of the term itself, "subjective" knowledge need not be knowledge whose concern is the individual subject (or subjects), nor need it be knowledge restricted to emotions and feelings. By the same token, "objective" knowledge is not necessarily knowledge having to do with extramental objects. Whether a piece of knowledge can rightly be called "subjective" or "objective" is not a matter of its constructional history or of the means by which one came by that presumptive knowledge. Objectivity in beliefs and knowledge has to do with the future, not the past—my belief that p is objective when, despite the fact that I might now be fully justified in maintaining p, it is possible that I will be proved wrong about p. In other words, my presumptive knowledge counts as objective when, even though I have been as careful as I can be in checking that p holds, I could still be surprised; I could still discover that p fails. Briefly put, my belief in p is objective when, apart from matters of language and justification, there is still something in p about which I might be making a mistake. My belief or knowledge is subjective when such surprises are ruled out. For example, under ordinary conditions, my belief that I am hungry is subjective, since my feeling hungry and believing that I am hungry are one and the same. In normal cases, there is no room here for mistake or surprise. This is so even when I come to realize that I feel hungry via so-called "objective" processes of observation and inference. Indeed, it sometimes happens that, near the end of the afternoon, I notice that I am answering friendly questions curtly and cutting people off in conversation. On that basis, I suddenly recognize that I'm feeling hungry. Even though, this time, the knowledge that I'm feeling hungry comes by way of observation and inference (from my own external behavior), the knowledge itself remains subjective: my knowledge and my feeling coincide. Conversely, I can also have objective beliefs, that is, fully justified beliefs that admit the prospect of error, even about my own feelings. For example, it is often possible to mistake feelings of lust and sexual gratification for those of love and affection, even when one is fully convinced at the time that the feelings are correctly classified. Famously, when it comes to such states as health, there is room in knowledge for surprises aplenty. One can firmly believe oneself healthy and yet discover through a visit to a doctor one's terrible mistake. It seems strange to us that anyone would want to deny the possibility of such real mistakes or real surprises of this kind, but in one or another way von Glasersfeld and Gergen, by denying objective knowledge, wish to do so. That is their joint, official position. Objective, knowledge-engendering truth claims are abandoned in favor of subjective, individual constructions, or constructions embedded in social conversation.[68]

It is important to recognize that, paradoxically enough, there remain in constructivism and constructionism unacknowledged commitments to objectivity in knowledge. Knowledge, on both accounts, remains perfectly objective, despite various claims of Gergen and von Glasersfeld to the contrary. The precise spot in which the objectivity in knowledge reappears varies. For von Glasersfeld, criteria for the acceptability of knowledge claims, particularly within scientific inquiry, include fit and viability. The cybernetic and evolutionary premises on which von Glasersfeld relies to explain these criteria leave plenty of room for the prospect of error, for, as even the post-Kuhnian history of science shows, one can be perfectly and completely wrong in one's assessment of the viability of a strategy. Consider, for example, the remedies late medieval medicos concocted for treating bubonic plague. These prized strategies were, most often, hopelessly nonviable as cures, even as ameliorations, of Black Death. Some actually accelerated the spread of disease. Of course, this negative assessment of late medieval medicine requires no one to suppose the existence of a non-mental world standing over and against the knower. In short, given that fit and viability can be mistaken by humans as readily as truth, von Glasersfeld should allow for objective knowledge, that is, for knowledge coming to exist in a battle against the prospect of real error. Further, if one is really free to construct one's world as she chooses, then one should be able to construct it with mistakes and surprises built in and, hence, objective knowledge built in. (Of course, if we are *really free* to construct our mental worlds as we choose, then the whole issue of viability is moot: one need simply construct all constraints to be satisfied instantaneously. If such a world construction is prohibited, then, even on the radical constructivist picture, there remains an external world, namely the set of constraints which I am not free to construct as I wish.)

POSTMODERNISM AS POSE: THE COLOR OF THE WRAPPER

Von Glasersfeld has written, "I agree wholeheartedly with Noddings when she says, . . . that radical constructivism should be offered as a 'post-epistemological perspective.'"[69] In an article entitled "Knowing without Metaphysics" he proclaims that "Radical Constructivism makes no ontological claims."[70] One can see from the expositions of constructivism and constructionism in earlier parts of this chapter that it is patently absurd, even hilarious, to consider describing either von Glasersfeld's views or those of Gergen as "antifoundational" or "post-epistemological." Both positions are foundational metaphysics in the full sense of the term. Both authors want everything in their respective world views to dance to one or the other metaphysical tune. In von Glasersfeld's case, that tune is the lure of an imaginary inner world of the individual and his or her constructions. We have already seen that he claims to deduce outright a full-blown Kantian ethics from this metaphysical/epistemological basis, to be specific, from the constraints he imposes on the fit and viability of mental constructions. Gergen insists that the ongoing cultural conversation answers philosophically or morally to no set of norms outside its limits: everything is to be judged in virtue of its prospect for positive or negative contributions to dialogue. Gergen's very notion of human being is warped to fit his vision of chitchat as the sole good, as the following illustrates:

[T]he individual self has run its course. The view of the private self . . . is no longer viable—not only on conceptual grounds but in terms of the societal patterns it invites. For many, the present challenge is how to replace the self as the critical unit of social life. Accounts that emphasize contextual embeddedness, relational formations, and dialogic process are under development.[71]

When one scheme, be it individual construction or social construction, is the thread from which an entire worldview is to be spun, on which the answer to every philosophical question is to be hung, then that scheme is foundational, and its author a foundationalist, regardless of the color of the wrapper.

CONSTRUCTION: THE VERY IDEA

If construction is to be any kind of act, then two preconditions, at least, have to be satisfied. First, the act has to have some sort of agent, an individual or group to serve as constructors, to do the constructing. Second, there has to be something there on which the agent is to act. In other words, there has to be material that gets "put together" in the construction process. Here, by "material," we do not mean "material substance." We refer only to whatever the initial inputs or objects of constructive processes are. Now, according to the constructivists, everything is construction: self, mind, world. Is this possible? Is it possible that everything, including agents and materials, be constructed?

The answer must be a resounding "No," if we make two uncontroversial assumptions: (1) individual minds and individual societies are not eternal in the past but first come into existence at some time or other; (2) agents and materials always pre-exist the act for which they are agents or materials, that is, whenever there is a process of constructing, the agent who is to construct and the materials on which the process is to unfold have to be ready and in place before the process can start. Now, if (1) holds, there is some first act of constructing for individuals and groups, some first time at which the presumptive agent or agents get down to the business of construction. If (2), then the agents and materials had to exist before that first act of constructing could start. Therefore, agents and materials have to be unconstructed items or givens in the construction process and it is impossible that literally everything be constructed. Therefore, if (as seems reasonable when construction is modeled on evolution) in von Glasersfeld's constructed world construction assumes an actual constructing agent who has to start at some initial point with given materials on which to construct, we know of two kinds of entities which are not constructed: agents and materials. In Gergen's case, there are also ontological givens; they seem to be relationship, community, and bits of language, all of which serve as inputs to Gergen's conception of dialogue. In neither case, therefore, does a constructive reconstrual of knowledge save one from objective ontological commitment. Very simply, neither brand of construction makes sense unless there are some unconstructed things there from the start.

CAN THERE BE "LOCAL KNOWLEDGE?"

Both von Glasersfeld and Gergen season their attacks on objective knowledge claims with the adoption of one or another form of epistemic localism: a view that the validity of knowledge claims is always local, holding good only within the limits of the individual constructing mind (for von Glasersfeld) or within the limits of a dialogic community (for Gergen), that is, limited to the mental or social realm in which the knowledge was first constructed. Epistemic relativism is one manifestation of localism in this sense, for it is a consequence of both philosophies under review that it is in principle possible that there exist two sets of constructing minds, A and B, such that, for all the members of A, the claim "2 + 3 = 5" counts as an expression of knowledge in the full sense of the term, while for all members of group B, the claim "2 + 3 = 5" fails to count as knowledge, without either group having committed an error or made a mistake. Put crudely, the relativistic consequences of localism can be captured by the slogan, "So you say! What you construct as knowledge may be viable or felicitous for you, but has no *prima facie* claim to validity for me!"

Von Glasersfeld gives vigorous endorsement to this notion of epistemic localism as an interpretation, which he adopts for himself, of the philosophy of Vico and the psychology of Piaget:

One of Vico's basic ideas was that epistemic agents can *know* nothing but the cognitive structures they themselves have put together. . . . the human knower can know only what the human knower has constructed. . . . [Knowledge] is the collection of conceptual structures that turn out to be adapted or, as I would say, *viable* within the knowing subject's range of experience.[72]

Gergen's epistemological localism follows directly from his explicit adoption of semantical internalism, the assertion that concepts and the meanings of symbolic items exist and maintain their validity only within the context of their original constructions:

[Semantic] agreements are typically generated for local purposes, and there is no principled means of insuring their generality outside such circumstances. . . . Further, there is no means of guaranteeing consistency of meaning outside the conditions of agreement because there is nothing about the nature of propositions that defines the conditions under which they apply.[73]

It would seem then that neither constructivism nor constructionism provides an adequate account of knowledge. For the very nature of a claim to knowledge is such that it is binding *prima facie* on anyone, in any situation, and the range of that binding is not localized or limited to the circumstances in which the presumptive knowledge originally arose. Therefore, once a claim is certified as expressing knowledge, then it is binding *prima facie* on all those who understand the claim and the certification. The claim to knowledge binds others into agreement. The qualification *"prima facie"* here means "unless good evidence is brought forward that would cause relevant persons to call the claim into question." We emphasize that, in speaking of the *prima facie* binding power of claims to knowledge, there is no implicit assumption at work that the knowledge in question pertains to objective or extramental situations. Quite the contrary. Under ordinary circumstances, where no effort at deception is discernible, the claim, "I feel really sick," as a claim to subjective knowledge, is accorded immediate binding power over all those who understand the claim. Doctors and nurses infer immediately from the mere fact that the patient makes such a claim with honest mien that he or she is in need of attention. That is, in all but unusual cases, doctors and nurses treat these kinds of claims, although notoriously subjective, as true and as requests, binding upon them, for medical attention. In this respect, what goes for the general binding power of "I feel really sick" applies to all knowledge claims. To put it simply, the very idea of knowledge loses a great deal of its point if its potential for binding others to agreement and action is not admitted. The *prima facie* binding power of a knowledge claim over those who did not originate the claim or who are not in a position to construct it for themselves is unintelligible within the constructivistic worldview where the power of knowledge is always local.

Moreover, to treat a claim as expressing knowledge, independently of whether the claim purports to present subjective conditions in a mental realm as opposed to objective mathematical or physical realms, is to ascribe to the claim a certain kind of epistemic portability inconsistent with constructivism. This means that, *prima facie*, anyone who understands a claim and takes it as knowledge, even if he or she did not discover that knowledge, can put it to work, regardless of his or her cognitive or linguistic circumstances. For example, we read newspapers to gain knowledge because we believe that, among other things, the validity of the reports therein are, in general, not limited to the particular circumstances in which the reporters who gathered the information found themselves. To take another example, medieval Arab mathematicians of the tenth century who so eagerly adopted the geometrical techniques of Archimedes were delighted to have this new knowledge, despite the fact that it was originally "constructed" in a cultural, linguistic, and social setting of which they perhaps had little other knowledge. Neither von Glasersfeld nor Gergen can make sense of this well-known portability, because their strict localism prohibits it. As the above quotation shows, Gergen has to maintain that even the Arabs who could read the words in Greek manuscripts written a millennium earlier were incapable of discerning their meanings, for meanings are valid only for the cultures in which they are constructed. On constructivist accounts, our practice of reading newspapers and books in order to gain information becomes a mystery.

ILLUSORY FREEDOMS, NEW CHAINS

Constructivists and constructionists alike endeavor to foster the impression that the constructive agents they envision partake in freedoms far more extensive than those human beings would have on other, opposing theories. Readers are led to believe that, by discarding old metaphysical and epistemological baggage, they are opening themselves to new and liberatory conceptions of individual mind or linguistic community and that, by ridding themselves of traditional philosophical constraints at the level of theory, they are thereby introducing revolutionary and creative ways of acting in concrete circumstances, either intramental or intrasocial. In truth, constructivists and constructionists pretend to offer us new freedoms while forging us new kinds of chains. The new chains are so strong that, on constructivist views, we cannot think or imagine ourselves unshackled.

Both von Glasersfeld and Gergen admit that the constructive processes they so prize occur only under the tight control of constraints. Von Glasersfeld writes of the resistance to construction provided by an experiential reality against which successful constructions have to struggle to be viable. Gergen refers repeatedly to the social conventions and norms that limit dialogic constructions. Thanks to the internalism of both views, however, these seemingly innocuous constraints become far more serious in consequence than their authors make out. In the case of von Glasersfeld, there is nothing outside the mental processing of the individual mind. With Gergen, there is nothing outside the conversation of the linguistic community. On these positions, therefore, not only is there no such thing as "getting outside the mind" or "leaving the community," these expressions (given localism about knowledge and meaning) don't make any sense; they are constructivistic contradictions. It is impossible even to think oneself free of the constraints set by one's own psychology or one's own society because, on the views considered, no concept (as a scheme constructed to serve purely internal purposes) applies "outside the mind" or "outside the community."

In these circumstances, a significant freedom evaporates; it becomes meaningless to speak of it. This is the freedom, essential to honest education, to make something different, even radically different, of yourself, from anything fitting neatly within the conceptual resources of the self or its current community. To take Gergen's view as an example (an analogous objection, relativized to the individual, holds for von Glasersfeld), it would not be possible, on this view, for members of a thoroughly violent and racist community, a linguistic group whose linguistic and nonlinguistic behaviors are shot through with hatred and threat, to extricate themselves from racism through thinking, learning, or education. Why not? Because, according to Gergen, the members of the group in question cannot think the thought that they are either outside the community and not subject to its linguistic constraints or that the community around them has changed in significantly linguistic ways. For everything is to be constructed linguistically, within the confines of the community, within the constraints that the community sets, including the concepts employed by its thinkers and the meanings of the words they use. If the community is wholly violent and racist, then the language and all the thinking it constructs is so earmarked. There are supposed to be no meanings or standards outside of or alternative to those of the community to which community members can appeal. There is no such thing, on this view, as another community, a just community, whose principles of justice have binding power over the community of racists. In effect, Gergen thereby creates a social prison for the individual in comparison with which the world of Orwell's *1984* is a pale shadow. Gergen's is indeed a prison of thought.

CONSTRUCTIVISM AND ITS EDUCATIONAL POLITICS

Education is and has always been a business of understanding the other, that is, of fathoming persons and groups distinctly unlike us. There can be little doubt among educators about the value and importance of learning opportunities that expand a student's native abilities and interests. Were we to restrict consideration to word origins alone, from the Latin *educare* as a "leading out," we see that education was intended, from the start, to involve the transcending of local constraints, whether intramental, intrapersonal, or intragroup. If this were otherwise, our continued efforts to encourage local students to enroll in programs of information and exchange with students and educational institutions from distant lands would make little sense. Multicultural education, to take one example, is a way of making this implicit goal explicit. Public education generally, and American public education specifically, represent yet further routes to the other. In public education, we strive to bring students a multiplicity of perspectives, to chart with them ways through John Stuart Mill's "marketplace of ideas." In America, public education takes the furthering of American democracy as among the first of its objectives. Therefore, our public education will have failed to the extent that it impedes access to a national perspective, a fairly accurate image of the nation as a whole. Crucially, American public education must grant students opportunities to transcend the limits on opinion and viewpoint set arbitrarily by accidents of locality: by the particular family, community, state or region in which the student happens to live. All these we take to be fairly uncontroversial truths about contemporary education, whether multicultural, public, democratic, or "just plain" education. Yet constructivism, if it is consistent, must take all of these truths to be falsehoods; it must deny them all. For internalism, either of individual mind or of individual community, has no room for the educational goal of the other, perhaps those very goals most characteristic of education per se. To repeat, on either view, the other (either outside the mind or the group) is no more than a constructional figment, governed not by its own rules but entirely by rules of viability or of language set for it within the mind or within the community. There is and can be no free and independent other.

On von Glasersfeld's combination of internalism and relativism or on Gergen's, there can be no commitment to democratic values. As described above, both constructivistic philosophers claim to be apolitical and to endorse a studied abstinence from moral principle. Even so, their respective writings strongly suggest that they indeed recognize a simple truth: that justice, equality, and human rights respect no limits, not to mention limits set for a single individual or community. There simply is no such thing as a special justice or equality for one person or for one group that does not apply to everyone equally. The very idea of a principle of equality is that it does not matter to whom, *ceteris paribus*, the principle is to be applied. Hence, neither constructivism nor constructionism can be consistent with such political principles as justice, human rights, and equality for all, because both views rule out as completely meaningless efforts to state and apply principles to all humans equally. For Gergen, we cannot meaningfully state, let alone apply, a principle which is to govern members of all human cultures. For von Glasersfeld, there can be no principle that constrains all constructing agents equally.

There is, we think, yet more reason for worry. These worries are motivated not *a priori* by the logical structure of constructivism, but *a posteriori*. In addition to being inconsistent with universal democratic values, constructivism and constructionism both seem far more at home with non-democratic forms of educational and governmental practice. To take one example, von Glasersfeld allows that we possess a kind of responsibility for others, presumably on the grounds that we have constructed them. Yet constructivism can provide no guidelines to govern the proper means by which that responsibility is to be exercised, because individualistic constructivism is officially opposed to universalistic moral stands. Hence, responsibility is assigned and, at the same time, proper ways to fulfill that responsibility are left wholly open. Herein lies the danger. A responsibility for others does not necessarily entail any positive regard. Even the most brutal slaveholder or abusive parent remains responsible for those under his care. Although God himself is responsible for the creatures He created, it does not follow that He may not consign half of them to eternal damnation, while remaining true to His responsibility. That is to say, proclamations of responsibility for others remain relatively empty, unless accompanied by overarching principles telling us how to enact that responsibility. In other words, "responsibility for" is, in this sense, no more than a ghostly skeleton in search of a moral body.

As these examples suggest and a study of history will confirm, it is a far easier and more commonplace solution to the problem of responsibility untempered by moral constraint to take full charge of those for whom we are responsible. Just as the single-minded Stalinist wished to fulfill his responsibility to the people's freedom by taking complete charge of the people's every thought and movement, the determined constructivist, one fears, may succumb to a similar line. As we have seen, there is nothing in the constructivist's philosophy to stop him. As Vaclav Havel stressed, the strongest moral brake on Stalinism has been truth—specifically, the truth that happiness and freedom can exist outside the Stalinist system. Yet this is just the truth Gergen and von Glasersfeld would deny us, the truth that there is an "outside." If Havel is right, the skeleton of responsibility for others must remain, within constructivism, a specter. One can, therefore, only worry that the sole means available to the constructivist for fulfilling the responsibility assigned to him or her is the easy, common way of totalitarianism, rather than the hard, always uphill, path of democracy.

CONSTRUCTIVISTS AND CONSTRUCTIONISTS ON
TEACHING AND LEARNING

Constructivism and constructionism offer monolithic, "one size fits all," pictures of teaching and learning. This is despite the fact that both perspectives officially disparage behaviorism in precisely these terms: as a monolithic conception of student motivation, instruction, and learning. We maintain that, in place of behaviorism, constructivists and constructionists propose an equally simplistic, though vaguer, image of what goes on in the classroom. Anyone who has ever tried to teach knows that there is no such thing as the best way to present a topic. The art of teaching, like the art of painting, calls for a flexible and varied approach. Sometimes lecture works best, sometimes participant discussion, sometimes role-playing, sometimes group projects, sometimes none of these. The artful teacher has a full palette of approaches and can mix more educational colors to suit. Even the most time-honored of objective subjects, such as mathematics or physical science, involve a plethora of kinds of knowledge: teachers present propositional knowledge (a knowledge that x) as well as procedural knowledge (knowing how to x). Therefore, no one kind of knowledge, no one style or approach can be singled out *a priori*. Constructionists and constructivists do their respective best to deny the variety required in teaching.

Furthermore, the simple thought of "no best way in teaching" remains true regardless of one's metaphysics of knowledge. The philosophical characterization of a kind of knowledge, whether objective or subjective, tells us nothing about how best to convey it. Why shouldn't a subjective impression be conveyed, and effectively, in the form of a lecture? Why can't objective knowledge be learned "constructively," that is, by encouraging each student to find his or her own favorite approach to the subject? Hence, constructivists and constructionists err in their belief that a theory of best teaching can be derived from a theory of knowing.

There must then be something amiss in Gergen and von Glasersfeld's shared belief that objective knowledge leads necessarily to a didactic or "banking method" of teaching in which students are mental pastry shells waiting for an epistemic filling. There are no grounds to support such a claim; it is a simple non sequitur.[74] Nor are grounds available for rejecting or disparaging certain versions of didactics, as constructivists and constructionists both strive to do. It is nowise clear that didactic, lecture-centered styles of teaching are always bad teaching. To condemn any one approach whole cloth is not only absolutist thinking about teaching but wholly antithetical to the educational values our authors themselves proclaim, that is, antithetical to encouraging individuals or groups (including teachers) to "construct things as they deem best." We have little recourse but to apply the principles of constructivist and/or constructionist epistemology to the teacher as well as to the learner. On those principles, one cannot prove outright that occasional reliance upon time-honored didactic methods are not viable for the teaching individual, in his or her efforts to construct a world. Why couldn't lecturing—or even simple telling—turn out to be more viable for the construction of a teacher's world than dialogue or Socratic questioning? Constructivists and constructionists cannot defend the idea that they refrain from imposing objective claims upon anyone, while prohibiting the teacher outright from constructing the classroom as he or she sees fit.

Now we turn to the picture of the student. Here, an absolutism is equally and painfully obvious. First, constructivists and constructionists alike cast all students *a priori* into one of two molds: active or passive learners, a dualism that just isn't viable. How should a teacher judge a bright but shy student who never "actively" participates in class but presents excellent written work? Conversely, what of the student who compulsively participates in classroom conversation (an "active" student by Gergen's lights) despite the fact that this very activity seems to impede the student's effective learning of writing? Again, as in the case of teachers, there are just too many varieties of student. Second, we find that constructivists and constructionists alike treat a particular image of one aspect of one phase of learning as if it were the key to all of learning, for any learner, at any stage of personal development. The model of constructivist learner is that of the solitary infant. Von Glasersfeld draws explicitly upon (his interpretation of) Piaget's theory of early childhood cognitive development. Somehow, in von Glasersfeld's hands, this image of a child's learning is applied generally and without further ado to learning altogether. Here, learning is nowise social and is never within or among people as equals. It remains the inner mental act of an individual organism.

Gergen, by contrast, imagines the constructionist learner on the model of the adult in social relationships. He seems to assume, from the start, complete linguistic, social, and dialogic ability in his participants. Without these assumptions, he could hardly suggest that the educational process "is to generate the kinds of contexts in which the value and meaning of the constituent dialogues may be most fully realized, conditions under which dialogues may be linked to the ongoing practical pursuits of persons, communities, or nations."[75] John Shotter seems right when he calls Gergen's notions of teaching and learning largely "social skills and practices developed in conversational settings."[76] For Gergen, there is no mental act of individual learning but only social learning through cooperative conversation. These generalities are illicit, as becomes obvious once we confront them with a plain fact: that socializing and constructing have themselves to be learned. Neither is a skill or aptitude that "comes naturally." Since each carries its own criteria for success or failure, mistakes are possible and we have to learn to avoid them.

For learning to construct, von Glasersfeld has no account: if all learning is constructing, there can be no explanation of how one first learns to construct. For Gergen, there can be no learning to socialize or to converse, because there is no state in which the actor is incapable of either of these features; the whole existence of agents is already dependent ontologically upon socializing and conversing. Social agents are to be constructed within the network of social acts. Hence, those agents have to be fully social from the beginning.

Concluding Summary

Despite the serious problems we have identified in the epistemological and educational aspects of radical constructivism and social constructionism, these philosophies remain seductive to educators. The allure we feel has less to do with content than with symbol. Both radical constructivism and social constructionism fit with contemporary politically correct language about construction of gender, self, and identity. They resonate with a popular anti-establishment, anti-authoritarian ideology and ironic attitude—they are anti-metaphysics, against traditional epistemology, against positivism, against "authoritarian" forms of pedagogy. Both approaches tap into pedagogical language and jargon that were features of a variety of earlier educational approaches (child-centeredness, child as active participator, self-determined learning and curriculum, freedom to determine own speed of learning, teacher as guide, facilitator). Both lend support to broad-scale attacks on behaviorist psychology, which lie at the root of much current dissatisfaction with pedagogy. Hence, constructivism in its various guises is thought to provide a philosophical grounding for the ideas that teachers ought to be free of bureaucratic and discipline-based structures so they can determine curriculum activities themselves; that both teachers and students ought to be more creative and experimental; and that everyone has something valuable to contribute to the classroom as laboratory in which all are more or less equal actors. Both philosophies embrace what appear to be novel classroom strategies aimed at increasing students' motivation to learn, locating the responsibility for learning with the student and not primarily the teacher, and emphasizing classroom communication and ways of learning.

Matters of who should teach and who should decide about what should be taught and about the aims of education are, of course, perdurable and contentious issues for the educational philosopher, the curriculum theorist, the educational historian, the classroom teacher. They call for reason and argument, description and evaluation, and we find it hard to believe that the philosophies of constructivism provide us with a set of resources for these important tasks.

NOTES

1. Patricia Teague Ashton, "Editorial," *Journal of Teacher Education* 43, no 5 (1992): 322.

2. Jacqueline Grennon Brooks and Martin G. Brooks, *In Search of Understanding. The Case for Constructivist Classrooms* (Alexandria, VA: Association for Supervision and Curriculum Development, 1993): 13.

3. Denis Phillips, "Coming to Grips with Radical Social Constructivism," *Science and Education* 6 (1997): 85-104.

4. Mark H. Bickhard, "Constructivism and Relativism: A Shopper's Guide," *Science and Education* 6 (1997): 29-42; Denis C. Phillips, "How, Why, What, When, and Where: Perspectives on Constructivism in Psychology and Education," *Issues in Education* 3, no. 2 (1997): 151-194; Denis C. Phillips, "The Good, the Bad, and the Ugly: The Many Faces of Constructivism" *Educational Researcher* 24, no. 7 (1995): 5-12; John Shotter, "In Dialogue: Social Constructionism and Radical Constructivism" in *Construction in Education*, eds. Leslie Steffe and Jerry Gale (Hillsdale, NJ: Lawrence Erlbaum, 1995): 41-56.

5. Some of Gergen's and von Glasersfeld's criticisms of one another can be found in their replies to Phillips in *Issues in Education* 3, no. 2 (1997).

6. Epistemological solipsism is radical skepticism about the existence of an external world (including other minds); semantic solipsism is the view that the meanings or referents of all words are mental entities accessible only to the individual language user.

7. Ernst von Glasersfeld, "Knowing without Metaphysics: Aspects of the Radical Constructivist Position" in *Research and Reflexivity*, ed. F. Steier (London: Sage, 1991): 13.

8. von Glasersfeld, "Knowing without Metaphysics," p. 25-26.

9. Ibid., p. 16.

10. Ernst von Glasersfeld, "Cognition, Construction of Knowledge, and Teaching." *Synthese* 80 (1989): 126f.

11. Ernst von Glasersfeld, *Wissen, Sprache und Wirklichkeit* [*Knowledge, Language and Reality*] (Braunschweig: Vieweg, 1992): 184.

12. von Glasersfeld, "Cognition, Construction of Knowledge, and Teaching," p. 133.

13. von Glasersfeld, *Wissen, Sprache und Wirklichkeit*, p. 194.

14. Ibid, p. 20

15. Kant, cited in von Glasersfeld, "Cognition, Construction of Knowledge, and Teaching," p. 130.

16. Ernst von Glasersfeld, *Radical Constructivism: A Way of Knowing and Learning* (London: Falmer Press, 1995): 128.

17. Ibid., p. 127.

18. von Glasersfeld, "Knowing without Metaphysics," p. 27.

19. von Glasersfeld, "Cognition, Construction of Knowledge, and Teaching," p. 134.

20. von Glasersfeld, *Radical Constructivism: A Way of Knowing and Learning*, p. 113.

21. Rosalind Driver et al., quoted in Michael R. Matthews, "Introductory Comments on Philosophy and Constructivism in Science Education," *Science and Education* 6, nos. 1-2 (1997): 13.

22. Charles Taylor, "Charles Taylor Replies" in *Philosophy in an Age of Pluralism*, ed. James Tully (Cambridge: Cambridge University Press, 1994): 234.

23. Kenneth J. Gergen, *Toward Transformation in Social Knowledge*, 2nd edition (Thousand Oaks, CA: Sage Publications, 1994); 1st edition, 1982; Kenneth J. Gergen, *Realities and Relationships. Soundings in Social Construction* (Cambridge, MA: Harvard University Press, 1994).

24. *Realities and Relationships*, p. 78.

25. Ibid., p. 113, 62-63.

26. See the discussion in Gergen, *Toward Transformation of Social Knowledge*, pp. 174-191 and in Kenneth J. Gergen, "Social Construction and the Educational Process" in *Construction in Education*, pp. 17-39.

27. See Kenneth J. Gergen, "The Mechanical Self and the Rhetoric of Objectivity," *Annals of Scholarship* 9 (1992): 87-109. Gergen's recounting of the origin of social constructionism has much in common with Charles Taylor's criticisms in *Philosophical Arguments* (Cambridge, MA: Harvard University Press, 1995) of the representational model of knowledge and its picture of human agency. We will not rehearse here these myriad criticisms and rejoinders that are the stock in trade of all efforts to make sense of the interpretive turn in the social sciences. This scene is well-covered elsewhere, see for example, Brian Fay, *Contemporary Philosophy of Social Science* (Oxford: Blackwell, 1996); Denis C. Phillips, *Philosophy, Science, and Social Inquiry* (Oxford: Pergamon, 1987); Thomas A. Schwandt, "Interpretivism, Hermeneutics, and Constructionism," in the *Handbook of Qualitative Research*, 2nd edition, ed. Norman K. Denzin and Yvonna S. Lincoln (Newbury Park: Sage, forthcoming). We are primarily concerned with the particular conclusions that Gergen draws from the classic critiques of epistemology mounted by Heidegger, Wittgenstein, and the continental philosophers in general; conclusions that define the contours of social constructionism.

28. Richard Bernstein, *Beyond Objectivism and Relativism: Science, Hermeneutics, and Praxis* (Philadelphia: University of Pennsylvania Press, 1983). Bernstein endeavors to find a way beyond the dichotomies of objectivism vs. relativism, certainty vs. uncertainty. He defends a fallibilism grounded in pragmatic, practical philosophy. Gergen, although appearing to accept epistemic fallibilism, finds it impossible to defend it.

29. *Realities and Relationships*, p. 72.

30. Ibid., pp. 69-70.

31. Ibid., pp. 59, 101.

32. Gergen, "The Mechanical Self and the Rhetoric of Objectivity," p. 105.

33. *Realities and Relationships*, p. 207.

34. Fay, *Contemporary Philosophy of Social Science*, p. 77.

35. See note 28 as well as Nicholas L. Smith, *Strong Hermeneutics: Contingency and Moral Identity* (London: Routledge, 1997).

36. *Realities and Relationships*, p. 103.

37. Nel Noddings, "On Community," *Educational Theory* 46, no. 3 (1996): 258.

38. *Realities and Relationships*, pp. 79-80.

39. Ibid., p. 112.

40. Ibid.

41. Ibid., p. 111.

42. Ibid., p. 253.

43. Ibid., pp. 59, 62-63.

44. Gergen, "Social Construction and the Educational Process," p. 23.

45. Ibid., p. 30.

46. Ibid., p. 34.

47. Ibid., p. 31.

48. Ibid., p. 32

49. Ibid., p. 33.

50. Ibid., p. 35.

51. See Gert J. J. Biesta, "Mead, Intersubjectivity, and Education: The Early Writings," *Studies in Philosophy and Education* 17, no. 3 (1998): 73-99.

52. Ken Plummer, "Symbolic Interactionism in the Twentieth Century: The Rise of Empirical Social Theory," in *The Blackwell Companion to Social Theory*, ed., Bryan S. Turner (Oxford: Blackwell, 1996): 224.

53. *Realities and Relationships*, p. 51.

54. Gergen, "The Mechanical Self and the Rhetoric of Objectivity," p. 105.

55. *Realities and Relationships*, p. 69.

56. Shotter, "In Dialogue: Social Constructionism and Radical Constructivism," p. 45.

57. Richard Rorty, *Consequences of Pragmatism* (Minneapolis: University of Minnesota Press, 1982): 139.

58. Charles B. Guignon, "Pragmatism or Hermeneutics? Epistemology after Foundationalism," in *The Interpretive Turn*, ed., David R. Hiley, James F. Bohman, and Richard Shusterman (Ithaca, NY: Cornell University Press, 1991): 90.

59. See Taylor, *Philosophical Arguments*.

60. Guignon, "Pragmatism or Hermeneutics? Epistemology after Foundationalism," p. 99.

61. *Realities and Relationships*, p. 82.

62. Kenneth J. Gergen, "If Persons are Texts," in *Hermeneutics and Psychology*, ed. Stanley B. Messer, Louis A. Sass, and Richard L. Woolfolk (New Brunswick, NJ: Rutgers University Press, 1988): 39. Charles Taylor replies to Gergen's paper in this volume and argues that Gergen wrongly interprets Wittgenstein to mean that all concerns with validity in interpreting the meaning of human action and utterances disappear once one endorses the notion of language games.

63. Susan Haack, *Manifesto of a Passionate Moderate* (Chicago: University of Chicago Press, 1998): 117.

64. Gergen seems happy to accept the label 'skeptic' as a self-description. See *Realities and Relationships*, pp. 76ff. Von Glasersfeld tries to extricate himself from the negative connotations of the term "skepticism." See Ernst von Glasersfeld, *Wege des Wissens. Konstruktivistische Erkundungen durch unser Denken* [*Paths of Knowledge. Constructivist Explorations of Our Thinking*] (Heidelberg: Carl-Auer-Systeme, 1997): 48.

65. von Glasersfeld, *Wege des Wissens*, pp. 45-61.

66. Gergen, "Social Construction and the Educational Process," p. 24.

67. Ibid., p. 32.

68. See *Realities and Relationships*, pp. 50-51 and Chapter 7.

69. von Glasersfeld, cited in Clemens Diesbergen, *Radikal-konstruktivistische Paedagogik als problematische Konstruktion [Radical-constructivist Pedagogy as Problematic Construction]*(Frankfurt, M.: Peter Lang, 1998): 19.

70. von Glasersfeld, "Knowing without Metaphysics," p. 26.

71. *Realities and Relationships*, p. 181.

72. von Glasersfeld, "Cognition, Construction of Knowledge and Teaching," pp. 123-125.

73. Gergen, "Social Construction and the Educational Process," pp. 25-26.

74. Robert Nola, "Book Review," *Science and Education* 80, no. 1 (1996): 210.

75. Gergen, "Social Construction and the Educational Process," p. 35.

76. Shotter, "In Dialogue: Social Constructionism and Radical Constructivism," p. 49.

Section Two

Social Constructivism

Editor's Introduction

The pair of chapters that follow take as their focus the hotly disputed social constructivist territory. (Joan Solomon also devotes some space to this dispute in Chapter X.) Peter Slezak, a philosopher and a cognitive scientist, describes (and makes his own contribution to) the so-called science wars. He sees great problems—philosophical and educational—in the work of sociologists of knowledge who advance the very strong thesis that knowledge is entirely socially constructed (the aptly named Strong Program in sociology of knowledge). On the other hand, Eric Bredo, who works at the intersection of philosophy of education, social psychology, and sociology and who is also not enamored of the Strong Program, favors a more moderate version of social constructivism that is nascent in the work of the American pragmatists George Herbert Mead and John Dewey (a form of constructivism that is not the target of Slezak's critique). Together their chapters give a good mapping of the complex social constructivist terrain.

Participants on both sides of the science wars have become quite intemperate, and as Slezak notes, there has been a great deal of purple prose in the literature (a little of which will be found to have crept into his own work).

Why all this heat? The answer was sketched in the opening chapter of this volume, and Bredo and Slezak also discuss it (the latter has it as the main thread of his chapter). There is a lot at stake in the disputes over social constructivism, chiefly the status of science as a form of knowledge that is warranted (and tested) by evidence and rigorous logical and mathematical argumentation. But as might be expected, there are several complex issues lying beneath the surface. First, as explained in the introductory chapter, if bodies of knowledge are (strongly) socially constructed—that is, if they are not shaped in any significant way by the realms of external nature that they appear to be about, but rather are determined by social forces of one kind or another—then the contents of these bodies of knowledge can only be accounted for in sociological terms. In effect, sociology of knowledge replaces epistemology; the issue of the warrant for our knowledge-claims gets relegated to the trash can of history. Philosophers (and many scientists) cannot be expected to take this news lying down.

A second and somewhat related issue is that the adherents of the Strong Program, and others who are like-minded, believe that it should be possible to explain all social phenomena in causal terms. Thus, it should be possible to give a causal account both of why the disciplines have the content that they do, and why it is that so many individuals come to believe or accept them as being the "truth." The field of sociology of knowledge can provide the requisite causal accounts but, according to these constructivists, philosophy cannot. Another way to put this is that the sociologists of knowledge reject the attempt made both by philosophers and members of disciplinary fields such as physics to give *internal* accounts of the development of those fields in terms of the reasons, evidence, data, and arguments that are the focus of internal discussions among the scientists who work in those fields. When scientists and epistemologists espouse this view, the radical sociologists of knowledge argue, they are supposing that acceptance of items of knowledge into the disciplines is *uncaused*. However, critics of the Strong Program, such as Slezak, argue that a serious error has been committed here; the evidence and arguments and deductions that are current inside a field such as physics are indeed *part of the causal nexus that is operating*. Physicists accept or reject hypotheses partly and sometimes wholly *because* of the evidence that is available (reasons are indeed helping to cause this aspect of the physicists' behavior). In their turn, sociologists of knowledge are not receptive to this opposing view because they take it as denigrating the contributions that their own discipline can make. And so the arguments rage on.

It should be clear that these two issues have great significance for all who think about the nature of education in the various disciplines represented in the school curriculum. But it also should be clear that the concepts we use, whether in everyday life or in the scholarly disciplines, did not descend—fully formed—out of the blue. There was a time when the concepts of "energy" or "mass" or "molecule" or "psychosis" or "working class" did not exist; and the halting and interactive process can be traced by which these concepts and the very things or categories themselves were developed. It is to this issue, where a moderate type of social constructivism would appear to be able to shed some light, that Eric Bredo turns. How did our conceptual apparatus come into being?

Bredo steers a course between, on the one hand, the traditional account of the origin of our knowledge that does not explicitly admit any social factors and, on the other hand, the radical sociological position of the Strong Program that seems to neglect any input from the external physical environment. He develops an account of the social construction of concepts that is based on a close reading of the work of John Dewey and his friend and one-time colleague George Herbert Mead. Several strands get woven together in this corpus of work. First, to the pragmatists, concepts or ideas are *tools* whose function it is to guide our actions so that we may better survive in the oftentimes hostile environment in which we are located. (There is an interesting similarity here between this aspect of classic pragmatism and some of the work of Ernst von Glasersfeld, who also sees our knowledge as being a tool for survival, but of course his account is tainted, so far as the pragmatists and social constructivists are concerned, by being so individualistically oriented.) It is important to note the centrality in the work of the pragmatists of the actual physical interaction with the environment—the tugging and pushing and manipulating by which we make objects and then use them to advance our purposes. (Jean Piaget has a somewhat similar view here, although his account also veers towards the individualistic.) Second, for Dewey and Mead the development of concepts takes place through the social medium of language, which above all is a medium for communication among members of a cultural group.

It is best to think of these pragmatists as being interested in both psychological and social constructivism; they think individuals learn by being part of a sociocultural nexus, but they also think that the public bodies of knowledge, or the disciplines, are *public* and hence are socially constructed. But neither Dewey nor Mead—nor Bredo, for that matter—moves significantly in the direction taken by members of the Edinburgh School. Dewey is famous for having written about the *warrants* that entitle us to make assertions about the world (warrants, that is, for our knowledge-claims); these include evidence or data or theoretical arguments, and they come from what he called *competent inquiry*.

CHAPTER IV

A Critique of Radical Social Constructivism

PETER SLEZAK

Introduction: Science Wars

The dispute concerning Social Constructivism has emerged from being an isolated and esoteric epistemological debate among relatively few academic scholars to being a notorious and widespread public scandal. Challenges to traditional conceptions of science which severely polarized philosophers, historians and sociologists have erupted into heated public disputes—the so-called Science Wars. The issues at stake concern the most fundamental questions about the nature of science, and inevitably these controversies have become prominent among educators where a variety of constructivist doctrines have become entangled.[1]

Undeniably, if radical social constructivist doctrines are correct, the implications for science education are revolutionary for, on these views, knowledge is merely consensus upon arbitrary convention; and education involves not learning as a cognitive process of reason and understanding, but merely conformity to power and political interests. As I will suggest, there could be no more fundamental challenge to education than the one posed by the radical form of social constructivism, since it purports to overturn the very conception of knowledge in the Western Tradition: The self-advertising grandiosely proclaims, "The foundations of modern thought are at stake here."[2]

A major battle in these Science Wars has been fought over the book *Higher Superstition* by Paul Gross and Norman Levitt, which brought the polemics surrounding social constructivism to wide popular attention.[3] Adding piquancy and creating even greater public attention to social constructivism was the fallout from the so-called "Sokal Hoax."

Peter Slezak is director of the program in cognitive science at the University of New South Wales. His areas of research and publication include the work of Descartes, problems of mental representation and visual imagery, rational decision theory, and sociology of scientific knowledge.

This heightening of controversy arose from the unwitting publication by the journal *Social Text* of a spoof article written in the postmodernist style by the mathematical physicist Alan Sokal, which was deliberate nonsense.[4]

In their different ways, the Sokal article and the Gross and Levitt book provided exposés of what they claim to be the bankrupt—indeed, fraudulent and pernicious—nature of social constructivism in a broad variety of postmodern guises. Thus, the popular polemics, colorful epithets and purple prose, while out of place in academic texts, succeeded in conveying a widely shared sense of the enormity of what Gross and Levitt call the postmodernist game of "intellectual subversion"[5] and "philosophical styrofoam."[6]

Even among the more temperate critiques in the academic literature there had been a scandalized outrage about social constructivism going well beyond normal intellectual disagreement. The disputes in the technical journals have been characterized by vituperative *ad hominem* assaults and exchanges of an unusual ferocity. For example, Mario Bunge has described most of the work in the field as "a grotesque cartoon of scientific research."[7] In a similar vein, the philosopher David Stove has written of these doctrines as a form of lunacy which is "so absurd, that it eludes the force of all argument," a "philosophical folly" and "a stupid and discreditable business" whose authors are "beneath philosophical notice and unlikely to benefit from it." In his scathing remarks, Stove describes such ideas as an illustration of the "fatal affliction" and "corruption of thought" in which people say things which are bizarre and which even they must know to be false.[8] Larry Laudan, who was among the first philosophers to make systematic critical analyses of social constructivism, has characterized this "rampant relativism" as "the most prominent and pernicious manifestation of anti-intellectualism in our time."[9] Laudan's charge of anti-intellectualism clearly points to the source of concern for educators.

Ideas or Ideology? Pedagogy or Propaganda?

In important clarifications of the various doctrines conflated under the label "constructivism," D.C. Phillips has noted, "Arguably it is the dominant theoretical position in science and mathematics education,"[10] and he remarks, "Across the broad fields of educational theory and research, constructivism has become something akin to a secular religion."[11] Phillips distinguishes the sociological form of constructivism of interest here from the psychological variety,[12] and he observes, "It is the work of the social constructivists that had drawn the most dramatic attention in recent years; clearly they have touched a raw nerve."[13] As Phillips notes elsewhere, the reason for this is that "There is a lot at stake. For it can be argued that if the more radical of the sociologists of scientific knowledge . . . are right, then the validity of the traditional philosophic/epistemological enterprise is effectively undermined, and so indeed is the pursuit of science itself."[14] The doctrines of radical social constructivism take scientific theories to reflect the social milieu in which they emerge and, therefore, rather than being founded on logic, evidence, and reason, beliefs are taken to be the causal effects of the historically contingent, local context. Accordingly, if knowledge is intrinsically the product of "external" factors rather than "internal" considerations of evidence and reason, then it is an illusion to imagine that education might serve to instill a capacity for critical thought or rational belief. On these views education becomes indoctrination, pedagogy is propaganda, and ideas are merely conventional conformity to social consensus.

Before examining these doctrines in detail, it is worth observing a symptomatic view of education and its goals arising from radical social constructivism. Where traditional views see scientific knowledge as a source of profound awe, insight, inspiration, creativity, and aesthetic pleasure, sociologists see something less exalted. Instead of fostering independent thought and the pleasures of intellectual curiosity, science is offered as having a mere utilitarian, pragmatic value, at best. Thus Harry Collins and Trevor Pinch, writing specifically on science education in schools, suggest, "It is nice to know the content of science—it helps one to do a lot of things such as repair the car, wire a plug, build a model aeroplane. . . ."[15] To be sure, science has such practical uses, but this prosaic view seems to leave out something essential—namely, the intellectual dimension, the role of the creative mind in providing an understanding of the world. Instead of conceiving of science education as fostering such intellectual values as understanding and critical thinking, Collins and Pinch recommend that science education should attend to the social negotiation, "myths" and "tricks of frontier science" as "the important thing."[16]

Perhaps most importantly from an educational point of view, the relativism inherent in radical social constructivist theories makes it impossible for teachers to offer the usual intellectual grounds for distinguishing science from nonsense. Since the rational virtues of theories are taken to be irrelevant to their status, one cannot complain that some views are false or implausible or otherwise lacking rational, cognitive merit. For example, one cannot teach that Soviet Lysenkoism or Hitler's racialism were perversions of scientific truth. Their success in winning consensus must count *ipso facto* as exemplary scientific achievement according to social constructivist doctrines.

What Is Radical Social Constructivism?

A few special difficulties must be faced in attempting to characterize the radical end of the field of social constructivism. First, in the years since its recent reinvention and promotion by the Edinburgh School,[17] there has been a fragmentation and doctrinal divergence among various factions which cannot be traced in detail here. Second, as we will see presently, the history of these changes is made somewhat difficult to understand by the questionable tactics of constructivists. Nevertheless, there are certain underlying, fundamental ideas which have motivated the enterprise throughout, and these must be understood despite having become obscured in its more recent manifestations.

In 1976, David Bloor's book *Knowledge and Social Imagery*[18] launched the so-called "Edinburgh Strong Program" in the sociology of scientific knowledge (SSK), and the undoubted appeal of this work to many was its iconoclastic approach to old-fashioned theories. Bloor was self-consciously heralding a strong or radical enterprise intended to displace traditional philosophy and epistemology. In brief, the essential, astonishing stance was the rejection of "the very idea" of science as a distinctive enterprise. This effacing of any distinction between science and other institutions is summarized by Steve Woolgar as the rejection of the following traditional "core assumption":

> The persistent idea that science is something special and distinct from other forms of cultural and social activity . . . Instead of treating them as rhetorical accomplishments, many analysts continue to respect the boundaries which delineate science from non-science.[19]

On this view, not only is the very distinctiveness of science merely some kind of propaganda victory, a further "assumption" to be rejected is the curiously persistent view "that the objects of the natural world are real, objective and enjoy an independent pre-existence."[20] Such astonishing claims made outside the academic seminar room would be evidence of clinical derangement. In place of the traditional "misconceptions" about science and the independent pre-existence of the world, strong social constructivism proposed an amalgam of idealism and relativism according to which scientific theories are merely "fictions," the product of social forces, interests, and other contingent, historical aspects of the milieu in which they arise. That is, the very substantive ideas and content of scientific theories are not explanatory or descriptive of the world, but are "rhetorical accomplishments" by some community of discourse and constituted entirely by social consensus. Even scientific discovery is a matter of "interpretative practice," and "genius has no bearing on the pattern of discovery in science."[21]

These are not merely radical or even revolutionary claims. They can only be described as staggering and extravagant doctrines which might be expected to require compelling arguments. The equanimity with which they were received by historians and sociologists is itself a psychological and sociological fact deserving explanation. In the absence of compelling, or indeed any, arguments, sociologists had a ready explanation for the predictable incredulity of philosophers. Foreshadowing the provocation of later works, Bloor's preface to the first edition of his book already hints darkly that the inevitable resistance by philosophers to his doctrines will be due, not to the unargued absurdity of the ideas, but to uncomfortable secrets that philosophers would wish to hide. Bloor asserts that his approach to science from a sociological point of view encounters resistance because "some nerve has been touched." He announces his bold intention to "despoil academic boundaries" which "contrive to keep some things well hidden."[22] Bloor was right about some nerve having been touched, though he misdiagnosed the nature of the irritation. He devotes an entire chapter of his landmark book to a kind of psychoanalysis of his opponents by speculating about the "sources of resistance" to the Strong Program which he attributes to hidden, indeed primitive, motives involving the fear of sociology's desacralizing of science and its mysteries. One might suggest alternative reasons for the resistance to his sociological doctrines, but Bloor sees only repressed impulses concerning the "sacred" and the "profane" leading to "a superstitious desire to avoid treating knowledge naturalistically."[23] Bloor imagines that the "threatening" nature of any investigation into science itself has been the cause of a "positive disinclination to examine the nature of knowledge in a candid and scientific way."[24] However, this disinclination to examine knowledge and the need to keep it mystified through fear of desecration is difficult to reconcile with the fact that every philosopher since Plato has been centrally concerned with the problem of knowledge and its justification. The inordinate space devoted to such fatuous *ad hominem* speculations signifies the pre-eminent place they occupy in the social constructivist enterprise as a substitute for serious, or indeed any, philosophical analysis.

"Knowledge As Such": Contexts, Contents and Causes

In his manifesto, Bloor had declared that the central claims of the Strong Program that he had launched were "beyond dispute,"[25] and Barry Barnes begins an article asserting that in the short time since its advent "developments have occurred with breathtaking speed" and "the view that scientific culture is constructed like any other is now well elaborated and exemplified."[26]

This level of self-congratulatory hyperbole has prompted Thomas Gieryn to comment upon these "defenses and re-affirmations" as "expressions of hubris" and "exaggerations passing as fact."[27] Gieryn has suggested that the radical findings of the new sociology of science "are 'new' only in a fictionalized reading of antecedent work."[28] In particular, Robert Merton's chapter on "The Sociology of Knowledge" had specifically enunciated the very central doctrine of the Strong Program. Merton wrote:

> The "Copernican revolution" in this area of inquiry consisted in the hypothesis that not only error or illusion or unauthenticated belief but also the discovery of truth was socially (historically) conditioned. . . . The sociology of knowledge came into being with the signal hypothesis that even truths were to be held socially accountable, were to be related to the historical society in which they emerged.[29]

Though it had appeared earlier in different guises in G. W. F. Hegel, Karl Marx, and Emile Durkheim, the radical idea at the heart of the Strong Program was to go beyond those sociological studies which stopped short of considering the actual substantive content, the *ideas*, of scientific theories as an appropriate domain for sociological investigation. Previously, sociological studies paid attention only to such things as institutional politics, citation patterns and other such peripheral social phenomena surrounding the production of science, but had not ventured to explain the *cognitive contents* of theories in sociological terms. Since this crucial point has been obscured, its importance for appreciating subsequent developments cannot be overstated. The opening sentence of Bloor's book asks, "Can the sociology of knowledge investigate and explain the very content and nature of scientific knowledge?"—that is, of "knowledge as such, as distinct from the circumstances of production."[30]

The alleged failure of previous sociological studies to touch on the contents of scientific belief was portrayed by Bloor as a loss of nerve and a failure to be consistent.[31] Karl Mannheim, among the founders of the sociology of knowledge, is characterized as failing to make the logical extension of his approach from knowledge of society to the knowledge of nature as well. The epistemological pretensions of the Strong Program—its relativist challenge—derive from this thoroughgoing application of the sociological principle which seeks to explain the hitherto exempted knowledge claims. The ambitions of Bloor's program are explicit from the outset, for he complains that previous sociologists, in "a betrayal of their disciplinary standpoint" had failed to "expand and generalize" their claims to all knowledge: ". . . the sociology of knowledge might well have pressed more strongly into the area currently occupied by philosophers, who have been allowed to take upon themselves the task of defining the nature of knowledge."[32]

Causes and Case Studies

The extensive body of case studies repeatedly invoked by sociologists to answer their critics has been taken to establish the thesis that the contents of scientific theories and beliefs have social causes, in contradistinction to psychological ones. The causal claim concerns such things as "connections between the gross social structure of groups and the general form of the cosmologies to which they have subscribed."[33] That is, the very cognitive content of the beliefs is claimed to be causally connected with immediate, local aspects of the social milieu. Of this general thesis, Bloor asserts, "The causal link is beyond dispute."[34] Indeed, Bloor and Steven Shapin[35] were evidently unable to believe that anyone might question the causal claims of the Strong Program except on the assumption that they must be unfamiliar with the extensive literature of the case studies. However, in a precise parallel with Emile Durkheim and Marcel Mauss[36] to be noted presently, the claims of social determination of beliefs are all the more extraordinary in view of the utter failure of these case studies to support them. Critics have challenged precisely the bearing of these studies on the causal claims, and so repeatedly citing the burgeoning literature is to entirely miss the point.

Of course, scientific discoveries have always necessarily arisen in some social milieu or other, but this is merely a truism holding equally for most human activity not thought to have been actually caused in this way by social factors. However, to the extent that social factors are indeed ubiquitous, establishing a causal connection requires more than merely characterizing in detail the social milieu which must have existed. These more stringent demands have not been met anywhere in the voluminous case studies in the SSK literature. Thus, although Shapin has acknowledged that "the task is the refinement and clarification of the ways in which scientific knowledge is to be referred to the various contextual factors and interests which produce it," and that "we need to ascertain the exact nature of the links between accounts of natural reality and the social order," nevertheless his much-cited case study of phrenology offers only a variety of anthropological approaches leading at best to a postulation of "homologies" between society and theories which may serve as "expressive symbolism" or perhaps function to further social interests in their "context of use." This falls far short of demonstrating the strong claims of social determination which abound in the rhetoric of programmatic statements and their "social epistemology." Thus, it is a truism to assert, as Shapin does, merely that "Culture [taken to include science] is developed and evaluated in particular historical situations."[37] Shapin undertakes to refute the accusations of empirical sterility by a lengthy recounting of the "considerable empirical achievements" of the sociology of scientific knowledge.[38] But he is simply begging the question with his advice that "one can either debate the possibility of the sociology of scientific knowledge or one can do it."[39]

When Is a Cigar Just a Cigar?

Taken to be an empirical claim—as intended by adherents of the Strong Program—the contingent, historical determination of scientific theories by local social context entails that the substantive content of theories would have been different had the milieu been different. We are inevitably led to ask: Would Isaac Newton have enunciated an inverse *cube* law of gravitation, perhaps, had the society been different? The model of such empirical studies was Forman's[40] much-cited work which attributes the development of quantum physics to the prevailing milieu in Weimar Germany. However, in the same vein, we might inquire: Did Kurt Gödel's Incompleteness Theorem arise from some lacunae in the Viennese social order of 1930? This admittedly facetious example merely invokes the same suggestive metaphorical connections adduced by social constructivist case studies. There is, at best, a kind of affinity claimed between the social context and the contents of the theory in question. Thus, Shapin cites "homologies between society and nature" and sees theories as "expressive symbolism" which can be exploited to serve social interests. Given the tenuous nature of such "homologies" between theories and the zeitgeist, the distinction between parody and serious claims is difficult to discern. Shapin's recherché homologies between theory content and social context recall the Freudian interpretation of dreams, which involved a similar decoding of an allegedly symbolic connection. Likewise, sociology pretends to disclose the hidden meaning underlying our scientific theories. We may have imagined that nineteenth century theories of phrenology were about the brain, but they were really "expressing a social experience" and were about the "differentiation and specialization [in the social order] perceived by the bourgeois groups."[41] Gödel's Incompleteness Theorem, too, undoubtedly expresses a collective longing for wholeness and fulfillment among the Viennese intelligentsia. However, in the spirit of Freud's famous remark one is tempted to ask: When is a cigar just a cigar?

The Social Construction of Social Constructivism

Having briefly indicated some of the foundational doctrines, it is instructive to look at a recent, authoritative, and sympathetic statement of strong social constructivism in a book whose co-authors include two of its founders—*Scientific Knowledge: A Sociological Analysis* by Barnes, Bloor, and Jules Henry.[42] As founders of the field, these authors are uniquely well qualified to offer the book to anyone "seeking a text in the sociology of scientific knowledge." However, borrowing earlier words of one of its authors, this sociological enterprise appears to "contrive to keep some things well hidden."[43] A study of the index is revealing. Georg Cantor, infinite cardinal numbers, and the continuum hypothesis get several entries whereas social constructivism and the Strong Program get none at all. In view of the Strong Program being proclaimed with great fanfare as the radical new approach revolutionizing the study of science and epistemology, its omission from the index is revealing. The Duhem-Quine Thesis, mentioned *en passant* in an obscure footnote, gets no index entry either, though the book is, in fact, an extended essay on the alleged consequences of this philosophical doctrine. Other omissions from the index are equally curious. The truth of a certain "teleological" view of rationalist philosophers was originally presented by Bloor as entailing the falsity of the sociological program, and he has recently[44] reaffirmed his commitment to the tenets of the original Program. In view of the decisive, foundational status of this diametrical opposition between the scientific/rationalist account and that of the Strong Program, it is striking that this issue, too, has disappeared without trace. This rewriting of history makes it impossible to understand both the social constructivist doctrines themselves and the scandal they have generated.

The following questions encapsulate some of the fundamental issues on which the disputes about social constructivism have centered and are a kind of diagnostic class test for "Social Studies of Science 101":

1. What is the Edinburgh Strong Program in the sociology of scientific knowledge, what were its central tenets, and what was its self-proclaimed radical novelty regarding the *content* of scientific theories?

2. What is the essential characteristic doctrine of radical social constructivism and what is its relation to "rationalist," "teleological" and "psychologistic" approaches of traditional epistemology? How are the latest views in the sociology of science related to their formulations of twenty years ago?

3. What is the Duhem-Quine thesis of underdetermination of theory by evidence? How does it relate to the "theory-laden" nature of observation? What follows from these theses for the determinants of theory-choice in science?

4. What kinds of empirical evidence have been offered as support for the theories of the radical sociologists of scientific knowledge and how exactly does any evidence bear upon the claims? Are theory contents caused by social contexts?

5. Which epistemological stance does the new sociology of science adopt? (a) Realism (b) Idealism (c) Relativism (d) All of the above (e) None of the above.

6. What are the scope and limits of sociological approaches to science in relation to individual psychology?

As indicated, students who might wish to use the latest book of Barnes, Bloor and Henry as a text to study for the foregoing class test would fail. These questions cannot be answered by a conscientious study of the book, though any teacher would recognize them as elementary ones basic to understanding the field. Cryptic references to issues such as the "rationalist" philosophies against which the entire sociological enterprise was directed are left entirely unexplained and so the innocent reader will not be able to understand or assess the current claims. Accordingly, the questions serve usefully as a thematic framework to organize the present discussion.

Idealism

The book by Barnes, Bloor, and Henry begins encouragingly, if somewhat mystifyingly for the newcomer, by acknowledging the existence of reality. This will undoubtedly be comforting to those who were harboring doubts about the matter, but it arises at all only through certain naive confusions. For their part, the three authors are concerned to distance themselves from those other sociologists who they say "[o]ccasionally . . . may have given this impression" of denying the existence of tables and chairs. Nevertheless, they admit that *most* other sociology of knowledge is, in fact, idealist. In repudiating this stance these authors emphasize their own contrasting "naturalistic" view, but on such good authority, then, idealism must be regarded as a central philosophical issue for the understanding of social constructivism.

Notwithstanding these authors' disclaimers, warrant for the charge of "idealism" against them as well arises partly from their own misconceptions regarding the "rationalist" theories they oppose and partly from the strong social constructivism to which they remain firmly committed, which is actually an amalgam of idealism and relativism. As we have seen in the remark by Woolgar, an unavoidable temptation towards idealism arises from the sociologists' desire to deny that science describes an independent world. Consequently, by contrast, the "rationalist" philosophy of science against which social constructivism has been opposed, has been consistently misconstrued as being committed to a metaphysical realism as some kind of epistemic access to absolute truth about a world behind appearances. While science is undoubtedly committed to discovering the nature of an independently existing reality, this is not a metaphysical thesis about some Kantian realm of "things-in-themselves." It is simply the truism that we take our best theories literally to be talking *about something*. The reaction to the ordinary practice of science as some kind of philosophical error requiring sociological remedy is simply a mistake, since the virtues and status of science as an enterprise are independent of such metaphysical questions. Realists and idealists alike can enjoy the fruits of scientific knowledge. Specifically, whether or not scientific theories are socially constructed is an issue to be determined by arguments entirely independent of idealism. Nevertheless, Barnes and his co-authors offer their own "naturalist" stance as the contrast with "idealism," but their "naturalism" is simply a demand for empirical explanation in terms of causes. However, Bishop George Berkeley, like all other idealists, was an empiricist in good standing in this sense, and one can be an idealist at the same time as being committed to empirical, naturalistic science. Idealism is a metaphysical doctrine concerning the overall status of our scientific theories as such, and not a specific approach to explanation within the overall enterprise like naturalism. The dispute concerning idealism is entirely indifferent to any debate about the practices of empirical inquiry as such and, therefore, asserting credentials as "naturalistic" does not even amount to a plea of "innocent" to the charge of idealism, much less grounds for acquittal.

Revealing comments support the charge of idealism despite their disavowals. Barnes, Bloor, and Henry point out that it is not "the existence of nature" which accounts for certain behaviors and that "attention to nature" will not adjudicate the merits of our theories and classifications.[45] Of course, if appeal to nature (meaning to empirical evidence) cannot adjudicate our theories, it is not clear what would do so. We see here the radical social constructivist dogma that scientific theories are somehow *unconstrained by the way things are in the world*. However, the writers are confusing the supposed indirectness of our knowledge of the world, its inaccessibility beyond the "veil of ideas," with the bearing of empirical evidence on our scientific theories. Stressing the former kind of inaccessibility does not establish the latter kind. This is precisely to confuse idealism with relativism.

The declaration of Barnes, Bloor and Henry that they are not idealists, then, is somewhat paradoxical since it poses the following dilemma: Which reality is the one the sociologists profess to believe in? Do they believe in an inaccessible Kantian *ding an sich* after all? Or do they believe in the rationalists' world as conveyed by our true (i.e., best) theories? In wishing to deny the former, they end up denying the latter and thereby become idealists as well as relativists.[46] In brief, their needless entanglement in such notorious problems is symptomatic of the radical sociologists' absurd pretensions to overthrow "the subject that used to be called philosophy."[47]

Relativism

Despite characterizing their book as focused on "basic foundations," Barnes et al. explain that it "gives little prominence" to such issues as relativism, *inter alia*. Indeed, this prefatory mention of relativism is the only one in the book. However, even more than idealism, relativism has been the central, distinctive theoretical doctrine of strong social constructivism and the source of most disputes.[48] Neglecting to discuss it is somewhat like a text on evolution professing to concentrate on basic foundations and yet choosing to give little prominence to natural selection. The authors' recent reticence about their own central, and previously explicitly embraced, doctrines is a curious, though telling, feature of their work, as already noted.[49]

Relativism is the claim that knowledge has no warrant beyond individual opinion. In part, it is often a *non sequitur* from the recognition that there is no absolute truth or certainty. However, given that there can be no absolutely secure knowledge, the alternative to relativism is fallibilism, that is, the idea that reliable knowledge is possible through revision and improvement. Relativism is at the heart of radical social constructivism because the supposed absence from the constraints of independent "reality" is assumed to leave no other grounds for adjudicating scientific claims. Specifically, this is taken to warrant appeal to a sociological account of theory acceptance. Relativism, then, is the spurious assumption that there can be nothing more to say about the goodness of our theories if one can't meaningfully compare them to an independent, inaccessible reality. However, the question of realism has been the subject of a vast philosophical literature, and both sides of these philosophical arguments accept the rational force of evidence and the usual considerations of explanatory virtue such as comprehensiveness, coherence, and simplicity as grounds for rational theory choice. Thus, Cardinal Bellarmine's instrumentalism did not involve a challenge to the intellectual merits of Galileo's Copernicanism as such. More recently, Bas van Fraassen's celebrated "constructive empiricism"[50] is concerned to "save the phenomena" without postulating a hidden underlying reality, but this does not entail rejection of the usual rational considerations governing theory choice. Social constructivists mistakenly conclude that the inaccessibility of "things in themselves" behind the veil of our theories (whatever this might mean) precludes saying anything sensible about their cognitive virtues.

However, "rationalist" talk of observation, confirmation, evidence, and truth is *within* the sociologists' own preferred framework, on our side of the veil, as it were—according to which, as Bloor says, all we have and all we need are the theories themselves. Indeed, this could be a succinct statement of Willard Quine's[51] well-known metaphor of the fabric or web of our knowledge, also articulated in his famous example from Otto Neurath—when doing science we are like a sailor who must repair his boat at sea; the boat is all we have, and we can only repair it one plank at a time while sailing in it. That is, we are inescapably dependent on our theories even as we seek to revise them. But to continue the metaphor, what counts as a repair is not a matter of arbitrary convention. Radical social constructivism, however, wants to scuttle the boat.

Theory Choice: Underdetermination of Theory by Evidence

One consideration, above all, has been widely taken to warrant the appeal to sociological factors in the explanation of scientific theory choice. This is an argument which attempts to exploit the so-called Quine-Duhem thesis concerning the underdetermination of theory by evidence—the thesis that there can be no direct inference from observational data to any particular theory, since indefinitely many theories are equally compatible with the same empirical evidence.[52] Therefore, other considerations must be invoked to explain the preference of scientists for one theory over others which are equally consistent with the observational or experimental data. However, a *non sequitur* from this thesis has become one of the foundational tenets of the social constructivist enterprise. Thus, when distilled to its essence, the entire case underlying Bloor's[53] manifesto is a spurious inference from underdetermination to social construction. However, underdetermination is completely neutral among the various alternative resources which might be invoked to explain theory choice beyond conformity with the evidence. Clearly, it has to be shown *independently* why it might be *social* factors rather than some others (say, astrological) which are the operative ones in determining theory choice between the various alternative theories that are consistent with the evidence in hand.

Setting the pattern for subsequent discussions, Bloor relies on this issue as the central thesis of his book. Evidently no argument is thought necessary for this egregious *non sequitur* and Bloor gives none. In view of the foundational status which this book and this "argument" have acquired, the situation is sufficiently peculiar to deserve emphasis: The problem with Bloor's discussion and the general reliance on this doctrine in radical social constructivism is not merely that the arguments are weak or open to challenge in some way. Rather, *no* arguments of any kind whatsoever are offered.

Christopher Boorse has pointed out that the underdetermination of theories by all possible observational evidence does not make them indistinguishable on other criteria such as simplicity, fecundity, coherence, comprehensiveness, explanatory power, and so on.[54] These are, of course, the kinds of rational considerations typically invoked by the rationalist or teleological account of the growth of scientific knowledge. Part of the problem may have arisen from an excessively literal construal of theory choice which cannot be considered as an actual selection among equivalent available alternatives; historians, above all, should recognize that the problem in science is typically to find even a single theory which is consistent with the observations. Accordingly, what is termed "choice" is more appropriately described as the psychology of scientific invention or discovery—the subject of a burgeoning research literature.[55]

Consensus as Conventional

Radical social constructivism rests on this idea that alternative theory choices are not only available but equally "good," for theories are adopted by convention—a view that opens the way to sociological relativism. Barnes, Bloor and Henry assert, "Conventions could always be otherwise . . .,"[56] suggesting that knowledge might have been negotiated differently had the local interpretive milieu been different and, thereby, inviting the facetious question about Newton's inverse cube law. Indeed, undaunted by its absurdity, the authors embrace precisely such a paradoxical idea even in the case of arithmetical laws.[57] According to their own account, given the underdetermination of theory by evidence, sociologists must be committed to the possibility of a consensus settling on a vast range of possible laws via the contingent "collective accomplishment" of "fact production" by "local cultural traditions." Unconvincingly, they suggest that the consensus on "2 + 2 = 4" is due merely to "pragmatic reasons connected with the organization of collective action" and the fact that "it is probably easier to organize" than a different convention such as "2 + 2 = 5." Indeed! The fact that the former might also be easier to *believe* is somehow not considered relevant from a sociological perspective.

Revisiting Durkheim: "Plus ça change . . ."

These central ideas of strong social constructivism have a notable pedigree. Emile Durkheim and Marcel Mauss[58] in their work *Primitive Classification* claimed that the cosmologies of groups such as the Zuñi reflected precise features of their social structure. In his paper "Revisiting Durkheim and Mauss,"[59] Bloor invokes them in support of "one of the central propositions of the sociology of knowledge"[60]—namely, their view that "the classification of things reproduces the classification of men." Bloor recommends that Durkheim and Mauss should be rehabilitated after having been consigned to the history books since their work is important for "showing not merely how society influences knowledge, but how it is constitutive of it."[61]

It is understandable, of course, that Bloor should commend the virtues of Durkheim and Mauss, for they offer essentially the same metaphorical links between concepts and contexts which have been the stock in trade of the recent sociology of science, but the Strong Program emulates *Primitive Classification* to the extent of exactly reproducing its severe shortcomings. Thus, a rather different picture emerges if one takes Bloor's invitation seriously to revisit Durkheim's work in the edition cited by him—including the introduction by Rodney Needham. It is striking that Needham makes trenchant criticisms of Durkheim and Mauss, which are identical with those which have subsequently been leveled against Bloor's Strong Program.

Needham draws attention to Durkheim's "tendency to argument by *petitio principii*" in his claim that the classification of non-social things "reproduces" the classification of people—the claim which Bloor characterizes without demurral as a "bold unifying principle" but which Needham describes as an unwarranted, abrupt inference and logical error which flaws the entire work. On the alleged parallelism between primitive societies and their concepts, Needham writes:

> Now society is alleged to be the model on which classification is based, yet in society after society examined no formal correspondence can be shown to exist. Different forms of classification are found with identical types of social organization, and similar forms with different types of society. . . . There is very little sign of the constant correspondence of symbolic classification with social order which the argument leads one to expect, and which indeed the argument is intended to explain.[62]

In the same vein, Needham notes further that with respect to one of their claims their "evidences on this point lend their argument no support whatever" and on another claim "nowhere in the course of their argument do the authors report the slightest empirical evidence, from any society of any form, which might justify their statement."[63] Needham's judgment is considerably more damning than Bloor reveals, suggesting "Durkheim and Mauss's entire venture to have been misconceived."[64] In view of the more recent airing of identical concerns, the following remarks are worth quoting in full:

> Yet all such particular objections of logic and method fade in significance before two criticisms which apply generally to the entire argument. One is that there is no logical necessity to postulate a causal connection between

society and symbolic classification, and in the absence of factual indications to this effect there are no grounds for attempting to do so. . . . If we allow ourselves to be guided by the facts themselves, i.e. by the correspondences, we have to conclude that there are no empirical grounds for a causal explanation. In no single case is there any compulsion to believe that society is the cause or even the model of the classification; and it is only the strength of their preoccupation with cause that leads Durkheim and Mauss to cast their argument and present the facts as though this were the case.[65]

These remarks take on special significance in light of the fact that identical claims by the Strong Program have been repeatedly asserted and repeatedly challenged. Needham draws attention to the extensive evidence which actually suggests a conclusion exactly the reverse of that which Durkheim and Mauss suppose. "That is, forms of classification and modes of symbolic thought display very many more similarities than do the societies in which they are found."[66] Needham's sober judgment is:

We have to conclude that Durkheim and Mauss's argument is logically fallacious, and that it is methodologically unsound. There are grave reasons, indeed, to deny it any validity whatever.[67]

Needham expresses an attitude to the work of Durkheim and Mauss which provides a striking sense of *déjà vu*, saying, "It is difficult not to recoil in dismay" from their "unevidenced and unreasoned" explanations for the complexities of social and symbolic classification.[68]

Impartiality

Robert Merton, like Karl Mannheim, argued that theories judged to be correct and founded on rational considerations are not in need of sociological explanation in the way that false and irrational theories are. In this sense, traditional conceptions relegated sociological accounts to only the dross of science, to account for the residue of false and irrational beliefs. Bloor's revival of the Durkheimian view was explicitly rescuing sociology from this ignominious role by asserting the appropriateness of sociological explanations for *all* of science regardless of evaluative judgments such as truth and falsity, rationality and irrationality, success or failure. Our own cosmology and science in general, like those of the Zuñi, were to be shown to be in their entirety reflections of the social milieu.

Bloor's complaint is directed at asymmetrical approaches such as Imre Lakatos's "rational reconstruction" of episodes in the history of

science which sought to explain correct scientific theories as products
of reasoned thought and, therefore, not requiring resort to sociological
explanations. Bloor regards this approach as having the effect of ren-
dering science "safe from the indignity of empirical explanation,"[69] but
for Lakatos only *sociology* was to be excluded from accounts of successful science since good reasons are a species of explanation themselves.
Analogously, veridical perception does not need explanation in the
same way as misperception or illusion. We do not ordinarily seek
explanatory causes in the case of normal veridical perception, not because we assume that there is no scientific explanation, but because we
assume it to be of a certain general sort. Thus, we don't explain normal
vision, but seek only the cause of failure (such as the influence of alco-
hol or disease). In the same way, we do not seek to explain why the
train stays on the tracks but only why it fails to do so. Again, this asym-
metry does not mean that we believe there is no cause or no explanation for the train staying on the tracks. However, this is the absurd view which Bloor imputes to rationalist philosophers such as
Lakatos. Notice that Bloor takes Lakatos to hold that a rational reconstruction of beliefs implies that they are thereby shown to lack *empirical
explanation altogether.*[70] In his *Knowledge and Social Imagery* (1976), Bloor
characterized the "autonomy of science" view he is opposing:

> One important set of objections to the sociology of knowledge derives
> from the conviction that some beliefs *do not stand in need of any explanation, or do
> not stand in need of a causal explanation.* This feeling is particularly strong when
> the beliefs in question are taken to be true, rational, scientific or objective.[71]

Elsewhere Bloor characterizes the "rationalistic" view that he
opposes as "the claim that nothing makes people do things that are
correct but something does make, or cause, them to go wrong," and
that in the case of true beliefs "causes do not need to be invoked."[72]
Bloor intends to make an absolute distinction between the "teleological" or "rationalist" view which inclines its proponents to "reject
causality"[73] on the one hand, and *"the* causal view," that is, the sociological approach of the Strong Program. On Bloor's own account, the viability of the Strong Program rests on the tenability of this dichotomy
and, in particular, the falsity of the "teleological model." There could
be no more crucial issue for the strong constructivist program.

Larry Laudan has characterized Bloor's acausal attribution to
philosophers as an absurd view which cannot plausibly be attributed to
any philosopher at all.[74] In particular, the approach of Lakatos does

not deny the existence of causes in cases of rationally held beliefs, but only assumes that reasons are themselves a species of cause.[75] However, in a remarkable passage, Bloor responded to Laudan by attempting to deny these patent and quite explicit earlier intentions.[76] Bloor's discomfort was understandable, since the entire edifice of the Strong Program rests on this claimed opposition. Indeed, in the second edition of his classic book, in the crucial section on the "Autonomy of Knowledge" dealing with the problem of causation, we discover certain judicious changes to the original text whose rationale is clearly to avoid the criticisms made by Laudan.[77] It must be noted that these alterations to the original text are somewhat difficult to reconcile with Bloor's prefatorial assertion that "attacks by critics have not convinced me of the need to give ground on any matter of substance" and, therefore, he says, "I have resisted the temptation to alter the original presentation of the case for the sociology of knowledge" apart from minor spelling and stylistic changes.[78]

Bloor's predicament, if not his tactic, is understandable since his statement of the conditions under which the program retains its plausibility left no room for compromise and no way out. Bloor had declared forthrightly, "There is no doubt that if the teleological model is true then the strong programme [sic] is false. The teleological and causal models, then, represent programmatic alternatives which quite exclude one another."[79]

If the "rationalist, teleological, autonomy" view is not the acausal, anti-empirical straw man that Bloor imagined, then its merits need to be confronted seriously. However, this means finding a way to reconcile radical social constructivism with the full weight of considerations from cognitive science. This, in turn, means trying to downplay or expunge the hostility to internal, mental or psychological accounts of rational belief which was a central plank of the Strong Program.

Social Constructivism as Born-again Behaviorism

The purported causal connection between ideas and social context is actually a version of stimulus-control theory akin to that of Skinnerian behaviorism and, not surprisingly, in his later work Bloor explicitly endorses such notorious theories.[80] In characterizing opposing rationalist or teleological views, and quoting Ludwig Wittgenstein, Bloor refers to explanations which postulate mental states as infected by the "disease" of "psychologism."[81] Bloor's frontal assault on the explanatory force of mental states is an intrinsic part of the defense of the radical alternative sociological approach to explaining science, but this bold stance left his program vulnerable to a case on the other side whose strength he had grievously underestimated. For example, anachronistically Bloor's program depends on rejecting the reality of mental states such as images. However, this position is thirty years—and a major scientific revolution—too late.

The pattern of such egregious solecisms is consistent and instructive. Thus, Bloor has dismissed Noam Chomsky's review of B. F. Skinner's *Verbal Behavior* with a passing footnote, and a reference to it as the "fashionable" and "standard" criticism of behaviorism.[82] But this reveals a complete failure to comprehend its significance. One might have expected some indication of the weaknesses of the review and why this merely "fashionable" criticism is to be ignored—particularly since neither Skinner himself nor other behaviorists replied to it.[83] In fact, the Chomsky review is generally regarded as having precipitated the downfall of the entire tradition of behaviorism in psychology. Bloor's cavalier handwaving is rather more misleading than these comments suggest. Chomsky's ideas foreshadowed in this review became the foundations of the dramatic developments of the so-called "Cognitive Revolution."[84] Bloor's failure to indicate the magnitude and import of these developments is comparable to defending Creationism today by dismissing the *Origin of Species* as merely "fashionable" and failing to let one's readers know anything of modern biology founded on Darwin's theory.

Newton's "Principia" as Conditioned Response

Since behaviorism is a doctrine concerning psychology, it is at first sight surprising that it has been recruited to the cause of radical social constructivism. However, behaviorism serves Bloor as an ally, since it denies the explanatory role of internal mental states and is thereby in diametrical opposition to the rationalist or teleological point of view that the Strong Program is also battling. If scientific beliefs are to be construed as the causal effects of an external stimulus, they are precisely analogous to Skinnerian "respondents" or "operants" and, therefore, science is the result of conditioning. In short, the deep insight of radical social constructivism is that Isaac Newton's *Principia* is to be explained just like a rat's bar-pressing in response to food pellets.

Bloor's recent protest that his views are entirely consistent with cognitive science cannot be taken seriously and can be asserted at all only because Bloor now pretends that the sociological thesis at stake is merely whether or not there are social aspects to science.[85] This is significantly different from the claim that knowledge is entirely socially constructed and constituted. This new weak and uncontroversial thesis is not the original doctrine he propounded, whose inconsistency with cognitive science was evident from the accompanying assault on the postulation of mental states. The truism that there are social dimensions to science would hardly have generated the opposition and controversy evoked by the Strong Program. Significantly, Bloor's radical sociological colleagues have reacted differently: their vehement attacks on cognitive science and artificial intelligence have been both telling and more ingenuous. Their strenuous attempts to discredit the claims of cognitive science have given tacit acknowledgment to the threat these pose to the central sociological doctrines.[86] Indeed, Harry Collins,[87] among others, has been perfectly explicit on this point, seeing the claims of artificial intelligence as a crucial test case for the sociology of scientific knowledge.[88]

Revolt Against Reason

Recent strong social constructivism is essentially the same doctrine characterized in an earlier generation by Karl Popper as the "revolt against reason"—a rejection of certain ideals of truth and rationality which, however difficult to explicate, are nonetheless central to the Western heritage. Popper saw the same tendencies in Hegel which he bitterly denounced as "this despicable perversion of everything that is decent." There can be little doubt about the close affinities between Hegel's doctrines and those of radical social constructivism: Popper observes that for Hegel, "History is our judge. Since History and Providence have brought the existing powers into being, their might must be right. . . ."[89] The unmistakable parallel is seen in their essentially similar answers to Popper's fundamental question, "who is to judge what is, and what is not, objective truth?" He reports Hegel's reply: "The state has, in general . . . to make up its own mind concerning what is to be considered as objective truth," and adds, "With this reply, freedom of thought, and the claims of science to set its own standards, give way, finally, to their opposites."[90] Hegel's doctrine expressed in terms of the "State" is essentially the same idea that political success is *ipso facto* the criterion of truth. As we will see presently, precisely this idea is resuscitated by Bruno Latour and Steve Woolgar, Trevor Pinch and Harry Collins, and the entire enterprise of contemporary radical social constructivism. This is a historical relativism according to which truth is merely political and dependent on the *zeitgeist* or spirit of the age. It is a view which Popper charges with helping to destroy the tradition of respecting the truth,[91] and his discussion of Hegel's "bombastic and mystifying cant" is striking in its aptness to recent sociology of science, and is echoed by Paul Gross and Norman Levitt, Larry Laudan and David Stove, among others. Popper warns against the "magic of high-sounding words" and the "power of jargon" to be found in doctrines which are

> . . . full of logical mistakes and of tricks, presented with pretentious impressiveness. This undermined and eventually lowered the traditional standards of intellectual responsibility and honesty. It also contributed to the rise of totalitarian philosophizing and, even more serious, to the lack of any determined intellectual resistance to it.[92]

Laboratory Life Under the Microscope

Perhaps the most obvious cause for such concern is another foundational classic of radical social constructivism, *Laboratory Life* by Bruno Latour and Steve Woolgar.[93] This work is self-consciously subversive, rejecting the rules of logic and rationality as a merely "coercive orthodoxy";[94] it has the avowed goal of deflating the pretensions of science both in its knowledge claims and in its claims to the possession of a special method. Among its iconoclastic goals, the book professes to "penetrate the mystique,"[95] dissolve the appearances, and reveal the hidden realities of science-in-the-making at the laboratory workbench. By contrast with our alleged ignorance concerning the details of scientific practice, this study purports to give an exposé of the "internal workings of scientific activity."[96]

Discovering certain puzzling questions concerning the nature of science, Latour and Woolgar conclude that all of science is merely the "construction of fictions."[97] Latour explains the profound insights emerging from the new discipline:

> Now that field studies of laboratory practice are starting to pour in, we are beginning to have a better picture of what scientists do inside the walls of these strange places called "laboratories." . . . The result, to summarize it in one sentence, was that nothing extraordinary and nothing "scientific" was happening inside the sacred walls of these temples.[98]

> . . . the moment sociologists walked into laboratories and started checking all these theories about the strength of science, they just disappeared. Nothing special, nothing extraordinary, in fact nothing of any cognitive quality was occurring there.[99]

Needless to say, the implications of such insights must be revolutionary, not least of all for science education, the foregoing remarks being approvingly quoted in a teachers' journal in an article recommending a radical new vision of "the reality of the scientific process."[100] Science education is presumably only socialization into power, persuasion, and propaganda. Rather than learning as a cognitive process involving reasoning, logic, and understanding, education involves merely the observance of arbitrary practices and political interest. Although Latour and Woolgar do not explicitly address the questions of most direct interest to educators as such, their characterization of science clearly suggests the appropriate role of the teacher:

> Each text, laboratory, author and discipline strives to establish a world in which its own interpretation is made more likely by virtue of the increasing number of people from whom it extracts compliance.[101]

On this conception, presumably the function of science teacher is that of principal agent for the extraction of compliance—more like camp commandant than traditional instructor.

Constructing the World

The state government of Indiana in the last century considered a bill which would have conveniently legislated the value of the mathematical constant "pi" to be exactly 3. This is a paradigm, if rather literal, example of negotiating or legislating the truth. As a *façon de parler*, the thesis of "constructing facts" permits a sensible reading according to which the theory or description of a substance is settled upon and in a certain sense perhaps even "socially negotiated." However, playing on the words, one can also choose to construe such banalities as something more paradoxical and seemingly profound—namely, that objects and substances themselves did not have an independent existence and were socially constructed. In like manner, one might say that Copernicus "removed the earth from the center of the universe," but asserting this literally would be an attempt at humor or evidence of derangement. Nevertheless, it is just this sort of claim for which the work of Latour and Woolgar has been acclaimed and accorded status as a defining text in the genre of ethnomethodology of science.

Witchcraft, Oracles, and Magic Among the Academics

On the face of it, the authors' own description of their project in *Laboratory Life* reads more like a parody than a serious inquiry. Upon entering the Salk Institute for a two-year study, "Professor Latour's knowledge of science was non-existent; his mastery of English was very poor; and he was completely unaware of the existence of the social studies of science."[102] It is from this auspicious beginning that the "revolutionary" insights into science were to emerge.

Of course, these apparent liabilities are portrayed by Latour and Woolgar as a unique advantage, since "he was thus in the classic position of the ethnographer sent to a completely foreign environment."[103] However, the idea that the inability to understand one's human subjects is a positive methodological virtue is surely a bizarre conception even for anthropology. For Latour and Woolgar, however, it is intimately connected with their doctrine of "inscriptions." The meaninglessness of the "traces, spots, points" and other recordings being made by workers in the laboratory is a direct consequence of Latour's admitted scientific illiteracy. Predictably enough, all these meaningful symbols are indiscriminable to an observer who is completely ignorant, and they must, therefore, be placed in the category of unintelligible markings or "inscriptions." Avoiding the possibility of understanding their subjects' behavior is justified on the grounds that, just as the anthropologist does not wish to accept the witch doctor's own explanations, so one should remain uncommitted to the scientists' rationalizations too. The absurdity of such an attitude follows from the simple failure to appreciate the difference between *understanding* the native and *believing* him.

Persuasion by Literary Inscription and Achieving Objects by Modalities

It is from a point of view of ignorance and incomprehension that Latour comes to rely on a "simple grammatical technique" in order to discern the true significance of the papers accumulating in the laboratory in which he was doing the fieldwork. Undeniably this method has great merit as an alternative to undertaking many years of undergraduate study and postgraduate research in the relevant science. On this flimsy basis, then, Latour and Woolgar obtain their profound insight: "Activity in the laboratory had the effect of transforming statements from one type to another."[104] Specifically, the rationale of the laboratory activities was the linguistic exercise of transforming statements in various ways in order to enhance their "facticity." Thus, we see how Latour and Woolgar arrive at their celebrated radical social constructivist conclusions. They maintain that "a laboratory is constantly performing operations on statements,"[105] and it is through this process that "a fact has then been constituted"[106] by social negotiation and construction. In short, the laboratory must be understood "as the organization of persuasion through literary inscription."[107] These are the grounds on which we must understand their claims that substances studied in the laboratory "did not exist" prior to operations on statements.[108] "An object can be said to exist solely in terms of the difference between two inscriptions."[109]

Poison Oracles and Other Laboratory Experiments

From the meaninglessness of the "inscriptions" and his revelation that "the 'scientificity' of science has disappeared,"[110] Latour is led inexorably to a "naive but nagging question"—namely, "if nothing scientific is happening in laboratories, why are there laboratories to begin with and why, strangely enough, is the society surrounding them paying for these places where nothing special is produced?"[111] This is undoubtedly a deep mystery if one systematically refuses to understand the meaningfulness of the "inscriptions" on these papers. From this vantage point, Newton's notebooks would be indiscriminable from random fly droppings—undoubtedly an important lesson for the science classroom.

On the analogy of "anthropologist's refusal to bow before the knowledge of a primitive sorcerer,"[112] Latour and Woolgar refuse to accept the authority of our best science, saying, "We take the apparent superiority of the members of our laboratory in technical matters to be insignificant, in the sense that we do not regard prior cognition . . . as a necessary prerequisite for understanding scientists' work."[113] Ironically, though rejecting our best science in this way, they happily countenance the magical transformation of physical substances into inscriptions. However, more than being an absurd affectation, their "irreverent" approach amounts to an arrogance which elevates ignorance to a methodology and a sophisticated intellectual virtue. Since "prior cognition" is not necessary for understanding a scientist's work, Latour and Woolgar see themselves as competent to adjudicate the merits of advanced scientific theories.[114] Presumably we may conclude that decades of intense study and high levels of intellectual achievement are unnecessary in order to appreciate the technical concepts of other fields such as quantum physics or relativity theory. Such astonishing anti-intellectual nonsense defies comment and should not require serious response. Equally, the corrosive educational values implied in such an outlook should be obvious.

This affectation that in his fieldwork Latour was like an Evans-Pritchard among the Azande is "anthropological strangeness" in a rather different sense of the term: no anthropologist was ever so strange. Given his method, predictably enough, Latour finds the activities in the laboratory completely incomprehensible. Undaunted, and unwilling to allow this to become a liability, it becomes, in fact, the deep insight of *Laboratory Life*. The behavior of the scientists not only *appears* meaningless, it *is* meaningless. In their conclusion, Latour and Woolgar reveal that "[a] laboratory is constantly performing operations on statements . . .,"[115] and the activities of the laboratory consist in manufacturing "traces, spots and points" with their "inscription devices." The production of papers with such meaningless marks is taken to be the main objective of the participants in essentially the same way that the production of manufactured goods is the goal of any industrial process. This is the view of science as sausage factory.

There is some unintended irony when Latour and Woolgar take their own confusion to be typical and presumptuously extrapolate their own predicament, asking, "Is there any essential distinction between the nature of our own construction and that used by our subjects?"[116] To their rhetorical question they say, "Emphatically, the answer must be no."[117] Based on their own experience, it is not difficult to see why Latour and Woolgar might arrive at the conclusion that science is a more or less arbitrary construction and negotiation with fictions and that "nothing of any cognitive quality was occurring" in scientific laboratories.

"Derridadaism": Readers as Writers of the Text

A measure of the perversity of this work is the fact that in the new edition of their book, Latour and Woolgar tell us that laboratory studies such as their own should, after all, *not* be understood as providing a closer look at the actual production of science at the workbench, as everyone had thought. This view would be "both arrogant and misleading,"[118] and would presume they had some "privileged access to the 'real truth' about science" which emerged from a more detailed observation of the technical practices. Instead, Latour and Woolgar explain that their work "recognizes itself as the construction of fictions about fiction constructions."[119] This is the textualism of Jacques Derrida combined with a much-vaunted "reflexivity." They continue: ". . . all texts are stories. This applies as much to the facts of our scientists as to the fictions 'through which' we display their work." Their own work, then, just like all of science, has no determinate meaning since "[i]t is the reader who writes the text."[120]

Here we see a notorious deconstructionist affectation which conveniently serves to protect Latour and Woolgar against any conceivable criticism. The contrast between the work of Bloor and that of Latour and Woolgar is interesting: Where Bloor professes to adhere to the usual principles of scientific inquiry, Latour and Woolgar engage in a game which David Lehman has aptly called "Derridadaism."[121] They manage to evade criticism only by adopting deconstructionist double-talk and affecting a posture of nihilistic indifference to the ultimate cogency of their own thesis. In keeping with the principle of reflexivity, they embrace the notion that their own text (like the science they describe) has no "real meaning," being "an illusory, or at least, infinitely renegotiable concept."[122] Reflecting on the controversies surrounding their work, Latour and Woolgar observe that defenders and critics alike have engaged in this futile "spectacle" in which they have debated the presumed intentions of the authors. This "spectacle" is, of course, just the exercise of scholarly criticism. Latour and Woolgar now reveal that the "real" meaning of a text must be recognized as illusory and indeterminate. Questions of what the authors intended or what is reported to have happened "are now very much up to the reader." This Rorschach inkblot view of their own work is undoubtedly correct in one sense, if only because *Laboratory Life* is in many respects completely incoherent and unintelligible. For example, some of the diagrams offered as explanatory schemas are impossible to decipher. Above all, it is sobering to consider how science teaching might be conducted in accordance with this model of scholarship.

Balance of Forces

Though the implications of radical social constructivism are not drawn out by the authors, these are close to the surface and not difficult to discern. Thus, once Latour and Woolgar reject "the intrinsic existence of accurate and fictitious accounts per se," the only remaining criterion for judgment is judgment itself. They say that "the degree of accuracy (or fiction) of an account depends on what is subsequently made of the story, not on the story itself."[123] There are no grounds for judging the merits of any claim besides the "modalizing and demodalizing of statements," a purely political question of persuasion, propaganda, and power. Thus they suggest that the very idea of "plausibility" of any work, including their own, is not an intellectual or cognitive question, but simply a matter of political redefinition of the field and other such transformations involving shift in the "balance of forces." In particular, the current implausibility of their own theory is only due to its relative political disadvantages rather than the lack of any intellectual merits.[124] Apart from being a self-serving justification of any nonsense at all, one could hardly find a more open endorsement of the doctrine that "might is right." The very distinction between education and indoctrination becomes impossible to draw.

Education: Truth as Power

There could be no more fundamental challenge to education than the one posed by these approaches, since their radical claims purport to overturn the very foundations of knowledge in the Western intellectual tradition. Thus, a leading partisan of the radical sociology of scientific knowledge has suggested that no less than the "foundations of modern thought are at stake here."[125] All sides of the dispute may agree on this, at least.

Social constructivist writings not only encourage but exemplify the kind of discourse which George Orwell described as giving "an appearance of solidity to pure wind" and which is "largely the defense of the indefensible."[126] Orwell's essay "Politics and the English Language" spoke of the abuse of language which he says is "like a cuttlefish squirting out ink" and has the effect of preventing clear, critical thinking and, thereby, the capacity to see through ideological mystification. The educational import of such approaches scarcely needs drawing out explicitly. Orwell sees the proper use of language as "an instrument for expressing and not for concealing or preventing thought," and he argues that subverting this function will have a deleterious effect by producing a "reduced state of consciousness," the anesthesia of a portion of one's brain.

Clearly, in this connection teachers have a special responsibility to foster clear thinking. The extent to which citizens are capable of exercising a capacity for critical independent thought will have immense consequences for our lives and very survival. In the spirit of Orwell's concerns, Noam Chomsky has documented the extent to which elite culture—the so-called "intellectuals" and the education system—perform a crucial propaganda function fostering "necessary illusions" and, thereby, serve the interests of privilege and power. In the face of such forces, he suggests that what is needed is the kind of intellectual self-defense which has always been the ideal of a liberal education.

. . . traditionally the role of the intellectual, or at least his self image, has been that of a dispassionate critic. Insofar as that role has been lost, the relation of the schools to intellectuals should, in fact be one of self-defense.[127]

The bearing of radical social constructivist doctrines on these educational questions is starkly brought out in Chomsky's further remarks:

It is the responsibility of intellectuals to speak the truth and to expose lies. This, at least, may seem enough of a truism to pass without comment. Not so, however. For the modern intellectual, it is not at all obvious. . . .[128]

Chomsky goes on to quote Martin Heidegger, who remained a card-carrying Nazi even after the Second World War. In a pro-Hitler declaration, echoing social constructivist ideas, Heidegger asserted that "truth is the revelation of that which makes a people certain, clear and strong in its action and knowledge." Chomsky remarks ironically that for Heidegger it seems that it is only this kind of "truth" that one has a responsibility to speak, that is, the "truth" which comes from power. In the same vein, we have seen Latour and Woolgar assert that the success of any theory is entirely a matter of, not persuasion, but politics and power extracting compliance. On this theory a repressive totalitarian regime must count as a model of scientific success.

Mertonian Norms: The Ethos of Science

On such a theory, it is impossible to distinguish fairness from fraud in science since, after all, both are ways of constructing fiction. In the absence of the usual distinctions, the scientist who fraudulently manufactures his evidence cannot be meaningfully distinguished from the honest researcher whose data are also "constructed," albeit in different ways. The problem arises from the radical social constructivists' rejection of the famous Mertonian norms of universalism, communism, disinterestedness, and organized skepticism which constitute the "ethos of science."[129] Merton described these as institutional imperatives, being "moral as well as technical prescriptions," that is, "that affectively toned complex of values and norms which is held to be binding" on the scientist. As Merton observes, these institutional values are transmitted by precept and example, presumably in the course of the scientist's education. It is difficult to see how someone committed to the radical social constructivist view can either teach or conduct science according to the usual rules in which truth, honesty, and other intellectual and ethical measures of worth are taken seriously.

Facticity and Maintaining One's Position

In articulating the same political view of scientific claims, social constructivist authors stop short of openly encouraging cheating and other forms of dishonesty in science, but there can be no mistake about what their theory clearly entails. Thus, when examining a dispute concerning the claims of parapsychology or astrology, Pinch and Collins draw attention to symmetries in the attempts of opponents to maintain their commitments—in one case, to orthodox science and, in the other, to the paranormal.[130] However, from the standpoint of scrupulous sociological "neutrality" or "impartiality" regarding the intellectual merits of the case on each side, there can be no way to discriminate the relative merits of either the arguments or the evidence itself.

In the case study offered by Pinch and Collins, both sides make questionable attempts to protect their favored theory against contrary evidence and, indeed, the scientists appear to have been less than completely forthright about some disconfirming evidence. Pinch and Collins wish to generalize from this to a thesis about science as a whole by construing it as a typical case, that is, as evidence of the way in which public scrutiny removes the mystique of science and exposes its socially constructed, negotiated character. Such exposé serves to "dissolve the facticity of the claims."

Pinch and Collins are unwilling to see such episodes as anything other than the way science always operates—not because all scientists are dishonest, but because the very distinction relies on being able to discriminate fact from fiction. When the scientists finally admit their error and revise their earlier stance in the light of falsifying evidence, they are ridiculed by Pinch and Collins for their grandiose, mythical pretensions and for appearing to adopt "a mantle of almost Olympian magnanimity."[131] The scientists are reproached for failing to "re-appraise their understanding of scientific method" and to learn about its "active" character, that is, about the way in which "facts, previously established by their presentation in the formal literature [sic], can be deconstructed"[132] by public scrutiny of the informal, behind-the-scenes reality of science. Remarkably, however, Pinch and Collins suggest that the right lesson about science was that "provided they had been prepared to endorse the canonical model in public while operating in a rather different way in private, they could have maintained their position."[133] In other words, if they had been even more dishonest, they would have been right—in the only sense of "right" possible, that is, they would have "maintained their position." The status or "facticity" of a claim is just a matter of how the claim is publicly presented, and the literature can either construct or "dissolve the facticity of the claims."[134] If we drop all this jargon, their point is simply that truth is what you can get away with. Heidegger would be impressed.

Altering the Grounds of Consensus: Affirmative Action?

In practice, through the feigned suspension of judgment, radical social constructivism has led to a tacit, or even explicit, advocacy of discredited or disreputable pseudoscience. Trevor Pinch[135] and Malcolm Ashmore[136] go so far as to defend the supposed "merits" of unorthodox and rejected theories on the grounds of equity. Not least, this policy is evidently taken to include the case of fraud since this "is to be seen as an attributed category, something made in a particular context which may become unmade later."[137] Ashmore proposes a radical skepticism concerning the exposé of notorious cases of misguided science such as that of Blondlot's N-rays. Amid the usual jargon-laden pseudotechnicality, such an approach amounts to actually promoting the alleged scientific merits or deserts of such discredited cases. Thus, Pinch writes of "making plausible the rejected view"[138] and Ashmore is perfectly explicit: "To put it very starkly, I am looking for justice! . . . in a rhetorically self-conscious effort to alter the grounds of consensus."[139] Again, the educational implications for the curriculum should hardly need drawing out. The "impartiality" defended by radical social constructivism has come to mean something like affirmative action for nonsense if not something worse.

NOTES

1. See D. C. Phillips, "How, Why, What, When, and Where: Perspectives on Constructivism in Psychology and Education," *Issues in Education* 3, 2 (1997): 151-194. See also articles in M. R. Matthews, ed., *Constructivism in Science Education: A Philosophical Examination* (Dordrecht: Kluwer Academic Publishers, 1998).

2. Andrew Pickering, *Science as Practice and Culture* (Chicago: University of Chicago Press, 1992).

3. Paul Gross and Norman Levitt, *Higher Superstition: The Academic Left and its Quarrels with Science* (Baltimore: Johns Hopkins University Press, 1994).

4. Alan Sokal and Jean Bricmont, *Intellectual Impostures* (London: Profile Books, 1997).

5. Gross and Levitt, *Higher Superstition*, p. 85.

6. Ibid., p. 98.

7. Mario Bunge, A Critical Examination of the New Sociology of Science, *Philosophy of the Social Sciences* 21, 4 (1991): 524-60.

8. David Stove, *The Plato Cult and Other Philosophical Follies* (Oxford: Basil Blackwell, 1991).

9. Larry Laudan, *Science and Relativism* (Chicago: University of Chicago Press, 1990), p. x.

10. Phillips, "How, Why, What, When, and Where: Perspectives on Constructivism in Psychology and Education," p. 152.

11. D. C. Phillips, "The Good, the Bad, and the Ugly: The Many Faces of Constructivism," *Educational Researcher* 24, 7 (October 1995): p. 5.

12. See Ernst von Glasersfeld, *Radical Constructivism: A Way of Knowing and Learning* (London: Falmer Press, 1995).

13. D. C. Phillips, Op. cit. note 10, p. 154.

14. D. C. Phillips, "Coming to Grips with Radical Social Constructivisms," *Science & Education* 6, 1-2 (1997): p. 86; also in M. R. Matthews, ed., *Constructivism in Science Education*.

15. Harry M. Collins and Trevor Pinch, *The Golem: What Everyone Should Know About Science* (Cambridge: Cambridge University Press, 1992).

16. Ibid., p. 150.

17. Ibid., p. 151.

18. David Bloor, *Knowledge and Social Imagery* (London: Routledge & Kegan Paul, 1976); Barry Barnes, *Scientific Knowledge and Sociological Theory* (London: Routledge & Kegan Paul, 1974).

19. Steven Woolgar, *Science: The Very Idea* (London: Tavistock Publications, 1988).

20. Ibid., p. 26.

21. Ibid., p. 26.

22. Bloor, *Knowledge and Social Imagery*, p. ix.

23. Ibid., p. 73.

24. Ibid., p. 42.

25. Ibid., p. 3.

26. Barry Barnes, "On the Hows and Whys of Cultural Change," *Social Studies of Science* 11 (1981): p. 481.

27. Thomas F. Gieryn, "Relativist/Constructivist Programmes in the Sociology of Science: Redundance and Retreat," *Social Studies of Science* 12 (1982): p. 280.

28. Ibid., p. 293.

29. Robert K. Merton, "The Sociology of Knowledge," in his *Social Theory and Social Structure* (New York: Free Press, 1957). The work of Merton and others who had already formulated the ideas of the current sociology of science are largely ignored today, and so there is some irony in reading Merton's remarks written in 1949 which acknowledge the source of these ideas among his own antecedents. Merton writes: "The last generation has witnessed the emergence of a special field of sociological inquiry: the sociology of knowledge (Wissenssoziologie)" (p. 456). Noting the long history of the problems, Merton observes further: "The antecedents of Wissenssoziologie only go to support Whitehead's observation that '. . . Everything of importance has been said before by somebody who did not discover it.'" (p. 456).

30. Bloor, *Knowledge and Social Imagery* , p. 1.

31. The disappearance of this bold new stance in subsequent work suggests something more that a mere loss of nerve among social constructivists, to say the least.

32. Bloor, *Knowledge and Social Imagery*, p. 1.

33. Ibid., p. 3.

34. Bloor, 1981, Op. cit., note 59.

35. Steven Shapin, "Homo Phrenologicus: Anthropological Perspectives on an Historical Problem," in Barry Barnes and Steven Shapin, eds., *Natural Order: Historical Studies of Scientific Culture* (London: Sage Publications, 1979).

36. Emile Durkheim and Marcel Mauss, *Primitive Classification*, translated and edited with introduction by Rodney Needham (Chicago: University of Chicago Press, 1903/1963).

37. Shapin, Op. cit. p. 42.

38. Ibid., p. 65.

39. Steven Shapin, "History of Science and Its Sociological Reconstructions," *History of Science* 20 (1982): 157-211 at 158.

40. P. Forman, "Weimar Culture, Causality and Quantum Theory 1918-1927," in R. McCormmach, ed., *Historical Studies in the Physical Sciences* (Philadelphia: University of Philadelphia Press, 1971): 1-115.

41. Shapin 1979, Op. cit. note 68, p. 57.

42. Barry Barnes, David Bloor and Jules Henry, *Scientific Knowledge: A Sociological Analysis* (Chicago: University of Chicago Press, 1996).

43. Bloor, *Knowledge and Social Imagery*.

44. David Bloor, *Knowledge and Social Imagery*, Second Edition (Chicago: University of Chicago Press, 1991).

45. Barnes, Bloor, and Henry, *Scientific Knowledge: A Sociological Analysis*, p. 48.

46. It is perhaps worth noting the curious and persistent appearance of idealism in discussions of the philosophical foundations of education. It is surely difficult to see how such a question can have the slightest implications for education (or for anything else for that matter). Nevertheless, idealism appears prominently among the central concerns of the quite different psychological variant of 'constructivism' associated principally with Ernst von Glasersfeld, *Radical Constructivism: A Way of Knowing and Learning* (London: Falmer Press, 1995).

47. David Bloor, *Wittgenstein: A Social Theory of Knowledge* (New York: Columbia University Press, 1983).

48. See below, note 72.

49. Barry Barnes and David Bloor, "Relativism, Rationalism and the Sociology of Knowledge," in M. Hollis and S. Lukes, eds., *Rationality and Relativism* (Oxford: Basil Blackwell, 1982), pp. 21-47.

50. Bas van Fraassen, *The Scientific Image* (Oxford: Oxford University Press, 1980).

51. W. V. Quine, *Word and Object* (Cambridge, MA: MIT Press, 1960).

52. See Larry Laudan, "Demystifying Underdetermination," C. Wade Savage, ed., *Scientific Theories, Minnesota Studies in the Philosophy of Science, Vol. XIV* (Minneapolis: University of Minnesota Press, 1990), p. 6.

53. Bloor, *Knowledge and Social Imagery*.

54. Christopher Boorse, "The Origins of the Indeterminacy Thesis," *Journal of Philosophy* 72 (1975): 369-887.

55. See Pat Langley, H. A. Simon, G. L. Bradshaw and J. M. Zytkow, *Scientific Discovery: Computational Explorations of the Creative Process* (Cambridge, MA: MIT Press, 1987); Ryan Tweney, M. E. Doherty and C. R. Mynatt, eds., *On Scientific Thinking* (New York: Columbia University Press, 1981); M. E. Gorman, *Simulating Science: Heuristics, Mental Models and Technoscientific Thinking* (Bloomington: Indiana University Press, 1992); Ronald Giere, ed., *Cognitive Models of Science, Minnesota Studies in the Philosophy of Science, Volume XV* (Minneapolis: University of Minnesota Press, 1992); Peter Slezak, "Scientific Discovery by Computer as Empirical Refutation of the Strong Programme," *Social Studies of Science* 19 (1989): 563-600.

56. Barnes, Bloor, and Henry, *Scientific Knowledge: A Sociological Analysis*, p. 154.

57. Ibid., p. 184.

58. Durkheim and Mauss, *Primitive Classification*.

59. David Bloor, "Durkheim and Mauss Revisited: Classification and the Sociology of Knowledge," *Studies in History and Philosophy of Science* 13, 4 (1982): 267-297.

60. Ibid., p. 267.

61. Ibid., p. 297.

62. Durkheim and Mauss, *Primitive Classification*, p. xvi.

63. Ibid., p. xxii.

64. Ibid., p. xxvi.

65. Ibid., pp. xxiv-xxv.

66. Ibid., p. xxvi.

67. Ibid., p. xxix.

68. Ibid., p. xxiii.

69. Bloor, *Knowledge and Social Imagery*, p. 7.

70. Ibid., p. 7.

71. Ibid., p. 5; emphasis added.

72. Ibid., p. 6.

73. Ibid., p. 10.

74. Larry Laudan, "The Pseudo Science of Science," *Philosophy of the Social Sciences* 11 (1981): p. 178. Reprinted in J. R. Brown, ed., *Scientific Rationality: The Sociological Turn* (Dordrecht: Reidel, 1984).

75. See discussion in D. C. Phillips, "Coming to Grips with Radical Constructivism," *Science & Education* 6 (1997): p. 100, reprinted in M. R. Matthews, ed., *Constructivism in Science Education*.

76. David Bloor, "The Strengths of the Strong Programme," *Philosophy of Social Sciences* 11 (1981): 199-213.

77. See Peter Slezak, "Bloor's Bluff: Behaviourism and the Strong Programme," *International Studies in the Philosophy of Science* 5, 3 (1991): 241-256.

78. Bloor, *Knowledge and Social Imagery*, Second Edition, p. ix. For discussion of these alterations and their significance see Peter Slezak, "The Social Construction of Social Constructionism," *Inquiry* 37 (1994): 139-57.

79. Bloor, *Knowledge and Social Imagery*, 1976, p. 9.

80. David Bloor, *Wittgenstein: A Social Theory of Knowledge* (New York: Columbia University Press, 1983).

81. Ibid., p. 6.

82. Ibid., p. 191.

83. In fact, ten years later, at the height of the Chomskyan Revolution, a belated and lame response appeared by Kenneth MacCorquodale, editor of the series in which Skinner's book had appeared. Implausibly, he suggests that the principal reason that no one had replied to Chomsky's review was its "tone." See Kenneth MacCorquodale, "On Chomsky's Review of Skinner's Verbal Behaviour," *Journal of the Experimental Analysis of Behaviour*, Vol. 13 (1970), 83-99.

84. Howard Gardner, *The Mind's New Science: A History of the Cognitive Revolution* (New York: Basic Books, 1987).

85. Bloor, *Knowledge and Social Imagery*, Second Edition.

86. Peter Slezak, "Scientific Discovery by Computer as Refutation of the Strong Programme," *Social Studies of Science* 19, 4 (1989): 563-600. See responses in same issue.

87. Harry M. Collins, *Artificial Experts: Social Knowledge and Intelligent Machines* (Cambridge, MA: MIT Press, 1990).

88. Peter Slezak, "Artificial Experts," *Social Studies of Science* 21 (1991): 175-201.

89. Karl R. Popper, *The Open Society and Its Enemies, Volume 2, Hegel and Marx* (London: Routledge & Kegan Paul, 1966), p. 49.

90. Ibid., p. 43.

91. Ibid., p. 308, note 30.

92. Ibid., p. 395.

93. Bruno Latour and Steve Woolgar, *Laboratory Life: The Social Construction of Scientific Facts* (London: Sage, 1979).

94. Woolgar, ed., *Knowledge and Reflexivity* (London: Sage, 1988).

95. Latour and Woolgar, *Laboratory Life*, p. 18.

96. Ibid., p. 17.

97. Ibid., p. 284.

98. Bruno Latour, "Give Me a Laboratory and I Will Raise the World," in K. Knorr-Cetina and M. Mulkay, eds., *Science Observed: Perspectives on the Social Study of Science* (New York: Sage, 1983), p. 141.

99. Ibid., p. 160.

100. N. W. Gough, "Laboratories in Schools: Material Places, Mythic Spaces," *The Australian Science Teachers Journal* 39 (1993): 29-33.

101. Bruno Latour and Steve Woolgar, *Laboratory Life: The Construction of Scientific Facts*, 2nd Edition (Princeton University Press, Princeton, 1986), p. 285.

102. Ibid., p. 273.

103. Ibid., p. 273.

104. Ibid., p. 81.

105. Ibid., p. 86.

106. Ibid., p. 87.

107. Ibid., p. 88.

108. Ibid., pp. 110, 121.

109. Ibid., p. 127.

110. Latour, 1983, Op. cit. note 86, p. 142.

111. Ibid., pp. 141, 2.

112. Ibid., p. 29.

113. Ibid., p. 29.

114. Of course, at the same time they pretend to disavow any such judgments. Even if they seek only to discover how the scientists themselves make such judgments, Latour and Woolgar can hardly avoid understanding the content of the theories and the criteria for scientific merit.

115. Ibid., p. 86.

116. Ibid., p. 254.

117. Ibid., p. 254.

118. Ibid., p. 282.

119. Ibid., p. 282.

120. Ibid., p. 273.

121. David Lehman, *Signs of the Times: Deconstruction and the Fall of Paul de Man* (New York: Simon & Schuster, 1991).

122. Latour and Woolgar, *Laboratory Life*, 2nd ed., p. 273.

123. Ibid., p. 284.

124. Ibid., p. 285.

125. Pickering, *Science as Practice and Culture*, p. 22.

126. George Orwell, "Politics and the English Language" in *The Penguin Essays of George Orwell* (Harmondsworth: Penguin Books, 1984).

127. Noam Chomsky, *American Power and the New Mandarins* (Harmondsworth: Penguin Books, 1969), p. 251.

128. Ibid., p. 257.

129. R. K. Merton, "Science and Technology in a Democratic Order," *Journal of Legal and Political Sociology* 1 (1942), reprinted as "Science and Democratic Social Structure," in his *Social Theory and Social Structure* (New York: Free Press, 1957).

130. Trevor J. Pinch and H. M. Collins, "Private Science and Public Knowledge: The Committee for the Scientific Investigation of the Paranormal and its Use of the Literature," *Social Studies of Science* 14 (1984): 521-46.

131. Ibid., p. 536.

132. Ibid., p. 538.

133. Ibid., p. 539.

134. Ibid., p. 523.

135. Trevor J. Pinch, "Generations of SSK," *Social Studies of Science* 23 (1993): 363-73.

136. Malcolm Ashmore, "The Theatre of the Blind: Starring a Promethean Prankster, a Phoney Phenomenon, a Prism, a Pocket and a Piece of Wood," *Social Studies of Science* 23 (1993): 67-106.

137. Pinch, Op. cit., note 124, p. 368.

138. Ibid., p. 371.

139. Ashmore, Op. cit. note 124, p. 71.

CHAPTER V

Reconsidering Social Constructivism: The Relevance of George Herbert Mead's Interactionism

ERIC BREDO

In the last decades constructivism has become an important intellectual movement in education as well as in many other fields. While interest in constructivism starts with seemingly innocuous questions about how children's knowledge develops, or how scientific knowledge has been formed, it quickly leads to much deeper philosophical issues concerning relations between knowledge and reality. Does knowledge mirror a given external reality, or is reality itself in some sense made or invented? Such issues touch, in turn, on relations between the sciences and humanities, with the sciences committed to finding lawful regularities in nature, while the humanities are committed to opening up new ways of being human. And the latter controversies themselves resonate with wider political issues, such as the "culture war" between conservatives seeking social order and progressives seeking freedom and diversity.[1] Whatever constructivism may be, it stirs up a lot of dust.

This essay will be concerned with a particular sub-species of constructivism, social constructivism. Its purpose is to help map this somewhat confusing terrain so that others may find their way more easily. It is also an attempt to defend a version of social constructivism against overly quick dismissal while acknowledging difficulties with some versions. As I will suggest, the source of many difficulties is a tendency to think in terms of polar oppositions between inner and outer factors, such as relations between "inner" humanity versus "outer" nature, or the "inner" individual versus the "outer" social environment. Reframing these issues in interactional terms can help resolve some of the conceptual difficulties that result from polarized thinking. To suggest how this can be done I will borrow heavily from the work of George Herbert Mead, who had many thoughtful things to say about the social construction of reality. He is a particularly interesting figure because

Eric Bredo is Professor of Education at the University of Virginia, where he teaches philosophy and sociology of education.

he avoided many of the conventional lines of polarization, being as much humanist as scientist, as much psychologist as sociologist. Since his work has hardly figured in the discussions of constructivism, it seemed a good time to "bring Mead back in."

The plan of this chapter is to begin by considering the meaning of constructivism—or at least *a* meaning of it. Social constructivism is then discussed along with some lines of social-constructivist thought. Following this, polarized ways of thinking about the issues are considered and briefly criticized. Mead's approach is then discussed in some detail, showing how it conceives of the social construction of physical, social, and scientific objects. Some lessons about the uses and abuses of social constructivism are drawn together in the conclusions.

What Is Constructivism?

Like most intellectual movements constructivism is both diverse and moving. The fact that the term has become so popular and used in such differing and changing ways makes its meaning uncertain. As Denis Phillips observes, simply learning that an individual is a constructivist "is to acquire no useful information whatsoever."[2] Others, like Mark Bickhard, suggest that the term provides only negative information about what an author opposes, while positively it indicates only a "wild multiplicity" of approaches.[3] Clearly it would help to be able to pin down the meaning of constructivism more definitely, but a paradox emerges at this point. Any conception of constructivism that fails to take into account the full variation and change in the way the term is used will itself be a humanly created construct. Evidently, constructivism (like philosophy) is its own first problem. My approach to this issue is simply to admit that the conception offered here is a simplifying idealization designed for certain purposes. It is a construct but, hopefully, a useful one.

Before considering present-day constructivism in however idealized form, it may be helpful to consider briefly some of its more distant philosophical precursors both to give some context to present-day discussion and to see some of the range of related thinking. The philosopher Immanuel Kant is undoubtedly the principal originator of constructivist thought in philosophy and psychology. Kant attempted to resolve the competing claims of rationalists like René Descartes,[4] who viewed knowledge as derived from intuitively clear and indubitable ideas, and empiricists like John Locke,[5] who viewed knowledge as synthesized from elementary sensory experiences. Kant argued that both mental organization and sensory input are involved in knowing. The mind provides the basic categories or relationships, such as spatial, temporal and causal relations, that give form to the flux of experience. Sensory experience, for its part, provides concrete particulars that give specific content to the mind's categories. In this view we can never know the "things in themselves" that cause perceptual experiences because even the phenomena of experience are shaped by mental relationships. As Kant put it, "our senses are affected in a particular manner by objects that are unknown in themselves and are entirely distinct from these phenomena . . . For we only know nature as the sum total of phenomena, i.e., as the sum total of images or representations in our mind."[6] Thus even the most basic experiences are constructs since they have been given form by mental categories and relationships. Considered in this way, there is no "innocent eye," no escape from the influence of our *a priori* assumptions. However, since the implicit categories of thought are universal, we all live in a common (albeit constructed) world.

Other philosophers, such as G. W. F. Hegel, have also had an influence on some lines of constructivist thought. Hegel attempted to synthesize opposing forms of thought by viewing them as phases, or "moments," in a process of sociocultural evolution (or so we would interpret it today).[7] Various forms of consciousness develop in different ages, with resulting changes in the qualitative character of subjects, objects, and methods of representation. In a sense, collective thought and reality evolve together and are parts of the same basically mental developmental process. History is a process in which mind evolves towards increased self-awareness and freedom. Hegel thus introduced an evolutionary or developmental approach to thinking about the relations between mind and nature, as opposed to Kant's static approach. He inspired later work in phenomenology, as well as Karl Marx's materialistic interpretation of social evolution. Marx, in turn, influenced Russian thinking on the social formation of mind, including that of the psychologist Lev Vygotsky. For philosophers like Hegel and Marx, individual thinkers, and individualism itself, play a role in the process of social evolution, but the emphasis was on collective evolution towards some ultimate state of permanent harmony and consensus.

Charles Darwin's work advanced an evolutionary approach much further while placing more emphasis on individual uniqueness and within-group variation and rejecting the notion that evolution has an ultimate goal. In effect, he more directly challenged conventional notions of essential sameness and rationality in nature while introducing individual diversity and contingency. American pragmatists like William James, John Dewey, and George Herbert Mead sought something of a synthesis between neo-Hegelian and Darwinian views. With Hegel, they saw mind as a social product and as a factor within nature and social life, helping to alter the course of its evolution. With Darwin, they saw mind as a practically adaptive function, rather than an aspect of Absolute Spirit, saw every individual as unique, and conceived of no fixed end to natural or social evolution. Seen in this way, mind is a partial and limited participant in the course of social—and natural—evolution, and not a mere spectator. This perspective will become clearer when Mead's approach is discussed more fully, but for the present the main point is merely that knower and known are, again, highly intertwined.

After the early decades of the twentieth century, evolutionary thinking tended to be rejected in many fields, such as philosophy, sociology, and psychology, in favor of the analysis of systems. With the linguistic and analytic turn in philosophy, beginning in the 1920s, formal logic and physics became the models of knowledge adopted by philosophers rather than biology.[8] Logical system builders like the philosopher Rudolf Carnap contributed to constructivist thought by viewing formal relationships in logical systems as defining distinctive "worlds." A set of logical primitives creates the basis for a world, not unlike the way a computer programming language creates a "micro-world." Systems based on different primitives then form different "worlds." This approach recalls Descartes' mathematical and deductive emphasis, but with multiple "worlds" constructed using different assumptions rather than a single world based on a single set of assumptions. Some contemporary constructivists such as Nelson Goodman were influenced by Carnap as was Herbert Simon, one of the originators of the cognitive revolution in psychology.[9]

This brief history, which is obviously greatly oversimplified, may at least suggest that ideas relating to "constructivism" have been around for a long time and have taken different form. Some have focused on the construction of objects within a single system. Others have emphasized diverse constitutive frameworks forming different worlds. Some have viewed minds and worlds as fixed, while others have seen them as co-evolving rather than fixed. Some have seen such evolution as having a fixed end, while others have left its course open and contingent. Finally, some have emphasized the importance of ideas, while others have seen material conditions as more important. One reason contemporary constructivism seems to lead in varied directions may be that these different strands of thought are being drawn upon, often unwittingly. Nevertheless, there may also be some commonalties that can help to give an overall sense of "constructivism."

The principal claim in some discussions of constructivism is that knowledge is made rather than found. This is hardly a surprising claim, however. Indeed, it is virtually trivial today. While some historical thinkers, such as Plato, viewed knowledge as basically static, to be found by remembering the soul's past life, the notion that knowledge is made would seem to be entirely non-controversial today. Our lives are constantly being affected by new discoveries that are the outcomes of specific lines of research so we take for granted that knowledge is a product of human activity. To see why constructivism is controversial we must evidently dig deeper.

The deeper and more controversial point, evident in the philosophical approaches just discussed, is that subject and object, knower and known, mind and reality, are intertwined or co-constructing. Conventionally, the object that is known has been viewed as having a separate identity from the knowing subject, who also has a separate and given identity. This might be viewed as traditional realism (there are many varieties of realism, some consistent with constructivism). It is this assumption of the fixed, separate, and well-defined identities of subject and object that is challenged by most constructivists. For constructivists subject and object are entangled with one another. They are also often seen as co-constructing or co-evolving, rather than fixed. Considered in this way what we take to be the objects making up "reality" are in some manner products of our own activity from which they cannot be fully distinguished or separated, like Kant's "phenomena." To put the point strongly, realists (of the traditional sort just mentioned) claim that natural objects are external to us and can be known as independent things, while constructivists claim that objects are in some sense humanly made and have an internal relation to us or to our activity.

The controversial claim or suggestion of constructivism, then, is not only that knowledge is made but, more fundamentally, that *the objects and properties that we experience and know are themselves in some manner products of human (mental or physical) activity*. This is the more radical claim that we live in an "invented reality."[10] Taken on its face, this may seem ridiculous, as though thinking made mountains, which is one of the reasons that constructivism has been controversial. However, it is important to be careful about what it means to be an "object" or to be "real" before jumping to such conclusions. How would you know that some set of experiences involves an "object"? And what does it mean for something to be "real"? To ask these questions is to begin to focus on the processes or activities by which one reaches such conclusions rather than merely taking the conclusion for granted.

To back off from these heady issues for a moment, however, we might also consider what "constructivism" means from a purely practical educational standpoint more concerned with "making" knowledge than with claims about objects or reality. Here constructivism seems to have two implications: (1) a concern for students' having an active role in learning and (2) their being allowed to redefine or discover new meanings for the objects with which they interact. By this definition, passive theories, such as traditional direct instruction or object lessons, are not constructivist because they allow little role for student activity. Some active approaches, like Skinnerian conditioning, are also not constructivist because they assume that the meaning of events is fixed by contingencies outside of the learner's control. Problem-solving approaches based on symbol-processing theories of cognition are superficially closer to the mark, since they consider both inner activity (symbolic operations) and changed cognitive structures as outcomes.[11] However, they tend to presuppose a fixed problem definition at base that is not up for reorganization (much like logical constructivists). Since these procedures and related "objects" may not be reconstructed such approaches are not fully constructivist, at least according to this definition.[12] What remain are approaches that emphasize active constructing and reconstructing all the way down. Such approaches are varied, as we will see momentarily, but all view the learner as a potential contributor to the remaking of "reality."

Varieties of Social Constructivism

As this discussion has suggested, constructivism is concerned not only with the social construction of knowledge, but also with the social construction of "reality." The focus of this essay is on social constructivism, however, and not on constructivism in general. Phillips distinguishes between psychological constructivism, which focuses on the construction of an individual's knowledge and social constructivism, which focuses on the creation of public bodies of knowledge like the sciences or other disciplines.[13] This is a sensible distinction between levels of analysis, like distinguishing between building a house or a whole town. All too often, however, the distinction can become rigid and exaggerated, with "individual" taken to mean "not social" and "social" as meaning "not individual." For instance, psychologists sometimes think they have to ignore social and cultural phenomena to be proper psychologists who are supposed to focus on "the individual." Sociologists and anthropologists sometimes seek similarly to ignore individuals, because they are supposed to study "groups" or "collectivities." An alternative approach is to take "social" to refer to processes of interaction at any level of aggregation. This is the way I will consider it later on, but for the moment it is good to keep in mind that the meaning of "social" can be just as contentious as the meaning of "constructivism."

While much of the educational interest in constructivism came initially from Jean Piaget's psychology, which viewed a child's activity as "constructing reality" in the child,[14] this has come to be seen as an overly individualistic approach.[15] For those seeking to bring social life and culture back into psychology, the work of the Russian psychologist Lev Vygotsky has become increasingly influential.[16] Vygotsky can be viewed as a constructivist because he considered basic forms (and contents) of minds to be socially constructed (and constructing). He viewed symbolically mediated thought as a social process, like a dialogue, that is "internalized" through participation in social interaction. (This is, again, highly oversimplified.) The kind of thinking that one learns from social interaction is itself dependent on the sociohistorical nature or level of society. As Russia modernized, for example, people's ways of thinking changed to become more formal-logical as a result of schooling and other experiences.[17] Seen in this way, society is not just an environmental variable or a content that one learns about. Rather, modern social life creates the very form of modern minds. Vygotsky's concerns went well beyond the traditional focus on isolated individuals to include a concern for stages of social development as well as the biological development of species. The stage theoretical part of his work reflects an inheritance from Marx that is among aspects being revised in current work.[18]

Much of the work in social constructivism has focused on the way social facts and identities are socially constructed while made to *appear* natural. This is a theme in much of the work in social reproduction theory. Borrowing from Marx, Weber, and linguistic structuralism among other sources, reproduction theorists have considered how social and political elites define "knowledge" and expertise in self-serving ways. Using such limited but tacit definitions of what counts as knowledge, schools make some students appear "naturally" smart or dumb depending on their familiar experiences. A variety of self-reinforcing processes serve to exaggerate these differences, including an evaluation process that defines educational success as getting ahead of others rather than becoming more competent. In the process, initial social differences are reproduced and converted into apparently "natural" differences in intelligence and the like.[19] While there has been a strong tendency towards social or cultural determinism in this work, there are also attempts to bring a greater sense of agency and even individual histories into the picture.[20]

Other forms of social constructivism contrast institutionalized "myths" with concrete practices, viewing the myths as creating social reality. Some of this work has been inspired by Peter Berger's conception of social reality as a kind of ritual construction of sacred objects that gain a reality because everyone must take them into account.[21] For instance, modern culture and institutions constitute the ritually sacred individual that is imbued with a plethora of rights.[22] They have also made rituals of rationality a fact of public life. As a result, people are often more concerned with following defensibly "rational" procedures or hiring properly certified personnel than with actual functioning in practice. Schools play a role in this drama by conforming to institutionalized categories and rules so as to gain legitimacy while also helping to define new categories of knowledge and expertise, such as "genetic counselor," that alter the social structure (rather than merely reproducing it).[23] In a sense, schools make and confirm the institutionalized "myths" that constitute social reality. This work also has tendencies towards social determinism, since institutionalized categories are viewed as affecting things irrespective of variations in individual belief or local practice.

Related work also views a rational world as an appearance or production, but focuses more specifically on the accounting practices by which this is accomplished. Work deriving from Harold Garfinkel's "ethnomethodology" studies the methods that people use to make things appear rational or publicly accountable.[24] An example would be the sort of documentation that a school or hospital might create to show that "the right thing" had been done when treating a client. Typically, a decision can be made to appear quite rational given the results of various tests, and so forth. However, in practice decisions are made in a much messier fashion involving contingencies that never appear in the documentation. An example is Hugh Mehan's study of the way "special education" decisions are made. The formal considerations entering into such decisions include a student's IQ scores and achievement test results. However, Mehan found that the strongest determinant of being placed in a given category was whether there was an opening in the relevant class.[25] Seen in this way, social "reality" is made much like sausage, which is neatly packaged and labeled on the outside, but you don't want to know what went into it. Garfinkel and other ethnomethodologists have adopted a posture of indifference as to whether some practices are more rational than others, preferring to study them as different ways of making things appear rational. However, this has raised questions about the status of their own "accounting" procedures. Such reflexivity affects all constructivists, who, to be consistent, must acknowledge the constructed character of their own accounts, an issue to which I will return in the conclusions.

Much of the work described so far has tried to show how social facts or identities are socially constructed, thus undermining the claim that they are simply "natural." Other work has attempted to show that nature itself is socially constructed. Sociological, anthropological, and historical studies of science, commonly lumped together as "social studies of science," attempt to show the influence of social conditions and practices on natural science. The implication is that science is affected by broader cultural assumptions and social interests, such as evolutionary theory being affected by utilitarianism and the social conflicts and reforms of the early decades of the nineteenth century. It is also implied that the course of science might have turned out differently but for slight differences in context and is therefore historically contingent. Thomas Kuhn's influential work on the role of paradigms in science and the extra-scientific factors entering into scientific revolutions helped open the door to this line of thinking.[26]

Some such work has tended to adopt a social reproductionist view, seeing science as subtly shaped by, and serving to reproduce, dominant social interests. Work by Barry Barnes, David Bloor and others of the Edinburgh school's "strong program in the sociology of knowledge," as well as Harry Collins and others of the "Bath school" has at times concluded that "nature" plays only a slight role, if any, in the creation of scientific knowledge.[27] Other work has adopted a microscopic focus on laboratory research practices, viewing scientific facts as a "text" that is collectively written, almost like the game in which a number of people write a story by each adding a sentence at a time. As Latour and Woolgar summarize their work, "Scientific activity is not 'about nature,' it is a fierce fight to *construct* reality. The *laboratory* is the workplace and the set of productive forces, which makes construction possible. Every time a statement stabilizes, it is reintroduced into the laboratory (in the guise of a machine . . . skill, routine . . . etc.), and it is used to increase the difference between statements. The cost of challenging the reified statement is (then) impossibly high. Reality is secreted."[28] Consistent with ethnomethodological indifference, these authors view their own social science, as well as the science of those they study, as "no more than fiction," even arguing in a draft of the book that the reader should not take their account seriously.[29] While there have been strong tendencies towards social determinism in some social studies of science, newer studies pay greater attention to individual scientists without losing a view of the networks and coalitions, strategies for advancing their positions, contingent battles with opponents, and so forth, that ultimately result in a scientific revolution.[30]

The view that science is socially constructed has offended many natural scientists, since it seems to suggest that their results are simple fictions, or driven by extrinsic interests outside of science, thereby undermining the legitimacy of their enterprise. Some have responded by arguing that they are merely humble reporters of reality.[31] Controversy over the character of scientific knowledge spills over into education because of its relationship to the way science is taught (constructed myth or sacred truth?)[32] and because of epistemological implications affecting educational thought and research more generally.[33]

Schism and Constructivism

This discussion has already hinted at some of the divisions between constructivists and their opponents, as well as some differences within constructivism. Three controversies seem particularly important to highlight. (See the helpful discussion in Phillips' essay[34] from which I have drawn upon in some of the following.)

The first and most dramatic is, of course, the contrast between the view that knowledge is shaped by external nature versus the view that knowledge, and perhaps "nature" itself, is in some sense made by human activity. When engaged in scientific or other inquiry one is likely to focus "outwards" on nature and the objects under investigation, seeing them as determining the conclusions of one's inquiries. Scientists involved in everyday work undoubtedly function as naïve realists whatever their more sophisticated thoughts at other moments. They recognize that errors may be made, but commonly suggest that the normal course of science serves to eliminate them. If one investigator makes an error, it is washed out by countervailing reports from others. If different scientists use different methods, they will converge on the same results, at least if the methods are used properly. As a result, science progresses, with successive theories representing ever closer approximations to a given external reality. Constructivists, on the other hand, tend to focus "inwards" on the taken-for-granted assumptions and habitual practices that shape an inquiry but are not part of what is typically focused upon. Seen in this way, scientific (and everyday) inquiry involves wider and more unconscious influences than are acknowledged in the official idealized story, and these influences affect the conclusions reached. To presume that the results of science are independent of such influences then seems like assuming that it is entirely other-worldly, rather than merely a specialized part of wider social life at the time. It also overlooks the fact that some of yesterday's scientific objects, like phlogiston, are today's subjective illusions. Mightn't the same be true of today's scientific objects? In short, the first controversy is between the view that knowledge is shaped by an external reality independent of the inquirer versus the view that the objects being known, and perhaps reality itself, are in some way internal to the inquirer's activities.

A second point of controversy occurs among constructivists themselves. Is knowledge or reality constructed by individuals or by societies? For some, knowledge and reality are individual and basically subjective. We all have our own distinct experiences and as a result construct our own distinctive realities. Ernst von Glasersfeld's work has this quality, viewing knowledge as subjective and constrained only by its working for an individual. For those adopting such a view, society is often seen as an external environment "outside" of the individual. This has been a common approach in psychology, which has treated social and cultural matters as external to the individual. This individualistic approach makes it hard to understand how people can communicate common meanings or how all of the students in a class might learn the "same" lesson. Piaget tried to solve this problem by assuming that everyone converges on the same types of cognitive structures, but this view has been challenged by those who note that discrepancies between fact and theory may be accommodated in many different ways.[35] The opposing position is that individual minds are entirely socially constructed, making the individual a clone of a collective way of thought and thereby unable to gain independent perspective on it. Michel Foucault asks, for example, whether "subjects responsible for scientific discourse are not determined in their situation, their function, their perceptive capacity, and their practical possibilities by conditions that dominate and even overwhelm them."[36] In his account, individual scientists are products of a form of discourse, pawns in a collective language game which constitutes their mentalities. Individual knowers are, then, entirely internal to society, as opposed to society being external to the individual. This second point of controversy thus contrasts a psychological approach to constructivism that treats "reality" as individually constructed, with a sociological approach that treats both "reality" and the individual knower as socially constituted.

A third point of controversy concerns the kind of constraints or influences affecting knowledge (and reality) construction. Are the principal influences ideal or material? Some social constructivists, especially those drawing on Marx, view concrete material conditions such as those involved in the use of technology and work as constituting minds and realities. Other social constructivists, drawing on Kant or Emile Durkheim are likely to view cultural or linguistic norms as giving form to experience. Similar differences arise among individually oriented constructivists, some emphasizing the influence of learned beliefs or assumptions; others, genetically determined structures in the brain (such as Noam Chomsky's hypothetical "language acquisition device").

Thought is often polarized between such internal-versus-external perspectives.[37] These perspectives conflict with one another because one is based on a distinction that the other denies. One draws a line distinguishing between the inside and outside of some entity such as a boundary separating knower and known, while the other denies that this line exists. There are also practical conflicts between these views, since one cannot focus "outwards" on the objects of inquiry and at the same time focus "inwards" on the assumptions or processes by which that object is distinguished. There are also conflicts between those who have an interest in keeping things defined in a conventional way and those who seek to redefine such conventions. For these reasons debate often becomes sharply polarized, forcing one into one camp or the other. Either science is an unfiltered account of reality, or it is fiction. Either knowledge is individually constructed, or it is socially constructed. Much of the rashness of the debate derives from such polarized, either-or, thinking, as though there were only two possibilities. As Phillips observes, "this descent into sectarianism . . . is the ideological or ugly side of the present scene."[38] Such divisions organize a great deal of thought in philosophy and education. As Arthur Bentley noted, the boundary of the skin is traditional philosophy's "last line of defense."[39]

While constructivists and their opponents often take—or are forced into—polarized positions, this discussion suggests four forms of polarized constructivism that can also develop. These may be briefly summarized as follows:

1. *Individual Idealist Constructivism*

Reality is a product of the basic categories of thought of each individual mind. These structures give form to knowledge and reality for the individual. The shared character of the world derives from the fact that these assumptions all happen to be the same or tend to converge on the same structures over time. Most constructivism of this sort derives from Kant's work. Piaget's psychology and Ernst von Glasersfeld's more recent version have roots in this tradition. A principal difficulty is accounting for shared meanings and a shared reality.

2. *Individual Realist Constructivism*

Reality is constructed by the material structure of the brain or genetic structures of the body. These constrain the kinds of perceptions and ideas that one can have. Noam Chomsky's notion that all languages have a common deep structure because of an "innate language acquisition device" in the brain is an example. Gestalt psychologists also tended to posit innate structures in the brain determining good perceptual form, hence the objects perceived. Individual learning then involves only a minor variation within these general constraints.

3. *Social Idealist Constructivism*

Reality, including the mind and self of the knower, is a product of a society's language, culture, or other norms and ideals. Benjamin Whorf[40] and Emile Durkheim[41] would be historical examples, the former emphasizing the power of linguistic terms, the latter the use of ritual distinctions to constitute the basic forms of thought. Nelson Goodman and Richard Rorty would be contemporary examples emphasizing the constitutive influence of "symbol systems" or "vocabularies," respectively. A concern is accounting for individual variation and for differences among classes or other categories of people in the "same" culture.

4. *Social Realist Constructivism:*

Reality, including the minds and selves of knowers, is a product of the economic or political divisions within a society, such as its economic class system or power structure. Contingencies of practical work and politically dominated forms of discourse create different realities for different classes of people. Vygotsky and A. R. Luria drew on this Marxist approach, as seen in their rejection of Durkheim's idealism.[42] Current activity theory and some work on situated cognition also derive from this tradition.[43] An important difficulty can be accounting for individual variation as well as for commonalties among those facing different practical situations.

To the extent that one adopts an exclusive version of any of these approaches, the resulting position would seem to face a dilemma between inconsistency and implausibility. Those who adopt an internalist position at a given level and an externalist position at another will tend to be inconsistent, or so I would suggest. To see knowledge as socially rather than individually constructed, for example, and yet to insist that nature does not play a strong role in this process, seems to me to court inconsistency because whatever arguments are used against external natural constraint should apply against external social constraint on an individual. On the other hand, the more a version adopts the internal option at every level, the more implausible it becomes. If nature, social and cultural structure, material habit, and brain structure all play no role in constraining knowledge, then "knowledge" would seem to be entirely imagined. This argument should clearly be carried out in greater detail, but for the present I would suggest that dualistic constructivisms are caught in a dilemma in which the choice is between inconsistency and implausibility.

If this analysis is correct, it suggests that things have taken a wrong turn somewhere. The obvious place to look for this wrong turning is with the premises common to all of these approaches. One common premise is the inner-versus-outer way in which the problem of knowledge or reality is framed. In fact, it would seem obvious that an either/or framing is incorrect. One is not human *or* natural, individual *or* social, mental *or* material. These are not either/or choices. To be human is to be *part* of nature, not other than nature. By the same token the natural includes everything that is human within it, including all of the subtleties of human psychological, social, and cultural life. Similarly, one is not individual *or* social. Each of us is a social being, but our unique ways of being social contribute to and alter, however slightly, the character of the social life of which we are a part. Finally, activities and artifacts are not material *or* ideal. They have an ideal aspect having to do with purposeful patterning, but this pattern must also have a material substrate.[44] While there is a strong tendency to fall or be pushed into these dichotomized positions (as I may be in danger of doing to some of those cited above), there are fortunately more than two flavors available.

Interactional Constructivism

But where can one begin if not with an inside and an outside, a subject and an object, as defined by the boundaries of the skin or the geopolitical boundaries of a society? The principal alternative is an interactional (or transactional) approach deriving, ultimately, from evolutionary thought.[45] Whatever their other differences and occasional polarizing tendencies, most of the earlier "constructivists" of the late nineteenth or early twentieth century, such as William James, Jean Piaget, Lev Vygotsky, John Dewey, and George Herbert Mead, attempted to develop such an approach.

An interactional approach attempts to avoid the inside-versus-outside dichotomy by giving priority to *doing* rather than *knowing*. As just suggested, most of the discussion of constructivism has had a strongly cognitive focus. Once the focus is on knowledge, there is a tendency to think in dichotomized terms about how the subject knows the object, or how the subject invents the object. Either the object is given, to be known by the subject, or the subject is given, to invent the object. Subject/object dualism already infects the analysis, even among those attempting to avoid it. The remedy explored by the pragmatists and other classical constructivists was to begin with activity and view conscious thought or awareness as emerging within conflicted activity, which it helps to reorganize to help action proceed. This view leads to a pragmatic or *cogency* theory of truth,[46] which contrasts with the *correspondence* theory of traditional realism as well as with the *coherence* theory of traditional idealism. In the pragmatic account a proposition that works as advertised in a situation becomes "true," if judged to do so by competent inquirers—at least until it fails. Such beliefs are tools for changing conditions and facilitating future inquiry rather than statements that passively mirror affairs in an external world (correspondence) or are internally consistent with other beliefs (coherence). As Dewey put it, "Confirmation, corroboration, verification lie in works, consequences. . . . When the claim or pretension or plan is acted upon it guides us truly or falsely; it leads us to our end or away from it . . . [I]n the quality of activity induced by it lies all of its truth and falsity."[47]

To make an interactional perspective clearer, I will use George Herbert Mead's work to show how various types of objects are socially constructed. By way of brief preview it may help to know that Mead thought of "objects" as aspects of functions in activity, not as metaphysical entities. A crumpled ball of newspaper may be a "soccer ball" if it is treated in that way and serves to sustain the activity of playing soccer. Mead's use of the term "social" may also be surprising.[48] He held that "[s]ociality is the capacity of being several things at once."[49] For instance, one may be both a symbolic thinker and an animal, or both an animal and a piece of matter. One *is* both of these different things at the same time. Thus "sociality" has to do with being in a relationship which alters one's qualities, since new consequences are brought out as a result of the relationship, while not being subsumed by the relationship. Of course, we may look at ourselves in only one way or the other at different times, but the relationships in which we participate are not just ways of looking; they are ways we *are*. Nelson Goodman made a similar point when he suggested that "the world *is* many ways."[50] Mead's friend, John Dewey, was also making an analogous point when he wrote, "There is a peculiar absurdity in the question of how individuals become social, if the question is taken literally. Human beings illustrate the same traits of both immediate uniqueness and connection . . . as do other things . . . Everything that exists in as far as it is known and knowable is in interaction with other things. It is associated, as well as solitary. . . . "[51] Bearing in mind this broadened notion of the "social," consider how physical, social, and scientific objects may be socially constructed.

CONSTRUCTING THE PHYSICAL OBJECT

Physical objects seem particularly definitive of what we take to be "reality." When Dr. Johnson wanted to make a point about obdurate reality, he spoke of kicking a stone. Many philosophers have borrowed this example, undoubtedly because it seems so convincing. But what does it mean to be a physical object? And in what (if any) sense are physical objects social constructs?

Mead approached this question by asking about the role an "object" plays in an organism's behavior. Consider a child who reaches out for something bright and shiny, grasps it, and puts it in its mouth. The bright and shiny stimulus is full of promise; it is an implicit sign of possibilities. The reaching and grasping response is a way of bringing the bright "thing" closer to ingest. And the pleasure or distress upon eating it is the consummation that implicitly confirms or disconfirms the initial promise. For Mead a physical "object" is, fundamentally, whatever can be detected at a distance, grasped with one's hands or other appendages, and used to bring about some consummation.

Seen in this way an "object" is the objective of a response. It is what the child reaches for, the stimulus for the response of reaching. On the other hand, it is also a means to some further consummation, since it is used to achieve some purpose, however unconscious and implicit.[52] Objects are thus both ends of a perceptual act and means for further activity. They must play successfully the role of something sought and used to accomplish a purpose to be an "object." A physical object, in particular, is whatever can be brought to play these roles in the close, manipulatory region in which one's hands or other appendages can function. This experience may later be extended to other objects that cannot be brought close to manipulate, like distant planets, which are treated as if they could be handled if they were near to hand.

This view of "objects" suggests that they are defined by organismic activity. As Mead put it, "Organic processes or responses in a sense constitute the objects to which they are responses; that is to say, any given biological organism is in a way responsible for the existence (in the sense of the meanings they have for it) of the objects to which it physiologically and chemically responds. There would, for example, "be no food-no edible objects-if there were no organisms which could digest it."[53] Put another way, the notion of an "object" implies an objective. Since only organisms have aims or objectives, it takes an organism to make something an "object." If there were no organisms with distance perceptors (e.g., eyes and ears) and appendages to manipulate things, there would be no physical *objects*.

Just because an organism's activity plays a role in making something function as an object does not mean that this is a unilateral accomplishment, however. The child may reach out and not be able to grab hold of anything. Or the thing may not serve to bring about the end that its shiny quality seems to promise. If it does function as it is taken, however, this experience provides a basis for the object's "reality." As Mead put it, "[I]t is the adequacy of the response which . . . determines the reality of the stimulation . . . The response is functionally the reality of the stimulation; the end of the act, the reality of its beginning."[54] Those who have endured a severe earthquake undoubtedly understand how "reality" may be shaken when it no longer functions reliably as a partner in activity.

The boundaries of physical objects as well as their other properties are also the result of activity. If one holds a physical object in one hand and presses against it with the other, the hand holding the object must act back against the pressing hand if it is to remain steady. In effect, the hand holding the object acts as the object would when pressed; it takes the role of the object. Mead argued that this is the origin of object boundaries: "The suggestion which I have . . . made is that the pressures of bodily surfaces against each other, preeminently of one hand against the other, are transferred to the object . . . It is only in so far as the organism thus takes the attitude of the thing that the thing acquires such an inside."[55] When squeezing, "it" exerts an equal force back, making it (potentially) "hard." When throwing, "it" resists the accelerating force. Traditional Newtonian properties like extension, mass, and inertia are directly *reflected* to the organism when an object is acted upon.

This approach dissolves the traditional metaphysical object, the object that is assumed to be given prior to activity, and makes both boundaries and properties dependent upon activity. The same blob may be smeared around the table like finger-paint or put in one's mouth like food. What it "is" for an organism depends on what is done with it. This is not to say that nothing exists prior to action, only that such unknown "things" or "existences" are not objects. Making an object's definition and meaning (its consequences when acted upon) dependent on how it is used may seem to make it insubstantial or unreal, the perennial fear of constructivism's opponents. However, as Mead was careful to suggest, objects are not defined unilaterally. They are effectively partners in the act and must function in the requisite way for an act to succeed. For something to function as food, it has to reduce hunger; if it does so, it *really is* food. All of the normal constraints on the object's behavior remain; only traditional metaphysical claims are dissolved.

CONSTRUCTING THE SOCIAL OBJECT

Words in a language and institutions such as "schools" and nation-states like the United States may all be thought of as social objects. The boundaries of these objects depend rather obviously upon conjoint social practices and conventions. When the bell rings and everyone attends to this fact, in whatever way, "school" has suddenly come into existence. Institutional facts and categorizations like being considered "gifted" or "disabled" or "retarded" (to use an older term) may also be considered social constructs, since they hold relative to the practices of a given institution. Before age-graded schools with a yearly progression of grades there was little conception of being "advanced" or "retarded." Finally, selves and minds may also be thought of as socially constructed "objects."

Mead's approach to the social construction of social objects was to treat them also as functions rather than as metaphysical entities. In this case, however, they were considered to be functions in social life. I will consider his argument in some detail because I believe it clarifies many issues relating to social constructivism. It is also essential for understanding how education alters minds and selves, which are among the most important ends its practitioners can hope to accomplish.

At its most basic, human interaction is like interaction among non-language-using animals. When such animals are interdependent, they become sensitive to signs of the way each is likely to behave. Borrowing from Charles Darwin and Wilhelm Wundt, Mead suggested that "gestures," or the slight beginning of acts, become signals of the rest of the act to follow. Animals learn to respond to the beginnings of acts as signs of what is coming. A boxer begins to respond to a minor change in an opponent's orientation, for example, as though a blow were coming. This gesture functions as stimulus for a readjustive response of the second person, such as raising an arm to block the impending blow. The response, in turn, becomes a stimulus for a readjustive response of the first person, who may alter the developing blow, and so on. Mead termed such a series of (largely unconscious) feints and counter-feints "a conversation of gestures, a field of palaver within the social conduct of animals."[56]

The regularities that emerge in interaction are important because they create social meaning. Mead's analysis of meaning is particularly helpful because it makes this frequently murky concept clear and un-mystified. To continue with the example of the boxers, if the second boxer responds to a change in the first's orientation (the initial gesture or stimulus) by raising an arm as if to block a blow, then this response implicitly defines the initial gesture as a "blow." The initial stimulus *means* a "blow" because this is the end, or completed act, to which it is evidently a means. The social meaning of a gesture is, then, the end it is a *means* to, as interpreted by the anticipatory response of those with whom one is interacting. Of course, a certain regularity or degree of predictability is necessary for an act to have meaning, but over time interaction will have followed various repeated patterns that the interactants unconsciously take into account. Seen in this way meaning arises in joint interaction and is visible in the anticipatory behavior of the interactants. It is not some picture or a subjective *thing* inside of either actor's head. As Mead put it, "Meaning is . . . a development of something objectively there as a relation between certain phases of the social act; it is not a psychical addition to that act and it is not an 'idea' as traditionally conceived."[57]

The conversation of gestures and the social meanings that these regularities of mutually anticipatory behavior create are themselves important because they form the basis for the development of reflective intelligence. In the interaction of animals or infants each actor responds to meaningful stimuli from the other, but does not treat its *own* behavior as meaningful. The actor does not respond to his or her *own* gestures in terms of the ends to which they are likely to lead. In other words, outer events are responded to as though meaningful, but one's own response to these events is not treated as though it had meaning. There is no "reflection" on the meaning of what one is doing. But suppose one has a conflicted response in a situation. A very tentative or conflicted response might make a child conscious of his or her own action, since the act will be disorganized or disrupted. If the other person responds to this conflicted act in a certain way, it makes its meaning evident. It becomes a means to what is now a determinate end. In such cases the child might begin to become conscious of the meaning of its own gestures. If so, it can then begin to respond to its own gestures as the other would, effectively carrying on an internalized "conversation of gestures" with itself. This process is what Mead meant by "reflective intelligence." It is a process through which the organism takes its own emerging behavior in a certain way, that is, in terms of a certain interpretation or meaning, responds to this response, and so on, until a way is found that clarifies the meaning of the initial conflicted situation, showing its meaning, or what ends it may lead to.

Gestures that have the same meaning for different actors play an important role in this process, enabling one to indicate aspects of one's behavior to oneself and to respond to them as another would, just as they can do the same in reverse. Such shared gestures or "significant symbols" are the basis for language. In effect, reflective intelligence, which is made possible by such symbols, enables a creature to select the aspects of the situation to which it responds. By being able to "take" things in different ways it becomes in many respects self-stimulating, freeing it from merely responding to the most obvious or intense or immediately present stimulus. This process of responding to one's own behavior, treating one's own responses as "objects," also implies that one has a self, since acting toward oneself as an object is what it means to have a self, at least when considered functionally.[58] Seen in this way, both mind and self are socially constructed functions, not preexistent entities.

The point of this analysis for the present is that social interaction using linguistic symbols constitutes whole new classes of objects. The use of language changes the practical character of physical objects by allowing one to respond to selected aspects of them, or respond when they are not present. The use of symbols also creates social processes or functions, like minds and selves, that are a whole new type of self-interactive "object." Similar processes also constitute social institutions like school, family, business, etc. Such institutions involve taking the role or attitude of a "generalized other" that one learns through participation in more complex and widespread activities. When one takes the attitude of a generic member of the public into account in one's action, such as taking into account what "school" implies for all participants, this becomes the basis for institutionalized behavior. Thus, whole new classes of objects are constituted as a result of social interaction using language. As Mead wrote, "Symbolization constitutes objects not constituted before, objects which would not exist except for the context of social relationships wherein symbolization occurs. Language does not simply symbolize a situation or object which is already there in advance; it makes possible the existence or the appearance of that situation or object, for it is a part of the mechanism whereby that situation or object is created."[59]

While new classes of objects are constructed in this way, Mead's analysis obviously implies no lack of "reality" or constraint. Unlike the literature on teacher expectations that was popular some years ago, there is no suggestion that thinking makes it so. A gesture may be taken in many ways, but only some ways will work out in the interaction. This "working out" is the result of the mutually selected contingencies of interaction, as constrained by language, convention, and habit. Such social constraints may seem highly uncertain, and at times they are, but their outcomes are nevertheless as "real" as being forced to drive on the right hand side of the road so as to avoid colliding with other drivers.

CONSTRUCTING THE SCIENTIFIC OBJECT

Scientific objects like atoms, quarks, black holes, or genes have a peculiar status. On the one hand, they are highly abstract and often invisible, giving them a kind of fictive quality. On the other hand, they are often taken to be the most real or substantial things that there are, the things of which everything else is made. The difference between everyday objects that we know so well at first hand and scientific objects that are known only through specialized inquiry leads to a contrast between appearance and reality. It seems that scientists peer behind appearances to learn how things really are, while everyday actors know only illusion.

There is something to this view, since science involves some of the most careful, systematic, and tested inquiry that we know. Shouldn't well-tested inquiry supplant mere prejudice and convention? On the other hand, there is also a kind of Platonism in it and a hint of self-interest. The notion that scientists find the "real" objects behind lay appearances sounds not unlike ancient priests claiming to be the only ones in direct contact with God.

Mead, like Dewey, sought to recognize the value of science without turning it into a priesthood.[60] He did so by placing science *within* everyday life rather than outside of it. Despite fancy theory and apparatus, scientific inquiry begins and ends with everyday objects in the everyday world. It begins with a taken-for-granted "world that is there," including near-at-hand dials and levers that are directly observed and manipulated. This unquestioned material world and set of unquestioned objects forms the background of scientific inquiry.[61] Scientific inquiry focuses on only a small, problematic part of the "world that is there," everything else being simply taken for granted. A new fact may be found, for example, that makes the meaning of old objects unclear. People are known to have lower rates of malaria if they live in the highlands, for example, yet malaria is not cured by simply moving to higher ground. How can this be?

· This is where scientific objects come in. The hypothesis that malaria is caused by a certain parasite posits a "scientific object" as the cause. If the parasite is found to be transmitted by mosquitoes who thrive in lowland swamps yet are able to live in a host at higher altitudes, then the anomaly is resolved, at least hypothetically. The theory based on a mosquito-borne parasite can then be tested to see if the elimination of mosquitoes reduces the incidence of disease. The role of a scientific object, such as a possibly invisible parasite, in this process is to aid problem solving. It is an abstract entity that helps in causal reasoning and, by extension, practical problem solving.

Like other types of objects, scientific objects are both stimuli that are sought and means to ends. They are tools of instrumental thought, not metaphysical givens. As Dewey put it, "The objects of physics subsist precisely in order to bring about this transformation" (of things immediately had or felt into those whose causal relations are understood).[62] Science begins with the everyday world, uses abstract objects to infer the implications of various actions, and ends with the everyday world in which these consequences are tested. The role of the scientific object is to focus attention on certain aspects of the situation, such as vectors by which a parasite might be transmitted, and suggest implications leading to consequences that can be put to experimental (or other) test. Seen in this way science produces what are in essence transformation rules for changing one state of affairs into another. The differential equations commonly used in physics, for example, are statements about how change in one variable affects change in another, not metaphysical statements about "reality." To cite Dewey again, "The notion of matter actually found in the practice of scientists has nothing in common with the matter of materialists . . . The matter of science is a character of natural events and changes. . . . Objects of natural science are not metaphysical rivals of historical events; they are means of directing the latter."[63] In other words, scientific objects are also to be understood functionally rather than metaphysically.

It is interesting to note in this regard how different scientific objects are from everyday objects, the former often seeming to have a kind of fictive quality. Many have been invisible but nevertheless useful, such as neutrinos, atoms, viruses, and black holes (some of which are now visible due to the development of new instruments and inquiries). Many, like black holes or superstrings, seemed like outrageous fictions when first proposed, although they are now becoming conventional. Some like "space-time" are so abstract it is impossible to conceive what directly "seeing" them could possibly entail. Of course, many scientific objects eventually become parts of everyday life when they serve their functions well and become used more widely. They become part of the "world that is there," furnishing the taken-for-granted background of new inquiries. Those that do not serve well their function of guiding manipulations to predictable ends become subjective fictions, like phlogiston or the ether. Either way their original function is to guide action and inquiry in an instrumental fashion so that different observers may produce similar results from similar manipulations. Their *scientific* role is to be tools of inquiry.

In this view, scientific objects are constructs that help to reconstruct the world. The results of scientific inquiry literally change reality, rather than merely reflecting it. As Mead put it, "[A] world within which an essential scientific problem has arisen is a different world from . . . the world that is there when this problem has been solved."[64] One might say that the only thing changed is human conduct, but this is also a part of nature. If people respond to circumstances in new ways, old objects acquire new properties. The sun may be in the sky as before, but prior to sun-based religions it did not have the property of invoking ritual obeisance. As Dewey remarked, "Changing the meaning of the world (when the New World was discovered) effected an existential change. . . . In some degree, every genuine discovery creates some such transformation of both the meanings and the existences of nature."[65] Even the physical properties of matter depend, at least at the extremes, on variations in the observer's behavior or standpoint. The Heisenberg uncertainty principle, Einstein's relativity theory, Bohr's complementarity theory, and Bell's theorem in quantum mechanics all relate observer and observed.[66] As an article on quantum mechanics in *Scientific American* suggested, "The doctrine that the world is made up of objects whose existence is independent of human consciousness turns out to be in conflict with quantum mechanics and the facts established by experiment."[67]

The upshot of this analysis is Mead's suggestion that scientists can solve problems as they arise in their fields without having to turn into metaphysicians proclaiming a monopoly on reality. As he put it, "I have . . . insisted that as a scientist his goal in the pursuit of knowledge is not a final world but the solution to his problem in the world that is there."[68] Viewed in this non-dogmatic way a scientific conclusion represents the conclusion of the latest inquiry, not *the* conclusion of inquiry. This approach allows science itself to evolve, reconstructing present conclusions when new facts call for it. When science is placed within the world, rather than outside of it, the rigid division between the natural and human is also eliminated, leaving in its place various sciences with differing aims and objects, all of which involve some form of participation in the phenomena being studied.

Conclusions

While the constructivism controversy has appeared to be about whether knowledge is made or found, as we have seen the issue actually goes much deeper. The deeper issue is whether the objects that are known are given independently of the knower, or are in some way made or constituted by the knower's activities. Put another way, the contentious issue is not whether knowledge is made or found, but whether "reality" is made or found.

As we have also seen, views on this issue tend too often to polarize into mutually exclusive positions. One is either a realist or a constructivist, a psychological constructivist or a sociological constructivist, and so forth. Since the contending positions seem to make opposing claims about the way the world is, if one is right the other must be wrong. If one side views objects as completely given, the other must see them as entirely made up; if one side emphasizes individual construction, the other rejects all individualism in favor of collective construction, and so forth.

Clearly the problem is to find some balance between these competing claims or attitudes, but how? One approach is to suggest that the real answer consists of a "bit of each." But the trouble with this approach is that it says nothing about how much of each or when. It sounds like a nice compromise but like a recipe that says "add a bit of each" or a will that says that each relative gets a "bit of the estate" it ends up saying nothing that is specific enough to be of any help.

A second approach is to partition the problem. Some facts and objects seem more obviously "made" than others. Social facts and identities, such as being ticketed for speeding or labeled a speeder, seem

obviously constructed. The speed limit varies by state and its specific
application is a matter of interpretation and possible negotiation. Many
natural facts and objects, on the other hand, seem more enduring and
universal. Every atom of gold behaves in ways that are unlike every
atom of silver, making each seem to be a "natural kind." If we could
only separate these two types of objects, we could resolve the controversy by agreeing that some are constructed while others are not. The
natural sciences could then study the natural kinds, while the social sciences could study the artificial ones. The difficulty with this approach
is that it does not tell us how to treat the objects whose status is in dispute. Whether a given fact or object is "natural" or "artifactual" is precisely what the dispute is about.[69] How should we treat "intelligence"
or "attention deficit disorder"? Are these natural or artificial kinds?
Even if we did develop a method for determining when an object is a
natural kind or not, that method would itself be based on assumptions
or interests that are open to question, thereby reintroducing the
human element. For these and other reasons, it seems unlikely that the
issue can be resolved by simply partitioning fact from artifact.

A third strategy is to take each position as merely a way of talking.
(As Stephen Toulmin remarked, philosophy tends to oscillate between
boldly proclaiming "This is the way it is" and whimpering "It's just a
way of talking.") This fall-back position seems virtually required of constructivists when they recognize that their positions imply that their
own claims must also be constructs. As noted earlier, Latour and Woolgar acknowledge that their account is only one "story" among others,
all equally "fictitious."[70] They were trying to make the postmodern
point that things may be constructed many ways, and construction is an
ongoing "playful" affair, but asking the reader not to take one's work
seriously seems seriously self-defeating. Reflective realists may also be
driven to a similar position when they acknowledge that realism is not
itself a scientifically discoverable fact about "reality." The trouble with
retreating to "mere talk," then, is that it makes it hard to take the
resulting position seriously. Surely more is involved than mere chatter?

An interactive approach, like Mead's, can be helpful in dealing with
these difficulties. It acknowledges both possibilities for constructive
freedom and the constraints imposed by actual functioning. By viewing
action as like a mutual dance with a partner who responds in turn to
one's actions, there is clearly room for both initiative and constraint.
One can lead the "dance" a certain way, but the response is not always
what one expects since it involves more than one's will or intent. The
other dancer is neither a total dictator who cannot be swayed (realism),

nor mere putty in one's hands (some constructivisms). There is both constraint and opportunity for initiative. Nor is there a clean separation between humans who propose and nature that disposes, because the relevant characteristics of the environment (the "partner") depend on what an organism can detect and what it is attempting to do. What the object is, in terms of its definition or meaning, depends on how it is taken and on its functioning successfully in that way. The "same" object may be taken in many different ways, just as one might treat the biologically identical individual as a superior or a subordinate, or in some other way. If these ways of taking work out, then the object *is* those ways. Thus a plurality of ways of taking and making need not dissolve into merely various ways of seeing or talking.

Mead introduced a series of refinements to this approach, bringing in different kinds of constraints. A person may interact with a physical object and be constrained by the way in which "it" responds to physical efforts, like handling and throwing. In a sense, the classical Newtonian properties of the object are directly reflected back to the actor. Social interaction introduces a new set of constraints, since one must then coordinate one's actions with others and with a new set of tools, language. For the same term to apply to something or for it to have the same explicitly indicated properties, it must function as indicated for those who are members of the linguistic community. The scientific community then introduces both new constraints and wider generality by approaching objects in a purely instrumental fashion and insisting that anyone who performs the appropriate experiment (or equivalent) should get the same results. These specialized purposes require a new set of objects. For an object to play these various roles it must satisfy the constraints of successful physical action, social intercourse, and scientific experimentation. Thus Mead's view is hardly one that suggests that things are made up any way one likes. Of course, Mead did not deny that there are "things" in the external world, but these vague postulates are not "*objects*" since they do not (yet) function in people's conduct. Like Kant's unknown "thing in itself," they are latent differences that do not yet make a difference in how we behave.

This approach helps to resolve the dispute between the position that claims "This is *the* way it is" versus "It is all just talk." It suggests that the world actually *is* many ways.[70] There is no single way of taking things that captures all of the possibilities. While there is multiplicity, this involves more than talk or writing, more than stories or texts. We talk to be able to meet at the same place and time, to be able to accomplish grand projects using a division of labor, to negotiate political arrangements, to get married, and so forth. These consequences extend beyond the bounds of the same "discourse" or "text," making "good" or "true" or otherwise valued talk more than simply arbitrary words. Good stories are those that are good *for* something. They may be good for many purposes, whether for guiding instrumental action truly or for sheer entertainment, but to be good in one of these ways they have to successfully aid in the performance of the relevant function. Seen in this way, the world *is* many ways, and these ways are not "just talk"— although talk is one form of behavior that helps to create new objects, new opportunities, and new constraints.

Mead's approach also helps resolve the tension between a world that is mechanically determined and one that has room for novelty and emergence. Natural science generally attempts to construe the world in terms of mechanical laws, while the humanities, and many constructivists, emphasize its continual indeterminateness. Mead's approach was to place the knower inside of a world that is evolving, and whose evolution the knower affects. In order to act effectively in an instrumental fashion, we attempt to build closed systems of laws that account for past regularities. But since every interaction is unique, at least when considered as a whole (we change, the world changes, etc.), many factors are omitted in any system of laws, and outcomes may change because of the omitted factors. However helpful laws describing the past may be, there are no guarantees, so every law is ultimately hypothetical. When things do not work out as expected, making new facts evident, then we rework the laws to try to incorporate or otherwise handle them. Seen in this way, new facts are both the products of our activity (experiments, inquiries, etc.) and independent of prior knowledge. In this way Mead maintains both the externality of fact to prior knowledge and its internal relation to action. Of course, similar processes occur in social interaction when we attempt to anticipate one another's behavior, or the behavior of generalized members of the public, but then have to adjust our expectations as contradictory events occur (to which we ourselves contribute). The upshot is that we seek a closed mechanical interpretation of the world for purposes of instrumental action, but this activity is only a small part of living in and contributing to the evolution of an open universe. If a scientific interest is uppermost, this is still just a phase or aspect of things, one emphasizing causal or instrumental relationships. As long as it is not taken as *the* way the world is, there is no necessary conflict with other human values.

The point of this approach for education is, in part, to help find a way of thinking that helps reunify the pre-verbal world of the infant, the verbally mediated world of everyday life, and the specialized world

of science or other disciplined inquiry. Each increasingly more specialized form of interaction is a development based on less specialized
precursors. While later or more specialized developments modify earlier ones, as well as creating new objects of their own, they do not supplant the earlier and must ultimately both begin from and return to
them. Scientists begin with immediately manipulable events at hand,
like knobs and dials, use everyday language to talk to one another, and
then develop specialized, abstract terms and relations to manage indirect contingencies, and, ultimately, predict differences in the same
immediacies at hand. Seen in this way, education builds from where
one is, utilizing and transforming this base, but not destroying or
entirely supplanting it. When properly done, more specialized education and inquiry is a function within a wider life rather than a competitor with it. Of course, the wider philosophical point is much the
same as William James's when he declared the universe both "pluralistic" and "open." We are among the existences and agents helping to
alter the universe (in however limited a way) in interaction with others. Education can help prepare us for shared and evolving roles.

Finally, what is the status of Mead's own approach? Is his approach
to constructivism also a "mere" construct? Is it *the* way the world is or
just another fiction? To be consistent, this approach has to be acknowledged as a construct. If it is helpful and its use truly resolves the shared
difficulties to which it is addressed, then it would seem to be at least *a*
way the world is. But, of course, this is an hypothesis.

Thanks to Ryan Babineaux, Walter Feinberg, Sophie Haratounian-Gordon, Laura
Kerr, Jon Levinson, Denis Phillips, and Susan Verducci for their very helpful thoughts,
suggestions, and criticisms.

Notes

1. James Hunter, *Culture Wars: The Struggle to Define America* (New York: Basic
Books, 1991).
2. D. C. Phillips, "Coming to Grips with Radical Social Constructivisms," in *Constructivism in Science Education*, ed. Michael R. Matthews (Dordrecht, NL: Kluwer,
1998), 139.
3. M. C. Bickhard, "Constructivisms and Relativisms: A Shopper's Guide," in *Constructivism in Science Education*, ed. Michael R. Matthews (Dordrecht, NL: Kluwer,
1998), 99.
4. René Descartes, *Discourse on Method and Meditations on First Philosophy*, trans.
Donald A. Cress (Indianapolis: Hackett Publishing Co., 1980).
5. John Locke, "An Essay Concerning Human Understanding," in *The Empiricists*,
ed. Richard Taylor (Garden City, NY: Doubleday and Co., 1974).
6. Immanuel Kant, "Prolegomena to Every Future Metaphysics That May Be Presented as a Science," in *The Philosophy of Kant*, ed. Carl J. Friedrich (New York: The
Modern Library, 1783/1949), 88.
7. G. W. F. Hegel, *Phenomenology of Spirit* (Oxford, UK: Oxford University Press,
1977); *The Philosophy of History* (New York: Dover Publications, Inc., 1956).

8. A. J. Ayer et al., *The Revolution in Philosophy* (London: Macmillan and Co., 1963).

9. Nelson Goodman, *Ways of Worldmaking* (Indianapolis: Hackett Press, 1978); Nelson Goodman and Catherine Z. Elgin, *Reconceptions in Philosophy and Other Arts and Sciences* (Indianapolis: Hackett Publishing Co., 1988).

10. Paul Watzlawick, ed., *The Invented Reality* (New York: Norton, 1984).

11. Alan Newell and Herbert A. Simon, *Human Problem Solving* (Engelwood Cliffs, NJ: Prentice-Hall, 1972); Pat Langley et al., *Scientific Discovery: Computational Explorations of the Creative Process* (Cambridge, MA: MIT Press, 1987).

12. Hubert L. Dreyfus, *What Computers Can't Do* (New York: Harper and Row, 1972/1979); Terry Winograd and Carlos Fernando Flores, *Understanding Computers and Cognition* (Reading, MA: Addison-Wesley, 1986); Eric Bredo, "Reconstructing Educational Psychology: Situated Cognition and Deweyan Pragmatism," *Educational Psychologist* 29, no. 1 (1994): 23-35.

13. D. C. Phillips, "Coming to Grips with Radical Social Constructivisms."

14. Jean Piaget, *The Construction of Reality in the Child*, trans. Margaret Cook (New York: Basic Books, 1954).

15. Jerome Bruner, "Vygotsky: A Historical and Conceptual Perspective," in *Culture, Communication, and Cognition*, ed. James V. Wertsch (Cambridge, UK: Cambridge University Press, 1985), 21-34.

16. L. S. Vygotsky, *Thought and Language*, trans., E. Hanfmann and G. Vakar, 1966. Revised and edited by Alex Kozulin, 1986. (Cambridge, MA: MIT Press, 1934); L. S. Vygotsky, *Mind in Society: The Development of Higher Psychological Processes* (Cambridge, MA: Harvard University Press, 1978); James V. Wertsch, *Vygotsky and the Social Formation of Mind* (Cambridge, MA: Harvard University Press, 1985); J. V. Wertsch, ed., *Culture, Communication, and Cognition* (Cambridge, UK: Cambridge University Press, 1985); James V. Wertsch, *Voices of the Mind: A Sociocultural Approach to Mediated Action* (Cambridge, MA: Harvard University Press, 1991); Michael Cole, *Cultural Psychology: A Once and Future Discipline* (Cambridge, MA: Harvard University Press, 1996); Michael Cole, Yro Engestrom, and Olga Vasquez, eds., *Mind, Culture, and Activity: Seminal Papers from The Laboratory of Comparative Human Cognition* (Cambridge, UK: Cambridge University Press, 1997).

17. A. R. Luria, *Cognitive Development: Its Cultural and Social Foundations* (Cambridge, MA: Harvard University Press, 1976).

18. Michael Cole, *Cultural Psychology: A Once and Future Discipline* (Cambridge, MA: Harvard University Press, 1996).

19. Basil Bernstein, *Class, Codes and Control*, 4 vols. (London: Routledge and Kegan Paul, 1971-75); Pierre Bourdieu and J. C. Passeron, *Reproduction in Education, Society and Culture*, vol. 5 (Sage, 1977); Pierre Bourdieu, *Outline of a Theory of Practice*, trans., Richard Nice (New York: Cambridge University Press, 1977); Pierre Bourdieu and Loic J. D. Wacquant, *An Invitation to Reflexive Sociology* (Chicago: University of Chicago Press, 1992); Bradley A. Levinson, Douglas E. Foley, and Dorothy C. Holland, *The Cultural Production of the Educated Person* (Albany: SUNY Press, 1996); Herve Varenne and Ray McDermott, *Successful Failure: The School America Builds* (Boulder, CO: Westview Press, 1999).

20. Jay MacLeod, *Ain't No Makin' It* (Boulder, CO: Westview Press, 1987).

21. Peter L. Berger and Thomas Luckmann, *The Social Construction of Reality: A Treatise in the Sociology of Knowledge* (Garden City, NY: Doubleday, 1966).

22. G. M. Thomas et al., *Institutional Structure: Constituting State, Society, and the Individual* (Newbury Park, CA: Sage, 1987).

23. J. W. Meyer and B. F. Rowan, "Organizational Structure as Myth and Ritual," in *Environment and Organization*, ed. Marshall W. Meyer (New York: Jossey-Bass, 1978); J. W. Meyer, "Types of Explanation in Sociology of Education," in *Handbook of Theory and Research for the Sociology of Education*, ed. J. G. Richardson (New York: Greenwood Press, 1986), 341-359; J. W. Meyer, "The Effects of Education as an Institution," *American Journal of Sociology* 83, no. 1 (1977): 55-77.

24. Harold Garfinkel, *Studies in Ethnomethodology* (New York: Prentice-Hall, 1967).

25. Hugh Mehan, Alma Hertweck, and J. Lee Meihls, *Handicapping the Handicapped* (Stanford: Stanford University Press, 1986).

26. Thomas S. Kuhn, *The Structure of Scientific Revolutions* (Chicago: University of Chicago Press, 1970).

27. Harry M. Collins and Trevor J. Pinch, *Frames of Meaning: The Social Construction of Extraordinary Science* (London: Routledge and Kegan Paul, 1982); Harry Collins, *Changing Order: Replication and Induction in Scientific Practice* (London: Sage, 1985).

28. Bruno Latour and Steven Woolgar, *Laboratory Life: The Social Construction of Scientific Facts* (Beverly Hills: Sage Publishing Co., 1979), 243.

29. Ibid., 257.

30. Adrian Desmond, *Huxley: From Devil's Disciple to Evolution's High Priest* (Reading, MA: Addison-Wesley, 1997).

31. Paul R. Gross and Norman Levitt, *Higher Superstition: The Academic Left and its Quarrels with Science* (Baltimore, MD: Johns Hopkins University Press, 1994). But see the rejoinder by another scientist in R. C. Lewontin, "Survival of the Nicest?," *The New York Review of Books*, October 22 (1998): 59-63.

32. Michael R. Matthews, ed., *Constructivism in Science Education* (Dordrecht, NL: Kluwer, 1998).

33. D. C. Phillips, "The Good, the Bad, and the Ugly: The Many Faces of Constructivism," *Educational Researcher*, October, 1995 (1995): 5-12.

34. Denis Phillips, "How, Why, What, When, and Where: Perspectives on Constructivism in Psychology and Education," in *Issues in Education: Contributions from Educational Psychology*, ed. Jerry S. Carlson (Stamford, CT: JAI Press, 1997), 151-194.

35. D. C. Phillips, *Philosophy, Science, and Social Inquiry* (Elmsford, NY: Pergamon Press, 1987).

36. Michel Foucault, *The Order of Things* (New York: Random House, 1970), xiv.

37. Peter Godfrey-Smith, *Complexity and the Function of Mind in Nature* (Cambridge, UK: Cambridge University Press, 1996).

38. Phillips, "The Good, the Bad, and the Ugly," 5.

39. Arthur F. Bentley, "The Human Skin: Philosophy's Last Line of Defense," in *Inquiry into Inquiries: Essays in Social Theory*, ed. Arthur F. Bentley (Westport, CT: Greenwood Press, 1954), 195-211.

40. John B. Carroll, ed., *Language, Thought, and Reality: Selected Writings* (Cambridge, MA: MIT Press, 1956).

41. Emile Durkheim, *The Elementary Forms of the Religious Life* (New York: The Free Press, 1965).

42. Luria, *Cognitive Development*.

43. Michael Cole, Yro Engestrom, and Olga Vasquez, eds., *Mind, Culture and Activity* (Cambridge, UK: Cambridge University Press, 1997); Jean Lave and Etienne Wenger, *Situated Learning: Legitimate Peripheral Participation* (Cambridge, UK: Cambridge University Press, 1991).

44. Cole, *Cultural Psychology*.

45. John Dewey, *The Influence of Darwin on Philosophy* (Amherst, NY: Prometheus, 1910/1997); George Herbert Mead, "Evolution Becomes a General Idea," in *George*

Herbert Mead: On Social Psychology, ed. Anselm Strauss (Chicago: University of Chicago Press, 1934/1962), 1-16; John Dewey and Arthur F. Bentley, *Knowing and the Known* (Boston, MA: Beacon Press, 1949).

46. G. H. Mead, "A Pragmatic Theory of Truth," in *Selected Writings: George Herbert Mead*, ed. Andrew J. Reck (Indianapolis: Bobbs-Merrill, 1964), 320-344 (See especially p. 330).

47. John Dewey, *Reconstruction in Philosophy* (New York: Henry Holt and Co., 1920), 128-129.

48. See Arthur E. Murphy, "Introduction," in *The Philosophy of the Present*, ed. Arthur E. Murphy (La Salle, IL: Open Court, 1959), xi-xxxi. For a different interpretation see Hans Joas, *G. H. Mead: A Contemporary Re-examination of His Thought* (Cambridge, MA: MIT Press, 1985).

49. George Herbert Mead, *The Philosophy of the Present* (La Salle, IL: Open Court, 1932/1959).

50. Nelson Goodman, "The Way the World Is," in *Problems and Projects* (Indianapolis, IN: Hackett Publishing Co., 1972).

51. John Dewey, *Experience and Nature* (New York: Dover Publications, 1958), 174-175.

52. George Herbert Mead, "The Process of Mind in Nature," in *The Social Psychology of George Herbert Mead*, ed. Anselm Strauss (Chicago: University of Chicago Press, 1934/1956), 77.

53. George H. Mead, *Mind, Self, and Society: From the Standpoint of a Social Behaviorist* (Chicago: University of Chicago Press, 1934), 179.

54. Mead, "The Process of Mind in Nature," 76-77.

55. Mead, *The Philosophy of the Present*, 121,122. See also pp. 124-125.

56. George Herbert Mead, "Social Consciousness and the Consciousness of Meaning," in *Pragmatism: The Classic Writings*, ed. H. Standish Thayer (New York: Mentor Books, 1910/1970), 342.

57. Mead, *Mind, Self, and Society*, 178.

58. William James, *The Principles of Psychology*, vol. I and II (New York: Dover Publications, Inc., 1890/1950).

59. Mead, *Mind, Self, and Society*, 180.

60. John Dewey, *Experience and Nature* (New York: Dover Publications, Inc., 1929/ 1958).

61. Mead, *The Philosophy of the Present*, 140.

62. Dewey, *Experience and Nature*, 140.

63. Dewey, *Experience and Nature*, 74, 148.

64. Mead, *The Philosophy of the Present*, 57-58.

65. Dewey, *Experience and Nature*, 156-157.

66. Mead, *The Philosophy of the Present*, discusses relativity theory. The other examples are my own.

67. Bernard d'Espagnat, "The Quantum Theory and Reality," *Scientific American* (1979): 158.

68. Mead, "The Nature of Scientific Knowledge," 58.

69. See the discussion of these issues in Ian Hacking, *The Social Construction of What?* (Cambridge, MA: Harvard University Press, 1999).

70. Latour and Woolgar, *Laboratory Life*, 257.

Section Three

Constructivism in Science and Mathematics Education

Editor's Introduction

Constructivist ideas have been of great interest in many areas of education—the teaching of reading and writing, teacher education, curriculum theory, and philosophy of education, among others; but their influence has been particularly great in the fields of science and mathematics education. Researchers who focus upon what happens in science and mathematics classrooms, those who train mathematics or science teachers, the teachers themselves, curriculum developers, and those who wish to see the history and philosophy of each of these subjects playing a more central role in the curriculum as enacted in classrooms have all come into contact with constructivist ideas of one form or another, and many either have had their work significantly impacted or at least have had to come to terms with them in some way (as can be seen in the chapters by Tobin and Gunstone).

Michael Matthews, the author of Chapter VI, and Deborah Loewenberg Ball and Hyman Bass, who wrote Chapter VII, were charged with reflecting upon the impact of constructivism in their respective fields of interest, and whether overall it has been beneficial or not. In common with the authors of other pairs of chapters, they chose to pursue their charge in quite different ways (they "constructed" their task remarkably differently!). It will be seen, however, that the chapter by Ball and Bass depicts a teacher struggling with an important problem for constructivists that Matthews identifies, a problem that he suggests many constructivists "skirt around."

Matthews is a philosopher of education, with special expertise in the history and philosophy of science; he has been the leading player on the international stage who has worked to arouse the interest of philosophers and historians of science in science education and the interest of science educators in the philosophy and history of their field. Anyone who reads his chapter cannot but be impressed by the volume of literature that exists on constructivism in science education.

159

Indeed, his chapter is an extraordinary bibliographic resource (even for those whose interest lies in other subject domains). Naturally enough, he approached his charge from his unique philosophical and historical perspective. He finds psychological constructivism, and strong social constructivism, wanting both philosophically and when considered as an influence on science education. For example, Matthews sees the work of von Glasersfeld and those in science education who have been influenced by him, as suffering from defects similar to those found in the philosophy of classic empiricists such as John Locke (compare with the views of Howe and Berv.) His criticisms of social constructivism parallel those made by Peter Slezak. When he turns to constructivism's impact on science education, he raises the important point ("skirted around by constructivists," he says, although Dewey was certainly sensitive to it) that in order to understand science, a student must understand current theories (many of which are complex and quite abstract) and also have some appreciation of the methods used by scientists to test or warrant their conjectures. It is unrealistic to expect that these aspects of science could be "constructed" entirely by the student— teachers probably have to "convey something to pupils."

Deborah Ball works in the field of mathematics education, and her co-author Hyman Bass is a distinguished mathematician. While Ball also has philosophical interests, she is noted for her important studies of the learning, and construction, of mathematical knowledge by young students in classes she herself teaches. In various ways her constructivism bears the stamp of Deweyan ideas, and also is closer to Vygotsky than to von Glasersfeld. Ball and Bass approached their charge from this general perspective, examining constructivism as put into practice in the elementary mathematics classroom. In Ball's teaching in these settings, students have been treated as members of a learning community to which she, as teacher, also belongs.

In their chapter, Ball and Bass focus in depth on the development of mathematical reasoning in a third grade classroom and the elements that play a crucial role in this process—one of which is the base of common knowledge that sets the boundaries of what they call the "granularity of acceptable mathematical reasoning." They take very seriously the fact that the classroom construction of knowledge is taking place within a disciplinary framework. In a sense, then, the authors are showing us some aspects of "social construction" in practice (although their work is quite different in emphasis from that of the radical "social constructivists"), and they are grappling with the important issue that Matthews said is too often "skirted around" in the constructivist literature.

CHAPTER VI

Appraising Constructivism in Science and Mathematics Education

MICHAEL R. MATTHEWS

Constructivism is undoubtedly a major theoretical influence in contemporary science and mathematics education; many would say it is *the* major influence. It is also a significant influence in literary, artistic, social science, and religious education. Frequently feminist and multiculturalist proposals in science and mathematics education are put forward in a way that simply *assumes* constructivist pedagogical, epistemological, and ontological positions. For many, constructivism has become part of the educational furniture. And although constructivism began as a theory of learning, it has progressively expanded its dominion, becoming a theory of teaching, a theory of education, a theory of educational administration, a theory of the origin of ideas, a theory of both personal knowledge and scientific knowledge, and even a metaphysical and ideological position. Constructivism has become education's version of a grand unified theory.

Although there have been some critics of constructivism,[1] and some who have urged caution in its adoption,[2] few would dispute Peter Fensham's claim that, "The most conspicuous psychological influence on curriculum thinking in science since 1980 has been the constructivist view of learning."[3]

The Scope of Constructivism

Constructivism has certainly spread its wings from its learning theory origins. The range of expanded constructivist concerns can be seen in the subheadings of a science education article where the reader is informed of "a constructivist view of learning," "a constructivist view of teaching," "a view of science," "aims of science education," "a constructivist view of curriculum," and "a constructivist view of curriculum

Michael R. Matthews is an Associate Professor in the School of Education at the University of New South Wales. He is the founding editor of the journal *Science & Education*.

development."[4] The spread of constructivist interest, or theorizing, is apparent in the remarks of one adherent who writes, "This approach [constructivism] holds promise for the pursuit of educational objectives other than those associated exclusively with cognitive development . . . the constructivist point of view makes it possible to develop a vision of the whole educational phenomena which is comprehensive and penetrating."[5] Another writes, "Constructivism is a postmodern theory of knowledge with the potential to transform educational theory."[6] It is thus not surprising that, "For several years now, across the country, preservice and inservice teachers have been considering constructivism as a referent for their philosophies of education."[7]

And constructivism is not just a theory about learning, teaching, and philosophy of education, significant though those subjects are; some also propose it as a theory about one of culture's greatest and most enduring achievements, namely science. As one author says, "Indeed as an epistemology, constructivism speaks to the nature of science."[8] If it does so speak, then it certainly has a claim to our attention: few things are more important than understanding the nature of science.

But even the nature of science and the nature of education do not between them exhaust the putative explanatory reach of constructivism, which increasingly presents itself as an ethical and political theory, as well as a learning, a teaching, and an epistemological theory. As is stated in a recent paper, "There is also a sense in which constructivism implies caring—caring for ideas, personal theories, self image, human development, professional esteem, people—it is not a take-it-or-leave-it epistemology."[9] This ethical dimension is manifest in the frequency with which notions of emancipation and empowerment occur in constructivist writing; constructivism is thought to be a morally superior position to its rivals in learning theory and pedagogy.

There is also a political and administrative dimension to much constructivist writing. Two constructivist writers say that they are "committed to the philosophy and principles of composite grades and mixed-ability groupings."[10] Another writer has identified the Progressive Education tradition as constructivist, and sees the British Plowden Report of the mid-1960s as the embodiment of constructivist school organization.[11] There are even constructivist accounts of school leadership.

A number of constructivists align themselves with the Critical Theory of Michael Apple, Henry Giroux, and Stanley Aronowitz. One New Zealand commentator writes, "There are many parallels between the literature on the development of critical pedagogy [and] the literature on constructivist learning."[12] This is because "[c]ritical theorists question the value of such concepts as individualism, efficiency, rationality and objectivity, and the forms of curriculum and pedagogy that have developed from these concepts."[13]

For some, constructivism is even larger than a theory of learning, education, and science; it is almost a worldview or *weltanschuung*. Yvon Pépin, quoted above, goes on to say that constructivism "also offers a global perspective on the meaning of the human adventure, on the way human beings impart meaning to their whole existence in order to survive and adapt."[14] Another constructivist writes:

To become a constructivist is to use constructivism as a referent for thoughts and actions. That is to say, when thinking or acting, beliefs associated with constructivism assume a higher value than other beliefs. For a variety of reasons the process is not easy.[15]

Thus one problem posed for the appraisal of constructivism is being clear about what aspect of constructivism is being evaluated: the learning theory, theory of knowledge, pedagogical theory, theory of science, educational theory, or the all-encompassing worldview. Frequently the different aspects are treated as a package deal, whereby being a constructivist in learning theory is deemed to flow on to being a constructivist in all the other areas, and being a constructivist in pedagogy is deemed to imply a constructivist epistemology and educational theory. But these aspects can all be separated and each can stand alone. Thomas Kuhn, for instance, held a constructivist theory of science yet was an advocate of anti-constructivist pedagogy.[16] Socrates might be seen to be a constructivist in pedagogy, yet he was an anti-constructivist in his theory of knowledge. On the other hand, Ernst Mach was a most vigorous champion of instrumentalist (constructivist?) views of science, yet was quite didactic in his pedagogy.

Thus at least the following dimensions, or fields, of constructivism need to be separated:

- Constructivism as a theory of cognition
- Constructivism as a theory of learning
- Constructivism as a theory of teaching
- Constructivism as a theory of education
- Constructivism as a theory of personal knowledge
- Constructivism as a theory of scientific knowledge
- Constructivism as a theory of educational ethics and politics
- Constructivism as a worldview

Cutting across these divisions is the fundamental distinction between constructivism as a theory of meaning (a semantical theory) and constructivism as a theory of knowledge (an epistemological theory). These categories are frequently, and erroneously, merged. To give an account of how meaning is generated, or how ideas are formed, is not to give an account of the correctness of the ideas or propositions. Too often in the research literature, studies of children's beliefs are reported as studies of "children's knowledge." There is a fundamental distinction, recognized since at least Plato's time, between belief and knowledge. When this distinction is lost sight of, psychology and psychological investigation masquerade as epistemology and philosophical investigation. In each of the above fields of constructivist research, one can find *both* semantical and epistemological claims being made.

A second problem is that a good deal of constructivist writing is theoretically undernourished. As one constructivist remarked, "In summary then the term 'constructivism' appears to be fashionable, mostly used loosely with no clear definition of the term, and is used without clear links to an epistemological base."[17] Although there are countless thousands of constructivist articles, it is rare to find ones with fully worked out epistemology, learning theory, educational theory, or ethical and political positions. This makes appraisal difficult.

SCHOLARLY INFLUENCE

A former president of the National Association for Research in Science Teaching (NARST) has said, "A unification of thinking, research, curriculum development, and teacher education appears to now be occurring under the theme of constructivism . . . there is a lack of polarized debate."[18] Another president of NARST wrote that "there is a paradigm war waging in education. Evidence of conflict is seen in nearly every facet of educational practice . . . [but] there is evidence of widespread acceptance of alternatives to objectivism, one of which is constructivism."[19] A review of research in mathematics education notes that "In the second half of the 1980s public statements urging the introduction of radical constructivist ideas in school mathematics programs also began to assume bandwagon proportions."[20]

A 1990 bibliography produced at Leeds University, a major center of constructivist research, listed over one thousand works.[21] Reinders Duit, at the Institute for Science Education in Kiel, has been performing the Herculean task of keeping up to date with research in this field, and in the early 1990s he estimated that there were 2,500 constructivist-inspired scholarly research articles in journals and anthologies.[22]

At the end of the 1990s, that number could probably be quadrupled. A periodic series of research conferences held at Cornell University under the guidance of Joseph Novak reflects this same almost exponential growth of constructivist scholarship. Sixty papers were presented at the first international conference in 1983, 160 papers at the second conference in 1987, 300 at the third conference in 1993, and about 300 at the fourth in 1995.

In the past decade there have been scores of constructivist-inspired books and anthologies in science and mathematics education.[23] There have been numerous special issues of journals such as *Educational Studies in Mathematics, Journal for Research in Mathematics Education,* and *Educational Researcher* devoted to constructivism. And at annual conferences of groups such as NARST, prominent constructivists (although not necessarily the same kinds of constructivist) such as Ernst von Glasersfeld and the late Rosalind Driver have been invited plenary speakers.

CURRICULAR INFLUENCE

Constructivist influence has extended beyond just the research and scholarly community: it has had an impact on a number of national curricular documents and national education statements. Speaking of recent science and mathematics education reforms in the United States, Catherine Fosnot has commented, "Most recent reforms advocated by national professional groups are based on constructivism. For example the National Council of Teachers of Mathematics . . . and . . . the National Science Teachers Association."[24] The National Science Teachers Association's *Standards for Teacher Preparation*—standards according to which the value of institutions' teacher education programs are to be evaluated—is replete with the endorsement of constructivism. The mathematics components of the National Profiles in Australia and the National Curriculum in England are influenced by constructivist thought.

Constructivism influenced the recently released National Science Education Standards.[25] The 1992 *Draft Standards* recognized that the history, philosophy, and sociology of science ought to contribute to the formation of the science curriculum. But when the contribution of philosophy of science was included in an elaborated Appendix, it turned out to be *constructivist* philosophy of science. After dismissing a caricature of logical empiricism, the document endorses, "A more contemporary approach, often called postmodernism [which] questions the objectivity of observation and the truth of scientific knowledge." It proceeds to state that "science is a mental representation constructed by the individual," and concludes, in case there has been any doubt, "The National Science Education Standards are based on the postmodernist view of the nature of science." Not surprisingly these endorsements caused some scientific and philosophical eyebrows to be raised, and sleeves to be rolled up.[26]

The revised 1994 *Draft* emerged *without* the Appendix, but its constructivist content was not rejected, merely relocated. Learning science was still identified with "constructing personal meaning." And the history of science was seen in terms of the "changing commitments of scientists [which] forge changes commonly referred to as advances in science." As one commentator sympathetic to constructivism remarked:

even though the term *constructivism* is not used even once in the NSES, it is clear that individual constructivism . . . is the driving theory of teaching and learning throughout the document . . . the theoretical underpinning of the document is made to be invisible.[27]

And constructivist influence is not confined to the United States. The New Zealand National Science Curriculum is heavily influenced by constructivist theories and ideals. Comparable documents in Spain, the United Kingdom, Israel, Australia, and Canada to varying degrees bear the imprint of constructivist theory.

REVOLUTIONARY EXPECTATIONS

High hopes are held for constructivism, with two proponents in science education saying that it "can serve as an alternative to the hunches, guesses, and folklore that have guided our profession for over 100 years."[28] The introductory essay of a recent constructivist anthology announces that: "'critical-constructivism' stands in opposition to the unmitigated socio-political vaporousness only too frequently encountered nowadays."[29] Another leading advocate has said in an understatement: "If the theory of knowing that constructivism builds upon were adopted as a working hypothesis, it could bring about some rather profound changes in the general practice of education."[30]

These comments resonate with a certain Manichaeism commonly found in constructivism. There is a widespread sense that constructivism will lead teachers, students, and researchers out of the wilderness and into the educational Promised Land; that one's back can be turned on "sociopolitical vaporousness" and emancipation achieved. There are goodies and baddies, and references to "warfare." Jeremy Kilpatrick, in his plenary address to a major international mathematics education conference in 1987, criticized the insularity and fervor of constructivists, observing that constructivism was akin to waves of religious fundamentalism that periodically sweep America. He said of constructivism:

[It has a] siege mentality that seeks to spread the word to an uncomprehending, fallen world; a band of true believers whose credo demands absolute faith and unquestioning commitment, whose tolerance for debate is minimal, and who view compromise as sin; an apocalyptic vision that governs all of life, answers all questions, and puts an end to doubt.[31]

And constructivism is understood as not just another flag to march behind; it is not just an ideal, or purely normative theory: it purports to give scientific guidance about human learning and the process of knowledge production, and philosophical guidance about the epistemological status of what is being learned, especially the nature of scientific and mathematical knowledge claims. Constructivism is not just a banner flapping idly in the breeze, as Luis Althusser once said of the role of Marxism in the French Communist Party and as could be said of so many educational slogans. Rather constructivism is meant to connect with the reality of human cognitive processes and thus guide effective teaching and learning across the curriculum: in science, mathematics, literature, religion, and history. Children are said to learn in a certain way, and what they learn is said to be characterized in a certain way and thus teaching, curriculum, school organization are all supposed to reflect these realities, not just hopes or aspirations.

AN EVIDENTIAL DILEMMA

Although constructivists appeal to realities about human learning and science, there is a problem because for many constructivists reality collapses into "my experience of reality." This is comparable, and not accidentally so, to what happened to reality in the classic empiricism of Bishop George Berkeley. Antonio Bettencourt is just one of many constructivists who say "constructivism, like idealism, maintains that we are cognitively isolated from the nature of reality. . . . Our knowledge is, at best, a mapping of transformations allowed by that reality."[32]

Thus there is an "evidential dilemma" for constructivists: they wish to appeal to the nature of cognitive realities (learning processes) and epistemological realities (especially the history of science and mathematics) to support their pedagogical, curricular, and epistemological proposals. Thus one researcher who champions "sociotransformative constructivism" (STC), and who supports the position with a study of 18 students in a secondary science methods class, is impelled to remark:

Note that by using the term *empirical evidence*, I am not taking a realist or empiricist stance, nor any other Western orientation. I use the term "empirical evidence" with the understanding that knowledge is socially constructed and always partial. By "empirical evidence" I mean that information was systematically gathered and exposed to a variety of methodology checks. Hence in this study I do not pretend to capture the real world of the research participants (realism), nor do I pretend to capture their experiential world (empiricism). What I do attempt is to provide spaces where the participants' voices and subjectivities are represented along with my own voice and subjectivities.[33]

That constructivists suffer this "evidential dilemma" or "evidential discomfort" is not surprising. As a prominent constructivist in mathematics education has written:

Put into simple terms, constructivism can be described as essentially a theory about the limits of human knowledge, a belief that all knowledge is necessarily a product of our own cognitive acts. We can have no direct or unmediated knowledge of any external or objective reality. We construct our understanding through our experiences, and the character of our experience is influenced profoundly by our cognitive lens.[34]

As lenses change, so seemingly does reality, and researchers with different lenses live in different worlds, and necessarily have to appeal to different "realities" to support their claims. Just whose reality is the most real, or whose reality ought to drive education policy and funding, is left obscure. Two constructivists, citing the work of Egon Guba and Yvonne Lincoln, say, "The notions of reliability and validity are incommensurable with constructivist research and evaluation and are replaced by the parallel criteria of credibility and trustworthiness."[35]

There are of course difficult interpretative problems regarding the relationship of evidence to theory, and there are problems in defining reliability and validity for research instruments and data. Good researchers are aware of these difficulties and subtleties and do their best to overcome them. Constructivists, however, create an *in principle* barrier between evidence and theory. This then leaves space for ideology, personal and group self-interest, or just "feel-goodness" to determine theory choice and educational policy.

Varieties of Constructivism

There are three major constructivist traditions: educational constructivism, philosophical constructivism, and sociological constructivism. Educational constructivism itself divides into personal constructivism having its origin with Jean Piaget and at present most clearly enunciated by Ernst von Glasersfeld; and social constructivism which has its origins with Lev Vygotsky, the Soviet contemporary of Piaget, and has been enunciated by researchers such as Rosalind Driver in science education and Paul Ernest in mathematics education. Philosophical constructivism has its immediate origins in Thomas Kuhn's work, and is most robustly represented by Bas van Fraasen, a recent president of the Philosophy of Science Association. This philosophical constructivism has its roots in Berkeley's philosophy of science, and further back in intrumentalist philosophy of ancient Greece. This tradition has been, since Aristotle, opposed by realists in the philosophy of science.[36] Sociological constructivism is identified with the Edinburgh "Strong Program" and their research on the Sociology of Scientific Knowledge (SSK). In this latter tradition, the growth of science and changes in its theories and philosophical commitments are interpreted in terms of changing social conditions and interests. The explanatory power of cognitive content and rational reasoning is discounted. Psychological processes are not much referred to in this tradition: the individual mind is treated like a "black box," with the sociologists concentrating mainly on sociological inputs or context and theoretical outputs or statements of belief. That is, that something is true and reasonable is not thought by adherents to the Edinburgh Program to constitute an explanation of why it is believed. They believe in the Symmetry Principle: the explanation of false beliefs and of true beliefs has to be of the same form.[37]

This chapter will be concerned chiefly with the first tradition, educational constructivism. Even here there are many varieties; one review identified seventeen varieties, including contextual, dialectical, empirical, information-processing, methodological, moderate, Piagetian, post-epistemological, pragmatic, radical, realist, and socio-historical.[38] To this list could be added humanistic constructivism,[39] didactic constructivism,[40] sociocultural constructivism,[41] pragmatic social constructivism,[42] sociotransformative constructivism,[43] and critical constructivism.[44]

Thus constructivism is clearly a "Broad Church" doctrine, and this presents problems for its appraisal. These "identity problems" are exacerbated when some educational constructivists simply identify constructivism with non-behaviorist learning theory. Indeed for many writers, teachers, and students this is what constructivism means. Dennis and Valentina McInerney, for instance, in their text on educational psychology state: "We discuss the cognitive theories of Gestalt Psychology and of Bruner as examples of personal constructivism."[45] This identification is a cause of some confusion: what is a reasonable necessary condition for constructivism becomes both a necessary and sufficient condition. Bruner and the Gestalt theorists paid little attention to epistemology, which is the defining feature of serious constructivism. Certainly many realists in epistemology embrace non-behaviorist learning theory: to label these people "constructivists" is to invite confusion. For instance, Karl Popper was a realist and defender of science; yet he recognized, against crass empiricists, that "we are not passive receptors of sense data, but active organisms . . . ideas are produced by us, and not by the world around us; they are not merely traces of repeated sensations or stimuli."[46] To give credit to the human intellect and its creativity is not tantamount to becoming a constructivist.

These identity problems are likewise exacerbated when writers simply identify constructivism with all views that recognize the social, cultural, and historical dimension of cognition. Many persons, at least since G. W. F. Hegel and Karl Marx, have recognized that the "we think" determines and sets limits on the "I think." Paulo Freire is one of many who have championed this view.[47] Constructivists rightly stress this insight, but are frequently blind to its major import: the individual does not confront the world and experience as a Robinson Crusoe figure, but needs to absorb, learn, and be formed by his or her social milieu and language. Language, especially scientific and mathematical language, needs to be mastered and, at the end of the day, transmitted. Many constructivists want the "historical-cultural omelet" but are reluctant to break the "knowledge cannot be transmitted" egg.

Constructivists' paradigmatic case of knowledge is the individual confronting the world and making sense of his or her experiences: socialization, enculturation, and language are pushed into the background. Alan Morf, for instance, in an article elaborating constructivist epistemology, wrote, "I consider knowledge as *experience-generated potentialities for action*,"[48] and he refers to an infant's first interactions with the environment as exemplary of this kind of knowledge. Anthony

Lorsbach and Kenneth Tobin, in an article explaining the implications of constructivism for practicing science teachers, wrote:

The constructivist epistemology asserts that the only tools available to a knower are the senses. It is only through seeing, hearing, touching, smelling, and tasting that an individual interacts with the environment. With these messages from the senses the individual builds a picture of the world. Therefore, constructivism asserts that knowledge resides in individuals.[49]

This Lockean-individualist picture of the origin of concepts is deeply flawed. Unfortunately it is the plank upon which much constructivist analysis and pedagogical recommendations rest. People do not build up meanings from sensory inputs: they learn meanings, and they may learn them more or less accurately and well. We push against an object and receive varied sensory inputs. None of this converts to ideas of pressure, elasticity, force, stress or strain—until we learn the words and how they are defined. Definitions (meanings) are not "built up" by the individual, they are "learned" by the individual. Meanings are in the public domain; they have to be enculturated. Notions and ideas are in the private domain; their etiology is varied.

RADICAL CONSTRUCTIVISM

Ernst von Glasersfeld has had great influence on the development of constructivist theory in mathematics and science education in the past decade. He has published well over one hundred papers, book chapters, and books in fields such as mathematics and science education, cybernetics, semantics, and epistemology. Von Glasersfeld is an advocate of "Radical Constructivism," a position based on "the practice of psycholinguistics, cognitive psychology, and . . . the works of Jean Piaget."[50] As he provides perhaps the most systematic account of the epistemological and ontological underpinnings of psychological constructivism that can be found in the educational literature, his work will be examined here in some detail. The examination intends to illustrate some philosophical problems with constructivist theory and, more generally, to illustrate how the history and philosophy of science can bear upon important disputes in educational theory.

Von Glasersfeld sees himself in a constructivist tradition begun in the "18th century by Giambattista Vico, the first true constructivist" and continued by "Silvio Ceccato and Jean Piaget in the more recent past." This tradition tends to undermine a large "part of the traditional view of the world," above all "the relation of knowledge and reality."[51] Von Glasersfeld concludes his discussion of Vico with the claim that for constructivists:

The word "knowledge" refers to a commodity that is radically different from the objective representation of an observer-independent world which the mainstream of the Western philosophical tradition has been looking for. Instead "knowledge" refers to conceptual structures that epistemic agents, given the range of present experience within their tradition of thought and language, consider *viable*.[52]

This can be referred to as von Glasersfeld's principle, or perhaps von Glasersfeld's philosophy (VGP), as it subsumes a number of epistemological and ontological theses, among which are the following:

1. Knowledge is not about an observer-independent world.
2. Knowledge does not represent such a world; correspondence theories of knowledge are mistaken.
3. Knowledge is created by individuals in a historical and cultural context.
4. Knowledge refers to individual experience rather than to the world.
5. Knowledge is constituted by individual conceptual structures.
6. Conceptual structures constitute knowledge when individuals regard them as viable in relationship to their experience; constructivism is a form of pragmatism.

There are some ambiguities and obscurities in this formulation, but there are other statements of VGP which illuminate some of these constitutive theses. In one place von Glasersfeld says:

Our knowledge is useful, relevant, viable, or however we want to call the positive end of the scale of evaluation, if it stands up to experience and enables us to make predictions and to bring about or avoid, as the case may be, certain phenomena (i.e., appearances, events, experiences). . . . Logically, that gives us no clue as to how the "objective" world might be; it merely means that we know one viable way to a goal that we have chosen under specific circumstances in our experiential world. It tells us nothing . . . about how many other ways there might be.[53]

This supports the foregoing delineation and suggests a further thesis implicit in the former statement:

7. There is no preferred epistemic conceptual structure; constructivism is a relativist doctrine.

And finally, in a move that many idealists before him have made, von Glasersfeld proceeds from an epistemological position to an ontological one:

Radical constructivism, thus, is *radical* because it breaks with convention and develops a theory of knowledge in which knowledge does not reflect an "objective" ontological reality, but exclusively an ordering and organization of a world constituted by our experience. The radical constructivist has relinquished "metaphysical realism" once and for all.[54]

This claim suggests two further constitutive theses of VGP:

8. Knowledge is the appropriate ordering of an experiential reality.
9. There is no rationally accessible, extraexperiential reality.

In his 1989 paper, von Glasersfeld quotes approvingly Ludwik Fleck and Richard Rorty. From a 1929 paper of Fleck's, he quotes: "The content of our knowledge must be considered the free creation of our culture. It resembles a traditional myth." From Rorty's 1982 book, he repeats that the pragmatist "drops the notion of truth as correspondence with reality altogether, and says that modern science does not enable us to cope because it corresponds, it just enables us to cope."[55] These endorsements strengthen the nine-part delineation of VGP proposed above.

In his 1995 book, perhaps the definitive statement of this position, von Glasersfeld states that for a radical constructivist:

Knowledge is not passively received either through the senses or by way of communication . . . knowledge is actively built up by the cognizing subject . . . the function of cognition is adaptive, in the biological sense of the term, tending towards fit or viability . . . cognition serves the subject's organization of the experiential world, not the discovery of an ontological reality.[56]

This basically repeats all of the above nine constitutive elements of VGP.

It is easy to see the influence of VGP in scores, if not hundreds, of constructivist publications. Stephen Fleury, for instance, writes that:

Two philosophical principles characterize constructivism. . . . The first is that knowledge is actively built by a cognizing subject. . . . A second foundational principle . . . [is that] the function of cognition is to organize one's experiential world, not to discover an ontological reality.[57]

Earlier, Grayson Wheatley offered a nearly identical summary of the epistemological core of constructivism, saying:

The theory of constructivism rests on two main principles . . . Principle one states that knowledge is not passively received, but is actively built up by the cognizing subject . . . Principle two states that the function of cognition is adaptive and serves the organization of the experiential world, not the discovery of ontological reality . . . Thus we do not find truth but construct viable explanations of our experiences.[58]

The late Rosalind Driver, although a leader of the "social constructivist" group in science education, nevertheless repeats crucial elements of VGP. For instance, she wrote:

Although we may assume the existence of an external world we do not have direct access to it; science as public knowledge is not so much a discovery as a carefully checked construction.[59]

Because of its enormous influence, von Glasersfeld's elaboration of constructivism warrants detailed attention. And it has major problems, specifically its empiricism, its confusion of real and theoretical objects of science, its individualism, its account of concept acquisition, and its idealism.

PROBLEMS WITH RADICAL CONSTRUCTIVISM

The basic problem with VGP is that it is a variant of the classic empiricist conception of knowledge which the scientific revolution discredited. All the root commitments of empiricism are preserved and endorsed in VGP: knowledge is something that individuals create and adjudicate; experience is both the raw material of knowledge claims and their arbiter; there is no immediate, epistemic access to the external world; once individual cognitive activity is recognized, it is assumed that cognitive claims are compromised and knowledge of an external reality becomes impossible. VGP (1-9) embraces and elaborates the consequences of orthodox empiricist epistemology.

Any epistemology which formulates the problem of knowledge in terms of a subject looking at an object and asking how well his or her experience or sensations reflect the nature or essence of the object is quintessentially Aristotelian, or more generally empiricist—even if the conclusion is that sensory experience does not reflect properties of objects at all. Aristotelians were direct realists about perception; that is, the objects of perception were material bodies. Later empiricists were largely indirect realists; that is, the objects of perception were sense impressions generated, it was supposed, by material objects. John Locke, an avowed opponent of Aristotle, puts the matter this way in his *Essay*: "The mind, in all its thoughts and reasonings, hath no other immediate object but its own ideas, which it alone does or can contemplate."

Variations of this Lockean problematic recur in modern constructivist formulations. Experience, rather than a means to knowledge, becomes the object of knowledge. This substitution is fatal. As is well known, Locke's formulation of the problem of knowledge was used by Berkeley to support idealism and relativism. Berkeley's argument in his *Treatise* was simple but devastating: "As for our senses, by them we have the knowledge *only of our sensations*, ideas, or those things that are immediately perceived by sense, call them what you will: but they do not inform us that things exist without the mind, or unperceived." It is not coincidental that modern constructivists, once having formulated the epistemological problem in Aristotelian-Lockean terms (VGP 4, 8), then endorse versions of Berkeley's savage critique of it and end up with relativism (VGP 7) and, for the more consistent, idealism (VGP 9). As when Yvon Pépin writes, "The visible world does not exist as such but assumes a form when it is constructed by the eye."[60]

INSTRUMENTALIST PROBLEMS

George Bodner, an American constructivist, provides a pleasingly frank endorsement of instrumentalism, saying: "The constructivist model is an instrumentalist view of knowledge. Knowledge is good if and when it works, if and when it allows us to achieve our goals." To his credit, at least for consistency, he went on to align himself with the sixteenth century theologian Andreas Osiander, the instrumentalist champion in one of the great showdowns between instrumentalism and realism in the history of science. Bodner admits, seemingly without embarrassment, that:

A similar view was taken by Osiander, who suggested in the preface of Copernicus' *De Revolutionibus* [that] "There is no need for these hypotheses to be true, or even to be at all like the truth; rather, one thing is sufficient for them—that they yield calculations which agree with the observations."[61]

If von Glasersfeld's instrumentalism is meant as a theory of knowledge, as an epistemology that accounts for bodies of putative propositional and theoretical knowledge as found in science, and not just as some low-level interpretation of how people and animals go about their everyday lives, then it is either flawed, or just a disguised way of talking about how predictions match the world. It reproduces in different language the "old" problem of epistemology and truth from which radical constructivism supposedly was to liberate us. He speaks (above) of knowledge being useful when it "makes predictions" that "stand up" and turn out to be correct. Elsewhere he speaks of predictions turning out to be "right." But this talk is simply a disguised way of talking about "truth": we predict observation O, and when it occurs or is observed, we say that "it is true that O." We have to check our prediction, a statement, against what occurs in the world, or what we see. Radical constructivism is then back with most other epistemologies, except that it has made no advance on the hard questions of theory growth, choice, refutation, and so on.[62]

A representative version of constructivist instrumentalism is put forward by Wolf-Michael Roth and Anita Roychoudhury, who claim that:

Knowledge "survives" when it is viable in the experiential world, but it is generally "abandoned" when individuals recognize that it cannot describe their experience. Thus, in constructivism, the classical notion of truth is replaced by the notion of viability.[63]

This formulation neatly captures the major difficulties of constructivism. First, the common constructivist device of using scare quotes renders the assertion unintelligible. Because knowledge is said to "survive" rather than simply survive, and "be abandoned" rather than simply be abandoned, the reader is left wondering just what it is that putatively happens to knowledge in the experiential world. Does it survive or is it abandoned when it is not viable? Second, the formulation nicely confuses psychological and epistemological matters, which is another common constructivist fault. Inasmuch as it is an assertion of anything, it is an assertion about individual *beliefs*, not *knowledge*. Whether beliefs survive or are abandoned, and under what circumstances, is a purely psychological matter on which there is likely to be much individual variation—some people are notoriously dogged in their beliefs, others are notoriously fickle. Whatever the case may be, what people do about their beliefs has nothing to do with the status of those beliefs as knowledge. Some people hang on to their belief that they are Napoleon, others abandon the belief; whatever they do is irrelevant to judging whether the belief is true or false and whether it constitutes knowledge or not. Some constructivists substitute psychology for epistemology, while others substitute sociology. In either case the substitution is a major error. Third, the Roth and Roychoudhury formulation nicely illustrates why constructivist epistemology cannot give a satisfactory account of the scientific revolution and modern science. It is precisely the abandonment of experience as the arbiter of knowledge claims that distinguishes the work of Galileo and Newton from their Aristotelian and empiricist opponents. Immediately after mathematically establishing his famous law of parabolic motion of projectiles, Galileo remarks:

> I grant that these conclusions proved in the abstract will be different when applied in the concrete and will be fallacious to this extent, that neither will the horizontal motion be uniform nor the natural acceleration be in the ratio assumed, nor the path of the projectile a parabola.[64]

Thankfully, constructivist dependence on experience did not sway Galileo and the other founders of modern science from their convictions. As Alexandre Koyré remarks:

> . . . observation and experience—in the meaning of brute, common-sense observation and experience—had a very small part in the edification of modern science; one could even say that they constituted the chief obstacles that it encountered on its way. . . . the empiricism of modern science is not *experiential*; it is *experimental*.[65]

INADEQUATE STATEMENT OF THE EPISTEMOLOGICAL PROBLEM

Following Kant, Piaget, and the host of postpositivist philosophers such as Stephen Toulmin, Thomas S. Kuhn, Paul Feyerabend, and Richard Rorty, modern constructivism asserts that, because individuals are active in knowledge acquisition, knowledge of an external reality is impossible. The constructivists conceive the epistemological problem as one of an observer facing the world and seeking knowledge of it. It is then argued that, inasmuch as the observer contributes to the resulting knowledge, it cannot be undiluted knowledge of reality. Human involvement, supposedly, compromises knowledge.

Within the Aristotelian-empiricist tradition the possibility of knowledge was weakened once it was pointed out that the mind is active in cognition. The possibility of knowledge evaporated once it was claimed that the immediate objects of the intellectual faculty were sense impressions rather than nature itself. Nature, or in Kant's terms, the thing-in-itself, became unknowable, because we only ever see it through a distorting lens, and there is no privileged position from which to check the correspondence of thought to reality.

Constructivism's acceptance of the fundamentals of the Aristotelian-empiricist epistemological problematic is indicated when von Glasersfeld speaks of "looking through distorting lens"; when Jere Confrey speaks of "cognitive lens"; when Desautels and Larochelle write of "making sense of observations which are themselves theory-laden"; and when numerous others have recourse to this looking/seeing/observing vocabulary for stating the problem of knowledge. The empiricist assumptions of constructivism are also revealed by the frequent use of the ambiguous or "hidden figures" examples to establish facts about the theory dependence of observation; or when the "gestalt-switch" terminology of Kuhn and N. R. Hanson is used to describe scientific revolutions. Whether subjects are seeing through the lens clearly or darkly, it is the metaphor of seeing through a lens which signals commitment to an empiricist theory of knowledge.

The one-step argument from the psychological premise (1) "the mind is active in knowledge acquisition" to the epistemological conclusion (2) "we cannot know reality" is endemic in constructivist writing. Stephen Lerman speaks for many when he says of these two theses that "the connections between hypothesis (1) and (2) seem to be quite strong."[66]

However, this conclusion only follows on the assumption that the empiricist tradition has correctly delineated the problem of knowledge. If one rejects the assumption that the problem of knowledge arises when a subject looks at an object and wonders whether his or her mental representation corresponds to the object, then none of the skeptical conclusions of radical constructivism follow. Non-empiricist theories of knowledge are not subject to this skeptical argument.

A number of these matters were developed by the philosopher Wallis Suchting, who concluded a long and detailed analysis of von Glasersfeld's radical constructivism with the opinion that:

First, much of the doctrine known as "constructivism" . . . is simply unintelligible. Second, to the extent that it is intelligible . . . it is simply confused. Third, there is a complete absence of any argument for whatever positions can be made out. . . . In general, far from being what it is claimed to be, namely, the New Age in philosophy of science, an even slightly perceptive ear can detect the familiar voice of a really quite primitive, traditional subjectivistic empiricism with some overtones of diverse provenance like Piaget and Kuhn.[67]

Constructivist Teaching of the Content of Science

One response to criticism of constructivist theory is to say that constructivist pedagogy is valuable and should be encouraged, even if the theory is debatable. This position is understandable, but it rests on a moot point: How efficacious is constructivist pedagogy in teaching science?

The difficulty for constructivism posed by teaching the content of science is not just a practical one; it is a difficulty that exposes a fundamental *theoretical* problem for constructivism. If knowledge cannot be imparted, and if knowledge must be a matter of personal construction, then how can children come to knowledge of complex conceptual schemes that have taken the best minds hundreds of years to build up?

Many science educators are interested in finding out how, on constructivist principles, one teaches a body of scientific knowledge that is in large part abstract (depending on notions such as velocity, acceleration, force, gene), that is removed from experience (propositions about atomic structure, cellular processes, astronomic events), that has no connection with prior conceptions (ideas of viruses, antibodies, molten core, evolution, electromagnetic radiation), and that is alien to common sense and in conflict with everyday experience, expectations and concepts? Teaching a body of knowledge involves not just teaching the concepts, but also the method, and something of the methodology or theory of method. How all of this is to be taught, without teachers actually conveying something to pupils, is a moot point.

Joan Solomon, a prominent British science educator, well articulates the problem:

Constructivism has always skirted round the actual learning of an established body of knowledge ... students will find that words are used in new and standardised ways: problems which were never even seen as being problems, are solved in a sense which needs to be learned and rehearsed. For a time all pupils may feel that they are on foreign land and no amount of recollection of their own remembered territory with shut eyes will help them to acclimatise.[68]

The constructivist research of the late Rosalind Driver and scholars at Leeds University illustrates the "skirting around" to which Solomon draws attention. In a recent book the Leeds group reasonably enough maintain that:

learning science involves being initiated into the culture of science. If learners are to be given access to the knowledge systems of science, the process of knowledge construction must go beyond personal empirical enquiry. Learners need to be given access not only to physical experiences but also to the concepts and models of conventional science.[69]

There is near unanimity on this claim—conservatives and progres-
sivists all agree, with perhaps just discovery-learners dissenting. The
claim echoes the Leeds group's oft-repeated assertion that constructivism is different from discovery learning. But having made the above
claim, the Leeds group go on to say:

The challenge for teachers lies in helping learners to construct these models
for themselves, to appreciate their domains of applicability and, within such
domains, to use them.[70]

One might reasonably ask, at this point, whether learning theory,
or ideology, is simply getting in the way of good teaching. Why must
learners construct for themselves the ideas of potential energy, mutation, linear inertia, photosynthesis, valency, and so on? Why not
explain these ideas to students, and do it in such a way that they understand them? This process may or may not be didactic: it all depends on the classroom circumstance. There are many ways to explain
science: didacticism is just one of them. Certainly a challenge for constructivist teachers lies in helping learners construct these ideas without violating constructivist learning principles. The Leeds group recognize this, and they continue:

If teaching is to lead pupils towards conventional science ideas, then the teacher's
intervention is essential, both through providing appropriate experiential evidence and making the theoretical ideas and conventions available to pupils.[71]

This is perhaps the precise point where Solomon's "skirting around" is
evidenced. How can a teacher make "the theoretical ideas and conventions available to pupils" without explaining them, without illustrating
them, without showing their interconnections, in brief, without *teaching* them to pupils?

Constructivists addressed the problem of the teaching of the content of science at an international seminar held at Monash University
in Melbourne, Australia in 1992. Its published proceedings were titled
*The Content of Science: A Constructivist Approach to its Teaching and
Learning*. Driver and colleagues made a contribution to the seminar on
"Planning and Teaching a Chemistry Topic from a Constructivist Perspective." They had children put nails in different places and observe
the rate at which they rusted. They remarked that:

The theory that rusting is a chemical reaction between iron, oxygen and water, resulting in the formation of a new substance, is not one that students are likely to generate for themselves.[72]

Indeed. After ten pages describing how the teacher tries to "keep faith with students' reasoning . . . yet lead them to the intended learning goals,"[73] we are told, "The process of investigating personal ideas and theories may lead students to reflect upon and question them. At the same time, it is unlikely to lead to the scientific view."[74] Quite so. But where does this leave constructivism as a putatively useful theory for science teachers?

Most science teachers realize this difficulty. They try their best to explain things clearly, to make use of metaphors, to use demonstrations and practical work to flesh out abstractions, to utilize projects and discussions for involving students in the subject matter, and so on. They realize that many, if not most, things in science are beyond the experience of students and the capabilities of school laboratories to demonstrate. The cellular, molecular, and atomic realms are out of reach of school laboratories, as is most of the astronomical realm. Most of the time even things that are within reach do not work. It is a rare school experiment that is successful. For children, a great deal of science has to be taken on faith. Good teachers do their best in the situation and try to point out why faith in science is warranted. They may refer to texts or studies that have better controlled for experimental conditions than is possible in school settings. They may get students to appreciate the general directions in which school laboratory results are heading. They may do various other things to get pupils to see that their particular experience of a situation falls short of the experience that scientific investigation requires.

NEW WORDS, SAME REALITIES

Constructivism has introduced some new words and meanings, it has borrowed terminology from progressive education traditions, and it has appropriated concepts from postmodernist sources. However, it is not clear that new realities have been identified, or that old realities are better explained. Nor is it clear that long-standing problems of epistemology have been avoided, transcended, or solved. Translations, such as the following, can easily be made from constructivist language to standard English and orthodox philosophy of science:

CONSTRUCTIVIST NEW SPEAK	ORTHODOX OLD SPEAK
perturbation	anomaly
viability	confirmation
construction of knowledge	learning
facilitating cognitive transformation	teaching
scheme	theory
conceptual ecology	ideas
accommodation	theory change
negotiation of meaning	student discussion
dialogical interactive processes	talking with each other
student engagement	paying attention
off-task behavior	not paying attention
community of discourse	group
distinctive discourse communities	different groups
personal construction of meaning	understanding
discourse	writing
verbal discourse	speaking
discursive resources	concepts
habitus	cultural environment
symbolic violence	learning something different
mediational tools	graphs
conversational artifacts	diagrams
inscription devices	drawings, diagrams, graphs
cognitive apprenticeship	education

Using such a translation manual, the following constructivist passages can be rewritten in simple everyday terms:

Constructivist Speak:

Since coparticipation involves the negotiation of a shared language, the focus is on sustaining a dynamic system in which discursive resources are evolving in a direction that is constrained by the values of the majority culture while demonstrating respect for the habitus of participants from minority cultures, all the time guarding against the debilitation of symbolic violence.[75]

Plain Speak:

Teach in a way that is sensitive to cultural values.

Constructivist Speak:

Through our presence as facilitators and mentors, we can provide settings that are constrained and have minimal complexity so that students can construct conceptual and procedural knowledge with low risks of failure.[76]

Plain Speak:

If students are taught simple things first, they are more likely to learn.

Constructivist Speak:

[Constructivism] suggests a commonality amongst school science students and research scientists as they struggle to make sense of perturbations in their respective experiential realities.[77]

Plain Speak:

Students and scientists adjust their theories when confronted with anomalies.

Constructivist Speak:

The discursive practices in science classrooms differ substantially from the practices of scientific argument and inquiry that take place within various communities of professional scientists.[78]

Plain Speak:

Student learning differs from scientific research.

Constructivist Speak:

Making meaning is thus a dialogic process involving persons-in-conversation, and learning is seen as the process by which individuals are introduced to a culture by more skilled members. As this happens they "appropriate" the cultural tools through their involvement in the activities of this culture.[79]

Plain Speak:

Students need the assistance of teachers when learning new concepts.

Constructivist Speak:

If students are to learn science as a form of discourse, then it is necessary for them to adapt their language resources as they practice science in settings in which those who know science assist them to learn by engaging activities of coparticipation occurs.[80]

Plain Speak:

Students need new concepts and vocabulary in order to learn science.

Constructivist Speak:

Our microanalytical view of the learning processes in one group showed how much the evolution of students' activities depended on features of the physical context, discourse contributions from individual group members, material actions on and with instructional artifacts, contingent interpretations, and the past history of the activity itself.[81]

Plain Speak:

Our study of 25 students showed that their learning is affected by peers and by the availability of educational resources.

There is no problem in principle with specialized vocabularies and theoretical terms: natural science is full of them. But whereas natural science uses theoretical terms to simplify complex matters, social science, at least in the above examples, is using theoretical terms to complicate simple matters.

Some would say that the constructivist/anti-constructivist argument thus reduces to a mere verbal preference: constructivist teachers perhaps do make the concepts available (in the sense of teaching them), but they prefer to talk of student construction, while traditionalists prefer to talk of transmission. Where there is a failure of match between the pupil's idea and the scientific idea, constructivists prefer to talk of imperfect construction, and traditionalists prefer to talk of failure of attention, imperfect comprehension, inadequate preparation. Provided both groups of teachers are doing the same thing, and judging the outcome by the degree to which the pupil understands the current scientific concept, then the argument could be seen as merely verbal.

But it is not just a verbal matter. A practical, but not insignificant, consideration is that science teachers are overwhelmed by challenges— pupils' lack of interest in science, teachers' inadequate knowledge of science, schools' lack of resources, society's lack of interest in education—so they do not need to be further weighed down by illusory challenges. One group of critical constructivists maintain that "teachers must possess critical awareness," by which they mean:

an understanding of themselves, their perspectives, their approaches to the construction of knowledge, and ways in which their own consciousness has been shaped by society (and schools) . . . pupils themselves, too, need to appreciate the nature of the innovation being practised on them.[82]

They admit that this is "very difficult to do." But it is not just difficult, verging on impossible; it is completely unnecessary. With all of the manifest burdens placed on teachers' shoulders, adding such enormous and utopian burdens is professionally irresponsible.

Another constructivist writes that "teachers need to understand what is in the mind of students—their ideas, explanations and understandings, questions, concerns, values, prior experiences and interests."[83] This surely is not only intrusive, but a flight of child-centered fantasy. Teachers do not need to concern themselves, unless asked, with the values, concerns and interests of their students. To make teachers of 160 high school students, or 1000 university students, feel that they must so concern themselves in order to be effective teachers is, again, irresponsible.

ETHICAL AND POLITICAL CONSIDERATIONS

Constructivism has spread beyond learning theory, epistemology, and education to increasingly encompass ethical and political domains. One constructivist writes of "critical constructivism" that it "offers an avowedly ethical basis for regulating the discursive practices of knowledge construction."[84] Paul Ernest utilizes constructivist epistemology to ground cultural relativist views:

Each culture, like each individual, has the right to integrity. Thus, the system of values of each culture are *ab initio* equally valid. In absolute terms, there is no basis for asserting that the values of one culture or society is superior to all others. It cannot be asserted, therefore, that Western mathematics is superior to any other form because of its greater power over nature.[85]

It is important, for constructivists and everybody else, that the ethical and political arguments for different multiculturalist positions not be confused with epistemological arguments.[86] In the foregoing quotation, the epistemological conclusion that different values, much less systems of mathematics, are equally valid simply does not follow from the ethical premise that each culture has a right to integrity. The ethical, or political, premise can be agreed to without any commitment at all to the relativistic epistemological conclusion. The right to individual or cultural integrity is simply not dependent upon individual beliefs, or cultural norms, being right. Being silly does not nullify one's right to respect from others.

And conversely, there are numerous occasions where the ethical and political premise should be denied, but it is difficult to see how constructivism can support the denial. Do we really want to say that "all systems of values are equally valid?" That the values of caste, racist and sexist societies and sub-groups are not to be criticized?

It is notorious that people have for centuries thought that the grossest injustices and the greatest evils have all made sense. The subjection of women to men did, and still does, make perfectly good sense to millions of people and to scores of societies; explaining illness in terms of possession by evil spirits makes perfectly good sense to countless millions; the intellectual inferiority of particular races is perfectly sensible to millions of people including some of the most advanced thinkers. The list of atrocities and stupidities that made perfect sense at some time or other, or in some place or other, goes on and on. It seems clear that the appeal to sense is not going to be sufficient to refute such views. The appeal to truth which is independent of human desires or power may be able, perhaps, to overturn such opinions. Certainly the interests of the less powerful and marginalized are not advanced by championing the view that power is truth; minority rights have always been better advanced by holding on to the view that truth is power. As Meera Nanda says, "The growth of local tyrannies, each justifying itself by culturally authentic standards, is not a far-fetched fear at all, and the proponents of ethnosciences cannot ignore the unintended— and frightening—consequences of their theories."[87]

The debate over constructivism in education is a component of the more general Science Wars that have been raging in the final decades of the twentieth century. The philosopher Michael Devitt has written:

I have a candidate for *the* most dangerous contemporary intellectual tendency, it is . . . constructivism. Constructivism is a combination of two Kantian ideas with twentieth-century relativism. The two Kantian ideas are, first, that we make the known world by imposing concepts, and, second, that the independent world is (at most) a mere "thing-in-itself" forever beyond our ken. . . . [considering] its role in France, in the social sciences, in literature departments, and in some largely well-meaning, but confused, political movements [it] has led to a veritable epidemic of "worldmaking." Constructivism attacks the immune system that saves us from silliness.[88]

It is not only realists who have drawn attention to the unsavory, and essentially conservative, social implications of constructivism. Some social constructivists have been at pains to point to the political limitations of their psychological brethren, with one writing an article titled "Constructivism as a Liberal Bourgeois Discourse,"[89] and another saying that "situated cognition and individual constructivism both ignore the agency that individuals have (or lack) to transform their own socio-cultural contexts and how those contexts provide (or deprive) individuals of agency."[90]

Conclusion

Constructivism has done a service to science and mathematics education by alerting teachers to the function of prior learning and extant concepts in the process of learning new material, by stressing the importance of understanding as a goal of science instruction, by fostering pupil engagement in lessons, and other such progressive matters. But liberal educationists can rightly say that these are pedagogical commonplaces, the recognition of which goes back at least to Socrates. It is clear that the best of constructivist pedagogy can be had without constructivist epistemology: Socrates, Michel de Montaigne, John Locke, John Stuart Mill, and Bertrand Russell are just some who have conjoined engaging, constructivist-like pedagogy with non-constructivist epistemology.

Constructivism has also done a service by making educators aware of the human dimension of science, its fallibility, its connection to culture and interests, the place of convention in scientific theory, the historicity of concepts, the complex procedures of theory appraisal, and much else. But again realist philosophers can rightly maintain that constructivism does not have a monopoly on these insights. They can be found in the work of thinkers as diverse as Ernst Mach, Pierre Duhem, Gaston Bachelard, Karl Popper, and Michael Polanyi.

Constructivism, in all its varieties, has been the subject of heated debate. The debate is not simply about the adequacy of a particular learning theory or the cogency of an epistemological position. Something more is at stake. Karl Popper recognized it when he wrote:

The belief of a liberal—the belief in the possibility of a rule of law, of equal justice, of fundamental rights, and a free society—can easily survive the recognition that judges are not omniscient and may make mistakes about facts . . . But the belief in the possibility of a rule of law, of justice, and of freedom, can hardly survive the acceptance of an epistemology which teaches that there are no objective facts; not merely in this particular case, but in any other case.[91]

NOTES

1. See Wallis Suchting, "Constructivism Deconstructed," *Science and Education* 1, no. 3 (1992): 223-254; Michael R. Matthews, "Old Wine in New Bottles: A Problem

with Constructivist Epistemology," in *Philosophy of Education 1992*, Proceedings of the Forty-Eighth Annual Meeting of the Philosophy of Education Society, ed. Henry Alexander (Urbana, IL: Philosophy of Education Society, 1992): 303-311; John Osborn, "Beyond Constructivism," *Science Education* 80, no. 1 (1996): 53-82; Peter Slezak, "Sociology of Science and Science Education: Parts I and II," *Science and Education* 3, nos. 3 and 4 (1994): 265-294, 329-356; Robert Nola, "Constructivism in Science and in Science Education: A Philosophical Critique," *Science and Education* 6, nos. 1-2 (1997): 55-83; Denis C. Phillips, "Coming to Grips with Radical Social Constructivisms," *Science and Education* 6, nos. 1-2 (1997): 85-104 [reprinted in Matthews, ed., *Constructivism in Science Education*]; Denis C. Phillips, "The Good, the Bad, and the Ugly: The Many Faces of Constructivism," *Educational Researcher* 24, no. 7 (1995): 5-12; Denis C. Phillips, "How, Why, What, When and Where: Perspectives on Constructivism in *Psychology and Education*," *Issues in Education* 3, no. 2 (1997): 151-194; Helga Kragh, "Social Constructivism, the Gospel of Science and the Teaching of Physics," *Science and Education* 7, no. 3 (1998): 231-243.

2. See Robin Millar, "Constructive Criticisms," *International Journal of Science Education* 221 (1989): 587-596; Joan Solomon, "The Rise and Fall of Constructivism," *Studies in Science Education* 23 (1994): 1-19; George Kelly, "Research Traditions in Comparative Context: A Philosophical Challenge to Radical Constructivism," *Science Education* 81, no. 3 (1997): 355-375; Richard Grandy, "Constructivism and Objectivity: Disentangling Metaphysics from Pedagogy," *Science and Education* 6, nos. 1-2 (1997): 43-53.

3. Peter Fensham, "Science and Technology," in P. W. Jackson, ed., *Handbook of Research on Teaching* (New York: Macmillan, 1992), p. 801.

4. Beverly F. Bell, "A Constructivist View of Learning and the Draft Forms 1-5 Science Syllabus," SAME Papers (1991): 154-180.

5. Yvon Pepin, "Practical Knowledge and School Knowledge: A Constructivist Representation of Education," in eds., Marie Larochelle, Nadine Bednarz, and James W. Garrison, *Constructivism and Education* (New York: Cambridge University Press, 1998), p. 173.

6. S. C. Fleury, "Social Studies, Trivial Constructivism, and the Politics of Social Knowledge," in *Constructivism and Education*, p. 156.

7. Michael L. Bentley, "Constructivism as a Referent for Reforming Science Education," in *Constructivism and Education*, p. 244.

8. Ibid., p. 243.

9. D. M. Watts, "Constructivism, Re-constructivism and Task-oriented Problem-solving," in eds., Peter Fensham, Richard Gunstone, and Richard White, *The Content of Science: A Constructivist Approach to Its Teaching and Learning* (London: Falmer Press, 1994), p. 52.

10. Kate Brass and Maureen Duke, "Primary Science in an Integrated Curriculum," in *The Content of Science: A Constructivist Approach to Its Teaching and Learning*, p. 100.

11. David Hawkins, "Constructivism: Some History," in *The Content of Science: A Constructivist Approach to Its Teaching and Learning*, pp. 9-13.

12. Jan Gilbert, "Constructivism and Critical Theory," in ed. Beverley Bell, *I Know About LISP But How Do I Put It into Practice: Final Report of the Learning in Science Project* (Teacher Development) (Hamilton, N.Z.: Centre for Science and Mathematics Education Research, University of Waikato, 1993), p. 35.

13. Ibid., p. 20.

14. Pepin, "Practical Knowledge and School Knowledge," p. 174.

15. Kenneth Tobin, "Constructivist Perspectives on Research in Science Education," paper presented at the Annual Meeting of the *National Association for Research in Science Teaching*, Lake Geneva, WI, 1991, p. 1.

16. Thomas S. Kuhn, *The Essential Tension*. (Chicago: University of Chicago Press, 1977).

17. Tony Featherston, "The Derivation of a Learning Approach Based on a Personal Construct Psychology," *International Journal of Science Education* 19, no. 7 (1997): 801-819.

18. Russell H. Yeany, "A Unifying Theme in Science Education?" NARST News 33, no. 2 (1991): 1-3.

19. Kenneth Tobin, ed., *The Practice of Constructivism in Science and Mathematics Education* (Washington, DC: AAAS Press, 1993), p. ix.

20. Nerida Ellerton and M. A. Clements, *Mathematics in Language: A Review of Language Factors in Mathematics Learning* (Geelong, Victoria, Australia: Deakin University Press, 1991), p. 58.

21. Philip Carmichael et al., *Research on Student's Conceptions in Science: A Bibliography* (Leeds, UK: Children's Learning in Science Project, University of Leeds, 1990).

22. Reinders Duit, "The Constructivist View: A Fashionable and Fruitful Paradigm for Science Education Research and Practice," in *Epistemological Foundations of Mathematical Experience*, ed. Leslie Steffe (New York: Springer-Verlag, 1993).

23. See, for example, Michael Matthews, "A Bibliography for Philosophy and Constructivism in Science Education," *Science and Education* 6, nos. 1-2 (1997): 197-201.

24. Catherine Fosnot, ed., *Constructivism: Theory, Perspectives, and Practice* (New York: Teachers College Press, 1996), p. x. Fosnot also comments on constructivism's influence in the domain of literacy.

25. National Research Council (NRC), *National Science Education Standards* (Washington, DC: National Academy Press, 1996). The revised draft was circulated in 1994.

26. Gerald Holton has documented efforts made to counteract constructivist interpretations of the history and philosophy of science in his "Science Education and the Sense of Self," in *The Flight from Science and Reason* (New York: New York Academy of Science, 1996): 551-560.

27. Antonio J. Rodriguez, "The Dangerous Discourse of Invisibility: A Critique of the National Research Council's National Science Education Standards," *Journal of Research in Science Teaching* 34, no. 1, 1997: 19-37.

28. Joel Mintzes and James H. Wandersee, "Reform and Innovation in Science Teaching: A Human Constructivist View," eds. Joel Mintzes, James H. Wandersee, and Joseph Novak, *Teaching Science for Understanding: A Human Constructivist View* (San Diego, CA: Academic Press, 1998), p. 30.

29. Marie Larochelle and Nadine Bednarz, "Constructivism and Education Beyond Epistemological Correctness," in *Constructivism and Education*, p. 20.

30. Ernst von Glasersfeld, "Cognition, Construction of Knowledge and Teaching," *Synthese* 80, no. 1, 1989: 135.

31. Jeremy Kilpatrick, "What Constructivism Might Be in Mathematics Education," in eds. J. C. Bergeron et al., *Psychology of Mathematics Education*, Proceedings of the Eleventh International Conference, Montreal, 1987, p. 4.

32. Antonio Bettencourt, "The Construction of Knowledge: A Radical Constructivist View," in ed. Kenneth Tobin, *The Practice of Constructivism in Science Education*, p. 46. For the relationship between constructivism and classic empiricism, see Matthews, "Old Wine in New Bottles" and Suchting, "Constructivism Deconstructed."

33. Antonio J. Rodriguez, "Strategies for Counterresistance: Toward Sociotransformative Constructivism and Learning to Teach Science for Diversity and for Understanding," *Journal of Research in Science Teaching* 35, no. 6, 1998: 618.

34. Jere Confrey, "What Constructivism Implies for Teaching," in eds. Richard Davis et al., *Constructivist Views on the Teaching and Learning of Mathematics* (Reston, VA: National Council of Teachers of Mathematics, 1990), p. 109.

35. Wolf-Michael Roth and Anita Roychoudhury, "Physics Students' Epistemologies and Views about Knowing and Learning," *Journal of Research in Science Teaching* 31, no. 1, 1994: 11.

36. Michael Matthews, *Science Teaching: The Role of History and Philosophy of Science* (New York: Routledge, 1994): Chapter 8.

37. For criticisms of the "Strong Program" see papers by Robert Nola, Denis Phillips, and Wallis Suchting in *Science and Education* 6, nos. 1-2, 1997; also Peter Slezak, "Sociology of Science and Science Education" 3(8), 1994: 265-94; and Kragh, "Social Constructivism, the Gospel of Science and the Teaching of Physics."

38. See, for instance, Ron Good, James Wandersee, and John St. Julian, "Cautionary Notes on the Appeal of the New "Ism" (Constructivism) in Science Education," ed. Kenneth Tobin, *Constructivism in Science and Mathematics Education*; Phillips, "The Good, the Bad, and the Ugly"; David Geelan, "Epistemological Anarchy and the Many Forms of Constructivism," *Science and Education* 6, nos. 1-2, 1997: 15-28; Phillips, "How, Why, What, When and Where."

39. K. C. Cheung and Robert Taylor, "Towards a Humanistic Constructivist Model of Science Learning: Changing Perspectives and Research Implications," *Journal of Curriculum Studies* 23, no. 1 (1991).

40. Jan van den Brink, "Didactic Constructivism," in ed. Ernst von Glasersfeld, *Radical Constructivism in Mathematics Education* (Dordrecht, The Netherlands: Kluwer, 1991), pp. 195-227.

41. Marjorie O'Laughlin, "Rethinking Science Education: Beyond Piagetian Constructivism Toward a Sociocultural Model of Teaching and Learning," *Journal of Research in Science Teaching* 29, no. 8, 1992: 791-820.

42. James Garrison, "Toward a Pragmatic Social Constructivism," in *Constructivism and Education*, eds., Larochelle, Bednarz and Garrison, pp. 43-60.

43. Rodriguez, "Strategies for Counterresistance."

44. D. M. Watts, Zelia Jofili, and Risonilta Bezerra, "A Case for Critical Constructivism and Critical Thinking in Science Education," *Research in Science Education* 27, no. 2, 1997: 309-322.

45. Dennis McInerney and Valentina McInerney, *Educational Psychology: Constructing Learning* (Sydney, Australia: Prentice-Hall, 1998), p. 90.

46. Karl Popper, *Conjectures and Refutations* (London: Routledge, 1963), p. 95.

47. Michael Matthews, "Knowledge, Action and Power," in ed. Robert Mackie, *Literacy and Revolution: The Pedagogy of Paulo Freire* (London: Pluto Press, 1980), pp. 82-92.

48. Alan Morf, "An Epistemology for Didactics: Speculations on Situating a Concept," in *Constructivism and Education*, p. 36.

49. Anthony Lorsbach and Kenneth Tobin, "Constructivism as a Referent for Science Teaching," *NARST Newsletter* 30 (1992): 5.

50. Ernst von Glasersfeld, *Radical Constructivism in Mathematics Education*, p. 1. See also his *Construction of Knowledge* (Salinas, CA: Intersystems Publications, 1987); "Cognition, Construction of Knowledge and Teaching"; "Questions and Answers about Radical Constructivism," in ed. M. K. Pearsall, *Scope, Sequence, and Coordination of Secondary School Science* 11, Relevant Research (Washington, DC: NSTA): 169-182; *Radical Constructivism: A Way of Knowing and Learning* (London: Falmer Press, 1995).

51. von Glasersfeld, *Construction of Knowledge*, p. 193.

52. von Glasersfeld, "Cognition, Construction of Knowledge and Teaching": 124.

53. von Glasersfeld, *Construction of Knowledge*, p. 199.

54. Ibid.

55. von Glasersfeld, "Cognition, Construction of Knowledge and Teaching": 122, 124.

56. von Glasersfeld, *Radical Constructivism*, p. 51.

57. Stephen C. Fleury, "Social Studies, Trivial Constructivism, and the Politics of Social Knowledge," in *Constructivism and Education*: 157, 158. See also Grayson Wheatley, "Constructivist Perspectives on Science and Mathematics Learning," *Science Education* 75, no. 1 (1991): 9-22.

58. Wheatley, "Constructivist Perspectives on Science and Mathematics Learning."

59. Rosalind Driver and Valerie Oldham, "A Constructivist Approach to Curriculum Development in Science," Studies in Science Education 13 (1996): 109. See also Roth and Roychoudhury, "Physics Students' Epistemologies and Views about Knowing and Learning": 6.

60. Pepin, "Practical Knowledge and School Knowledge."

61. George Bodner, "Constructivism: A Theory of Knowledge," *Journal of Chemical Education* 63, no. 10 (1986): 874.

62. On the incoherence of constructivism's instrumentalism, see Nola, "Constructivism in Science and in Science Education: A Philosophical Critique."

63. Roth and Roychoudhury, "Physics Students' Epistemologies and Views about Knowing and Learning": 6-7.

64. Galileo, *Dialogues Concerning Two New Sciences*, trans., H. Crew and A. de Salvio (New York: Dover, 1954).

65. Alexandre Koyre, *Metaphysics and Measurement* (Cambridge, MA: Harvard University Press, 1968), p. 90.

66. Stephen Lerman, "Constructivism, Mathematics, and Mathematics Education," *Education Studies in Mathematics* 20 (1989): 212.

67. Wallis Suchting, "Constructivism Deconstructed": 247. Suchting's paper and von Glasersfeld's response are reprinted in *Constructivism and Science Education: A Philosophical Examination*.

68. Joan Solomon, "The Rise and Fall of Constructivism": 16

69. Rosalind Driver et al., "Constructing Scientific Knowledge in the Classroom," *Educational Researcher* 23, no. 7 (1994): 6.

70. Ibid.

71. Ibid.

72. P. Scott et al., "Working from Children's Ideas: Planning and Teaching a Chemistry Topic from a Constructivist Perspective," in *The Content of Science: A Constructivist Approach to its Teaching and Learning*, eds., Fensham, Gunstone and White, p. 206.

73. Ibid., p. 207.

74. Ibid., p. 218.

75. Kenneth Tobin, "Sociocultural Perspectives on the Teaching and Learning of Science," in *Constructivism and Education*, p. 212.

76. Wolf-Michael Roth, "Construction Sites: Science Labs and Classrooms," in ed. Kenneth Tobin, *The Practice of Constructivism in Science Education*, p. 168.

77. Peter Taylor, "Constructivism: Value Added," in eds. Barry Fraser and Kenneth Tobin, *International Handbook of Science Education* (Dordrecht, The Netherlands: Kluwer, 1998), p. 1114.

78. Driver et al., "Constructing Scientific Knowledge in the Classroom": 9.

79. Ibid.: 7.

80. Kenneth Tobin, Cam McRobbie, and David Anderson, "Dialectical Constraints to the Discursive Practices of a High School Physics Community," *Journal of Research in Science Teaching* 34, no. 5, 1997: 493.

81. Reinders Duit et al., "Conceptual Change cum Discourse Analysis to Understand Cognition in a Unit on Chaotic Systems," *International Journal of Science Education* 20, no. 9, 1998: 1070.

82. Watts, Jofili, and Bezerra, "A Case for Critical Constructivism and Critical Thinking in Science Education," 312.

83. Bell, "A Constructivist View of Learning and the Draft Forms 1–5 Science Syllabus," 160.

84. Taylor, "Constructivism: Value Added,"1116.

85. Paul Ernest, *The Philosophy of Mathematics Education* (London: Falmer Press, 1991), p. 264.

86. See Michael Matthews, *Science Teaching: The Role of History and Philosophy of Science*, ch. 9.

87. Meera Nanda, "The Epistemic Charity of the Social Constructivist Critics of Science and Why the Third World Should Refuse the Office," in ed. Noretta Koertge, *A House Built on Sand: Exposing Postmodernist Myths about Science* (New York: Oxford University Press, 1998), p. 289.

88. Michael Devitt, *Realism and Truth* (Oxford: Blackwell, 1991), p. ix. For discussions of the "science wars" see John Passmore, *Science and Its Critics* (Rutgers, NJ: Rutgers University Press, 1978); Gerald Holton, *Science and Anti-Science* (Cambridge, MA: Harvard University Press, 1993); Paul Gross and Norman Levitt, *Higher Superstition: The Academic Left and Its Quarrels with Science* (Baltimore: Johns Hopkins Press, 1994); Phillips, "How, Why, What, When, and Where"; *The Flight from Science and Reason*, eds. Paul Gross, Norman Levitt, and Martin W. Lewis (New York: New York Academy of Sciences, 1996); Alan Sokal and Jean Bricmont, *Intellectual Impostures* (London: Profile Books, 1998); ed. Noretta Koertge, *A House Built on Sand*.

89. Robyn Zevenbergen, "Constructivism as a Liberal Bourgeois Discourse," *Educational Studies in Mathematics* 31, 1996: 95-113.

90. Rodriguez, "Strategies for Counterresistance," 597.

91. Popper, *Conjectures and Refutations*, p. 5.

CHAPTER VII

Making Believe: The Collective Construction of Public Mathematical Knowledge in the Elementary Classroom

DEBORAH LOEWENBERG BALL AND HYMAN BASS

Near the end of a class, third graders are concluding a discussion with their teacher.

Riba: (*to the class*) So, Sean is saying that some even numbers, in a pattern, can be even *and* odd and some can't. Four can't, because it's two groups. Six can. Eight can't. Ten can. (*Pointing at the number line above the chalkboard, she uses a pointer to mark off consecutive even numbers.*) Can't. Can. Can't. Can . . .

Ofala: Well, I just think that just because twenty-two is eleven groups, that doesn't mean it's an odd number. My conjecture, I think it's always true, is that if all twos are circled in a number, then it's an even number.

Sean: What conjecture?

Ball: Ofala, tell him what you're talking about when you talk about your conjecture. He's not sure what you're referring to.

Ofala: That conjecture I already . . .

Sean: That's not a conjecture. That's a *definition*.[1]

These children and their classmates are struggling with concepts of evenness and oddness as a consequence of one child's claim that six could be even and it could also be odd. His argument has challenged the group's previous complacency about definitions of even and odd, and they are reasoning about his claim. In the process, they are solidifying their understanding of the definitions. And they are *constructing* mathematical knowledge.

Deborah Loewenberg Ball is Professor of Mathematics Education and Teacher Education at the University of Michigan. Her work as a researcher and teacher is rooted in practice and draws directly and indirectly on her experience as a classroom teacher. Hyman Bass is the Roger Lyndon Collegiate Professor of Mathematics and Professor of Mathematics Education at the same institution. He is a member of the National Academy of Sciences and the American Academy of Arts and Sciences.

Perspectives on the Construction of Mathematical Knowledge

In this chapter, we examine the construction of mathematical knowledge in classroom teaching and learning. Much has been written in recent years about constructivist theories of learning and their implications for instruction. Indeed, "constructivism" has been arguably one of the most influential—and most multiply interpreted—ideas in mathematics education. From one perspective, learners are thought to construct their own understandings of content, based on their prior knowledge and experience.[2] What they bring shapes the sense they make of new experience. This perspective derives principally from cognitive theory and focuses generically on individual learning. A second increasingly significant theory of learning takes a sociocultural point of view.[3] On this view, individual learning takes place as a function of engagement in cultural activity within communities of practice. The focus of this work is on how participation in such communities, in the company of more experienced others, enables the development of competent practices and knowledge.

D. C. Phillips has written extensively about various interpretations of constructivism and has analyzed contemporary perspectives on how individuals construct knowledge, individually and as members of communities. These different views of constructivism, he points out, embed more than a perspective on how to teach mathematics or science—they involve particular epistemologies, theories of learning, and even interpretations of the philosophy and history of particular fields.[4] Worrying a bit that discussions of constructivism veer toward relativism, Phillips argues for preserving some focus on the external world and on attempts toward justification and truth. He writes that ". . . constructivists of both types—psychological and social—have to find room for the fact that our knowledge is *about* something. And whatever it is, it has to be granted a role in influencing our constructions . . ."[5] Phillips's is a call for a focus on *knowledge* in contemplations on its construction.

In our work, constructivism enters from a perspective distinct from either the individual cognitive or sociocultural views. We scrutinize classroom mathematics learning and teaching in light of ideas about the construction of knowledge that are rooted in mathematics as a discipline.[6] When students are at work in a *mathematics* class, we see them as constructing *mathematical* knowledge. Looking at the development of students' knowledge in this way illuminates some inherently mathematical dimensions of their work. The ways in which they seek to justify claims, convince their classmates and teacher, and participate in the collective development of publicly accepted mathematical knowledge have powerful resonances with mathematicians' work. As students explore problems, make and inspect claims, and seek to prove their validity, we see that even young children engage in forms of mathematical reasoning and make use of mathematical resources.[7] This mathematical perspective makes visible some critical aspects of mathematics teaching and learning that are hidden when viewed from a cognitive or sociocultural perspective. In particular, this analysis allows for and explores a subject-specific view of learning.

This work finds company in recent advances in other fields. Samuel Wineburg, an educational psychologist who studies historical knowing, argues for a new approach to the study of the learning and teaching of history which he terms "applied epistemology."[8] This perspective entails the examination of the learning of history through the perspective of the discipline. Wineburg points out that this would depart from the traditional psychologist's generic perspective on knowing and learning. Suzanne Wilson, a researcher on the teaching and learning of history, elaborates what this might mean for the study of teaching and learning:

An applied epistemology would . . . require that the historian and the psychologist listen to classrooms in new ways. As they do so, their own understanding might continue to unfold, as the words of a child or discourse of a classroom send them back to history and psychology in search of resonant ideas. They might see in a child's words central historical concepts like the role of human agency.[9]

Shari Levine Rose, in her study of fourth graders' learning of history in her own classroom,[10] distinguishes between what she was able to see in her students' work when she viewed it from the perspective of generic theories of learning and when she later began to view their work using a lens of historical sense-making. Initially, she explains, she was "influenced by constructivist theories of learning, . . . [believing] that children drew upon knowledge, values, and beliefs in actively making sense of new information." The generic perspective, however, she argues, did not help her see how the children were constructing meaning of historical events.[11] But with the historical lens, she was struck by the "historical nature" of children's sense-making. They repeatedly sought understanding through the construction of stories, much as historians fashion narratives, embedding meaning and interpretation in context.

Rose writes about how the historical perspectives that she brought to bear in hearing and interpreting her students made visible how the children came to know the past and constructed meaning of historical events in ways that were much more rooted in the nature of historical sense-making.

Our work is similar. As we began to develop and use mathematical lenses to look in on third graders, we noticed them working empirically and generating conjectures from that work. We saw them constructing arguments intended to make their classmates believe that what they had noticed was true. We even saw them confronting the very nature and challenge of mathematical proof. For example, after working on several problems that involved patterns of sums, they had noticed that even numbers added to other evens seemed to always equal even numbers, and that evens added to odds equaled odds, and so on. They formulated conjectures, such as an even number plus an even number equals an even number, and set out to try to prove that these were always true. For the first time, in the course of this, it had occurred to some of the children that really *proving* something was something they had not done before, and that doing so presented challenges they had not previously recognized. Jeannie and Sheena, who were working on the conjecture that an odd number plus an odd number equals an even number, reported on their work:

> Jeannie: Me and Sheena were arguing together, but we didn't find one that didn't work. We were trying to prove that . . . you can't prove that Betsy's conjecture always works. Because um there's um like numbers go on and on forever and that means odd numbers and even numbers go on forever, so you couldn't prove that all of them aren't.

Ofala protested that she had tried "almost eighteen" of them and even some special ones, and they had all "worked," and so she thought that "it can always work." Mei pointed to several conjectures posted above the chalkboard that had been previously made. There had been collective public agreement about these conjectures and they were functioning almost like theorems, even though the class had not tested those with all numbers. Since numbers go on and on forever, she asked, "Why don't you say that those conjectures are not always true because we haven't tried every number there ever was?"

"I never said they were true all the time," replied Jeannie.

"Why didn't you disagree when like Lucy and everybody agreed with those conjectures?" continued Mei.

"She just thought about it," explained Sheena. "That's why we were trying to think about it today."

The disciplinary perspective from which we are viewing and interpreting classroom exchanges such as this one illuminates deeply mathematical qualities of children's work, just as Rose's historical perspective surfaces characteristically historical sense-making in fourth graders' efforts to understand the past. The children were encountering a central problem of constructing mathematical knowledge in the discipline: the challenge of proving that something is true when all cases cannot be checked. That this can be done is a fundamental achievement of mathematics, and these children were arriving at an appreciation of the need to be able to do so.

Before continuing, we comment briefly on the nature of the mathematics teaching and learning on which we focus. It is perhaps best characterized in terms of three fundamental commitments, not in terms of specific practices. First is the commitment to treat the discipline of mathematics with integrity; a second is to give serious respect to children's mathematical ideas, and a third commitment is to see mathematics as a collective intellectual endeavor situated within a community.[12] What it means to take seriously either mathematics or children's ideas, or to treat mathematical work as collective, is of course contestable. "Mathematics as discipline" is hardly a monolith; and "taking children's ideas seriously" can imply vastly different actions. Neither of these commitments provides clear guidance for practice, but together they function as twin imperatives for orienting the kind of substantive work children might do and how their learning might be fostered. Further, "collective intellectual work" has been too often distorted into a commitment to particular physical room layouts—group seating, for instance. Although not determinative of practice, these three commitments define a problem space for teaching and learning that shapes practical decisions, moves, interpretations, questions, and puzzles. This problem space also shapes the pedagogical and mathematical issues that arise.

Mathematical reasoning within a community, central to the development of mathematical knowledge, is the focus of the analysis in this chapter. We choose mathematical reasoning because it is the core technology by which mathematical knowledge is constructed in the discipline. Mathematical reasoning can serve as an instrument of inquiry in the discovery and exploration of new ideas. It also functions centrally in the justification of mathematical claims. Many discussions of mathematical reasoning in school mathematics focus on the reasoning of inquiry; because of its important role in establishing the validity of claims, we focus here on the reasoning of justification. We begin by describing core elements of such reasoning in order to develop a framework for viewing classroom teaching and learning. We turn next to examine a series of classroom interactions in which ideas are developing, in which children are producing, seeking to convince others, and coming to believe particular mathematical claims, solutions, methods, and ideas. We use the processes of mathematical reasoning as an analytic lens to illuminate the construction of the children's mathematical knowledge. We conclude by considering what this disciplinary perspective on classroom learning implies for the practice of teaching.

Studying Mathematics Teaching and Learning from the Perspective of Practice

This chapter draws on an interdisciplinary study of the interplay of mathematics and pedagogy in elementary mathematics teaching and learning. One of us is an educational researcher who is also an elementary school teacher, the other a professional mathematician. We use our distinct perspectives to analyze where and how mathematical knowledge and ideas, skills and sensibilities, commitments and orientations may play a role for both teachers and students in the course of their work together. Our principal interest is to uncover less exposed mathematical entailments of the work for teachers, seeking useful answers to questions about what teachers need to know and be able to do in order to teach. To do this, we study elementary teaching and learning, seeking to uncover, identify, and understand the mathematical work in which teachers and students are engaged. Some of the mathematical elements underlying classroom work can clearly be viewed as knowledge, while others might be more appropriately labeled mathematical sensibilities or sensitivities, mathematical appreciation, or mathematical skills. Some of what we have begun to notice would not appear on most itemizations of the elementary curriculum, nor are they things that practicing mathematicians would readily name when asked to talk about what there is to learn. The things we see are recognizable to mathematically fluent people, who rely on and use these in their own mathematical thinking, but for whom these things are almost ineffable.

One example is a sensibility that we are currently referring to as the *imperative to reconcile multiplicities* (of interpretation, definition, representation, solution paths and methods, solutions). What we mean is that, in the practice of mathematics, when more than one representation is offered for an idea or a problem, examining the extent to which these are mathematically isomorphic, equivalent, or similar is crucial. Doing so is part of the development as well as the verification of the work. The opportunity for this is actually ubiquitous in classrooms where students' ideas contribute substantially to the enacted curriculum.[13] For example, in one discussion in Ball's class, which we examine later in this chapter, three different definitions were offered for even numbers: as alternating whole numbers ("every other number" on the number line when you start with zero); as those numbers that can be divided into two equal groups of whole number size with no remainder (numbers of the form $2k$ where k is an integer); and as those numbers that can be divided into groups of two with none left ($k2$).[14] The mathematical imperative to reconcile the differences among these definitions would involve asking whether each of these produces the same set of numbers, and if so, whether and how the three versions map onto one another, or, at a more sophisticated level, asking whether they are all logically equivalent. Pursuing this leads to other mathematical ideas. Comparing the second and the third, for example, involves understanding commutativity, in this case understanding what it would take to establish that $2k = k2$. The issue of reconciling multiplicities in the course of classroom lessons has emerged repeatedly across our data, as well as in others' data on classroom teaching and learning. As children engage with interesting mathematical problems, they produce different solution strategies and solutions. Quite often, however, classes end with no comparative inspection of these. Instead, multiple representations, methods, and solutions are left to an uneasy coexistence, implying either a mathematically unverified equivalence, or the message that multiple solutions simply exist, much like multiple interpretations of text. But the disciplines of mathematics and literary interpretation differ, and the imperative to inspect and compare multiple ideas is central to mathematics. This sensitivity sometimes gets lost in the context of developing instructional approaches that are reactions against a "single right way" approach to teaching mathematics. Generating multiple solutions, representation, and explanations is often valued in its own right in "reform-oriented" classrooms, without the imperative to inspect and compare them. In mathematics, multiplicity can lead to illuminating relations or equivalence of representations or it can conceal mathematical contradiction, on which ensuing mathematical reasoning may founder. Unexpectedly, mathematical similarity, equivalence, and isomorphism, while often considered the province of advanced mathematical study, have repeatedly emerged in our analyses of elementary classroom lessons.

Our work turns the usual approach to the study of teacher knowledge on its head. Instead of asking what do teachers need to know, and making lists of topics based on the curriculum for which teachers are responsible, we ask, "What is teaching, and what does it take to teach mathematics?"

In order to ground our inquiry, we analyze data from elementary classroom teaching of mathematics. Primary is a large base of "records of practice" collected in Ball's third grade public school classroom during the 1989-90 school year.[15] Daily mathematics lessons were videotaped using two cameras each day, and audio tapes were made as well. The students' written work was photocopied and Ball's teacher journals and notes were preserved. There were tape-recorded semi-structured interviews with all the students, as well as informal conversations. Most lessons have been transcribed from the video and audio, and some have been closely improved to a point where the quality and faithfulness of the written transcript is high. These materials are catalogued and accessible, some supported with software designed for rapid access and navigation as well as manipulation of the material. They constitute a large primary collection of data on elementary mathematics teaching and learning. A second source of material consists of analogous materials (though not as extensive) from other teachers' classrooms and records from subsequent years of Ball's teaching.

One central analytic task we face is to probe the particulars of the cases we are examining: to uncover mathematical issues that can be seen to figure in particular moments of teaching practice, to seek connections with other moments, and to consider the role such mathematical ingredients play in teaching. The other is to identify what is generalizable and what is specific to particular approaches to teaching, or to the specific cases which we are studying. This is done both through logical analysis (focused on identifying elements of mathematical knowledge or insight that would be important in any approach to teaching) and through comparisons derived from further empirical analyses of other classroom data. Combing through records of classroom activity, records that document that activity from multiple perspectives (e.g., videotape, teacher's written notes) and represented in multiple forms (e.g., transcripts of classroom lessons, videotapes of those same lessons), we look for signs of mathematical activity, places where mathematical issues appear salient. Using a mathematical eye as a tool of the inquiry, we seek to annotate and index mathematical issues that shape an account of what is happening in the class. One form this takes is as interlinear annotation on the "texts" of classroom activity. Another is commentaries on segments of classroom activity, supported with particular evidence from those "texts." We seek to identify patterns, themes, mathematical issues and lacunae, and to support the identification of those with evidence in the records. In interaction with other members of the research group, our written and oral exchanges over the mathematical analyses enable us to meld mathematical issues to pedagogical patterns, issues, and events that we identify as intersecting with them. These emanate from analyses of teaching and learning from the perspective of practice.[16]

We turn now to examine mathematical reasoning as a lens for understanding the construction of mathematical knowledge in classroom teaching and learning.

MATHEMATICAL REASONING IN PRACTICE

Viewed from the perspective of the practicing mathematician, reasoning is one of the principal instruments for developing mathematical understanding and for the construction of new mathematical knowledge. Such reasoning rests on two foundations. One is a body of public knowledge on which to stand as a point of departure, and which defines the "granularity" of acceptable mathematical reasoning within a given context or community. The second foundation of mathematical reasoning is language—symbols, terms and other representations, and their definitions—and rules of logic and syntax for their meaningful use in formulating claims and the networks of relationships that are used to justify them.

We first discuss the *base of public knowledge*. We have struggled to come up with a term to describe this knowledge. Erna Yackel and Paul Cobb use the label "taken-as-shared" to refer to the meanings, norms, and ideas that are negotiated and used as common within a classroom.[17] Derek Edwards and Neil Mercer also write about the development of "common knowledge" in teaching and learning, and focus particularly on the discourse patterns whereby teachers establish such common knowledge.[18] Our focus is more than social or what Yackel and Cobb call *sociomathematical*.[19] Whereas Yackel and Cobb focus on the normative aspects of mathematics discussions specific to students' mathematical activity, such as agreements about what counts as "mathematically different" solutions or what counts as an "acceptable mathematical explanation," we focus on the *mathematical knowledge* that is available for public use by a particular community in constructing mathematical claims and for seeking to justify them to others. It is knowledge already assumed or developed, part of the record of the children's prior experience or the class's past work. We do not wish to imply that each member of the community *knows* it individually in the same way; this is an empirical question beyond the scope of our analysis. We mean to call attention to that knowledge that can comfortably be assumed and used publicly without additional explanation. We contrast such knowledge with ideas or procedures that are not shared, and must therefore be justified before they can be used in the collective discourse of a community.

This base of public knowledge is defined relative to a particular community of reasoners. In the case of professional mathematicians, it might consist of an axiom system for some mathematical structure (such as euclidean geometry or group theory), simply admitted as given, plus a body of previously developed and publicly accepted mathematical knowledge derived from those axioms. University instructors listing prerequisites for a course are prescribing part of the common knowledge upon which they wish to rely in developing the scope of the course's mathematical work. We argue that this idea is useful in understanding the work of a class of elementary school students as well, where this base of public knowledge comprises the expanding set of publicly established ideas and shared knowledge which can be used by the class in explanation or justification.

Take a simple example. On one day, early in September, in Ball's third grade class, the children were working on the problem, "Write number sentences for 10." In the early stages of their work, most students were writing simple equations: $4 + 6 = 10, 3 + 7 = 10, 8 + 2 = 10$. Pressing them gently into more complex solutions, Ball asked:

> I wonder if someone can think of a number sentence that uses more than two numbers here. Just so we have a bunch of ideas of how we could do this. Who can make a number sentence that equals 10, but has more than two numbers adding up to 10?

Quickly, Tembe[20] began:

> One plus one plus one plus one—

Ball wrote on the board as he rattled off: "One plus one plus one plus one plus one plus one plus one. Plus three."

"Why does that equal 10?" she asked, and called on Harooun to justify Tembe's claim. Harooun, repeating, said, "That's just one plus one plus one plus one . . ." Ball asked the students, "How do we know that that equals 10?" Riba, eager to respond, explained, "Because one plus one plus one plus one plus one plus one plus one and plus three equals 10." Ball, still not satisfied, said, "You're just sort of reading it. How could you *prove* it to somebody who wasn't sure?"

Riba: Because I counted it.

Ball: What did you count? What did you find out?

Riba: There's one and the next one is two and the next one is three, next one is four, next one is five, next one is six, next one is seven, next one is—seven, and then three more, eight, nine, ten.

In this simple segment, Tembe's offered solution, the first that included more than two terms, was not something automatically presumed to be within the common knowledge of the class and Ball asked for justification. If this had been a fifth grade class, one might presume differently. A young child's initial sense of addition comes from counting, which is adding one at a time. Adding many terms at once, or adding, in a single step, two numbers larger than one, is a higher order operation, not only for young children, but also mathematically. When Riba is called upon to explain why the string of terms equals 10, she first just recites the equation. When Ball presses her, "But how could you *prove* it to somebody who wasn't sure?" Riba replies that she "counted," and Ball then encourages her further to make this counting public. In response, Riba expands her explanation:

> There's one and the next one is two and the next one is three, next one is four, next one is five, next one is six, next one is seven, next one is—seven, and then three more, eight, nine, ten.

Perhaps it is through this counting that Riba first proved *to herself* that Tembe's formulation was valid. The teacher was requiring that this reasoning be made public, to persuade the class as well. The teacher then publicly validates Riba's work, underlining early in the year a standard for explanation and justification that is more than simple restating of the assertion:

> Do you see the difference in Riba's second explanation? Did you see how she really showed us how it equals 10? The first time you just read it. And the second time you explained it. That was really nice.

A process of reasoning typically consists of a sequence of steps, each of which has the form of justifying one claim by invocation of another, to which the first claim is logically reduced. This process, which merely transforms one claim into another, is not a vicious circle because the reduced claim is typically of a more elementary or accessible nature, and, in a finite number of such steps, one arrives at *a claim which requires no further warrant*, because it is part of the base of publicly shared knowledge, and is therefore universally persuasive within a particular community of reasoners. Thus, the base of public knowledge defines the primordial steps, requiring no further warrant, which form the stepping stones of an argument. In this sense, what is publicly shared knowledge defines the *granularity of acceptable mathematical reasoning* within a given context. In the example above, the addition represented in the equation $1 + 1 + 1 + 1 + 1 + 1 + 1 + 3 = 10$ was not presumed to be part of the base of established knowledge of this class, and so Riba was pressed to reduce the claim to an iterated counting, keeping track of the total as she counted. At this point, Tembe's assertion was sufficiently reduced to a level that relied on knowledge common to the class, and required no further justification.

The crucial issue is: *How can one justify a mathematical claim?* One way is to state a claim, and to undergird its truth by the sheer force of authority. Students often receive mathematical knowledge in school that is justified by little else than the textbook's or the teacher's assertion. By default the book has epistemic authority: Teachers explain assignments to pupils by saying, "This is what *they* want you to do here," and the right answers are found in the answer key. Learning to "play by the rules" often entails a "suspension of sense-making" in school mathematics.[21] But that route is the antithesis of warranting claims through a process of mathematical reasoning.

The base of publicly shared knowledge consists of knowledge of certain facts and concepts, of the meanings of mathematical terms and expressions, of procedures and resources for calculation and other problem solving. It is always present, in both latent and active forms, though it may be tacit, and only implicit in the discourse of the community, whether they be mathematicians or third graders.

Whether a particular piece of knowledge is in fact commonly shared is an empirical question, one that a teacher must often appraise. Did everyone in the class understand and agree that Riba's enumerated explanation satisfactorily proved Tembe's claim? And, further, how many children were not already adequately convinced by his initial statement? These are difficult questions to resolve fully; they are also not completely within a teacher's or students' view as a class discussion proceeds. Still, reasoning within a community depends on the *presumption* of common knowledge and shared established methods. This is most often represented by the use of knowledge already used and established publicly. Arguments that do not build on publicly shared knowledge are unlikely to be effective in convincing others. At the same time, the process of reasoning can in fact help to build and extend a group's common knowledge. As claims are proved, and ideas developed, they may become part of the legacy of public knowledge, on which subsequent claims may depend and build.

In our analysis, *mathematical language* is the foundation of mathematical reasoning complementary to the base of publicly shared knowledge. "Language" is used here expansively, comprising all of the linguistic infrastructure that supports mathematical communication, with its requirements for precision, clarity, and economy of expression. Language is crucial for mathematical reasoning and communication with others about mathematical ideas, claims, and explanations, and proofs. Mathematical language is not simply an inert canon, inherited and learned from a distant past. It is also a medium in which mathematics is enacted, used, and created.

Language in our framework includes the nature and role of definitions in mathematics, the nature and rules for manipulation of symbolic notation, and the conceptual compression afforded by timely use of such notation. Definitions and terms play a crucial role: Not simply delivered names to be memorized, they originate in and emerge from new ideas and concepts, and develop through active investigation and reflection. They facilitate reasoning about those new ideas by naming and specification. Decisions about what to name, when to name it, and how to specify that which is being named is an important component of mathematical sensibility and discrimination central to the construction of mathematical knowledge. Using symbolic and other representations to encode ideas, as well as decoding ideas represented in symbolic or other form are critical communicative tools for the construction of mathematical knowledge. Notation can be used to compress ideas into forms that, when done skillfully, reveal their structure. Wise use of notation can reduce computation and manipulation to manageable proportions; how and when to do this is an important skill of mathematical representation useful in reasoning.

Mathematical language is crucial to reasoning—to the construction of mathematical knowledge—for it provides the medium in which claims are developed, made, and justified. Magdalene Lampert writes:

Mathematical discourse is about figuring out what is true, once the members of the discourse community agree on their definitions and assumptions. These definitions and assumptions are not given, but are negotiated in the process of figuring out what is true.[22]

Some disagreements stem from divergent or unreconciled uses of terminology, while others are rooted in substantive and conflicting mathematical claims. The ability to distinguish these requires a sensitivity to the nature and role of language in mathematics. We return to this element of language in the examples analyzed in the next section of this chapter.

Constructing Knowledge in a Classroom: Mathematical Reasoning at Work

We turn next to a closer look at three examples from Ball's third grade classroom. Whereas other analyses of mathematics learning view the construction of knowledge as either an individual process of interpretation and sense-making based on what learners bring, or as a social process—the product of participation in a set of shared cultural practices—our examination looks through the lens of the discipline of mathematics. How are mathematical ideas developed and justified in a class of eight-year-olds? How is public mathematical knowledge used to validate claims, and how does an idea or a method become part of the shared knowledge to be used by the class? How do issues of formal and informal language play out in the students' reasoning about emergent and established mathematical ideas? Magdalene Lampert's studies of fifth graders engaged in mathematical discourse provide portraits of them seeking to validate what is true "not by the teacher, or another student, saying that an answer is right or wrong, but by mustering the evidence to prove or disprove an assertion."[23] We attempt in this chapter to probe closely the anatomy of children's mathematical reasoning, with the nature of reasoning and justification in the discipline of mathematics as our lens for examining the children's efforts to produce conviction.

We selected the three examples to portray different cases of mathematical reasoning in a group of young children's construction of mathematical knowledge. In the first example, two children attempt to reason about whether zero is even or odd. Their exchange provides a simple example of children's efforts at basic mathematical reasoning that relies both on the presumption of publicly shared knowledge and on mathematical language. The second example provides a case of failed collective mathematical reasoning: a child proposes a division sentence as a solution to a problem, and because the children lack the shared knowledge required to verify the validity of her claim, the solution is ultimately tabled. And the third, most complex, example reveals a portrait of the children's joint construction of mathematical knowledge. A child makes a mathematical observation that conflicts with the shared knowledge of the group and working definitions that they hold. As the children argue with his observation, their collective work that leads to the construction of a new mathematical idea reveals sophisticated use of a base of publicly shared knowledge and the development of mathematical language.

MUCH ADDUCED ABOUT NOTHING:
SEEKING COMMON GROUNDS FOR BELIEF ABOUT ZERO

In mid-January, the third graders' fascination with zero is in full bloom. They often bring zero up as a special or boundary case when exploring conjectures and they like using it in number sentences or in solutions to problems. They also wonder about its nature: Is it even or odd, or perhaps neither? Is it really a number? It is, after all, "nothing." Some ask their parents and bring to school their parents' views about zero.

Near the beginning of class one day, Sheena is musing about something she had heard the day before:

> Well, I didn't think that zero was—zero, um—even or odd until yesterday they said that it could be even because of the ones on each side is odd, so that couldn't be odd. So that helped me understand it.

A closer look at Sheena's statement reveals that it is a structured mathematical argument. She makes an implicit claim: Zero is even.

She provides a justification for her claim, relying on something she heard another student say. The justification has two elements, each part of the publicly shared knowledge of the group:

> The ones on each side is odd . . .
> . . . so that couldn't be odd.

"The ones on each side is odd" refers to the status of one and negative one, each of which Sheena believes to be odd. This is an interesting case: Although the number one has been publicly established to be odd, and although the children have worked with negative numbers, no explicit consideration has been given to the expansion of their definition of odd numbers used for whole numbers to the enlarged system of the integers. This is an aspect of the collective work with mathematical language that we refer to analytically as "expanding definitions," but in any case, it has not yet happened in the class. Still, Sheena seems confident that negative one is odd and uses it, presumably assuming that others share this idea by extension.

"So that couldn't be odd," the second step in Sheena's argument, refers to the zero, positioned on the integer number line which is mounted prominently above the chalkboard, between negative one and one. Here she is using one of the publicly shared definitions of even and odd numbers—that they alternate on the whole number line.

Sheena's argument, then, is that zero is even, and she provides an argument for her claim built on shared public knowledge and shared mathematical language.

Sean sits up, however, and takes issue with Sheena's claim:

> Um, I—I—I just want to say something to Sheena, when she—what she said about um that, that one, um—zero has to be an odd, an even number because—I disagree because, um, because what, what two things can you put together to make it?

Like Sheena's argument, Sean's has a clear structure of claim and reasons. His implicit claim is: Zero cannot be even.

His justification relies on just one piece of mathematical knowledge, one that he likely thinks is shared among his classmates:

> What two things can you put together to make it?

This one requires some translation. By asking Sheena, "What two things can you put together to make it?" he seems to be invoking another piece of public knowledge about even numbers—that is, that they are the sum of two other equal whole numbers. Eight is the sum of four plus four. Twenty is the sum of ten plus ten. Sean's test for whether or not a number is even is different from the one used by his classmates, although it relies on the class's current working definition:

> If you have a number that you can split up evenly without having to split one in half, then it's an even number.

Whereas other children determine whether a number is even or not by splitting it in half, Sean seeks a number that can be doubled to yield the given number: He has transformed the definition into a parallel form in which even numbers are those numbers that are "made up of" two equal whole numbers. But what is he saying here? "What two things can you put together to make [zero]?" implies that he does not think that zero can be written as the sum of two equal numbers. It is not clear what he is thinking, but he might be looking to negative numbers to find one that can be doubled to equal zero. With a positive even number, after all, the number that is doubled to produce it is to its left on the number line. For example, eight is "made up of" four plus four, and four is to the left of eight. He thus might be seeking, and failing to find, a number to the left of zero whose double is zero. He may be thinking something else; it is not clear. However, in any case, he does not seem to think of zero as "made up of" zero plus zero. This is an interesting instance of mathematical reasoning, in part, because he does invoke publicly shared knowledge (even numbers as double another number) but cannot apply it in this case, since he cannot think of a number that is half of zero. By claiming that negative one was odd, something that had not in fact been publicly determined, Sheena, too, was facing ambiguities in using the publicly shared definition of odd numbers.

Sheena moves to respond to Sean's challenge:

> Well, I could show you it. (*Moves toward the chalkboard and points to the number line above the chalkboard.*) This one (*points to the 1 on the number line*)—this one is odd and this one (*points to the -1 on the number line*) is odd, so this one (*points to the zero*) has to be even.

In her response, Sheena does not answer Sean's direct question, which is based on a different definition of even numbers than the one she is invoking.

Viewed from the perspective of the discipline, this is a striking mathematical exchange. Each child's argument is structured with a claim, and supported by smaller stepping stones of publicly shared mathematical knowledge. However, because they are using two shared, but different and unreconciled, definitions of even numbers, they are unable to find common ground for reaching agreement on the parity of zero. Neither seems convinced by the other's reasoning and the question is left unresolved. What is needed in particular is a process for comparing and reconciling these different definitions of even numbers so that Sheena and Sean can reason together about zero.

In the next example, the class considers a claim for which there is no supporting publicly shared knowledge or established mathematical language: a hundred divided by ten equals ten. After some efforts to verify this claim, it becomes clear that, lacking the resources for building the chain of reasoning, this valid claim must be set aside, unverified and, for now, unverifiable within this community.

UNCOMMON—AND UNCONVINCING—NUMBER SENTENCES FOR TEN

Early in September, Ball gives her third graders the problem referred to earlier, "Write number sentences for 10." After the early discussion described above, in which Ball presses the children to generate solutions that use more than two terms, they work alone and in pairs for about half an hour, generating many solutions to the problem. Later in the class period, Ball pulls them back together to begin sharing and inspecting solutions. She opens by inviting students to consider what they might want to bring up:

> Let's see if we can share some of the things you can come up with. Look over your list, and pick a couple that you feel especially—are especially interesting, that you think other people might not have thought of or that you were pleased to get or something. And I would like you to listen to each other's. If you liked one that somebody else brings up you can add it to your list. (*pause*) Lucy, do you have one that you like?

Lucy says she does, and announces "a hundred divided by ten equals ten." Ball tells the class to listen closely to Lucy, and repeats her solution.

> Ball: She said a hundred divided by ten equals ten. Lucy, can you explain that?
> Lucy: What do you mean by "explain"?
> Ball: How do we know that that's right?

Lucy begins to explain it and then pauses, "I don't know really." Ball asks who else can explain. "How do we know that what Lucy said is right?" Lisa volunteers. She says that she agrees with what Lucy had said about the number sentence. When Ball asks her why she thinks it is right, Lisa says she doesn't know, but she just thinks it's right "for some reason." Mei agrees: "I had it on my paper." Ball presses. "But how do you know it's right? Just because a couple of people have it on their paper doesn't mean it's right." Lucy ventures, "Mei said her mom taught her about dividing." She adds, "and so I believe Mei."

> Ball: Okay, so Mei told you, and her mother taught her, and so you believe her. Mei—
> Lucy: Um, well um, I have a lot of other ones, and like, if I had twenty divided by two, Mei said it was right, so then—when I said that, she said it was right, so if I—if I have ten divided—ten divided by one equals ten, and then I have it—and then I have like fifty divided by five equals ten, and Mei said that it was right, and so, like if you have a hundred divided by ten it would be right because—because if you went from like five then it would be five more, and then—'cause fifty is five less than a hundred so—so it would be ten cause if it's five divided by—fifty divided by five it would equal ten.

Ball wonders what others are understanding of Lucy's tumble of divisions. Lucy's enthusiasm notwithstanding, Ball is concerned whether others are following and whether the children will be able to justify her claims. The class have not yet worked on division, although they will later in the year. Ball asks others what they think. Betsy says she thinks she knows what Lucy is saying. "Like the fifty she just put—she just plussed fifty plus fifty and made it into a hundred, five plus five, made it into a ten, and then she divided it and put it into ten, made it ten." This doesn't exactly seem clear. "*Is* that what you are saying, Lucy?"

"Yeah, sort of," she replies doubtfully.

Ball turns out to the class: "Does anyone have anything they could say that would help us know whether we should believe this or not? Devin and Tembe? (*pause*) Mei, you think you have something?"

Mei: Those kinds of problems are really the opposite of times. And like if ten times five, it would be fifty, so fifty divided in five would be ten.

Multiplication has not yet been a topic in the class, although Ball suspects that some children may know some multiplication. In order to follow Lucy's and Mei's claims, and to justify them, they will have to be able to use knowledge of multiplication. Ball probes the class, "What does she mean, ten times five is fifty?" Jeannie says something vague about Mei writing up two numbers on the board, and no one else comments. The children do not seem to be rising into the discussion, and Lucy and Mei themselves do not seem able to construct a line of reasoning accessible to the others. The discussion appears to be grounded for now, lacking the base of publicly shared knowledge necessary for its development.

Ball: It seems like maybe we should go on right now. Other people seem to be working on other things and I'm not sure that everyone is thinking about whether or not we should believe this. I'm not sure we should—we should include this on our list until we have some way of showing that we know that it's right. Like, remember before when Riba explained one plus one plus one plus one plus one plus one plus three. She proved to us that it made sense. But right now we don't have any way of really knowing if these are right or not. And I'm not sure we should have them on our list unless we have a way to show that they make sense.

Ball places brackets around the division sentence, $100 \div 10 = 10$, commenting, "This doesn't mean that it's wrong, but until we have some way of deciding if it's right, we're not sure about it yet."

Ball's decision not to take up multiplication and division in the context of this problem, "Write number sentences that equal ten," may seem a puzzling pedagogical move, missing an opportunity to open a territory for the children's work. But considering what it takes to justify a mathematical claim reveals that the children, confronted with division sentences, did not share a base of public knowledge with which to reason about and validate them. Lucy herself, who introduced this, could not explain it. She believed that a hundred divided by ten was ten because Mei's mother taught Mei, and Lucy believed Mei. Although she did exhibit substantial signs of emergent understanding, her conviction seemed based more on her trust in Mei than her ability to reason mathematically about division herself. Her "explanation" did not seem to work to engage or persuade her classmates. Moreover, the group lacked the publicly shared knowledge to inspect and verify the division sentences. They did not share definitions for multiplication and division, and even the terms and notation were not shared. Without publicly shared knowledge or language with which claims can be discussed and validated, the discussion cannot be founded on mathematical reason, but is reduced to the authority of whoever puts forth an idea. The children were not yet equipped mathematically to reason about multiplication and division, at least not without some development, which Ball decided not to do on the fly. To develop knowledge of multiplication and division is not something to do by way of mention or quick illustration.

We turn next to an example, where drawing on a base of publicly shared knowledge and language, the children were successfully able to handle and develop a novel idea proposed by one child. In contrast with the example of division sentences above, in the following case, children are able to reason constructively about the mathematics in play.

SEAN NUMBERS: THE COLLECTIVE CONSTRUCTION OF A NEW MATHEMATICAL IDEA

One Friday in January, in the midst of a unit on even and odd numbers, Sean proposes to the class that the number six "can be even and it can be odd." After a few minutes, he clarifies: "Three twos to make that, and two threes make six." When he says this, many of the children appeared dubious and most seemed to think he was wrong. Six could not be considered odd. Several tried to persuade him of this.

Cassandra, using a pointer on the number line hung above the chalkboard, invokes the even-odd-even-odd pattern:

> I disagree with Sean when he says that six can be an odd number. I think six can't be an odd number because . . . look—(*she gets up and comes up to*

the board) . . . Six can't be an odd number because this is (*she points to the number line, starting with zero*) even, odd, even, odd, even, odd, even, how can it be an odd number because (*starting with zero again*) that's odd, even, odd, even, odd, even, odd. Because zero's not an odd *number*.

Sean continues his point:

There can be three of something to make six, and three of something is like *odd*, like see, um, you can make two, four, six. Three twos to make that and two threes make six.

Keith, unconvinced, looks at him:

That doesn't mean that six is *odd*.

Tembe requests that Sean "prove it to us," and Ball, sensing the need to clarify terms, asks what the "working definition of an even number is." Sean doesn't remember, but several other children do, and Jeannie articulates the current public working definition:

It is um, if you have a number that you can split up evenly without um, having, having to um, split one in half, then um, it's an even number.

Sean agrees that 6 is even. But, he says, "It can fit the definition of odd, too." "Prove it to us," demands Tembe. "*Prove* it to us." Sean does not appear to hear this as anything other than a reasonable request for justification. He walks slowly up to the board, where he draws six circles and places lines between each pair of circles:

$$\circ \; \circ | \circ \; \circ | \circ \; \circ$$

He explains:

Well, see, there's two, (*he draws*) number two over here, put that there. Put this here. There's two, two, and two. And that would make six.

It gradually dawns on Mei what Sean is saying. "I think I know what he is saying," she says. "I think what he is saying is that it's almost, see, I think what he's saying is that you have three groups of two. And three is an odd number so six can be an odd number *and* an even number." Ball looks at Sean and asks whether that is what he is claiming.

He nods. Mei becomes excited and says she disagrees. She asks Ball whether she can go to the board.

> It's not *according* to how many groups it is. Let's say that I have (*pauses*) Let's see. If you call six an odd number, why don't (*pause*) let's see (*pause*) let's see—ten. One, two . . . (*draws circles on board*) and here are ten circles. And then you would split them, let's say I wanted to split, spit them, split them by twos . . . (*she draws*)

$$\text{o o|o o|o o|o o|o o}$$

> one, two, three, four, five—then why do you not call *ten* a, like—a, an odd number and an even number, or why don't you call *other* numbers an odd number and an even number?

Sean looks carefully at what Mei has drawn and replies:

> I didn't think of it that way. Thank you for bringing it up, *so*—I say it's—ten can be an odd and an even.

Mei becomes agitated. If he goes "on like that," she says, maybe "it will turn out that all numbers will be odd and even" and that "wouldn't make sense. She continues excitedly:

> Then it won't make sense that all numbers should be odd and even, because if all numbers were odd *and* even, we wouldn't be even having this *discussion!*

In this segment, Sean has initially noticed something interesting about the number six. He sees suddenly, based on some discussion among his classmates about structure of even numbers, that there is something noteworthy about six—namely, that when it is divided into twos, there are three groups of two and three is an odd number . . . This seems to strike him as interesting and he proposes that it could therefore be considered "odd," too.

Sean is making a mathematical observation about the number six. Calling six "odd," however, conflicts with the current public definitions of even and odd, which are implicitly considered to be mutually exclusive. As Mei points out, the definition does not depend on the "number of groups it is." Sean's nonstandard use of terminology agitates his classmates. Moreover, six is already known to be even: This is public knowledge. Sean's efforts to make this new claim about the number six falters both because he is using the term "odd" in ways that do not correspond to the collective working definition, and because his argument is built on a way of understanding the concept of a number's parity that departs from where the class has been. In other words, the reasoning does not convince his classmates because it is not built on, and in fact conflicts with, publicly shared knowledge and common definitions of terms. Mei's sense is that if his argument were to erode all distinctions between evenness and oddness, then that would not make sense, and the discussion they were having would not even occur.

However, as the discussion unfolds, gradually his idea is liberated from its connection to the terms "even" and "odd." Mei's proposal to Sean, "Why don't you call *ten* an even and an odd number?" launches the class into a *generalization* of Sean's idea to all numbers which are an odd number of groups of two.

First, the class revisits the definition of an odd number. Matching Sean's drawings of numbers divided into groups of two, Ofala points out that "even numbers have two in them, and also odd numbers have two in them, except they have one left":

Prompted for a definition of odd numbers, she explains:

Ofala: Well, an odd number is something that has one number left over.
Ball: After you do what?
Ofala: After you circle the twos.

Ball guides the students through some experimentation with other numbers they know to be odd, testing Ofala's definition, when suddenly Riba calls out, "Twenty doesn't work. There's *ten* groups." Sean looks at her, "I'm not *saying* that twenty can be an odd number. I'm saying *twenty-two* can be an odd number." This fires up the class, as they race to locate other even numbers like six, ten, and twenty-two. When Ball asks whether there is a pattern to the ones that Sean is calling odd, several children chorus yes, and Sean says he knows what it is:

Every four numbers, like um, there's one starting out like that, and it can be an odd number, and then four more . . . The fourth one would be another odd number. Because you can split it in odd groups. Odd number of groups.

Riba, at the board, uses a pointer to underscore Sean's pattern: Four can't, six can, eight can't, ten can, can, can't, can, can't (*marking off alternating even numbers*). The number two surprises everyone, including Sean.

Sean: Two isn't, two isn't, because you can't make it an odd number. There's only one group there.
Riba: (*and several other students*) One's an odd!!
Riba recapitulates Sean's idea that some even numbers can be even and odd and some can't. "That's what I'm trying to say," agrees Sean.

In the unfolding of the class's work with Sean's original idea about the number six, his idea had been developed and become public. It was no longer an idea only about six, but about that subset of even numbers that are an odd multiple of two (e.g., 6, 10, 14, 18). An emergent new idea had been born from Sean's initial observation. Remaining was need of a name to detach it from its confounded interaction with evenness and oddness: "Sean numbers." Without a label, and without a developed sense of the importance of naming, Sean had quite reasonably used the names he knew—even and odd—and used them together to denote the properties he is noting. Sean numbers, as newly defined mathematical objects, then proved worthy of the same questions of interest that are asked of its cousins, even and odd numbers. What do you get, for instance, when you add a Sean number to another Sean number?

Many readers might puzzle over the significance of third graders developing a new idea that has to them no known place in mathematics. Sean numbers? What are they? What is the point of children constructing knowledge in school separate from the familiar body of knowledge we call "mathematics"? We take a closer look at the mathematical idea that the students have constructed. Just as even and odd numbers can be thought of as whole numbers leaving a remainder of zero or one, respectively, when divided by two, Sean numbers are characterized as those leaving a remainder of two when divided by four. Six, ten, and twenty-two are all Sean numbers—even numbers with an odd number of groups of two. Six divided by four is one with two left over. Ten divided by four is two with a remainder of two. Twenty-two divided by four is five with a remainder of two. And so on. The arithmetic study of the remainders upon division by a fixed number m (m is the "modulus," the number being used as the divisor) is a domain of mathematics called "modular arithmetic." This is useful, for example, in studying periodic phenomena; a familiar example is "every other number" which is period two. This topic is sometimes referred to as "clock arithmetic," since the analog clock is period twelve. Thus, Sean's idea took the class from modular arithmetic mod two (the study of evenness and oddness) to an encounter with a phenomenon of period four, since Sean numbers occur in steps of four (2, 6, 10, 14, and so on). This led to the class construction of a piece of modular arithmetic mod four, a natural mathematical idea.

Labeled and defined, Sean's idea had traveled from an initial isolated observation (or confusion) to a maturely developed mathematical concept as a result of the class's collective work on his claim. While his original argument faltered because it violated publicly shared knowledge and did not fit the collective working definition of the term "odd," the children together built up a core of publicly shared knowledge about this newly discovered set of "Sean numbers." They relied on, and in the process improved, their publicly shared knowledge of even and odd numbers. Making it clearer that the number of groups of two into which a number may be divided is not a relevant part of the definition of evenness or oddness helped to build the concept of "even" and "odd." The children also struggled with the imprecision of their working definitions, and through their work, improved those, too. When Sean argued, "Six can be split fairly and six can be shared not fairly," he was still able to use the currently shared working definitions to permit six to be considered odd. This helped to point out not that six was odd, but that the definition needed to be sharpened. That the children were working with three different definitions of even numbers also complicated the class's reasoning. When she went to the board to use the number line as a tool to reason about Sean's claim, Cassandra used the definition of even numbers as alternating whole numbers ("every other number" on the number line when you start with 0). Several other children were using as their definition for even those numbers that can be divided into two equal whole-number groups with no remainder ($2k$). Sean, and later Ofala, were working from the definition that specifies even numbers as those numbers that can be divided into groups of two with none left ($k2$). These three definitions, while all viable, had not been compared and each called attention to a different aspect of evenness. The children's work with Sean's claim and his reasoning helped to reveal the need to compare and reconcile the three definitions.

In this example, the children constructed a new idea together. Initiated by the private musings of one child, his observation gradually evolved into a public object of first, dispute, and later, exploration.[24] His claim, built on the use of ideas that at first seemed to conflict with the provisional publicly shared knowledge, became more clearly a site where names and definitions emerged as crucial to the group's work. Calling what he was noticing about the number six "odd and even" complicated the children's explorations of the idea. As they focused increasingly on the structure and pattern of these numbers that they together identified, they were able to move from an argument about terms to the development of a mathematical idea, which was eventually given its own name, unconfounded with the working definitions of even and odd numbers. On the unit quiz given two weeks later, all the children were correctly able to place even and odd numbers into a Venn diagram. Despite the fact that two of the even numbers given were Sean numbers, no one placed those in the intersection (as even and odd). The base of public knowledge was a critical resource in their work, as was their sensitivity to definitions and use of terms.

Making Believe: Mathematics and Elementary Teaching and Learning

A recurrent dispute about school mathematics learning has been whether children should function as "little mathematicians." Our analysis does not take a position on whether or not they *should* function as such, but suggests that when their interactions and work are viewed from a disciplinary perspective, particular features of the construction of mathematical knowledge often unseen become visible. We do not advocate that students "make believe" they are mathematicians. Instead, we argue that "making believe," or producing conviction, is central to constructing mathematics and that it has special subject-specific characteristics with which even young children contend. Sheena's sudden insight that they had never really proved something—since numbers go on forever—presented her and her classmates with a special challenge of knowing that is unique to mathematics. Sheena's and Sean's struggles to talk with each other about whether zero was an even number similarly put them in a quintessentially mathematical situation—seeking common ground on which to reconcile disagreement, but finding it impossible to do when the linguistic components of their arguments lacked commonality. Similarly, the tabling of Lucy's effort to introduce advanced mathematics (division) into the third grade reveals what is required for a community to consider and verify a new idea, and the role played by publicly shared and established knowledge in constructing mathematics in a community. The example of Sean's observation about the number six and the ways in which his classmates picked up and challenged, argued against, and eventually developed the idea highlights the critical role played by mathematical definitions and other terms in constructive mathematical work.

What does this disciplinary perspective on students' learning of mathematics mean for the practice of mathematics teaching? Too often, the focus on "constructivism" has been transformed into imperatives about teaching: teachers are to listen more, to talk and tell less, and to create and orchestrate situations in which students will "construct understanding." Giving knowledge to students has been portrayed as being in conflict with constructivist theories, for students are supposed to construct their "own" ideas. Telling students things that they have not constructed themselves is sometimes seen as pointless, as if to assume that students could not develop understanding by listening or watching.[25] Helping students construct valid and usable knowledge of mathematics is a complex challenge of practice. Global imperatives and slogans tend to obscure the subtleties entailed in the active work of helping students construct knowledge. Our analysis of children's classroom mathematics learning seen as the construction of mathematical knowledge suggests to us a different path for the development of practice in support of students' learning. We highlight three elements that connect ideas about the construction of mathematical knowledge to the work of teaching. These elements are bound together by their role in the establishment of conviction, of *making believe*, in mathematics teaching and learning.

First is the centrality of the *reasoning of justification* in the construction of mathematical knowledge. Recognizing the role of such reasoning to investigate claims provides a medium for inspecting and verifying representations and solutions produced individually and in class. It suggests the need for the development of classroom participation structures and intellectual and social norms that would enable students to reach sound mathematical conclusions that are neither idiosyncratic ("this makes sense to me") nor rooted in assumptions of others' authority ("the book says so").

Placing an increased emphasis on the reasoning of justification does not suggest who should produce these explanations. However, whether teachers explain and justify or whether students do, reasoning should provide a chain of supporting knowledge, linked logically, in ways that establish the validity of a claim and that are at the level of granularity appropriate for the current understandings of a particular group of children. Justification should seek to establish warranted conviction, making oneself and others believe for good mathematical reasons. This is core to the construction of mathematical *knowledge*.

Second is attention to what it means to support the identification, use, and ongoing development of a base of publicly shared knowledge within a classroom. Calling attention to conclusions reached, to shared assumptions, to common understanding is one component. Another may be to develop practices that create public records and naming ideas on which subsequent mathematical work can draw. The third graders in Ball's class had accumulated a small set of conjectures that had been proposed and agreed upon across the school year, each labeled with a name and printed on construction paper and posted publicly in the room. Much as mathematicians use theorems in constructing proofs, the children used these "conjectures" by name as they reasoned about ideas, representation, and solutions. Betsy's conjecture, for example, was, "An even number plus an even number equals an even number," and was used to build other arguments. Several conjectures about fractions were proposed and validated; these formed some of the resources for the children's mathematical reasoning on other problems. With encouragement to do so, the children also perused and drew from their notebooks ideas that had been publicly determined and were hence usable for reasoning. If publicly shared knowledge constitutes a crucial foundation for sound mathematical reasoning in a community, then it is an essential resource for individuals' and groups' efforts to construct mathematical knowledge. Therefore, developing ways to develop and make it both visible and usable is crucial.

Closely related is the third component—the significance of mathematical language in reasoning. Definitions, notation, and terms, as well as the syntax of their use in representing mathematical ideas, are important resources in mathematical reasoning. Children will invent terms and notation; respecting, reinforcing, and using those at times, and linking them to formal mathematical language at others, is a third area in need of focused attention. How and when might what forms of precision be a goal? When are students' informal ways of representing ideas important? If language is a medium for the construction of mathematical knowledge, then concern for its development and use matters. Language must be comprehensible to oneself, and also to others. The construction of mathematical knowledge depends on the comprehensibility and validity of the forms in which new ideas are represented, and old ones used. Taking more seriously the development of children's usable mathematical language implies a kind of substantive attention to definitions, symbolic and other notations, and issues of naming that is not typical in most classrooms. As the third element that emerges from our analysis of the construction of mathematical knowledge, mathematical language is a crucial cornerstone of moving toward the construction of publicly shared and validated mathematical knowledge.

We close with a final glimpse at children engaged in constructing mathematical knowledge, a look back that entails the ideas of mathematical reasoning on which this chapter has focused. Betsy and three other children, late in the work on the problem, "Write number sentences for ten," decided that they had a way to show that the answers to this problem were infinite, and they presented it to the whole class. Here we see them seeking to convince others of their idea, drawing on publicly shared knowledge and language, and assisted by the teacher. The segment begins with Betsy's explanation of their reasoning: they could take any number, subtract that number from itself, and add ten, and that number sentences of this form would always produce sums of ten. They link this to the shared knowledge that "numbers go on forever," to show that solutions to this problem "go on and on and on":

> See, what we did is we would take any number, it wouldn't matter what number—say two hundred. And then we would minus two hundred, then we would plus, ten, and it would always equal ten. So you could go on for, oh, a long, long time, just keep on doing that. . . . So, since numbers they never stop, you could go on and on and on and on and on and on and on.

Betsy's explanation draws on several things that she presumes to be shared by her classmates. For example, she leaves unstated the fact that two hundred minus two hundred equals zero; she assumes that everyone knows this. The fact that numbers "never stop" was similarly assumed. She apparently also expected others to share the knowledge that "any number" could replace her example of two hundred in the expression.

Ball tries to call attention to these children's claim by writing it down for collective consideration, and by giving a name for the first time this year to the kind of significant mathematical thinking that it represents—a *conjecture*.

> Ball: Could you say what your idea was again? I want to write it down for us to think about.

(*Later.*) Okay. Now, I put a title on this piece of paper, it's important. I wrote, "Betsy, Riba, Mark and Nathan's Conjecture."

Sean: What does that mean?

Ball: Conjecture is an important word that we're going to use this year. A conjecture is when you come up with an idea, something you think is true, that you're trying to prove to other people. How did they prove to us that they think this is true? Who understands what they were doing, that tried to prove to us that the answers would go on forever? What did they show us? What did Betsy do on the board to try to make you believe that this is true? Jeannie, what did she do?

Jeannie: She wrote it up on the board until we thought that they were right.

At this response, Ball tries to focus Jeannie and the others more closely on the specifics of Betsy's reasoning so that they can examine the claim and its supporting argument.

Ball: Well, what kind of example did she use? Do you remember what she showed?

Jeannie: She took away two hundred, and then that's zero, and then she added ten. She said she had a number—Betsy had a number, then she took it away and that was zero, and then she added ten.

Ball: Why does that—why does that help us to think that this is true? Why does that show that the answers would go on forever? I thought maybe people weren't sure about that. Can you—this group say anything more about why you think—oh, Lisa, you think you know why that proves it?

Lisa: Because numbers go on forever, and you can go like infinity take away infinity plus ten equals ten. Because numbers go on and on.

What had started as a relatively ordinary mathematics problem was evolving toward a sophisticated moment of mathematical reasoning, and the construction of a solution to the problem well beyond two-addend sums. The children, engaged in mathematical reasoning, were at the mathematical work of making believe. Taking a disciplinary perspective on classroom teaching and learning can offer ideas for supporting the construction of mathematical knowledge in school by honoring the central role played by the reasoning of justification and seeing it in incipient and sometimes astonishingly developed form even among young children. How we can learn to see and make use of this in practice, linking theories of learning with ideas about the construction of mathematical knowledge in the discipline, is the challenge.

This work is supported, in part, by the Spencer Foundation for the project, "Crossing Boundaries: Probing the Interplay of Mathematics and Pedagogy in Elementary Teaching" (MG #199800202).

The ideas in this paper were vetted in the Mathematics Teaching and Learning to Teach Project at the University of Michigan. We gratefully acknowledge the contributions to the development of these ideas made by its members: Merrie Blunk, Mark Hoover, Deidre LeFevre, Jennifer Lewis, Geoffrey Phelps, Ed Wall, and Raven Wallace. We thank Joan Ferrini-Mundy and Suzanne Wilson for their helpful comments on earlier drafts of this paper.

NOTES

1. Transcript of Ball's third grade class, January 19, 1990.

2. See, for example, Ernst von Glasersfeld, "Learning as a Constructive Activity," in *Problems of Representation in the Teaching and Learning of Mathematics*, ed. Claude Janvier (Hillsdale, NJ: Erlbaum, 1987): 3-18.

3. Paul Cobb explores possible tensions and complementarities between individual and sociocultural views of learning in "Where Is the Mind? Constructivist and Sociocultural Perspectives on Mathematical Development," *Educational Researcher* 25 (October 1994): 13-20.

4. D. C. Phillips, "The Good, the Bad, and the Ugly: The Many Faces of Constructivism," *Educational Researcher* 24 (October 1995): 5-12.

5. D. C. Phillips, "How, Why, What, When, and Where: Perspectives on Constructivism in Psychology and Education," in *Issues in Education: Contributions from Educational Psychology* 3(2), ed. Jerry S. Carlson and Robert Calfee (Stamford, CT: JAI Press, 1997), p. 190.

6. Magdalene Lampert has been exploring similar resonances between the practices of knowing mathematics in school and in the discipline. See Magdalene Lampert, "When the Problem Is Not the Question and the Answer Is Not the Solution: Mathematical Knowing and Teaching," *American Educational Research Journal* 27 (Spring 1990): 29-63; also, Magdalene Lampert, "Practices and Problems in Teaching Authentic Mathematics," in *Effective and Responsible Teaching: The New Synthesis*, ed. Fritz Oser, D. Andreas, J. Patry (San Francisco: Jossey-Bass, 1992): pp. 295-314.

7. See Stephen P. Smith, *Children, Learning Theory, and Mathematics: An Analysis of the Role of Language and Representations in Children's Mathematical Reasoning* (PhD dissertation, Michigan State University, 1999). Smith analyzes four nine-year-olds' individual mathematical reasoning, focusing on their use of language and representations as they draw together and use mathematical resources to solve problems.

8. Samuel S. Wineburg, "The Psychology of Teaching and Learning History," in *Handbook of Educational Psychology*, ed. David Berliner and Robert Calfee (New York: Simon & Schuster, 1996): 423-437.

9. Suzanne M. Wilson, "Research on History Teaching," in *Handbook of Research on Teaching*, ed. Virginia Richardson (New York: Macmillan, in press).

10. Shari Levine Rose, *Understanding Children's Historical Sense-making: A View from the Classroom* (PhD dissertation, Michigan State University, 1999).

11. Ibid., p. 215.

12. We thank Raven Wallace for identifying the salience and significance of this third commitment. For a more complete explanation of this teaching and some of its attendant dilemmas, see Deborah Loewenberg Ball, "With an Eye on the Mathematical Horizon: Dilemmas of Teaching Elementary School Mathematics," *Elementary School Journal* 93 (1993): 373-397.

13. Erna Yackel and Paul Cobb describe inquiry classrooms in which producing and sharing *mathematically different* solutions was encouraged. See Erna Yackel and Paul Cobb, "Sociomathematical Norms, Argumentation, and Intellectual Autonomy in Mathematics," *Journal for Research in Mathematics Education* 27 (1996): 458-477.

14. Data from January 1990 lessons in Ball's third grade class.

15. These records were collected in Ball's third grade mathematics class and Magdalene Lampert's fifth grade, with support from the National Science Foundation, for a project in which we set out to investigate the potential of using new technologies together with extensive records of practice to design new approaches to the pedagogy and curriculum of teacher education. For a discussion of this project and its results, see Magdalene Lampert and Deborah Loewenberg Ball, *Teaching, Multimedia, and Mathematics: Investigations of Real Teaching* (New York: Teachers College Press, 1998).

16. For discussion of what it means to study teaching "from the perspective of practice," see Magdalene Lampert, "Studying Teaching as a Thinking Practice," in *Thinking Practices in Mathematics and Science*, ed. James Greeno and Shelly V. Goldman (Hillsdale, NJ: Lawrence Erlbaum and Associates, 1998): pp. 53-78. Also, see Deborah Loewenberg Ball and Magdalene Lampert, "Multiples of Evidence, Time, and Perspective: Revising the Study of Teaching and Learning," in *Issues in Education Research: Problems and Possibilities*, ed. Ellen Lagemann and Lee S. Shulman (San Francisco: Jossey-Bass, 1999): pp. 371-398.

17. Yackel and Cobb, "Sociomathematical Norms, Argumentation, and Intellectual Autonomy in Mathematics."

18. See Derek Edwards and Neil Mercer, *Common Knowledge* (London: Routledge, 1989); Derek Edwards and Neil Mercer, "Reconstructing Context: The Conventionalization of Classroom Knowledge," *Discourse Processes* 12 (1997): 91-104.

19. Yackel and Cobb, "Sociomathematical Norms, Argumentation, and Intellectual Autonomy in Mathematics."

20. All names are pseudonyms, standardized across published analyses of these data, and selected to be culturally similar to the children's real names. For example, Tembe was from Kenya, and his pseudonym was selected from among similar Kenyan boys' names.

21. Robert Davis, "Mathematics Teaching—With Special Reference to Epistemological Problems," *Journal of Research and Development in Education* (Monograph No. 1, 1967).

22. Lampert, "When the Problem Is Not the Question," p. 42.

23. Ibid., p. 55.

24. Rogers Hall and Andee Rubin propose three participation structures used in the course of the construction of mathematical knowledge—private, local, and public. In the story of Sean numbers, we see an interesting movement across those three. See Rogers Hall and Andee Rubin, ". . . There's Five Little Notches in Here: Dilemmas in Teaching and Learning the Conventional Structure of Rate," in *Thinking Practices in Mathematics and Science*, ed. James Greeno and Shelly V. Goldman (Hillsdale, NJ: Lawrence Erlbaum and Associates, 1998): pp. 189-235.

25. See Daniel Chazan and Deborah Loewenberg Ball, "Beyond Being Told What to Tell," *For the Learning of Mathematics* 9 (July 1999): 2-10, for an analysis of the teacher's role in the context of discussion-intensive approaches to teaching mathematics.

The Impact of Constructivism on Researchers

Editor's Introduction

There are various ways in which important new ideas, or the ideas of an exciting theorist, can impact the work of researchers. They can suddenly gain attention like a searing flash of light, one that brings unexpected illumination to a field; Charles Darwin's impact on biologists (and some philosophers) in the years immediately following the publication of his book in 1859 seems to have been of this kind. Sometimes they can win slow acceptance and have impact that grows over time. Sometimes the new ideas get co-opted into a movement or research program that is already in existence, in order to give it additional support. Herbert Spencer, the enormously popular late-nineteenth century essayist, treated Darwin's theory this way, regarding it as added proof that his own prior theories were valid. And no doubt there are other ways in which new ideas come to have an effect.

How have the major constructivist ideas impacted researchers? Probably in all the ways depicted above; but, like true love, the course of exciting new ideas does not always run smooth, as shall be seen in the pair of chapters by Kenneth Tobin and Richard Gunstone. Both are internationally known science educators. Tobin has as his main focus the preparation of teachers, and Gunstone is chiefly concerned with studying classroom learning (not that there is a clearcut division between these interests). Both also would identify themselves as constructivists although, as will become clear, they mean different things by this label.

Both Tobin and Gunstone were asked to reflect on the impact that constructivism has had upon them, and how it (whatever they interpreted "it" to be) has influenced their own research and the schools or traditions of research with which they were most familiar. What results are two interesting—and remarkably different—sets of personal reflections by individuals who have very detailed knowledge of the work of important groups of science education researchers around the globe.

In Tobin's reflections, the thing that stands out is how constructivism, particularly as developed by von Glasersfeld, was absorbed into—and had a strong and enduring impact upon—his ongoing work. But he stresses that his work has constantly changed as he has absorbed new ideas, tried them out, observed new things, and changed his focus as new issues became central and as he outgrew old interests and concerns. But he sees constructivism as having an enduring legacy in his work. In one passage he movingly describes how he struggled with his theoretical beliefs, and with his model of himself as a teacher educator, as he decided to work in an underprivileged school district in order to be better able to prepare new teachers for such settings.

Gunstone reflects in depth on work done over almost two decades by two research groups (in Britain and New Zealand) which had close relationships with his own group at Monash University. As he sees the history of these groups, their work grew from an overriding concern with how students learned, or often mislearned, science in their classrooms. It was the challenges that arose within the course of their empirical work in classrooms that drove them, and he and his overseas colleagues were eclectic in that they took ideas from whatever source they could if these ideas appeared to have mileage in helping them make sense of what they were finding. He does not see the more theoretical or philosophical aspects of constructivism as having much influence on them, and certainly these ideas did not significantly shape their work or change its direction.

Both these chapters give new, and nuanced, insight into the ways in which ideas associated with various forms of constructivism spread and were absorbed or accommodated. They force us to look more deeply and somewhat more skeptically into the common and somewhat glib accounts of how constructivism has come to have what many would regard as virtual hegemony in the literature of mathematics and science education.

CHAPTER VIII

Constructivism in Science Education: Moving on . . .

KENNETH TOBIN

When I began to teach science in 1964 I did not employ any explicit theories to frame my experience. I arrived at school each day and I taught. The biggest concerns for me were mastery of the science content I was to teach, and motivating my rural students to engage in practices perceived by them to have little direct relevance. My instincts were to build a community of learners and to lead by example. The building of community was not difficult in my first school because the town in which it was located was tiny and the students readily formed a coherent group. After two years, when I moved to a large suburban high school, my goals for improvement focused still on mastery of the subject matter I was to teach. Once again the students were relatively easy to manage and for the most part could be convinced of the value of learning science. Knowing about theories for teaching and learning was not of importance to me. I talked with colleagues about what worked and what did not. And when any of us learned about promising innovations or resources we readily shared them with others. I became aware of the advantages of applying theory to the practices of teaching and learning only when I became a curriculum developer and needed to persuade others of the appropriateness of alternative activities and approaches to the teaching and learning of science.

As a curriculum developer my chief role was to support a statewide effort to reform science education. All science teachers in my state (Western Australia) were provided with teacher's guides that recommended ways of teaching subject matter, materials to use, how to manage instruction, and strategies for assessment. I had many questions to consider. For example, what is teacher knowledge and how does it change? My initial responses were guided by Jean Piaget's clinical studies

Kenneth Tobin is Professor of Education and Director of Teacher Education at the University of Pennsylvania.

on the learning of children and adolescents.[1] The obligation to identify the most appropriate ways to teach and learn given subject matter required me to justify, at least to myself, why one approach to teaching was preferable to another. At the time there were numerous curriculum resource guides produced in many countries that encouraged me to use Piaget's developmental theories as a rationale for enacting science curricula.

However, there was no consensus on the most appropriate theoretical framework for science education, and my decision to pursue doctoral studies in the United States was a catalyst for changing my thinking about teaching and learning. When I came to the University of Georgia to pursue my studies, the science education group there was concerned with the students' learning of science process skills and with educating teachers to teach them effectively. The group's approach was oriented strongly toward the use of behaviorism.[2] The context at Georgia was framed by problems that were of critical concern to the larger science education community. The lifeworlds of the researchers in the science education department made it sensible for them to think about science education in terms of radical behaviorism.

In a relatively short period of time I had changed my understanding of science education and science teacher education; I had moved on from my initial atheoretical beginnings to a strong theoretical framework, initially shaped by Piaget's research and then by behaviorism. As I continued to do research after leaving the University of Georgia, I found myself as a learner who is continuously moving on in the process of seeking understanding. This chapter is about this journey as it relates to constructivism.

The first part of this chapter provides a brief overview of changes that have occurred since the mid-1970s in terms of the foci of publications in the *Journal of Research in Science Teaching* at intervals of approximately five years. The second part of the chapter describes the manner in which I have applied theory in science education in a context of the local communities in which I participated. I describe the ways in which constructivism became an important framework in a context of changes in which I practiced science education and concomitant changes occurring within the science education community at large. The foci for the autobiographical component of the paper are teacher learning, change, and teacher education. These are discussed in the chapter in terms of significant theoretical perspectives that include behaviorism, constructivism, and communities of practice.

Changes within the Science Education Community

In 1979 the *Journal of Research in Science Teaching* featured five articles on paradigms in science education. Three of these laid out the bases for the reception learning paradigm,[3] the hierarchical learning paradigm,[4] and the developmental paradigm,[5] respectively. From my perspective there was little effort on the part of the writers to locate the common ground or to forge a best way to proceed from the strengths and weaknesses of the three approaches. Instead the three articles each described and advocated one distinctive approach as the preferred way to proceed in science education. An example of the extent to which prominent science educators distanced themselves from opposing theoretical positions is evident in an exchange involving Joseph Novak and Dudley Herron. Novak noted:

For some years now this editor has been trying to suggest that the Piagetian paradigm for *cognitive development* is not the most useful paradigm to guide research in science education nor for planning of instructional programs. I cannot repeat my arguments here, but my students and I have tried to show in previous work that Ausubel's theory of *cognitive learning* can have more validity and more relevance to our work as researchers and instructional planners.[6]

In response Dudley Herron chided Novak for using "his position as Learning Section Editor of *Science Education* to argue against Piaget's theory of intellectual development and to promote David Ausubel's theory of meaningful learning as a theoretical basis for research in science education."[7] Herron went on to provide reasons for the Piagetian paradigm being appropriate for scholarly activity in science education.

Although the influence of Piaget was strong in the United States and researchers such as John Renner and Anton Lawson were influential thinkers,[8] the trend was not reflected in publications in the *Journal* in 1974 but was much more discernible in 1979 and subsequent years.

The Piagetian and conceptual change foci in science education were well represented in 1984. The theoretical underpinnings of the research reported in the *Journal of Research in Science Teaching* in 1984 were not always as explicit as they tend to be at present. However, an analysis of the studies shows that the Piagetian framework, as exemplified in the studies of Lawson, was quite dominant at the time. A second trend was a significant number of studies associated with conceptual change and misconceptions. Although there were several qualitative studies reported in the journal in 1984, the majority of the research involved some form of quantitative analysis and an interpretive frame that is oriented toward positivism. Collections of researchers in different universities tended to align with one approach or another. However, by the early 1980s research on conceptual change was well established and constructivism was becoming a force that would unite the Piagetian and Ausubelian research groups in science education.

The trends within the field in 1988, as reflected in articles in the *Journal of Research in Science Teaching*, show evidence of the growing importance of conceptual change research. The trend is even more pronounced in other journals, such as the *International Journal of Science Education* and *Science Education*. However, what is not apparent in these trends is the extent to which researchers were synthesizing perspectives in an endeavor to get the greatest possible interpretive power in their studies. Theoretical advances enabled researchers in science education to begin to employ theoretical frames from disciplines such as sociology, philosophy, anthropology, and phenomenology.

The analyses for 1994 were difficult to do because most articles published could easily be placed in different categories depending on my focus. The differences between the Piagetian and conceptual change studies were now almost not discernible, with researchers such as Lawson writing about each in the one study. Each of these studies also could have been classified as constructivist. Hence, the boundaries were blurring and more than fifty percent of the studies were placed in the categories of constructivism, conceptual change, and Piagetian.

The analyses of the 1998 publications were the most difficult of all because they dealt with many more issues than in previous years. A trend was for authors to employ explicit theoretical frames for their studies and to use more than one. Distinctions between Piagetian, conceptual change, and constructivism were at times nonexistent. Notably the Piagetian analytical frame is subtler and the ideas of Novak are much more in ascendancy, particularly in terms of the use of concept maps.[9] Partially due to a tendency to publish special issues of the journal on topics such as equity, alternative epistemologies, and policy, it is apparent that social justice, power, and feminism are now major issues in the teaching and learning of science and theoretical frames have evolved to reflect those emphases.

References to constructivism as a theoretical underpinning have become less explicit. Although most of the articles dealing with teaching and learning still are consistent with constructivism, the labels used to describe the theoretical frameworks are usually more social and emphasize communities and discourse. Just as I have moved on in my applications of theory to science education so too has the field. In the following sections I describe the evolution in the theoretical frame that applied to my praxis in science education throughout the 1980s and 1990s.

Behaviorism in Science Education

When I arrived at the University of Georgia in 1978 I was struck by the strong influence of Robert Gagné and derivative behaviorist ways of thinking about teaching and learning.[10] Although I was somewhat opposed to reductionist ways of thinking about knowing and learning, behaviorist models were pervasive within the science education group. For a time I was persuaded by the compelling logic of hierarchical models being used to represent complex modes of scientific reasoning. Our group developed and refined models for data processing and created a conceptual scheme for planning of investigations.[11] Once developed, conceptual models such as these served as tools for curriculum development, analysis of teaching, and teacher education.[12] The models also were used as a basis for strategy analysis, a process of analyzing teaching and providing feedback to teachers, students, and curriculum developers. Adherence to a model served as a criterion for examining the appropriateness of instruction. The approach to teacher education then became one of understanding and applying models of teaching and learning. For example, student teachers could build an understanding of a conceptual model, utilize that model to plan a sequence of activities, and apply the model as they enacted a science curriculum.[13]

In the five-year period in which I used strategy analysis as a primary tool in my teacher education courses, students and teachers developed considerable competence in using models to guide their teaching. Complex sets of cognitive actions, sometimes consisting of ten or more components, were enacted as a routine. Student teachers learned to teach through the use of a variety of methods that included the use of written conceptual models to plan and teach science in activities involving one-on-one tutoring and teaching in micro settings and whole classes. Sometimes the learners were peers and on other occasions they were K-12 students.[14] The models also were a basis for analyzing teaching in actual classrooms or micro settings, and from videotapes.

Although the results were persuasive, when I returned to Australia my research was shaped by the priorities of a new community of scholars. The theories I had employed at Georgia were no longer adequate, and as I canvassed alternative ways to understand teacher learning and change, I was propelled on a trajectory of evolving theoretical underpinnings. The search led me to radical constructivism and the research of Ernst von Glasersfeld.[15]

Constructivism in Science Education

Ever so slowly constructivism progressed from a peripheral way of thinking about knowledge and knowing science to a central theoretical underpinning for science education. In the late 1970s, scholars like Les Steffe had considerable difficulty in gaining acceptance from their peers for applying constructivism to the teaching and learning of mathematics. However, somewhere during the five-year period from 1978-1983 the seeds were sown for constructivism to become a dominant way of making sense of mathematics and then science education. Within the science education community arguments about epistemology were of considerable interest during the latter part of the 1980s. These debates occurred as the community sorted out its perspectives on issues that had been latent in the practices of many. They mirrored the earlier debates that polarized those using Ausubelian and Piagetian psychology to frame their professional activities.

By the beginning of the 1980s research groups from around the world were showing strong interest in children's ideas about science, variously described as intuitive knowledge, alternative frameworks,[16] and children's science.[17] Peter Fensham[18] observed that neo-Piagetians, such as Rosalind Driver,[19] who found the Piagetian criteria for identifying stages of development too rigid and restricting, were developing flexible criteria for examining students' descriptions of science. Others who were not rooted in Piagetian theory used similar research methods to explore the role of prior knowledge in making sense of science. These researchers were concerned primarily with the teaching and learning of science and did not address the ontology of the constructed science. Von Glasersfeld wanted to distance himself from this group and created the term radical constructivism to describe his orientation. He commented that:

A few years ago, when the term constructivism began to become fashionable and was adopted by people who had no intention of changing their epistemological orientation, I introduced the term trivial constructivism. My intent was to distinguish this fashion from the "radical" movement that broke with the movement of cognitive representation.[20]

I was most concerned with teachers learning to teach science and spent considerable time trying to work out what teacher knowledge was and how it could be re-presented and transformed. When finally I decided that constructivism was a useful way to think about learning, I looked in depth at the differences between radical constructivism and other versions of constructivism such as trivial, social, and critical. I wanted to know such details as whether what was being learned was an approximation to a knowable reality and how viability differed from validity. I carefully studied the work of von Glasersfeld[21] in comparison to other research undertaken from a constructivist perspective.

Ontological issues were of importance to me since I wanted to decide for my own research whether to regard knowledge as a social construction mediated by participants from a particular community or an estimate of truth that iterated gradually toward one correct way of knowing. Did it make any sense to argue that there were correct ways to know and do? Or was correctness inherently a matter of social choice? Because I knew and respected von Glasersfeld, my initial tendency was to read, learn, and think about radical constructivism and ascertain the extent to which it was a suitable framework for my praxis. An initial concern was to figure out, from a radical constructivist perspective, how teachers could mediate their students' learning of science. I also wanted to understand how from this perspective teachers could re-present and change teaching. Finally, as I began to adopt the principles of radical constructivism as a foundation for my role as a teacher educator and for the substantive foci of my research on teaching and learning, I began also to adapt my research methods to accord with radical constructivism.[22]

I regard constructivism as a framework for thinking about how students can learn in given situations, how others can mediate in the process of learning, and how artifacts from an activity setting afford opportunities to learn and participate in particular ways. As a way of thinking constructivism can be applied to any activity setting, and questions can be asked about how to change the roles of teacher and students to promote greater learning. Inevitably the use of constructivism as a frame will involve the changing not only of interaction patterns but also the structure of the activity itself. However, constructivism is not only useful as a way to think about managing learning in small classes but can be relevant to learning in any social setting, even to a lecture class in college biology consisting of more than a thousand students. From a constructivist perspective teachers should take account of what students know and what they can do, how students can negotiate meaning and build consensus by interacting with one another and with artifacts, and how students can put their knowledge to the test and receive feedback on its adequacy.

There has been a tendency in teacher education to provide prospective and practicing teachers with methods that are purported to be generically successful in promoting higher learning (e.g., cooperative learning, open-ended questions, and inquiry methods). This is not surprising because many practicing and prospective teachers seem to value recipes for teaching (just as I did when I commenced my teaching career). It is as if there is a best way to teach that transcends all contexts, and people want to know what it is. I have a problem with quests for "master narratives" and use a fishing metaphor to counter requests for recipes. Instead of giving my students the fish they appear to want so badly I attempt to teach them how to fish for themselves. Not surprisingly my failure to give them what they want frequently is met with significant resistance.[23] Often the quest for "methods that work" is subtle. For example, even though I speak about constructivism as a powerful referent for thinking about teaching, learning, and relating to others,[24] people often interpret what I have said as describing a method of teaching that they reject as inappropriate because of the contexts in which they operate. Their reasons usually include the difficulty of using small groups and highly interactive participation of learners, essential characteristics of what they perceive to be constructivist ways of teaching.

In the subsections below I address some of the main ideas associated with the use of constructivism as a framework for learning to teach science (i.e., metaphor, reflection on action, action, and teaching as knowledge in action). My acceptance of constructivism in this way catalyzed research and other scholarly activities in each of the above areas. Finally, I address debates about whether or not constructivism is a useful framework for science education.

METAPHOR

My research focus was on better understanding how prospective and practicing teachers learn to teach and then apply their knowledge to enact a science curriculum. When I returned to the University of Georgia in 1985, I realized that the adoption of constructivism as a theoretical framework necessitated a reconceptualization of most of what I knew about teaching and learning. Von Glasersfeld foreshadows this problem with the comment that "radical constructivism entails a *radical* rebuilding of the concepts of knowledge, truth, communication, and understanding, it cannot be assimilated with any traditional epistemology."[25] A critical breakthrough for me was to recognize that from a constructivist perspective a belief was a form of knowledge considered by an individual or community to be viable. But I was puzzled by the different ways in which individuals could construct knowledge. George

Lakoff and Mark Johnson[26] argued that metaphor was at the root of much of what we know. This idea appealed to me because I was using the oral and written texts of teachers as evidence of their knowledge of teaching. Within a context of interpretive research I was correlating what I learned from the analyses of oral and written texts with field notes based on intensive classroom observations. If the roots of much of what teachers knew were metaphorical, then there was a possibility that insights into the conceptualizations of their roles would be evident in their talk about teaching.

A metaphor can be regarded as a conceptual organizer that aggregates sets of beliefs and also constrains actions in given contexts.[27] What was striking to me was that for more than a decade I had worked with teachers to change discrete practices like wait time, and had experienced the difficulty teachers had in making and sustaining such changes.[28] Yet, in our first study involving metaphor, one of the teachers was switching metaphors and, in so doing, was changing sets of associated actions.[29] Throwing a master switch enabled him to teach in a radically different manner than previously when his actions were constrained by a different metaphor. When a teacher switched from one metaphor for teaching (i.e., captain of the ship) to another (i.e., entertainer), it appeared as if hundreds of practices changed as the new metaphor was enacted. From the perspective of teacher education I was interested to see if teachers could learn new metaphors for teaching and learning, adopt them in their teaching, and thereby make significant changes in their practices. This is precisely what happened and the use of metaphor became a significant tool in my teacher educator toolkit.[30]

I collaborated with teachers to identify the salient metaphors used to conceptualize their most significant roles and to ascertain through reflection the extent to which those metaphors were optimal and consistent with what they believed about teaching and learning. The application of metaphors while teaching occurs at a relatively macroscopic level (i.e., at the level of teacher and student roles) that has the potential for making marked changes in classroom environments. In contrast, reflection on the efficacy of alternative metaphors occurs at more of a microscopic level (i.e., more particularized and at a level of discrete actions) as roles are examined in terms of the constituent practices and their associated beliefs and values. Since many metaphors have textual and image components, they can be accessed conveniently while teaching, thereby making it relatively easy to use them as "seeds" for initiating and sustaining changes in the classroom.

I have had personal experience in constructing metaphors to frame my teaching. For example, some years ago when asked about my beliefs about teaching college science, I realized that I did not have a metaphor to conceptualize my teaching roles. The process of creating a suitable metaphor was protracted in that I related potential metaphors and the associated images to constructivism and practices I regarded as essential to my teaching. The verbal label I gave to my new metaphor was "provocateur." When it was appropriate I preferred to mentally "push and cajole" students in an effort to obtain deeper levels of understanding. In response to questions about this metaphor there was a considerable amount that I could say about the roles of both teacher and students and also about the nature of the learning environment. But as I discussed what I meant by "provocateur" I also accessed an image of the teacher as fencing master. I had in mind a duel in which a fencing master practices with an advanced student. There are times when the master allows the student to attack. At these times the student practices attacking skills and experiences the defense of the master. Then the master attacks. Attacking moves are selected to allow the student to build a successful defense. And so the duel proceeds with the teacher and student having the autonomy to initiate changes to test each other to the limit. There is mutual respect and nobody gets hurt. The student wants to demonstrate competence and is not about to hurt her teacher. Similarly, the fencing master is cognizant of what the student can and cannot do and acts accordingly. Trust is embedded in the metaphor and when the duel is over both teacher and student bow to show their mutual respect. As they remove their masks it is evident that the master and the student are exhausted at the end of a solid workout.

Having constructed this metaphor, I was able to use it as a framework for thinking about teaching and enacting the curriculum. It was relatively straightforward to plan teacher and student roles to cohere with the metaphor. At a later time, when I returned to teach in an urban high school as a researcher-teacher,[31] I once again had to construct a metaphor to constrain the way I interacted with students.

From my first day in the class Nicole caught my attention. Nicole followed the Muslim tradition of wearing a head cover and drew attention to herself with her volatile presence. The day prior to my beginning to teach the class, while I was observing, Nicole initiated a dispute with another female that ended in violence as each swung her fists at the other and tore at her hair and clothing. I did not know very much about teaching in circumstances like these. That incident led to my resolution not to push students to the point of conflict and to adopt a metaphor of being a cork on a stormy sea. I wanted to be sure that any action of mine would not catalyze physical conflict as had happened during my observation. My field notes just prior to the first lesson read as follows:

I will be a cork on a stormy ocean on Monday. They will be the waves, the currents, the winds, and the tides. At times I am certain to be pulled adrift and even under the surface. However, I will be resilient and bob on the surface, following their lead as I find my way toward a destination that is dynamic and probably never ending. I will have more metaphors by the time I arrive in class, but for now this is a reassuring way to think about my roles. I will not be a counter puncher. I will have no weapons. I will be totally responsive. Also I will mediate the learning of individuals whenever the waters are calm.[32]

Once again the use of the metaphor enabled me to monitor my teaching at times when the automatic nondeliberative approaches did not work as intended. At such times I was able to "step back" from practice and think carefully about the context and the most appropriate method of proceeding. For the initial three months of teaching, the metaphor served me well as I navigated my way through the teaching of chemistry in a large inner-city high school. However, as my comfort level with these students and the school grew, I realized that the metaphor had limitations and needed to be adapted to facilitate a more proactive set of teaching roles. I had learned enough to be proactive in my reading of the class and mediating in their participation.

REFLECTION IN AND ON ACTION

Reflection is central to a constructivist perspective on learning. One of the significant parts of testing the viability of knowledge is to examine its coherence with experience and with other concepts. That is, reflection is at the heart of the construction and reconstruction of knowledge. In a context of learning to teach it is essential for teachers to reflect on their teaching and the learning of their students. However, this might be easier to say than do. Reflection in action[33] always seemed something of an elusive goal for me. To think about your teaching while teaching implies multi-tasking and assumes that prospective or practicing teachers can monitor their knowledge in action. I do not regard this as possible or desirable, as my experiences in sports suggest that if you think too much about what you are doing you are certain to lose a close contest! From my perspective, reflection in action is most applicable to teacher education since it allows teaching acts to be reconstructed and serve as objects for reflection. This process can be facilitated by the use of oral and written texts either by teachers working alone or by interacting with others. Self-analysis, using audio and videotapes, also facilitates reflecting in action. However, it is quite important to note that reflection in action involves cognitive objects that may not be directly related to the knowledge enacted while teaching. Thus the objects of reflection can be adapted without necessarily impacting the knowledge of teaching.

Arranging opportunities for reflection in action is a significant part of all teacher education programs in which I have been involved. A constructivist perspective encourages learning from diverse sources and providing social contexts in which individuals can make sense and test their emerging understandings. Learning to teach can be enhanced by making it possible for prospective and practicing teachers to review the oral and written texts of others, to evaluate videotapes of their own teaching, and to view and critique others' teaching, either directly or on videotape.

RADICAL AND SOCIAL CONSTRUCTIVISM

Unlike many of my colleagues, I have always made intact classrooms the principal context for my research. Accordingly, even though my focus on constructivism was initially from the perspective of individual teachers and students negotiating meaning and arriving at consensus, the activities were always radically social. Hence, it was essential for me to include in my ways of thinking about teaching and learning a strong component of social processes. Whereas von Glasersfeld and others could focus on individual cognitions and personal sense-making, the contexts in which I was doing my research necessitated that I understand not only constructions by individuals but also constructions of self and others. Any suitable theory to illuminate teaching and learning has to take into account the presence of others and the manner in which interactions among participants can promote learning.

I did not regard constructivism as a "master narrative" that could be used as the underpinning framework for all other narratives. In the contexts of my praxis I used a constructivist perspective to think through critical issues about teaching and learning and to conceptualize the meaning and place of issues such as power, autonomy, and management in science classrooms. Over a period of a decade, constructivism assumed a central place in a semantic web that focused on issues concerning teaching, learning, and curriculum. My expectations always were that my frameworks for research would evolve, and I was actively seeking a coherent set of theories that would fit into a semantic web and enhance my praxis in science education. As concepts were added to the web, other parts of it were reconceptualized so as to maximize the internal consistency of the constituents.

RESEARCH METHODS

I began to do interpretive research at about the same time I adopted radical constructivism as a general framework for my thinking about teaching and learning. On a visit to Michigan State University I met Fred Erickson, who gave me a copy of his soon-to-be-published chapter on interpretive research in the *Handbook of Research on Teaching*.[34] I had already decided to change my approach to research because of my dissatisfaction with the inability of quasi-experiments and process-product research to explore what I considered to be the big problems in science education. The key people who shaped my thinking in science education, such as Mary Budd Rowe, were maintaining that it was useless to do research on variables such as wait time until we had figured out how assessment and reward schedules shaped the curriculum. I wanted to employ a methodology that would provide me with the tools and flexibility to explore the most significant issues and enable me to learn from my research. Interpretive research appealed because it was grounded in a long tradition of theory, and its methods were very reminiscent of what I had experienced as a physicist. Unlike the way physics is described in many written accounts, my experience was that we spent the great majority of our time trying to answer big questions associated with what is happening and why is it happening. Highly controlled experiments were only a small part of my experience in the laboratory when problems were explored, as distinct from the contrived laboratories undertaken in course work toward my physics degrees.

My journey into interpretive research was an adventure because, at the time, there were few researchers employing ethnography in science education. I collaborated with Jim Gallagher to apply Erickson's interpretive research to make sense of high school science. As is evident in the first studies we undertook, the changes in methods were slow to occur and rather than a revolution to ethnographic methods the changes can be regarded historically as an evolution.[35]

The initial methodological problem I had to address was a lack of coherence between my radical constructivist framework for the substantive research questions and the theoretical underpinnings of the methods I employed in my research. I felt liberated in being able to employ an emergent design to address issues that had salience to the contexts in which the study was being conducted. However, I was unconvinced about the purposes of triangulation and uncomfortable with the idea that the actors had a better understanding of why they did what they did than others in that community (including the researchers). A significant challenge for me was to work out how the methods of interpretive research could be adapted to cohere with my changing beliefs about knowledge and reality. My own version of qualitative inquiry over a 15-year period reflects the use of radical constructivism as a frame and the gradual incorporation of social theories of knowing and learning. I was learning by doing and figuring out what to do within my own research group. Although there was considerable activity elsewhere within the science education community in terms of the applications of constructivism and qualitative methods, I was not particularly influenced by those trends because of the distinctiveness of the substantive foci of my research. My interests in teacher education, teacher learning, and curricular change required me to think beyond alternative frameworks and the use of Piagetian-style methods to explore them. Furthermore, the differences between radical and trivial constructivism, in terms of ontology, were becoming important distinctions within the university community at Florida State University where I was located.[36] For the time being at least I was determined to work out how best to do research so as to find answers to critical issues associated with teacher learning and change, and also to describe my experiences in ways that would bring different problems to the fore. There was little time for me to critique the work of other groups and my chief goal in reading the literature and in attending sessions at public meetings was to identify kindred spirits from whom I could learn and extend my efforts within science teacher education.

Although I now cite the 1989 work of Egon Guba and Yvonna Lincoln[37] I was not aware of *Fourth Generation Evaluation* until about 1994 when my colleague Wolff-Michael Roth began to cite their work.[38] Prior to that I had written several papers describing the evolution of interpretive research and had taken a hand in teaching others how to incorporate multiple approaches into a smorgasbord of methods to use in addressing the critical issues in science education. Notably, I wanted research to be educative and transformative for the participants, not just for the researchers. When I learned of fourth generation evaluation, I was able to incorporate some of its refreshing perspectives on ontology and the necessity of preserving the voices of peripheral participants in research. My thinking about research was beginning to be shaped by the idea that commensurability and coherence may not be as important in the social sciences as they are in the hard sciences. I began to view myself as a bricoleur creating a bricolage consisting of a variety of methods and diverse voices of the participants in my studies. Finally I was learning to re-present the diversity of research as well as its central tendencies.

The concept of action is a critical part of teacher knowledge and teaching. Just what did I mean by action when I asked, for example, what actions are occurring and what do these actions mean from the perspectives of the actors? The meaning of action was elusive for a number of years as I undertook research in classrooms and explored its theoretical underpinnings from a constructivist perspective.[39] Because I regarded an understanding of action as essential to describing and changing teaching, I wanted to know about action in a deep way, not just to be able to define it in a sentence or a paragraph. From a social constructivist perspective I concluded that action is a holistic entity that can be described in a variety of ways. I conceptualized actions as: a set of behaviors, a set of associated beliefs and values that provide a warrant for those behaviors being considered viable in the contexts in which action is to occur, the constructed context for the action, and a set of the actor's goals. Thus, in the circumstances perceived to exist, an action is an enactment of knowledge, a complex whole that incorporates what a teacher knows and values.[40]

Knowing about action also makes it clear that learning to teach involves much more than learning from written and oral texts and having convictions about what to do to facilitate student learning. How the context is constructed always will be a significant component of action. Accordingly, it is imperative that prospective teachers have assignments that require them to identify the most salient parts of the contexts in which curricula are enacted. Having prospective teachers undertake ethnographies of their own and others' teaching can provide insights into the significance of context and the manner in which a variety of factors can shape learning environments.

A cautionary note is warranted here. The constructivist perspective led me to think of action in a rationalistic way and to almost totally ignore the significance of knowing as doing. My point in mentioning this here is to emphasize that as theory affords it also obscures. In bringing to the foreground issues of behavior, belief, and value, the idea soon developed that action was rational and deliberative. Later theorizing was to radically change my perspectives on how best to think about teaching and teacher change. These issues are addressed later in the chapter in a section focusing on communities of practice.

DEBATES ABOUT CONSTRUCTIVISM

Throughout the late 1980s and the 1990s there were debates about the usefulness of constructivism in science education.[41] The debates mirrored some of the earlier disputes within science education, such as clashes between those ascribing to Piagetian and Ausubelian ways of making sense of science education.[42] Initially I was interested in the conversations because my expectation was that scholars within different disciplines such as history, sociology, philosophy and science could collaborate and co-generate appropriate foundations for science education. However, I soon perceived this as an unlikely outcome. Several conferences on the history and philosophy of science and science teaching held over a period of more than a decade failed to produce the hoped-for consensus, providing instead forums for staking and defending claims. Those opposing constructivism seemed to have legitimate and well-intentioned concerns, but their critiques were, for the most part, lacking in detailed analyses and did not provide alternatives that would yield fresh research questions and the associated implications for practice. Rather than basing a critique on a set of articles and books, or uses of constructivism within the field, some critics seized the opportunity to attack constructivism without presenting evidence of having read a representative amount of the work of the individuals and the ideas they were attacking. Too often the critiques were based on analyses of the use of single words and sentences from one text.[43] Whereas "member checking" is at the heart of the research methodology I employ, there was a reticence on the part of those critiquing constructivism to check to see if they had a viable understanding of the perspectives they were critiquing. "Do I have your perspective right?" It seems as if asking this question and making sure that it is answered in the affirmative is a necessary prerequisite to scholarly critique. Re-presentations of the perspectives of those using constructivism did not employ member checks and tended to trivialize those perspectives. Furthermore, word-by-word and line-by-line analyses were not convincing when the authors regarded the meaning as constituted in entire texts or collections of texts. In the absence of viable alternatives from the opponents of constructivism, I regarded the best source of alternative theories to be co-researchers seeking to solve similar problems to those I regarded as salient. Accordingly, I did not participate in the debates and focused instead on the substance of my research, which was to improve the quality of science teaching and learning.

Communities of Practice

I wish now to describe in five stages an evolution toward the recognition of the significance of learning in communities. In the period I have been discussing (1980s and 1990s) the chief goal had shifted from endeavoring to better understand cognitive processes of individuals to one of enabling groups to be better able to participate in science. The shift reflected a radical departure from a focus on the learning of individuals to a focus on social and cultural phenomena.[44] However, rather than rejecting radical constructivism as a theoretical framework, the evolution involves the addition of coherent perspectives to enhance the interpretive capacity of my research. The process is driven by the problems encountered worldwide by reform-oriented educators seeking to enhance science education. For my own part the most significant challenges are associated with learning to teach science and enacting curricula that are appropriate for diverse learners. The following sections discuss co-participation and learning, teaching as knowledge in action, a vignette that describes my experiences in teaching low-track students in urban settings, and an interpretation of those experiences in terms of the extent to which my knowledge of teaching is applicable across contexts.

CO-PARTICIPATION AND LEARNING

The enduring problems in science education will not be solved with theoretical formulations that focus primarily on the sense that individuals make of ideas and a rationalistic model of beliefs and values shaping actions. A radically social way of thinking about teaching and learning is needed. Science teaching and learning may be viewed as forms of enculturation into a discourse community.[45] The New London Group regards "discourse" as a sociocultural and political entity that subsumes ways of saying, writing, doing, being, valuing, and believing.[46] A discourse facilitates communication and establishes social and cultural identity within a community. Two broad types of discourse exist: primary discourses (learned in the home) and secondary discourses (associated with communities one might later encounter). Teaching and learning of science are considered to occur in evolving communities of practice in which the discursive practices (e.g., talk, writing, cognition, argumentation, and re-presentation) of participants are constantly changing. The catalysts for change are interactions between participants and social structures such as conventions and norms.[47]

Given the appropriate conditions, in which particular interests in a group are supported, learning about science can lead students to develop an increasingly science-like discourse. An important criterion is the extent to which students can use their discursive resources to make sense of their experience and support claims with evidence. According to Angela Calabrese Barton, "the experiences of everyone need to become part of the language of science if the experiences, beliefs, values and essence of all people are truly to be incorporated into science."[48] Henry Giroux suggests that when students begin with their language—the language that they speak at home and in the streets—they are more likely to develop literacy skills that are the foundation for developing more canonical, mainstream discourses.[49] For this to happen students must have opportunities to apply what they know and, as necessary, make adjustments while working at the elbows of others who know science, are aware of its conventions, and can provide the necessary scaffolds to mediate appropriate changes in the shared discourse. However, there is a tendency for the primary discourses of children from homes of the working class or unemployed not to connect well to a scientific discourse.[50] Accordingly, teachers often enact the curriculum for such students to emphasize the learning of scientific facts and to de-emphasize conceptual learning, inquiry and scientific habits of mind.[51] Tendencies such as these can support the types of inequities that are all too common in science education. It is imperative, therefore, to identify teaching strategies to address possible inequities in the learning of students.

To paraphrase David Ausubel, on entry to a course a teacher should find out what students know and can do and teach them accordingly.[52] This premise implies that a teacher should assist students to find resources to connect from what they know and can do to what they need to know and be able to do. There always will be differences of opinion about the purposes of class time, how much learning needs to be done in class, and how much must be done out of class time. It is fine for teachers to adhere to their beliefs about such matters as long as they identify the most appropriate resources to support the learning of students in and out of class. Identifying the resources, and making it clear how and when to access them, is an initial step toward enhancing the learning of all students. Ways to improve instruction and learning cannot be regarded as generically applicable to all circumstances. The details of how to afford enhanced teaching and learning must be worked out for every possible context. Whatever those contextual details it is an imperative that all learners co-participate in the community to build knowledge of science and how to do it. Co-participation necessitates each student accessing and appropriating a discourse that leads to his or her attainment of the goals for the course. Co-participation implies access to others who already know and can do, including instructors, tutors, students from previous years, and peers. Approaches to teaching and learning that embrace co-participation can vary markedly in terms of the way students are organized and managed. All learners need structure, a scaffold to get from where they are to some place else. Some learners can provide their own scaffolds by reading books and accessing resources that they know about from their own lifeworlds, but others cannot provide the necessary structure and are more dependent on teachers in class, tutorials, and individual assistance during office hours. If teachers are sensitive to the need for all learners to have structure to support learning, then they can find opportunities to mediate learning in ways that make sense to them.

An issue that arises is the need for teachers to take into account the multiple frameworks that students carry with them to class. That might be easier said than done, particularly when classes are very large. However, whether or not teachers consider what the students bring to class as capital, constructivism assumes that the students themselves have no choices. They must use what they know and can do as a foundation for building their understandings of the science they are to learn. At any level, but particularly in high school and in college-level science courses, it is imperative that students access multiple resources to support their own learning. These can include books written by different authors and peer tutors.

TEACHING AS KNOWLEDGE IN ACTION

As a theory of knowing, constructivism must address the issue of how particular types of knowledge can be constructed. Teacher educators are obviously concerned with facilitating the learning of how to teach. Consequently, my search for a theoretical framework for my praxis in science education focused on teaching as a way of knowing.

In many respects teaching is analogous to participating in sports. I have known since I was a child that there is a great difference between the knowledge needed to play tennis and the written and oral texts associated with playing tennis. Usually I learned to play tennis by practicing with my coach and peers or hitting against a wall. At times oral instructions were used to let me know when my participation was and was not appropriate. However, to learn tennis required hours of practice and, until I reached a high level of skill with a particular stroke, I did not apply the stroke in competition. Conversations before and after practice or competition often resulted in new practice regimes; however, the learning always occurred by doing and it was evident from my performance whether or not I had learned.

The knowledge of teaching that is of importance is what is enacted in specific teaching and learning contexts. Particular teaching strategies depend on context in much the same way as context can determine how well tennis is played. For example, a strong backhand may not win points against all opponents, on all court surfaces, and in all weather conditions. Similarly, particular teaching strategies are unlikely to be successful for all students, grade levels, and schools. Just like planning a strategy for a tennis match, conversations and pre-planning can produce teaching plans that are considered appropriate. However, whether or not they *are* appropriate cannot be known until the plan is enacted. During teaching, knowledge is enacted and can be adapted to attain instructional goals within the unfolding events of the classroom.

Being able to speak and write about a teaching strategy or to conceptualize it in terms of a metaphor does not imply that the teaching can be enacted in ways that are coherent with the conceptualization. Envisioning teaching in a particular way, or describing strategies using language, enables teaching to become the object of critical reflection. However, when individuals speak about teaching they are speaking about reconstructions, and the knowledge that is teaching is not the object of the discussions and reflective analyses. Reflection enables the use of particular strategies to be encouraged, some to be targeted for change, and others to be dropped from a recommended repertoire. To teach in accordance with those plans arising from reflection involves knowledge in action. Although it is possible for a teacher to teach in ways that are consistent with the plans, at least to the level of a family resemblance, it also is possible that what happens will be quite discrepant from the plans.

Plans can serve as frameworks for enacting a curriculum. However, what happens when a teacher enacts a curriculum depends on what that teacher customarily does, the details of the plan, and the extent to which the students facilitate teaching as planned. Physical aspects of the school also can facilitate or inhibit teaching in particular ways. Just as oral and written texts, metaphors, and images of how to play tennis are not transformed into tennis performance, neither are similar knowledge forms pertaining to teaching transformed into teaching performance. Learning to teach necessitates practicing in authentic ways to build particular knowledge and skills. Subsequent application of the knowledge in action always is mediated by the social conditions that pertain to the settings in which teaching and learning occur.

Co-teaching, which occurs when two or more teachers teach a class together, is an activity that can support learning to teach. Within the context of student teaching I have begun recently to arrange for co-teaching to occur,[53] not only at the beginning of student teaching but throughout that experience so that a learner-teacher has opportunities to "become like the other" through co-participation. During co-teaching it is advantageous to have close at hand an experienced teacher who knows how to teach effectively in a particular context so that his or her teaching allows a learner-teacher to experience directly successful and responsive teaching. For example, if the learner-teacher does something that is not optimal the co-teacher can quickly (and seamlessly) act in a compensatory way, providing images of practice and opportunities for the learner-teacher to stand back and reflect on what does and does not work. In this way a learner-teacher not only learns by doing but also has opportunities to experience the teaching of others as it is enacted and how it is responsive to the unfolding events of the classroom. Although co-teaching situations create opportunities for reflective discussions after the teaching has happened (and to stand back and reflect during a lesson), opportunities also are provided to learn through co-participation those aspects of teaching that are beyond language. What is salient in this learning situation is that the knowledge of teaching, as it is enacted, is adapted *in situ*—as distinct from the reconstructed knowledge that is adapted during reflective analyses that occur after teaching has occurred.

Is it necessary for a teacher educator to be able to teach effectively in order to mediate others' learning to teach? I do not think so, although I do believe it is essential to put claims about teaching to the test. In my own case I found that much of what I had learned over the years was difficult to apply in inner-city schools populated mainly by African American students. The knowledge I had gleaned from reading research and theory and from my own practices as a high school and college teacher did not seem viable in urban science classes. When practicing and prospective teachers adopted my suggestions to solve classroom problems they had identified, they appeared unable to enact my recommendations and the problems were unresolved. I was faced with a growing realization that the contexts associated with teaching and learning in urban schools were radically different from those pertaining to most research and the literature on science education. Hence I decided to experience those contexts directly and put my knowledge of teaching science to the test in an urban high school class.

TEACHING LOW TRACK STUDENTS FROM AN URBAN HIGH SCHOOL

The following vignette provides a description of my thoughts immediately prior to commencing to teach chemistry and physics in the low track of a large urban high school in which the students were primarily African American from communities characterized by poverty. Resistance to the enacted curriculum was evident from the outset. For several days I had observed the classroom teacher teach the class and the following excerpt from my field notes reflects my thinking the evening before I was to assume primary responsibility for teaching:

The inevitability of Monday is looming. I have plan A but what are plans B, C, D and E as successive efforts end in failure? Pessimistic? No. I am determined to be successful and I am a believer in having alternatives. To be constructed as teacher I will have to earn their respect and the process will not be short. I must be sincere, friendly, persistent and present. I cannot be there only when it suits me and I cannot take the view that this is only research and hence it does not matter what happens to the students. No. My agency is that I must be there for them and have their learning and welfare as my paramount interests.

When I wrote the narrative I was optimistic that I would be successful. To me success lay in being well prepared. I knew that while I was teaching I would not have the time to come out of action to reflect on what was happening. I did not need lists of ideas against which to check the progress of my teaching. I knew that my knowledge of teaching would carry me forward and only when things went wrong would I need a plan to guide future actions. Hence, I constructed a metaphor (i.e., a cork in a stormy ocean) to quickly refocus or constrain my actions as needed. However, I did not predict the extent to which the resistance of students would be a major obstacle to my teaching. My efforts to raise the demands of the curriculum were resisted strenuously by the students.[54]

It has been more than five months since I took over the responsibility for teaching these low-track students. In that time I have tried many things and most of them fall short of what I expect. I adapt and always try to lift the bar on my expectations. Ever so slowly I am learning how to cope with the class, finding ways for my knowledge of teaching to make a difference to the learning of my students. From my perspective there is no real rush to be successful because I have made a four-year commitment to learn to teach students like these. But to say that I am challenged may be the greatest understatement I have ever made. My knowledge of teaching and self-identity as teacher have been shaken as I realize that years of teaching elsewhere did not prepare me for these learners and these contexts. Also, my reading of the literature on urban education, including Lois Weiner's book on *Preparing Teachers for Urban Schools*, only alerted me to some of the critical issues.[55] I was not ready to teach these students when the regular classroom teacher completed some instructions to a restless class, glanced at me, and with a gesture of his hand said: "Dr. Tobin—." From that moment, it seems, I was on my own.

The first class wasn't so bad because I had a lab planned and the students enjoyed the chance to engage in new ways. But when I came in with a follow-up lab the next day I was surprised by their resistance to engage in serious inquiry. From then on the struggle has continued in earnest as I have learned what it means to say "these students need structure." Telling me about the issues, or reading about them, would have been of little value. In fact, each day when I come to class I learn in a deeper way what it means to provide structure for a class that consists of African American students, mainly from homes characterized by poverty and instability, and with chronic patterns of failure and irregular attendance. Mostly I have to struggle alone and experience the failure of my teaching to make a positive difference to the learning of most students. Fortunately there are occasions when I co-teach with the regular classroom teacher and I am able to step back and watch him try different approaches. Although most of what he tries also is unsuccessful, his teaching is a resource for me to learn how to be a more effective teacher for these students.

What are sensible ways of thinking about what happened during my teaching of chemistry and then physics to these high school students? Constructivism? Perhaps to a limited extent, but I need more theoretical tools to figure out what is going on and how I can turn my learning of how to teach here into a success story for the students whose lives I want to transform through education. Constructivism cannot serve as a unifying theory to apply as a solution to all problems. As a way of thinking constructivism is taken for granted. I do not think of it explicitly any more. I have moved on and think of teaching as knowledge in action and learning as a social process that occurs through co-participation in communities.[56]

Since the contexts in which I was teaching science were radically different from those in which I had previously taught, it was essential that I adapt what I knew and could do as a teacher. When my knowledge was not equal to the task, the rupture in action was evident to me and I had to step out of action to reflect on what I was doing and what was best to do next. Videotapes showed my lack of flow and the uncertainty that I experienced as my knowledge broke down in my efforts to enact a curriculum that was resisted by most students in the class. The goals and motivations of the students did not fit readily with my own plans and, as a consequence, there were times when I did not know how to proceed. It is apparent that my knowledge of teaching is not generalizable to the circumstances in which I have been teaching. What I know from my experience as a high school science teacher (in the 1960s and 1970s), more than 30 years of doing research in science teaching, and a long history of teaching in universities is not viable in the classrooms of my most recent experience. Through research on my own teaching practice I expect to identify new ways to think about teaching and learning and, by continuing to teach, to construct strategies to enhance science learning for students like those I have been teaching this year. My evolving knowledge also will facilitate my roles as researcher and teacher educator.

Conclusion

As a way of thinking, constructivism became pervasive in science education, and as the contexts for its applications diversified other theoretical frameworks were appropriated to address a multitude of problems that emerged and persisted. Initially the number of science educators using constructivism as a theoretical frame was few, but gradually a majority came to apply it. Critics raised issues about the limits to its potential applicability and users elaborated what they meant by constructivism and through its applications in diverse contexts expanded its meanings. Now, as the trajectory of practices has continued to evolve in the community, it is easy to see the trace of constructivism and also to observe that scholars who are in the front line of the community have moved on. The critical mass of science educators are still making sense of their praxis in terms of constructivism, but in a short time we will be in another theoretical epoch. It is essential that our theoretical frameworks evolve to create new ways to conceptualize problems and expand the associated horizons of potential solutions that promise enhanced learning for all and social reformation for those seeking liberation through science education.

Some readers may wonder about the metaphor of "moving on" to describe my trajectory as a science teacher, teacher educator, and researcher. "Moving on" might be considered treason to earlier cherished ideas. Yet the hermeneutic sciences, and postmodern scholars, have been telling us that texts and experiences are continuously interpreted and reinterpreted in the light of new understandings. Thus, each time we develop some understanding, it not only changes our current horizon but also the way we understand past research, texts, and experiences. "Moving on" then does not constitute an abandonment of a theoretical frame that once was central to my practices as a science educator. Constructivism is an important part of my learning trajectory, and as a metaphor it is axiomatic in my thinking about the teaching and learning of science. As an axiom, however, constructivism is the ether for an expanding constellation of theories that illuminate my praxis in science education.

NOTES

1. Jean Piaget, *The Psychology of Intelligence* (Patterson, New Jersey: Littlefield Adams and Co., 1966).

2. James R. Okey, "Consequences of Training Teachers to use a Mastery Learning Strategy," *Journal of Teacher Education* 28 (1977): 57-62; Russell H. Yeany, Jr., "Effects of Microteaching with Videotaping and Strategy Analysis on the Teaching Strategies of Preservice Science Teachers," *Science Education* 62 (1978): 203-207.

3. Joseph D. Novak, "The Reception Learning Paradigm," *Journal of Research in Science Teaching* 16 (1979): 481-488.

4. Howard L. Jones and J. Michael Russell, "Hierarchical Learning Paradigm," *Journal of Research in Science Teaching* 16 (1979): 489-499.

5. Anton E. Lawson, "The Developmental Learning Paradigm," *Journal of Research in Science Teaching* 16 (1979): 501-515.

6. Joseph D. Novak, "Editorial Comment on 'Implications of Piagetian Research for High School Science Teaching: A Review of the Literature'," *Science Education* 62 (1978): p. 591.

7. J. Dudley Herron, "Role of Learning and Development: Critique of Novak's Comparison of Ausubel and Piaget," *Science Education* 62 (1978): 593-605.

8. Anton E. Lawson and John W. Renner, "A Quantitative Analysis of Responses to Piagetian Tasks and its Implications for Curriculum," *Science Education* 58 (1974): 545-559.

9. Joseph D. Novak, "Application of Advances in Learning Theory and Philosophy of Science to The Improvement of Chemistry Teaching," *Journal of Chemical Education* 61 (1984): 607-612.

10. Julie S. Vargas, *Writing Worthwhile Behavioral Objectives* (NY: Harper and Row, 1972).

11. Kenneth Tobin, "A Four Phase Model for Activity Oriented Science: K-10," *Australian Science Teachers Journal* 28, no. 3 (1982): 63-71; Kenneth Tobin, "Teaching Strategy Analysis Models in Middle School Science Education Courses," *Science Education* 69 (1985): 69-82.

12. Kenneth Tobin and William Capie, "Teaching Process Skills in the Middle School," *School Science and Mathematics* 80 (1980): 590-600.

13. Kenneth Tobin, "Teaching Strategy Analysis Models in Middle School Science Education Courses," *Science Education* 69 (1985): 69-82; Russell H. Jr. Yeany, "Effects of Microteaching with Videotaping and Strategy Analysis on the Teaching Strategies of Preservice Science Teachers," *Science Education* 62 (1978): 203-207.

14. Tobin, "Teaching Strategy Analysis Models."

15. Ernst von Glasersfeld, *Radical Constructivism: A Way of Knowing and Learning* (Washington, DC: Falmer Press, 1995).

16. Rosalind Driver, "Pupils' Alternative Frameworks in Science," *European Journal of Science Education* 3 (1981): 93-101.

17. Roger Osborne, "Conceptual Change—for Pupils and Teachers," *Research in Science Education* 12 (1982): 25-31.

18. Peter J. Fensham, "Science Education Research: Present and Future," *Research in Science Education* 9 (1979): 1-4.

19. Rosalind Driver and Jack Easley, "Pupils and Paradigms: A Review of Literature Related to Concept Development in Adolescent Science Students," *Studies in Science Education* 5 (1978): 61-84.

20. Ernst von Glasersfeld, "Questions and Answers About Radical Constructivism," in *The Practice of Constructivism in Science Education*, ed. Kenneth Tobin (Hillsdale, NJ: Lawrence Erlbaum Associates, 1993), p. 24.

21. Ernst von Glasersfeld, "The Concepts of Adaptation and Viability in a Radical Constructivist Theory of Knowledge," in *New Directions in Piagetian Theory and Practice*, eds. I. Sigel, D. Brodzinsky and R. M. Golinkoff (New Jersey: Lawrence Erlbaum Associates, 1981), pp. 87-95; Ernst von Glasersfeld, "Cognition, Construction of Knowledge, and Teaching," *Synthese* 80 (1989): 121-140.

22. Kenneth Tobin, ed. *The Practice of Constructivism in Science Education* (Hillsdale, NJ: Lawrence Erlbaum and Associates, 1993).

23. Kenneth Tobin, Gale Seiler, and Mackenzie W. Smith, "Educating Science Teachers for the Sociocultural Diversity of Urban Schools," *Research in Science Education* 29 (1999): 68-88.

24. Tobin, ed. *The Practice of Constructivism in Science Education.*

25. von Glasersfeld, *Radical Constructivism: A Way of Knowing and Learning*, p. 19.

26. George Lakoff and Mark Johnson, *Metaphors We Live By* (Chicago: The University of Chicago Press, 1980).

27. Kenneth Tobin, "Changing Metaphors and Beliefs: A Master Switch for Teaching," *Theory into Practice* 29 (1990): 122-127.

28. Kenneth Tobin, "The Role of Wait Time in Higher Cognitive Level Learning," *Review of Educational Research* 57 (1987): 69-95.

29. Kenneth Tobin, Jane Butler Kahle and Barry J. Fraser, eds. *Windows into Science Classrooms: Problems Associated with Higher-Level Learning* (London: Falmer Press, 1990).

30. Kenneth Tobin and Sarah LaMaster, "Relationships Between Metaphors, Beliefs and Actions in a Context of Science Curriculum Change," *Journal of Research in Science Teaching* 32 (1995): 225-242.

31. Kenneth Tobin, Gale Seiler and Edward Walls, "Reproduction of Social Class in the Teaching and Learning of Science in Urban High Schools," *Research in Science Education* 29 (1999): 171-187.

32. Fieldnotes 1/8/99

33. Donald Schön, *The Design Studio* (London: RIBA Publications Limited, 1985).

34. Frederick Erickson, "Qualitative Research on Teaching," in *Handbook of Research on Teaching* (3rd Ed.), ed. M. C. Wittrock (New York: Macmillan, 1986), pp. 119-161.

35. Kenneth Tobin and James J. Gallagher, "What Happens in High School Science Classrooms?" *Journal of Curriculum Studies* 19 (1987): 549-560.

36. Grayson H. Wheatley, "Constructivist Perspectives on Science and Mathematics Learning," *Science Education* 75 (1991): 9-21.

37. Egon Guba and Yvonna S. Lincoln, *Fourth Generation Evaluation* (Newbury Park, CA: Sage Publications, 1989).

38. Wolff-Michael Roth and Anita Roychoudhury, "The Social Construction of Scientific Concepts or the Concept Map as Conscription Device and Tool for Social Thinking in High School Science," *Science Education* 76 (1992): 531-557; Wolff-Michael Roth and Anita Roychoudhury, "Physics Students' Epistemologies and Views about Knowing and Learning," *Journal of Research in Science Teaching* 31 (1994): 5-30.

39. Campbell J. McRobbie and Kenneth Tobin, "Restraints to Reform: The Congruence of Teacher and Student Actions in a Chemistry Classroom," *Journal of Research in Science Teaching* 32 (1995): 373-385.

40. Ibid.

41. Beverley Bell, Malcolm Carr, and Alister Jones, "The Development of the Recent National New Zealand Science Curriculum," *Studies in Science Education* 26 (1995): 73-105; Michael R. Matthews, "Constructivism and Science Education: Some Epistemological Problems," *Journal of Science Education and Technology* 2 (1993): 359-370.

42. Novak, "Editorial Comment on 'Implications of Piagetian Research for High School Science Teaching: A Review of the Literature'," 591; Herron, "Role of Learning and Development," 593-605.

43. Wallis A. Suchting, "Constructivism Deconstructed," *Science and Education* 1 (1992): 223-254.

44. Wolff-Michael Roth, *Designing Communities* (Dordrecht, The Netherlands: Kluwer Academic Publishers, 1998).

45. William W. Cobern and Glen S. Aikenhead "Cultural Aspects of Learning Science," in *International Handbook of Science Education*, eds. B. J. Fraser and Kenneth Tobin (Dordrecht, The Netherlands: Kluwer Academic Publishers, 1998), pp. 39-52.

46. The New London Group, "A Pedagogy of Multiliteracies: Designing Social Futures," *Harvard Educational Review* 66 (1996): 60-92.

47. Wolff-Michael Roth, *Authentic School Science: Knowing and Learning in Open-inquiry Science Laboratories* (Dordrecht, The Netherlands: Kluwer Academic Publishers, 1995).

48. Angela C. Barton, "Liberatory Science Education: Weaving Connections Between Feminist Theory and Science Education," *Curriculum Inquiry* 27 (1997): p. 155.

49. Henry Giroux, *Border Crossings: Cultural Workers and the Politics of Education* (New York: Routledge, 1992).

50. Mary Atwater, "Social Constructivism: Infusion into the Multicultural Science Education Research Agenda," *Journal of Research in Science Teaching* 33 (1996): 821-838.

51. Jean Anyon, "Social Class and School Knowledge," *Curriculum Inquiry* 10 (1981): 55-76; Jay L. Lemke, "Analyzing Verbal Data: Principles, Methods, Problems," in *International Handbook of Science Education*, 1175-1190.03.

52. David P. Ausubel, *Educational Psychology: A Cognitive View* (New York: Holt, Rinehart and Winston, 1968).

53. Kenneth Tobin, Gale Seiler and Mackenzie W. Smith, "Educating Science Teachers for the Sociocultural Diversity of Urban Schools," *Research in Science Education* 29 (1999): 68-88.

54. Tobin, et.al., "Reproduction of Social Class in the Teaching and Learning of Science in Urban High Schools."

55. Lois Weiner, *Preparing Teachers for Urban Schools: Lessons from Thirty Years of School Reform* (New York: Teachers College Press, 1993).

56. Wolff-Michael Roth and Kenneth Tobin, "Toward an Epistemology of Teaching as Practice," *Journal of Research in Science Teaching* (1999, submitted).

CHAPTER IX

Constructivism and Learning Research in Science Education

RICHARD F. GUNSTONE

It is a trite but important observation that works claiming to be some form of constructivist consideration of classrooms, either research or description of practice, have been extraordinarily abundant in the last decade. For example, a search of ERIC at the beginning of 1999 using the specific phrase "constructivist classroom" produced well over two thousand items; an Internet search at the same time yielded well over one thousand. Those items uncovered in this simple search ranged across the whole spectrum of age groups and curriculum possibilities: kindergarten to post-baccalaureate teacher education, mathematics to creative writing, physical science to dramatic arts. And one Internet search using the more general term "constructivist" resulted in well over sixteen thousand items. A scanning of just a small number of these suggests that there are no areas of human activity to which the label "constructivist" is not currently being applied in some form!

This chapter has a somewhat more restricted focus. It is concerned with discussing, illustrating, and assessing both the impact of constructivist ideas on classroom research and the ways this research informs classroom practice. I will also consider some of the critiques directed at constructivism. All this will be done within the context of science education. The reasons for restricting consideration to this area alone are simple: Science education studies employing constructivist practice began considerably earlier and have been more numerous than is the case for other curriculum areas; concerns with the classroom implications of the research and the impact of classroom experience on research have been central to much of the science education work (and, particularly, most of the early work which has subsequently been an influence on other researchers). It is important to the

Richard F. Gunstone is Professor of Science and Technology Education in the Faculty of Education at Monash University in Clayton, Victoria, Australia.

development of arguments in this chapter to consider the basis for these two assertions, as well as the broad nature of the way the research has developed in science education contexts. Initially I do this in general terms and then, in the next section, consider some specific examples of long-term research programs.

The first wave of those investigations related to science classrooms that might well now be called constructivist focused on explorations of the ideas children held about natural phenomena. These investigations have therefore had, from earliest times, a concern with specific concepts or content or phenomena. Such investigations go back at least to G. Stanley Hall in 1880.[1] More substantive beginnings are in the works of Jean Piaget, in part in the adoption of his clinical interview methodology by many later science education researchers[2] but also in the use of Piaget's data and inferences about children's understandings of natural phenomena. While it is clear that Piaget's concerns in his research were not focused on classrooms, it is also certain that some of the research in science education that derived from Piaget was motivated by concerns with the quality of learning and teaching in science classrooms. There was a surprising number of such studies conducted prior to 1950.[3] However, this focus disappeared from science education research through the 1950s and 1960s, and the earlier work (other than that of Piaget) was forgotten.

The current concern with what are now described as constructivist explorations of science classrooms began in the early 1970s and has continued to grow almost exponentially ever since. It is contentious to select a single study as marking the beginning of this dramatic growth, but many researchers would point to the doctoral study of the late Rosalind Driver.[4] This influential study focused on the thinking and reasoning of young science students involved in a program that reflected the then current concern with discovery learning. It demonstrated both the nature of the ideas about natural phenomena that children brought to the study of these phenomena in science classes, and the influence of these ideas on the learning of individual children. Central to the interpretations and conclusions of this study was the significance of the concepts or content that students were to learn. Driver's concerns with thinking and reasoning were in terms of specific concepts or phenomena, not with broader patterns of intellectual reasoning. Her study was explicitly located in the context of the children's usual classroom and curriculum, and was concerned with the nature of the classroom experience and its relationships with the nature of children's learning in specific areas of science. As will be illustrated in the next section, the research programs that developed around the world soon after Driver's thesis appeared commonly had their origins in similar classroom concerns. Three influential interpretive reviews of the emerging research field published in England in the late 1970s and early 1980s[5] also included considerations of various aspects of the relationships between this research and the nature of science curriculum, teaching, and learning. Research-practice relationships were one significant dimension of all three reviews, and all showed clearly the ways in which researchers at that time saw the content to be a significant variable in the study. These concerns with the classroom implications of the research and the impact of specific content on student learning have remained a common focus among most of the large number of researchers[6] who have followed.

So science education research that today often describes itself as "constructivist" is extensive and commonly has classroom concerns as a main focus. The essential purpose of this chapter is to consider this research and to explore the nature of the constructivist ideas that researchers assert underpin their work. This chapter has two major sections. In the first, the nature of this research—its classroom concerns and the theoretical underpinnings claimed by the researchers—is illustrated through consideration of the work of three major and long-lived research groups on the world stage: University of Leeds (England), University of Waikato (New Zealand), and Monash University (Australia). Each of these groups has research programs in this area that have existed for over twenty years and have had considerable influence in the wider research community. In all three, the beginnings of the research programs were very much rooted in concerns with demonstrated weaknesses in the nature of individual students' science learning in school (and university) classrooms. The groups have had substantial contact with each other from the very early days of their activity, although as is shown below there are also differences among the groups. In the second major section, these examples—and other perspectives and contexts relevant to science education—are considered in terms of some of the critiques brought against constructivism.

Programs of Research into Science Learning

For each of the examples of research programs I attempt to show briefly something of the approaches adopted, the ways these research programs have developed, the consistent concern with classroom science learning as motivating and often directing the research, and something of the evolving theoretical links in the programs. Two significant and interrelated points will be shown to be common to all three groups and, because of the influence of these groups on the field, to have influenced much of this research over the last twenty years: (1) constructivism as it is elaborated today *was not a central initiating theory for any of these groups*; (2) the motivations of these researchers were derived from classroom concerns with the quality of student learning in science.

There is today a widespread view within science education (and outside) that constructivism has been the dominant theoretical influence shaping the field over the past decade or more. The two points above refute this view. Rather, science educators have been driven by problems noted in science classrooms and have used theoretical positions derived from areas other than constructivism to guide their explorations of these problems. They have not been driven by theory, rather they have been users of theory; their research has not been concerned with the philosophic debates about forms of constructivism that are today common. A further significant point, to which I return later in this section, is that their concerns have been to have students better learn the concepts of science. This point clearly refutes arguments sometimes advanced today that this field of research has seen as acceptable relativist epistemologies of science, and the learning of "concepts" and "explanations" different from those of science.

There are many sources to support the foregoing statements; perhaps two of the most interesting are reports of invited research seminars held in Ludwigsburg (Germany) in 1981 and Leicester (United Kingdom) in 1982. The Leicester participants included essentially all the then significant groups or individuals working in this field from the English-speaking world other than the United States; the Ludwigsburg participants included essentially all the then significant groups or individuals from mostly continental Europe and some from the United States. These two reports attempted to reflect something of the processes of the seminars rather than to be only polished products, and thus they are important historical records of thinking in the broad research field at this time. The report of the Leicester seminar[7] is particularly useful here as it contains considerable analysis and synthesis of the individual papers, in addition to summaries of the papers. The report describes the purpose of the Leicester seminar clearly:

In recent years there has been a marked increase in studies of the alternative 'frameworks of thought' that learners bring to the interpretation of what they meet in school science. The principal purpose of this meeting was to review critically the methods being used in such research, and their theoretical basis.

Some of the questions we had in mind in setting it up were: If learners have alternative and perhaps unexpected ideas, e.g. of what heat is . . . How do they arise? How do they change? Are some more resistant to change? Can changes be followed and described? How do the feelings about the subject matter, and about oneself, affect the structure of ideas, and its capacity for change? What are the consequences for research, and teaching?[8]

The basis for invitation to the seminar reinforces these purposes: "All are interested in children's thinking—or what is going on inside kids' heads . . . All also share an interest in content-related conceptual development, rather than in general intellectual development."[9] In the analysis of the seminar, the researchers and their work are considered in terms of intentions, methods, types of representations of results, theories about learning that the researchers draw on (with the obvious and central point also made that these are not independent, nor are the relationships between them static). The synthesis of intentions is revealing:

1. To identify students' alternative frameworks, which are then communicated to teachers, curriculum designers, etc.;
2. To understand how students try to make sense of their world and/or the scientists' world;
3. To develop improved teaching methods;
4. To provide alternative study methods for learners;
5. To test or refine theory, or gather evidence for particular positions.

Both the purposes for the seminar and the analysis of intentions show clearly the prime source of motivation for these researchers to be concerns with the quality of science learning in classrooms. This is not at all to suggest that the researchers were utterly pragmatic, or unconcerned with theory and its role in their investigations. However, these were not researchers driven by theory; they were informed users and developers of theory.

This analysis is given strong support by the section in the seminar report that discusses the nature of the theories on which the researchers draw. This shows that only two co-authors of one paper directly and explicitly drew on a theory to direct their research—the "Personal Construct Theory" of George Kelly.[10] For the other researchers theory is described in terms of "influence" rather than "direction." Writers cited in this way are all from the broad area of cognitive psychology and information processing. The report asserts that "[d]ifferences of approach [by the various participants] are not readily explained by adherence to a particular theory,"[11] an analysis that, with the exception of the work based on Kelly, is today still clearly supported by the positions of the researchers. A further point of relevance here is that there is only *one point* in the report where the word "constructivist" is used (in a summary of a contribution by Driver and Erickson, an early working paper of what later became their influential review.)[12]

The general picture that emerges from the Leicester report then is one of research motivated by classroom concerns, and largely directed towards understanding learning in order to improve the quality of science learning and teaching. (And, in passing, one of the questions in the statement of purposes above—"How do the feelings about the subject matter, and about oneself, affect the structure of ideas, and its capacity for change?"—shows that even in those early days the impact on science learning of noncognitive issues was a concern for researchers. This concern is still evident in much work today.) The role of theory, for most of this important group of researchers, was much more to support their research and aid interpretation than to drive the research. The most obvious reason for this is found in the report of the Ludwigsburg seminar.

The report of the Ludwigsburg seminar consists largely of reproductions of working papers, and thus does not provide the broader analyses and syntheses that characterize the Leicester report. However, an introduction by the German researcher Walter Jung gives an important perspective on the group of researchers and their motivations, a perspective that also applies to the Leicester participants:

First of all, we are—with one exception—not professional psychologists, but from our scientific rearing we are physicists, chemists and mathematicians. We got interested in problems of the teaching of science in secondary schools, and some of us have many years of teaching practice within these subjects. . . . [O]ur prime interest is in better learning of physics and chemistry in secondary school, which implies, of course, better teaching.[13]

Jung's statement shows the origins of the concerns with science learning for this group; a similar statement for the Leicester group would also have been correct. The prime motivations of the researchers at both these seminars derived from their own professional experiences as teachers of science and, for a number, their then-current roles as lecturers in methods of teaching science in preservice teacher education programs.

A reading of the papers in the Ludwigsburg report is also illuminating in terms of the theoretical positions asserted by the researchers. At no point in the 450-page report, I believe, is the word "constructivist" used. For those who were indeed science educators with professional concerns underpinning their research motivations, the references used to embed their work are from other science educators, cognitive psychologists and information processors, researchers concerned with problem solving, Piaget (never in a constructivist sense, always in the context of stages of intellectual development), and many non-English sources. As was the case for the Leicester group, theory for these researchers served to support rather than to direct their research and to aid interpretation. And again as for the Leicester group, the theories used in this way are not the theoretical positions that today might be used in a consideration of the origins of "constructivism."[14] The theories are a blend of cognitive psychology and information processing, problem solving, and evolving interpretations of the data of other science educators. The publications referenced in the two influential reviews that appeared in 1983 (see Note 5) show similar patterns, but with even less emphasis on the literature from cognitive psychology.

In summary, these two research seminars involved almost all the influential groups and individuals active in the world at the time. The reports of the seminars show most of these early researchers to be mostly motivated by concerns and insights from professional (and often extended) teaching experiences, to be therefore strongly concerned with research-practice linkages, and it is reasonable to assume that as a consequence they had what I would term an informed pragmatic perspective on theory. That is, the researchers understood well the importance of defensible theoretical positions to the framing of their methodologies and approaches and to the interpretation of their results. But theory did not initiate their research; these were never theoretical ideologues. Given the conspicuous absence of explicit reference to "constructivism" in the two reports, it is interesting that today these same researchers so commonly use "constructivism" in their writing and are so widely labeled "constructivist."

I now turn to examples of extended research programs promised in the introduction. For each, the nature of the underpinning theory that is elaborated by the researchers will be considered (where relevant for issues of both learning and epistemology), as will the origins of the research. Substantially greater consideration is given to the Leeds group and Driver because of Driver's central role in the development of these research and research-practice perspectives, and because the conclusions drawn for Driver's research will be quite similar to the conclusions drawn about the other programs. There is an obvious caveat to place on the following discussion—the publications that are considered as representative of the evolving positions of each of the research groups are my selections, not those of the research group.

THE LEEDS PROGRAM (ENGLAND) AND ROSALIND DRIVER

Rosalind Driver began her professional career as a high school physics teacher in England. She was appointed to Leeds in 1974 after completing doctoral work at the University of Illinois. As well as directing extensive funded research over many years (most notably the Children's Learning in Science Project), she was a central figure in the science component of the first national assessment project in England (the Assessment of Performance Unit, 1979). This work was a significant influence on her research, as was her continued close collaboration with many science teachers. A major component of her funded projects was always the development of approaches for working with teachers to consider research findings and their implications for science classrooms and curricula. In the last decade of her life she expanded her work to consider issues of student progression in conceptual understanding (again including extensive concern with implications of the research), students' perceptions of science and the impact of these on their learning, and the broad issue of scientific literacy. All these activities have an obvious link—Driver's motivations were very much for improved learning and teaching of science, seeking improvements that were firmly rooted in understandings of science learning. The need for improvement in learning and teaching was demonstrated by the work of her group (and many others) which showed the inadequacy of science learning in many contemporary classrooms.

Issues of Learning. The views of learning that underpinned Driver's work are clear from her publications, and, as one would expect for such a significant researcher, they evolved over time. In her doctoral thesis she argued the then radical position that students' interpretations of phenomena were for them coherent frameworks of ideas derived from interpretations of their experiences rather than "mistakes" resulting from their inability to learn. She also argued that student learning was dependent on already-existing ideas held by the student rather than being limited by the level of intellectual development of the student. With this work she sought to draw theoretical links to the then emerging field of information processing, as well as to supporters and critics of Piagetian stage theory, and to views of the nature of scientific knowledge.

In her doctoral research she studied a science class over an extended period of time as the students engaged with the learning tasks provided by the teacher. These tasks focused on investigations of phenomena. Her data sources included detailed observation of this engagement, discussions in groups of students, interactions between the groups and the teacher, and records of students' work. Her subsequent research also made extensive use of student interviews and collaborative development work with science teachers.

A fundamental aspect of her doctoral research was the nature of the concept or content to be learned—how students engaged with this content, how this impacted on their learning and approaches to learning, and how their understanding of the content evolved through class experiences. These issues remained at the core of her later work.

In a significant paper published in 1981[15] Driver presented her thinking about learning of science at that time. Importantly, she concluded this paper with "Implications for classroom practice," making four points that are summarized here:

1. In organizing learning experiences science curriculum development needs to consider the structure of the child's thinking as much as considering the structure of the discipline. The specific content is significant rather than Piagetian operations.
2. The logical order of a topic derived from views of the structure of the discipline may not correspond to appropriate psychological order of learning.
3. Activities in the science classroom should allow opportunity to disprove alternative interpretations as well as to affirm accepted views.
4. Students need opportunities to consider the implications of observations and measurements. "We must realize that our explanations do not spring clearly from the data."[16]

The view of learning to be inferred from these points is one quite consistent with the issues raised in the discussion of the Leicester seminar—that students come to science classrooms with ideas about natural phenomena, and that these ideas will determine the learning that occurs (whether or not one considers them in one's teaching); teaching and curriculum, therefore, should be informed by these ideas and their significance for learning. There is the unequivocal message in these four points that the purposes of science teaching are to have students develop an understanding of the concepts and terms of science. Driver's essential orientation was to have learning and teaching focused on the ideas of science, *not* on seeing the ideas students bring to classrooms as having science value in their own right. While there is no doubt of the central significance seen by Driver (and all other researchers in this field) for the ideas and beliefs students bring to the study of science, for Driver the chief focus is the learning of science, *not* the science to be learned. This, as we shall see, remains a constant thrust in her writing about classrooms and student learning.

I now consider her two significant papers published in 1986, one with a focus on student learning, the other on science curriculum development.[17] The research from which the papers are derived is of the same form as previously detailed—studies of student learning relevant to particular content in real classrooms, and explorations of the learning consequences of alternative approaches. The learning paper begins with a view of science (discussed below when issues of epistemology are addressed), and then describes a "constructivist view of learning" through elaborations of a set of six assertions that focus on examples of student learning of specific science content. The paper concludes:

In summary, a constructivist view of learning emphasizes:
1. Learning outcomes depend not only on the learning environment but also on the knowledge of the learner.
2. Learning involves the construction of meanings. Meanings constructed by students from what they see or hear may or may not be those intended. Construction of a meaning is influenced to a large extent by our existing knowledge.
3. The construction of meaning is a continuous and active process.
4. Meanings, once constructed are evaluated and can be accepted or rejected.
5. Learners have the final responsibility for their learning.
6. There are patterns in the types of meanings students construct due to shared experiences with the physical world and through natural language.[18]

The list is different from, yet consistent with, Driver's 1981 publication described above. The six assertions are a fair representation of the kinds of assertions that became very common in reports of science learning studies from the late 1980s. They focus on learners and their learning, not on the *purposes* of teaching and learning. The section "Implications for Science Education" strongly reinforces these six assertions. The explicit use of "constructivist" as a description for such assertions has become very common in reports of science learning research. However, the references to "constructivist" in this paper by Driver are only to other science education researchers, not to a wider "constructivist" literature.

In the paper focused on curriculum development, Driver makes a clear and significant statement of the purpose of her major research program of the 1980s, the Children's Learning in Science Project. To appreciate the significance of the statement, it is necessary to briefly consider a term that is almost emblematic of science education research—"conceptual change." Most science learning researchers have for the last two decades described their views of learning as at least *involving* "conceptual change," while some have described learning as *being* "conceptual change." Central to this view is the belief that when students come to science classes with ideas and beliefs that are at odds with the conceptions or explanations of science ("alternative conceptions"), it is appropriate for science educators to seek to change those conceptions. When science education researchers debate the nature and processes of "conceptual change,"[19] they are mostly debating ways students come to accept the scientific conception or explanation. Driver and Oldham write:

It is the purpose of the Children's Learning in Science Project to attempt to undertake . . . a reconsideration of the teaching of science in secondary schools. Specifically the central aim of the research programme is to: *devise, implement and evaluate teaching materials and strategies which attempt to promote conceptual change in selected topic areas.*[20]

Clearly, the essential concern of this researcher and her group was to understand ways to improve how students learn the *science of scientists*. This is strongly reinforced by the five components given in a constructivist teaching sequence that has been widely used by researchers and some curriculum developers. These components are: (1) Orientation; (2) Elicitation of students' ideas; (3) Restructuring of ideas through four stages—clarification and exchange of ideas, exposure to conflict situations, construction of new ideas, evaluation of new ideas; (4) application of ideas; (5) review of change in ideas (through comparison with previous ideas, from 2). The unequivocal intent of the sequence is that students will, through the nature of the experiences provided by the teacher, construct the relevant ideas of science. "Whether or not this has happened, the teacher will present and explain [the scientific view] at some point, providing opportunities for pupils to construct meanings for it by empirical tests, and language activities."[21]

In this paper on curriculum development, Driver makes a number of references to theorists who provide the underpinning to the approaches elaborated. These references include other science educators, cognitive psychologists and information processors, and constructivist writers from outside science education.

The final selections from Driver's writing to be considered here are both from 1994. One is a book chapter, the other a widely cited paper from *Educational Researcher*. The book chapter[22] reports on a classroom in which teacher and students work through a unit on rusting designed to reflect constructivist views of learning. The unit of work was planned together by the researchers and the classroom teacher, and it was based on what was known about the nature of the relevant alternative conceptions students would likely bring to the class. The chapter reports the classroom transactions and student work resulting from this planning and the chapter concludes with a consideration of "Teaching Science from a Constructivist Perspective." In this discussion epistemological issues are raised in terms of their importance to the science learning of students "developing a new rationality for knowledge"—one that values the generalizable explanation over the contextually dependent particular explanation and that demands internal consistency of theories. That is, the raising of epistemology here is solely in terms of issues that students need to accept if they are to understand and believe the explanations of science in preference to alternative explanations that they may have already constructed. Other points in this discussion reinforce the view that the fundamental purpose of Driver's research in this field has consistently been to develop better quality learning of the concepts of science in science classrooms.

The second 1994 publication, the paper in *Educational Researcher*, includes the following in its abstract:

This article, which presents a theoretical perspective on teaching and learning science in the social setting of classrooms, is informed by a view of scientific knowledge as socially constructed and by a perspective on the learning of science as knowledge construction involving both individual and social processes.[23]

As this extract makes clear, the paper considers both epistemology and learning. In discussing learning issues and theory, Driver articulates the links between the science education research of the last twenty years and that of Piaget; both view learning as individual and constructive; that is, the individual constructs meaning based on his or her existing knowledge (schemes). Driver's subsequent consideration of learning science as social construction of knowledge is important. It is a continuation of a consistent theme through her writings of the significance of social interaction about concepts during the learning of science, a theme seen in the approaches to research she adopted and the approaches to curriculum and to alternative classroom experiences that she used. In this 1994 paper she argues the significance of social construction for learning, not just in terms of this interaction fostering and influencing the construction of individual meaning, but also in terms of the ways this can foster the learner's introduction into the conventions and symbolic world of science. It is social construction and its impact on the nature of learning that is crucial in discriminating constructivist classrooms from "discovery learning" classrooms. In what is usually meant by discovery learning there is an underlying assumption that the experience that is provided is the essential vehicle for student learning. This is insufficient. In Driver's 1981 paper considered above, she makes essentially the same point in a different way and in a different context: "Activity by itself is not enough. It is the sense we make of it that matters."[24] This is also a common perspective of other researchers in science education.

The concluding summary of Driver's 1994 paper makes clear the complexity of the relationships between research and practice. The extract below is preceded by statements about the significance of the constructions students bring to classrooms, the impact on these constructions of the broader culture in which the students live, and the epistemological and ontological differences between "everyday" and scientific reasoning.

If everyday representations of particular natural phenomena are very different from scientific representations, learning may prove difficult. We have argued that the relationship between views of learning and pedagogy is problematic, and that no simple rules for pedagogical practice emerge from a constructivist view of learning. There are, however, important features of the mediation process [between everyday and scientific representations] that can be identified. If *students are to adopt scientific ways of knowing*, then intervention and negotiation with an authority, usually the teacher, is essential. (emphasis added)[25]

This position, which recognizes the complex and problematic links between research and practice, is broadly shared by the other research programs discussed below. It is not, however, shared by all researchers who would cast themselves as constructivist. As a consequence, some constructivist science education researchers have made claims about the classroom implications of their work that, because of unreasonably simple views of the research-practice relationships, I regard as extravagant and unsupportable.

The issue of epistemology has been raised at a number of points in the above discussion of Driver's research. This issue has significant linkages with arguments common today about constructivism and its current apparent popularity in science learning research. The relevance of epistemology to this chapter is foreshadowed in a statement made at the beginning of this section: ". . . [the researchers'] concerns have been to have students better learn the concepts of science. This point clearly refutes arguments sometimes advanced today that this field of research has seen as acceptable relativist epistemologies of science, and the learning of 'concepts' and 'explanations' different from those of science." The arguments referred to in this statement are of the form represented by the following:

The common constructivist move is from uncontroversial, almost self-evident premises stating that knowledge is a human creation, that it is historically and culturally bound, and that it is not absolute, to the conclusion that knowledge claims are either unfounded or relativist.[26]

I attempt to show below that these arguments are *not* reasonable interpretations of either the ways most science learning researchers have considered the epistemology of science, or of their motivations for this consideration. Whether or not constructivist epistemologies are an appropriate interpretation of science is *not* relevant here. What is relevant is that science education researchers have considered and discussed epistemological issues in terms of their relevance to understanding the learning and teaching of science. Their fundamental concerns that students learn better the science concepts advanced by science make it clear that suggestions of their advocating a view that all knowledge claims have equal status (a relativist epistemology) are quite unreasonable. I now support this position by considering again Driver's research and writing.

Issues of Epistemology. In her doctoral research Driver was concerned with issues of the epistemology of science, and this concern remained throughout her work. In the 1994 *Educational Researcher* paper the essence of Driver's views is clear:

Any account of teaching and learning science needs to consider the nature of the knowledge to be taught . . . The objects of science are not the phenomena of nature but constructs that are advanced by the scientific community to interpret nature . . . The point is that, even in relatively simple domains of science, the concepts used to describe and model the domain are not revealed in an obvious way by the "book of nature." Rather they have been invented and imposed on phenomena in attempts to interpret and explain them, often as results of considerable intellectual struggles.[27]

As a very simple example of the issues being argued here, even in "relatively simple domains of science," consider the fact that in Australia signs are placed at all freeway entrances stating "Animals not allowed past this point." The scientific meaning of the term "animal" is totally inconsistent with this directive, yet no one stops at these signs to consider whether they should enter the freeway. Living with a social definition of "animal" that is contrary to the scientific definition is not difficult for scientists or lay people. However, even in this trivial example, there are issues for the teaching and learning of science. If the purpose in teaching the scientific conception of *animal* is no more than to have the class reproduce a definition on a test, then there is no problem. But if the intention is to have the class understand the logic underlying the science definition and to see why scientists find value in this conception (and thus have students able to use the scientific conception when appropriate), then a very different content and teaching approach are needed. The simplistic view of the nature of scientific knowledge and the consequent simplistic approach—such as the mere learning of that definition—have been shown in endless studies of science learning to be that adopted by many students in many classrooms where the logic and value of the scientific conception has not been part of the teaching and assessment of learning.

While my animal example is extremely simple, the underlying principle is fundamental to understanding the ways many researchers on science learning see the links between learning and the nature of the knowledge to be learned. It is, among many significant issues, an understanding that the complexity of science knowledge needs appropriate recognition in teaching. Much of current science teaching, learning, and assessment ignores this complexity, with poor forms of student learning being the very common consequence.

The fundamental links between learning and epistemology that I see for Driver, and many other researchers, are these: Since science is a complex human construction, the learning of science must accept and accommodate this; a simple (and unsupportable) positivist view of science as empirical and unproblematic in any way, which is a fair characterization of much of the tacit epistemology of some school science, is utterly incompatible with what we now know about the learning of science. Driver may appear to make an exception to this view in a reference to the radical constructivist Ernst von Glasersfeld in the 1986 curriculum development paper. However, this reference is in a discussion of learning, not epistemology, and is in the context of an argument that learners can only "check" their knowledge by considering the extent to which their constructions fit their experience in a coherent and consistent way. Whether or not one should see this as indicating a relativist view of science knowledge has been the subject of some passing debate. However, it is not relevant to the links between epistemology and learning that are at the heart of Driver's concerns, as she makes clear in the paper in *Educational Researcher*:

Whether or not a relativist perspective is adopted, however, the view of scientific knowledge as socially constructed and validated has important implications for science education . . . Scientific entities and ideas, which are constructed, validated, and communicated through the cultural institutions of science, are unlikely to be discovered by individuals through their own empirical inquiry . . . This perspective on pedagogy, therefore, differs fundamentally from an empiricist perspective.[28]

Most constructivist science educators share the position that epistemology and learning should be seen as linked in order to better understand how to assist students to learn and value the concepts of science, but a constructivist view of learning does not imply a relativist epistemology. These researchers are not philosophers of science; they are users of philosophy of science in the pursuit of better learning and teaching of science.

THE WAIKATO GROUP (NEW ZEALAND)

Roger Osborne, the founder of this group, was an accomplished and experienced high school physics teacher in New Zealand, author of a widely used physics textbook and an examiner of final-year school physics in the national system. He was appointed to the Physics Department at the University of Waikato in the 1970s because of his teaching expertise, an unusual appointment, particularly given that this Physics Department was a very small one. His doctoral research was not the form of learning study for which he later became so well known, although his concerns for the quality of physics learning and teaching were central throughout his teaching career. His first "constructivist" work occurred during his first sabbatical leave, which he spent with John Gilbert at the University of Surrey. There Osborne and Gilbert developed the first form of a methodology which he used throughout his research—an interview approach that focused on either a series of instances or non-instances of a given concept, or on a series of events that all would be explained by scientists with the same concepts and patterns of reasoning. The book for which he is probably most widely known, *Learning in Science: The Implications of Children's Science*,[29] contains many examples of the methods and results of this methodology, and substantial discussions of the implications of this research for science classrooms. The work of the Waikato group has been extensive and wide-ranging in its focus on science learning, teaching, and teacher development. Osborne's fundamental motivation for the research program was, as for Driver, concern with the inadequacy of much science learning, and a consequent need to improve the quality of science learning and teaching. As with Driver, Osborne's motivations and those of his group and successors derive from extensive experience in teaching science, and the central purpose of his work was to evolve approaches that would lead to better student understanding of science.

Although Osborne's early writing makes reference to people such as cognitive psychologists and information processors, it does not seek to make any extensive links with theoretical positions. He was deeply concerned about the need for underpinning theory to guide his research.[30] This led him to a collaboration with the cognitive psychologist M. C. Wittrock at the University of California Los Angeles that resulted in a theoretical position which saw learning as a "generative process."[31] While this position is clearly consistent with the ways "constructivism" is currently used, it draws heavily from work in cognitive psychology and science education. This position guided Osborne's thinking until his death in the 1980s, and continued to influence the Waikato group under its subsequent leadership.

The nature of the links between epistemology and learning are also seen by the Waikato group in ways similar to Driver's. A chapter written by members of the group in 1994[32] provides a clear example. The basic purpose is to argue implications of constructivist perspectives seen by the group for science content and pedagogy. It begins with a description of what are asserted to be common views of science among science teachers (assertions with which I agree). These views suggest that scientific knowledge is unproblematic and is comprised of objective truths discovered via observation and experiment. The remainder of the

Waikato group's chapter is a powerful analysis, based largely on the concepts of floating and sinking, of the ways in which such views necessarily lead to inadequate teaching and thus inadequate learning. The essential argument is that recognition and accommodation of the complexities of scientific knowledge is necessary for students to understand science concepts and explanations. The same positions on conceptual change that permeate Driver's work were also central to the Waikato group.

One of the major concerns of the members of the Waikato group for a number of years has been the school science curriculum and the implications for the curriculum of their work on learning, on teacher development, and on the nature of scientific knowledge. In common with many researchers in this field, they see curriculum development as including development of teachers' thinking and actions in order that the curriculum perceived by students may also change.[33] A new curriculum for New Zealand school science that was developed in the early 1990s embraced some of the ideas of the Waikato group.[34]

THE MONASH GROUP (AUSTRALIA)

The origins and early thinking of the Monash group, which began in the late 60s, have been described elsewhere[35] including a discussion of broader contexts for the early work of the members, and so are only briefly outlined here. This group differs from the two previously discussed in that it formed slowly as a number of already active Monash researchers with common concerns but different starting points found their thinking converging in the mid-to-late 1970s. The common concerns were with the poor quality of science learning and the development of appropriate alternative approaches to teaching and learning with subsequent exploration of the consequences. All these researchers had developed these concerns from their previous extensive science teaching experience and their work in preservice teacher education; their different starting points also reflected the different theoretical positions that were being used to guide their existing work.

This group describes its formation in a number of ways. Of particular relevance here are their concerns that science learning should be of worth for all students, and the realization that a shift from a teacher perspective to a student perspective was required in the research stance. This shift in stance led the group to substantially move away from experimental research paradigms that focus on "treatments."[36] One significant consequence of this shift for the group has been extensive collaborative work with teachers, motivated by concerns both for the researchers' work to impact on classrooms and for the research to reflect, at least in substantial part, the concerns of science teachers.

In the 1980s much of the group's work involved explorations of conceptual change in students, conducted both in science classrooms and in teacher education programs, with the group considering parallels among students, teachers, and researchers in attempting to understand conceptual change. A major and closely related thrust that emerged at this time was a concern with metacognition, a thrust that continues to be central to their work today. Their view of metacognition is multi-faceted and based in classrooms; in brief, it refers to knowledge about, awareness of, and control of one's own learning. These are both outcomes of learning (and thus can be changed by learning experiences) and influences on approaches to and outcomes of current learning tasks.[37] This position derives from the work of J. R. Baird,[38] who, in investigating the learning of undergraduate biology students and high school science students, found a range of "poor learning tendencies."[39] For Baird and the rest of the Monash group these are seen as deriving from students' ideas and beliefs about learning and about the assessment of specific learning contexts. In science learning, for example, students who believe that it is the teacher's responsibility to provide them with understanding are unlikely to undertake the personal effort often needed to grasp abstract concepts, especially when they must reconcile the science explanation with a conflicting belief of their own. As a consequence, the Monash group over the last fifteen years has also been closely involved in work whose purpose is to understand how to develop more appropriate metacognition among learners.[40]

The initial theoretical positions of the Monash group prior to the start of their "constructivist" work have already been noted as various. As the group's work became more cohesive, some have had the development of theory about the classroom learning of science as one of their central concerns. Richard White's writings clearly show the evolving nature of theory for the group over the last twenty years: a blend of a range of positions on information processing and the inclusion of Piagetian concerns (but not stages of development), always in the context of science learning in "real" classrooms.[41]

The thinking of this group that relates to science content per se has been less directly concerned with epistemological issues than is the case for the Leeds and Waikato groups, although it is clear that acceptance of similar epistemological issues is important to their views of learning and teaching science. The Monash group's concerns have been more in terms of the implications of this research for the purposes of teaching science,[42] the appropriate sequencing of content,[43] and attempts to evolve a "theory of content" that predicts the properties of content that matter for different areas of science teaching and learning.[44]

A VIEW ACROSS THESE THREE GROUPS

The three groups considered in this chapter have significant common features. In all cases the origins of, and motivations for, their research have been very much rooted in concerns with the quality of science learning, concerns arising from their experiences as science teachers and from their initial research. Finding that students commonly continued to interpret situations using "old" ideas that were often at odds with the concepts and explanations of science, researchers in the three groups responded similarly. They sought to understand more about learning and the impact of particular science content on this learning in order to develop alternative approaches to science teaching, and they consistently involved practicing science teachers as collaborators.

The theories that have guided this work have often not been those that are today commonly labeled constructivist. In all cases the theories of information processing that have emerged in educational psychology over the last thirty years have been central. While today it seems that the statement "individuals construct their own understanding" is almost emblematic for science education researchers, at the time of the Ludwigsburg and Leicester seminars many researchers believed with David Ausubel that "The most important single factor influencing learning is what the learner already knows. Ascertain this and teach him accordingly."[45] The development of classroom-based research on the learning of science over the last three decades can reasonably be seen in terms of substantial advances in approaches to "ascertaining" what learners already know and substantial advances in what this implies about "teaching learners accordingly." The statement "individuals construct their own understanding" is by itself of little use in considering the complexity of fostering science learning. However, the adaptation of information processing to consideration of science classroom learning has led to significant advances in understanding this complexity, and in teasing out at least some of "ascertain" and "teach accordingly." Researchers today would want to add *and believes* after "what the learner already knows."

If one looks beyond emblematic statements and considers more specific theoretical statements, then there is still no clear evidence of explicit constructivist theory influencing the development of research in science teaching and learning. The single work of most influence on the development of this field is probably the first articulation of a theory of conceptual change by George Posner et al. (See Note 19.) This theory has been developed and restructured in various ways by different groups, but its significance for directing the ongoing field of research has been major.

Of course, it might be argued that this view is a function of the particular three groups considered here. However, the same broad conclusions come from a similar analysis of the research motivations, research methods, and theoretical links for many other influential individuals and groups—for example, Hans Neidderer and his group at the University of Bremen, Joseph Novak and his group at Cornell, David Treagust and his group at Curtin University of Technology (Australia), Lillian McDermott and her group at the University of Washington, and Reinders Duit, John Clement, David Brown, and Audrey Champagne. There are significant differences in the details of the motivations, approaches, and positions of these groups. Although this is true also for the three groups considered in this chapter, these differences do not detract from the broader commonalities asserted here.

Given all this, it may seem an obvious question to ask why these researchers so often use the term "constructivist." On the other hand, given the ways in which constructivist ideas have emerged in an extraordinarily wide range of educational writings over the same time period in which research in science education has undergone major growth, it would be much more surprising if this were not the case. In terms of their fundamental positions about learning, those science education researchers who focus on classroom learning of science are clearly "constructivist." In terms of their fundamental positions on the purpose and value of learning in various forms of cognitive class discussions, they are "social constructivists." Their uses of these terms as broad descriptors for their work reflect the common use of these terms in the literature.

One further point reinforces the argument that these researchers do not have particular forms of constructivism directing their work in ways that would differ by form of constructivism. It involves the work of von Glasersfeld, a radical constructivist. One of a number of statements he has given about this position is:

[F]rom the naive commonsense perspective, the elements that form [the] complex environment [of the student] belong to a *real* world of unquestionable objects, as *real* as the student, and these objects have an existence of their own, independent not only of the student but also the teacher. Radical Constructivism is a theory of *knowing* which, for reasons that have nothing to do with the teaching of mathematics or education, does not accept this common sense perspective. Instead, it takes seriously the no less venerable suggestion that what a teacher sees when he or she looks at a student is necessarily part of the particular teacher's experience and, as such, the result of the particular teacher's ways and means of perceiving and conceptualizing what is being perceived . . . Superficial or emotionally distracted readers of the constructivist literature have frequently interpreted this stance as a denial of "reality."[46]

As is clearly suggested by the last sentence, "radical constructivism" has been contentious and hotly debated in the literature, most obviously because of the epistemological issues implied. However, this debate is not relevant to my point here. What is relevant is the way in which von Glasersfeld is often cited in science education literature. Even a casual inspection shows that, at the very least, a substantial number of citations are to nothing more than the ubiquitous statement "individuals construct their own understanding." That is, there are a number of researchers in science education who describe themselves as "constructivist" who apparently do not discriminate between "radical constructivism" and less contentious positions. While this may not be a sensible stance, it certainly shows that a particular form of constructivism is not driving their thinking.

Some Critiques of Constructivist Research in Science Classrooms

Constructivist science educators have a relativist epistemology.

This critique links with the position of "radical constructivism" mentioned in the previous section. In essence, the criticism is that by adopting what is a relativist view of learning, constructivists are compelled to adopt a relativist view of knowledge. It is also sometimes asserted that this position is shown by the writings of some researchers in science learning about the nature of science knowledge (as discussed above for the Leeds group and mentioned in passing for the other two). A useful starting point in considering this critique is a statement made by Jeremy Kilpatrick, in which he argues there are two quite different principles which can be involved in a constructivist view:

Knowledge is actively constructed by the cognizing subject, not passively received from the environment. [and] Coming to know is an adaptive process that organizes one's experiential world; it does not discover an independent, pre-existing world outside the mind of the learner.[47]

The first of these two points is today very widely accepted (and, as already noted, it is seen by science educators to include the impact of a range of forms of context and to be more than an individual process). The second point is more widely debated, sometimes with passion (in the science education literature at least). However, this second point actually impinges very little on research on the learning of science, or the implications researchers claim for classrooms from their work. As argued above, these issues of epistemology are taken up by science educators in terms of exploring the complexities of science in order to better inform the learning and teaching of that science. Science education researchers seek to generate better-quality learning and teaching of the concepts accepted by science, not to explore alternative concepts for students to learn. One consequence of this argument, then, is that the position of radical constructivists has had a relatively minimal impact on research in science education. The most prominent writer in radical constructivism, von Glasersfeld, comes from the context of mathematics and mathematics education. It seems to me no accident that there has not emerged a similar figure in science education.

The products of research in constructivist science education are no more than good teaching.

My first reaction to this critique is to ask, with feeling: if this is the case, why would it be a problem? Good teaching (which must be taken to imply quality learning by students) is after all at the heart of the reasons researchers investigate classrooms. Even so, where the consequences of this area of research include "good teaching," it is good teaching based on a position sufficiently informed so as to provide explanations for that good teaching. As a result, the good teaching has possibilities for transfer (across classrooms, across teachers, across content) that is demonstrably not the case for good teaching not so informed by research.

Constructivist practices are not new; they are contemporary versions of the views advocated by Dewey and subsequent progressives.

I probably should not respond to this critique as I have no claims to be a scholar of Dewey and progressive education. However, there is at least one clear difference between progressive positions and the work of constructivist science educators. That is the central significance for the constructivist of the specific content being considered. This is a necessary consequence of the ways learning is influenced by those ideas and beliefs held by the student that the student sees as relevant to what is to be learned. To the constructivist the assertion that learning should be "active" or "child-centered" is by itself of no more value than the isolated assertion "individuals construct their own understanding." As already noted, the value of constructivist considerations in science classrooms lies in the ways in which the implications for specific content of "individuals construct their own understanding" have been unpacked. The interaction between learners' ideas and beliefs relevant to what is to be learned and the "activity" that is intended to result in that learning has not at any time been an issue for the progressive movement in the ways that it is central to constructivists.

One link between science constructivists and Dewey that has been as yet little considered is Dewey's conception of reflection[48] (usually seen in terms of reflective teaching practice) and the issue of metacognition and its relation to quality learning. Dewey outlined three attitudes as important in an individual predisposed to reflect—open-mindedness, whole-heartedness, responsibility—and he described five elements of reflective practice—suggestions, problem, hypothesis, reasoning, testing. These map well onto both the ways science constructivists have described teaching sequences (e.g., Driver's "Constructivist Teaching Sequence" outlined above) and the ways in which metacognition has been argued to be significant to quality learning.

Constructivist practices are just discovery learning again.

A quotation from Driver already noted in this chapter—"Activity by itself is not enough. It is the sense we make of it that matters."—indicates clearly the profound ways in which constructivist research and thinking about science education differ from discovery learning. The centrality to constructivists of considering how students think about the concepts to be learned and of fostering genuine intellectual engagement as a necessary component of quality learning is a long way from the notion that the provision of appropriate experience will lead to the desired student learning. There may be a superficial linkage between discovery learning and constructivism in that both are inclined to use terms like "active"; however, activity for the constructivist must involve intellectual activity. This has no necessary links with discovery learning.

NOTES

1. Hall's stated purpose in this work was to establish "an inventory of the contents of the minds of children"; see S. S. Colvin, *The Learning Process* (New York: Macmillan, 1911), p. 84.

2. See, for example, A. L. Pines et al., *The clinical interview: A method for evaluating cognitive structure. Research report No. 6* (Department of Education, Cornell University, 1978).

3. A review of much of this work, including a number of studies of his own, is in M. E. Oakes, *Children's Explanations of Natural Phenomena* (New York: Teachers College, Columbia University, 1947). Oakes's concerns with classrooms in the conduct of his research are shown by an extract from this book: "Other investigators [including Piaget] have been concerned primarily with *interpretational* classifications of explanations . . . in other words with the effort to interpret the nature of the child's thinking. The interest of the present author is not so much that of the psychologist as that of the elementary teacher in the explanations themselves." (p. 3).

4. Rosalind Driver, *The Representation of Conceptual Frameworks in Young Adolescent Science Students*. Unpublished PhD thesis, University of Illinois, Urbana, 1973. See also Rosalind Driver, *The Pupil as Scientist?* (Milton Keynes, UK: Open University Press, 1983).

5. Rosalind Driver and Jack Easley, "Pupils and Paradigms: A Review of Literature Related to Concept Development in Adolescent Science Students," *Studies in Science Education* 5 (1978): 61-84; Rosalind Driver and Gaalen Erickson, "Theories in Action: Some Conceptual and Empirical Issues in the Study of Students' Conceptual Frameworks in Science," *Studies in Science Education* 10 (1983): 37-60; John L. Gilbert and D. Michael Watts, "Concepts, Misconceptions and Alternative Conceptions: Changing Perspective in Science Education," *Studies in Science Education* 10 (1983): 61-98.

6. The number of researchers and studies in science education is well illustrated by the magnitude of a bibliography produced in Germany. The 1994 edition contains well over 3000 studies ranging across all content areas of science, all educational levels, and with a range of purposes; See Helga Pfundt and Reinders Duit, *Bibliography Students' Alternative Frameworks and Science Education* (4th edition) (Kiel, Germany: Institute for Science Education, 1994).

7. Clive Sutton and Leo West, *Investigating Children's Existing Ideas about Science* (Occasional paper, School of Education, Leicester University, 1982).

8. Ibid., p. 1.

9. Ibid., pp. 25-26.

10. George A. Kelly, *The Psychology of Personal Constructs* (New York: Norton, 1955).

11. Sutton and West, *Investigating Children's Existing Ideas about Science*, p. 25.

12. Driver and Erickson, "Theories in Action: Some Conceptual and Empirical Issues in the Study of Students' Conceptual Frameworks in Science."

13. Walter Jung, "Introduction to the Conference: Toward a Synthesis of Research Efforts," in *Proceedings of the International Workshop on Problems Concerning Students' Representation of Physics and Chemistry Knowledge*, eds. Walter Jung, Helga Pfundt and Christoph von Rhöneck (Pädagogische Hochschule Ludwigsburg: Ludwigsburg, 1982). It is clear that Jung is referring to the European participants here. A scan of the names of the participants from the United States shows that probably three of the five fit the Jung description; the other two were cognitive psychologists and information processors without substantive science teaching experience.

14. For example, see D. C. Phillips, "The Good, the Bad, and the Ugly: The Many Faces of Constructivism," *Educational Researcher* 24, no. 7 (1995): 5-12.

15. Rosalind Driver, "Pupils' Alternative Frameworks in Science," *European Journal of Science Education* 3 (1981): 93-101.

16. Ibid., p. 99.

17. Rosalind Driver and Beverley Bell, "Students' Thinking and the Learning of Science: A Constructivist View," *School Science Review* 67, no. 240 (1986): 443-456; Rosalind Driver and Valerie Oldham, "A Constructivist Approach to Curriculum Development in Science," *Studies in Science Education* 13 (1986): 105-122.

18. Driver and Bell, "Students' Thinking and the Learning of Science: A Constructivist View," pp. 453-454.

19. The term "conceptual change" is today somewhat misleading. It was introduced at a time when such thinking was focused on understanding the processes that underlie students' changing conceptions; today debates include issues such as whether or not conceptual "addition" might be appropriate, and, if so, when and with what content. Even so the term "conceptual change" remains the common generic descriptor for these concerns. The most influential writing in this area is that of George Posner et al., "Accommodation of a Scientific Conception: Towards a Theory of Conceptual Change," *Science Education* 66 (1982): 211-227. Their theory of conceptual change proposed that initially there needed to be dissatisfaction with the existing conception, then the new conception needed to be intelligible, plausible, fruitful. This view has been the driving structure for many studies of attempts to create conceptual change in science. An influential early consideration of broader perspectives on "conceptual change" is A. Leon Pines and Leo T. West, "Conceptual Understanding and Science Learning: An Interpretation of Research within a Sources-of-knowledge Framework," *Science Education* 70 (1986): 583-604.

20. Driver and Oldham, "A Constructivist Approach to Curriculum Development in Science," p. 108.

21. Ibid., p. 118.

22. Rosalind Driver et. al., "Working from Children's Ideas: Planning and Teaching a Chemistry Topic from a Constructivist Perspective," in *The Content of Science: A Constructivist Approach to its Teaching and Learning*, ed. Peter Fensham, Richard Gunstone, and Richard White (London: Falmer, 1994), pp. 201-220.

23. Rosalind Driver et al., "Constructing Scientific Knowledge in the Classroom," *Educational Researcher* 23, no. 7 (1994): 5-12.

24. Driver, "Pupils' Alternative Frameworks in Science," p. 100.

25. Driver et al., "Constructing Scientific Knowledge in the Classroom," p. 11.

26. Michael Matthews, *Science Teaching: The Role of History and Philosophy of Science* (London: Routledge, 1994), p. 143.

27. Driver et al., "Constructing Scientific Knowledge in the Classroom," p. 11.

28. Ibid., p. 6.

29. Roger Osborne and Peter Freyberg, *Learning in Science: The Implications of Children's Science* (Auckland, NZ: Heinemann, 1985).

30. Personal communication, circa 1980.

31. Roger Osborne and M. C. Wittrock, "Learning Science: A Generative Process," *Science Education* 67 (1983): 489-508.

32. Malcolm Carr et al., "The Constructivist Paradigm and Some Implications for Science Content and Pedagogy," in *The Content of Science: A Constructivist Approach to its Teaching and Learning*, pp. 147-160.

33. An account of the group's curriculum thinking which draws on Australasian sources is Beverley Bell, "Implications for Curriculum," in *Learning Science Viewed as Personal Construction*, ed. Jeff Northfield and David Symington (Perth: National Key Centre for School Science and Mathematics, Curtin University of Technology), pp. 34-51.

34. This produced public controversy, much of which was based on misinterpretation of the Waikato position and "constructivist" views of learning. The spark for much of this was a book by Michael Matthews, *Challenging New Zealand Science Education* (Palmerston North, NZ: Dunmore Press, 1995) which expressed very strong criticism of the curriculum and the Waikato group. A collection of subsequent newspaper pieces, radio transcripts, and responses to the Matthews book are in Beverley Bell, *Responses to 'Challenging New Zealand Science Education'* (Waikato: Centre for Science, Mathematics and Technology Education Research, University of Waikato, 1995).

35. Richard Gunstone, Richard White, and Peter Fensham, "Developments in Style and Purpose of Research on the Learning of Science," *Journal of Research in Science Teaching* 25 (1988): 513-529.

36. Ibid., p. 516.

37. See, for example, J. T. Baird and Jeff Northfield, eds., *Learning from the PEEL Experience* (Faculty of Education, Monash University, 1992); and Richard Gunstone, "The Importance of Specific Science Content in the Enhancement of Metacognition" in *The Content of Science: A Constructivist Approach to its Teaching and Learning*, pp. 131-146.

38. J. T. Baird, "Improving Learning Through Enhanced Metacognition," *European Journal of Science Education* 8 (1986): 263-282.

39. Baird and Northfield, eds., *Learning from the PEEL Experience*.

40. Much of this work has been in collaboration with teachers, in the Project for Enhancing Effective Learning (PEEL); see, for example, Baird and Northfield, eds., *Learning from the PEEL Experience*.

41. For examples which show development over time see Robert Gagne and Richard White, "Memory Structures and Learning Outcomes," *Review of Educational Research* 48 (1978): 187-222; Richard White, *Learning Science* (Oxford: Blackwell, 1988); Richard White, "Research, Theories of Learning, Principles of Teaching and Classroom Practice: Examples and Issues," *Studies in Science Education* 31 (1998): 55-70.

42. Peter Fensham, "A Research Base for New Objectives of Science Teaching," *Research in Science Education* 10 (1980): 23-33.

43. Peter Fensham, "Beginning to Teach Chemistry" in *The Content of Science: A Constructivist Approach to its Teaching and Learning*, pp. 14-28.

44. Richard White, "A Theory of Content" in *The Content of Science: A Constructivist Approach to its Teaching and Learning*, pp. 255-262.

45. David P. Ausubel, *Educational Psychology: A Cognitive View"* (New York: Holt, Rinehart and Winston, 1978).

46. Ernst von Glasersfeld, "Introduction" in *Radical Constructivism in Mathematics Education*, ed. Ernst von Glasersfeld (Dordrecht: Kluwer, 1991), p. xv.

47. Jeremy Kilpatrick, "What Constructivism Might Be in Education," in *Proceedings of the Eleventh Conference of the International Group for the Psychology of Mathematics Education*, eds. Jacques Bergeron, Nicholas Herescovics, and Carolyn Fiernan (Montréal: Université Montréal, 1987), p. 7.

48. John Dewey, *How We Think* (Boston: D. C. Heath, 1910).

Section Five

Final Opinions

Editor's Introduction

The authors of the preceding chapters, in the course of addressing the different charges that the editor had given them, presented evaluations of constructivism in one or other (or in several) of its common guises. Some of these evaluations have been fairly negative, some have given a mixed report card, and some have been cautiously positive. It may seem strange, then, to end with yet two more chapters that have as their *raison d'etre* the presentation of further assessments. It turns out, however, that the authors represented in this section of the book are uniquely qualified to take on the task with which they were charged—to look at the general constructivist landscape and to reflect on what they saw. Joan Solomon, a science educator in the United Kingdom who has broad constructivist sympathies, had written an important assessment of this kind in 1994, "The Rise and Fall of Constructivism," and she was invited to reflect on developments since then. Nicholas Burbules, a philosopher of education who is knowledgeable about John Dewey and who has written on dialogue and the importance of bridging paradigmatic differences in philosophy and elsewhere, was charged with reading, and reflecting upon, the chapters in the previous sections. Together they provide a provoking set of "final opinions."

Joan Solomon sees three major developments that have significance for the further elaboration of constructivism as the new millennium dawns. The first is the spreading realization that constructivism is a perspective that applies not only to students, but also to teachers and researchers. In each of the spheres of activity in which these individuals work, there is the need to make sense of the facts that accumulate. She quotes Rosalind Driver as having said that "*all* learners need to interpret and make sense of new learning experiences for themselves." The second development has been the realization that the individualistic epistemology of science is inadequate and needs to be replaced by a more social epistemology, a development she sees as reflected in the so-called Science Wars. Third, she points to the growing recognition that education is centrally concerned with the development of students as persons, or as she prefers to phrase it, the development of "children's selfhood"; she stresses the role that creativity and "mental fluidity" play in this process—a role that has clear relevance for constructivism.

After reading the chapters in the previous sections, Nicholas Burbules was struck by the tendency of constructivists and their critics to overemphasize the differences between them and to downplay the commonalities or points of possible agreement; he lists five points on which he thinks they both could build. He criticizes members of both camps for setting out the issues that divide them in misleading ways, and— perhaps surprisingly for a philosopher—he suggests that the epistemological and metaphysical cast that is given to their disputes is often counterproductive and misleading. He illustrates this with an interesting (and what some philosophers will regard as a controversial) discussion of the disputes that members of both camps get into about the existence of an "external reality," which he thinks constructivists would have been well advised to completely avoid. He also makes a powerful case that constructivist pedagogy is not logically related to the so-called constructivist epistemology on which it is often supposed to rest and again sees the linking of these as a mistake. Developing this line of argument, he suggests that the problem lies with constructivists (and their critics) not being constructivist enough! Many readers will see a similarity here between Burbules and John Dewey, who was fervently opposed to the setting up of opposing "dualisms" and the reification of these into fixed and uncompromising positions that served as the soil in which warring "sects" could develop. Dewey always tried to disarm the sects, and this is what Burbules is also attempting to do—indeed a fitting "final word" for this yearbook.

CHAPTER X

The Changing Perspectives of Constructivism: Science Wars and Children's Creativity

JOAN SOLOMON

This chapter will begin by picking up some of the themes in constructivism that were troublesome in 1993-94 when I last wrote about the subject. The most important of these concerns constructivism as a method of teaching and the various brands of constructivism which lie beyond what the students tell us they think about scientific phenomena (as though these were wholly invented or constructed by them). Then there are two almost completely new themes which we should explore because they are becoming more confusing but also more interesting. The first of these is the so-called Science Wars, where angry exchanges and polarized views about truth and constructivism between the relativists and the scientists are beginning to assail the quieter domain of science education in order to recruit teachers and youngsters to their sides of the argument. As a science educator I find this quite worrying. However, the final theme is new and it brings us back to the aspects of classroom constructivism which seemed to be so very exciting and creative when the whole subject was new and pristine. Students actively discussing ideas about the meaning of experiences, whether their own or others, seemed to be so near to the heart of the whole educational enterprise that, whatever the drawbacks of constructivism in action, it made constructivism continue to seem attractive.

Revisitation

The year 1993, when I wrote my last paper on this theme,[1] was a time which set its own stamp on the progress of thinking about constructivism in terms of children's ideas about scientific phenomena or, as Rosalind Driver called them, "pupils' alternative frameworks." Ideas

Joan Solomon is a member of the Center for Science Education at the Open University in the United Kingdom. She has had a long-standing interest in the impact of constructivist ideas on her field.

for my paper were conceived in the airplane returning from what seemed likely to be the last of a series of three important educational conferences on "Misconceptions in Science and Mathematics" held in Cornell University. And so it proved to be. How dry and self-confident the series title sounds now! We had argued fiercely at the first conference as to whether the opening word would not have been better as "preconceptions" or just "conceptions" in order to show more respect to "children as scientists," but eventually the title stood unchanged. We were at pains to describe children's thinking in similar terms to scientists' thinking, using the old philosophical model of the scientific process, and very few were ready to denigrate that. It seemed to be a case of simply exploring any mismatch between children's ideas and the correct and prestigious scientific ideas. The focus of the discussion has become quite different today.

One general theme in that 1994 paper was the effect of new vocabulary on how we saw educational problems. In the early years of the century Jean Piaget, writing in language somewhat reminiscent of psychoanalysis, had put talking with children about their ideas on a par with the psychiatric clinical interview. Indeed much of his work became diagnostic in this tradition, attempting to find out exactly what stage of cerebration the child had reached. The educational constructivists tried for a while to combine this tradition with a more ethnographic approach to match the revolution in anthropological thinking which owed so much to Evans-Prit chard and then Pierre Bourdieu, but this attempt made no contact at all with Piaget's internalist cognitive view. The numerous statistics and graphs drawn from constructivist interview data, purporting to show how children at different ages saw natural phenomena, might have suited the Piagetian tradition, but did not map on to the ethnographic perspective at all well.

Later the psychology of George Kelly started another route in constructivism.[2] Isolated thinkers reflected upon the world and tried out hypotheses about its phenomena, in a way which seemed to Kelly to be very like what scientists did. It may have been working with schizophrenic patients that gave his approach an individualist feel which later attempts to include a more social dimension did little to change. Seven years later, Thomas Kuhn's historical descriptions of the revolutionary changes undergone by paradigms, and his account of paradigms as forms of life "inhabited" by groups of scientists, produced much more powerful social metaphors for interpreting the difficulties that pupils experience in learning the concepts of science.[3] The argument in my last paper was that progression from the student's personal construction to a more orthodox view was produced by new descriptive language, which was often used analogically and which provided new ways of perceiving those things that had already been perceived in a different way. Clearly this process of change was going to be taxing for the student, as research confirmed. There was plenty of material from philosophers like Richard Rorty and Ludwig Wittgenstein to support the linguistic aspects of this change. So we could see that new vocabulary not only created a different perspective, it also often created new theory; in terms of education the arrival of what some called "naive constructivism" in the classroom was a prime example of this.

In at least one respect my earlier paper was at fault. Its title, "The Rise and Fall of Constructivism," was more a literary borrowing from Gibbons's famous history of ancient Rome than the outcome of serious thought. I had not reflected then that when an educational perspective is no longer new it is far more susceptible to change than to extinction. With a theory as widely and securely based in philosophy as constructivism appeared to be, it was most unlikely to fall in the catastrophic Humpty Dumpty sense. This paper, then, will not attempt to pick up the pieces but will follow the trail of changed perspectives and new slants.

Constructivist Teaching

There are at least two matters which have progressed more or less continuously from their status in 1994 and need to be pursued a little further. The first of these is constructivism as a method of teaching science. There had always been a problem here because the way constructivism was applied in the classroom involved asking the pupils how they interpreted what was going on, and then explaining that they were wrong either explicitly or by teaching them the received scientific interpretation. One point of view, expressed by Rosalind Driver and Valerie Oldham, was that the impasse between the pupils' articulated ideas and the received scientific view could be resolved by getting students to observe and discuss some experiment or data designed to stimulate conceptual change in them.[4] This turned out to be no easy process and Robin Millar,[5] among others, had already expressed some reservations about the program of constructivist teaching and conceptual change.

Other convinced constructivists of the Driver school had tried to use the riot of pupils' ideas produced by their "elicitation" sessions in the classroom as an illustration of scientific method. They considered the existence of a variety of interpretations to be more important than the teachers' demonstration of "experimental facts" which pupils can use to support more than one theoretical interpretation. (We can recall a little boy in Teresa Wightman's report who insisted that something was lighter because it had more air in it, rather than because the atoms in it were crowded closer together, which was suggested by a friend.[6] Expanded polystyrene is indeed lighter than most other plastics and also does contain more air. Those are facts; interpreting them is far more difficult.) In the end only one theory was to be considered correct, so this aspect of constructivism became a way of teaching science by another name, and it often seemed to be very good teaching if judged by the motivational level of the students.

Outside the school, too, facts often have a much longer life than their theoretical interpretations, which may have to go through many revisions. The beautiful line spectra of incandescent atoms, for example, were recognized for nearly a century before succeeding waves of quantum theory explained them in slightly different ways. In evolutionary biology, as Patricia Harding and Leo Vining point out,[7] facts provided by the fossil evidence did not go away, although they were enhanced by data from genetics, radioactivity, and molecular biology, to support ever more sophisticated but continually reconstructed theories. Andrew Boulton and Debra Panizzon make similar points about river ecology theory;[8] but then they argue that it was the processes of science and the warrants that are made for scientific claims which should be studied rather than the phenomena (facts) themselves.

We are fortunate that just before Rosalind Driver died so tragically early, she engaged in a lively public discussion on this and related problems with Stephen Norris and Tone Kvernbekk which, typically, she enjoyed tremendously. Both sets of closely argued positions are to be found in the same journal issue. Basically the discussion was about goal-directed theories in science education, under which label Norris and Kvernbekk assumed her form of constructivism must fit because it was used to guide teaching in the classroom. Driver, however, denied that her position was goal-directed in this sense. She had sometimes worked with teachers who wanted to elicit the pupils' ideas and then to change them, and sometimes with other teachers whose goal was to use the pupils' ideas to teach about the provisional nature of scientific theories. She wrote:

> I would say that insofar as it (constructivism) provides a framework for thinking about teaching and learning which can constrain choices and aid

decision making, it does constitute a theory. However, it is a theory which provides a perspective rather than a prescription and is perhaps appropriately described as a framework theory . . . our theory is not a normative goal-directed theory.[9]

It was precisely this point about constructivism as perspective which my earlier paper had made. Driver's article has now provided not only this excellent clarification of the problem of constructivism as a method of teaching, it has also focused on another closely related area—the role of educational theory in providing a theory for teaching.

If constructivism proposes that we use evidence, logic, common sense, experience, metaphors, and theories to put together our own credible picture of how the world is, then this process will apply in the cases of both teachers and educational researchers. Whenever members of either of these two constituencies talk about, and use, theories to describe science education, they will almost certainly construct different representations of the field. This does not mean that they will be unable to understand each other's perspective as a shallow reading of Kuhn's work about incommensurablity of paradigms might suggest. But the fact remains that they do come from different social institutions and, as Ludwig Fleck was the first to recognize,[10] all social institutions are "thought collectives" each with its own point of view. Driver knew about these different perspectives because she and her researchers had so often worked with teachers. Fortunately, perspectival differences are not unbreachable; because of the strength of human empathy, we can all make a good attempt to see at least part of the world as others see it (a subject to which we will return in the next section). However, the salience of the different perspectives, or as John Elliot and Clement Adelman wrote,[11] their different "relevances," will vary between teachers and researchers. This is another aspect of the quite general constructivist problem of seeing the world from different points of view. Take it too far one way and we have David Hargreaves' position that most educational research is, and moreover is bound to be, of little use to practitioners.[12] Go too far the other way and we bump up against Donald McIntyre's view that teachers cannot be researchers because they lack the essential professionalism,[13] so their task is only to apply the theory derived from research through their teaching. It is not the underlying scholarly elitism of this view which is worrying, but the idea that application is not problematic. Teachers who hold professional beliefs about their practice will find the application of ideas is every bit as perspective-driven as is their reflection on them, indeed probably more so considering the very strong bond that exists between belief and action. (See, for example, Daniel Dennett, John Ziman, and Karl Popper).[14] This being so, we need the closest possible collaboration between the two constituencies, with each influencing the other. It is not at all clear that constructivism could be expected to provide this for communities with different perspectives and different relevances. This whole problem area, which did not emerge in the earlier context of educational constructivism, was nicely laid out in Driver's last paper where she wrote once more that "all learners need to interpret and make sense of new learning experiences for themselves." And the context indicated that this should include teachers and researchers as well as students.

Subjectivist versus Communal Constructivism

When my previous paper was written, Ernst von Glasersfeld's argument for a more radical constructivist approach had already become known, but since then he has expanded his treatment.[15] His recent book, like his previous articles, uses an understanding of the old British philosophical tradition of the Empiricist group of philosophers— Locke, Berkeley and Hume—to write about perception and internal reflection on the world. These three philosophers had argued (a) that ideas are based on our perception of sensations from the outside world, and they bring us private understandings of some of its qualities, (b) that what is so perceived cannot be known to correspond to "reality" in the world, and (c) that it is impossible to determine the causes of events either by experience or by arguing from theory. Put these teachings together and you forge a front against the whole scientific enterprise that is essentially individual, subjectivist, and totally nondeterministic. Von Glasersfeld believes that this establishes a radical position where knowledge of every kind is not only personally constructed but essentially impossible to communicate to anyone else.

The state of scientific research in the last two centuries does not seem to have been impeded in the least by these skeptical arguments. This statement, the reader will note, is one that von Glasersfeld would clearly discount as quite irrelevant to the philosophical point at issue. However, philosophers such as Richard Rorty, for whom he professes admiration, might comment that this is where an ironic attitude has most to offer. Philosophical irony simply ignores ideas which claim that all reflection must strictly conform to logic because it perceives that the world is simply not like that. Thus the extreme solipsism of the empiricist tradition is no longer of deep interest and certainly cannot make real contact with those of us committed to science education who must be able to take science and its knowledge as a reputable "given" in an ongoing sense, as well as enabling the constructivist growth of their students' knowledge. But what sort of scientific knowledge are we thus promoting?

The eighteenth century saw a healthy growth in science, not only in its experiments and theories but also in its practices and institutions. This suggests that the kind of constructivist practices actually used in science were already becoming more social in nature, although no contemporary philosopher seemed ready to observe and comment on this, or to acknowledge its epistemological implications. The Royal Society of London was established to bring scientists together to watch each other's experiments and to argue about their theories. Watching experiments like those of Blaise Pascal, Otto von Guericke, and Robert Boyle was also becoming an almost common public occurrence. Sometimes its function was the stimulation of amusement and curiosity (for example, the famous "Hanging Boy" electrical experiment at which Benjamin Franklin marveled when he was in Europe and later used to such good effect), rather like exhibits in the Interactive Science Centers of today. However, other activities had a more epistemological function. For example, when Pascal instructed his son-in-law to take a barometer up a mountain to test his idea that atmospheric pressure was supporting the column of mercury, his first task was to collect five reliable witnesses to climb up to the summit with him and observe the experiment. He even included two monks from a monastery at the foot of the mountain to take readings from a control barometer throughout the day in order to note any fluctuations of atmospheric pressure. So far we can see the function of the witnesses as little more than checks on experimental reliability; however, it seems clear that the experiment was on the way to becoming part of social communication for an epistemological purpose.[16] At the other extreme from these publicists of science, the eighteenth century also saw the work of the retiring and eccentric aristocrat Henry Cavendish. Towards the end of his life, he carried out some careful measurements of the repulsion between charged spheres in his personal laboratory, and seems to have established the inverse square law of electrostatic repulsion. We only know about this because the data were recorded in his diaries, which came to light much later. Cavendish did not care to publish any accounts of his activities for collective appraisal or public argument. The French scientist Charles Auguste de Coulomb carried out a very similar set of investigations some twenty-five years later, but he did publish the results. Reflecting on the isolated activities of Cavendish, one wonders if his work should be considered as science at all. If it was an activity done for personal curiosity alone, could it be recognized as part of the larger cumulative social enterprise which we call science? So we see that the answer to the question "what sort of science?" might perhaps be that it is a communally constructed science.

The last half century has seen scholars like Thomas Kuhn[17] and John Ziman[18] beginning to describe this new socially oriented philosophy of science. They found it characterized by an epistemology which is dependent upon continuous communication through publications in specialist scientific journals in order to reach a consensus facilitated by scholarly controversy and controlled by communal norms.[19] This may seem quite remote from the extremely individualistic and "cerebral" philosophy of the eighteenth century but, as we have seen, social processes were already at work then, but they were not recognized for what they were. If the foregoing is an objective description of how scientific knowledge is itself constructed, it cannot but affect the way we interpret that knowledge. Sound descriptions of the growth of knowledge, as all philosophers are aware, are themselves on the way to becoming philosophies.

Social Constructivism

The old and outdated subjectivist and individualistic stance makes people in science education today feel uncomfortable because it is so divorced from the realm of the taken-for-granted objects and materials we deliberately use in science education. It has been the gift of the twentieth century phenomenologists like Edmund Husserl and George Herbert Mead that has helped us to go at least a little way into exploring the realm of the taken-for-granted. John Dewey was close, intellectually and personally, to Mead and the influence of this pioneer in sociology may be responsible for Dewey's strongly held view that language is an instrument of social co-operation and participation, and that mind itself is an outcome of this.[20] James Garrison believes that it is possible to find an alternative to subjectivist constructivism in Deweyan thinking which avoids the host of individual mental entities which threaten, in von Glasersfeld's account, to banish constructivism from the realm of any mutual practical experience, and hence from science. Dewey's democratic commitment, combined with an abiding interest in a practical education in science, was symptomatic of his pragmatic approach. But was it constructivist? In one respect it is—and—constructivist in a sense that Driver and her colleagues would have easily recognized. Dewey claimed that the learning by the young in any society "cannot take place through the direct conveyance of beliefs, emotions and knowledge."[21] Instead he saw the learning process being carried out through the influence of the environment, natural as well as social. Here there was no subjectivist hesitation about the reality of the individual's sensations, or of his or her conjectural explanations. (Practical education through experience is a subject to which we shall return in the last section.)

Dewey went further towards the social communalism of scientific knowledge than most philosophers of his time. Garrison quotes a passage from *"Experience and Nature"* which links Dewey's view of language, thought, and meaning with constructivism via the intersubjectivity which lies at the very core of science as a community endeavor:

> The heart of language is not "expression" of something antecedent, much less expression of antecedent thought. It is communication . . . Meaning is not indeed a psychic existence; it is primarily a property of (social) behavior and secondarily the property of objects . . . [It is] *co-operative*, in that response to another's act involves contemporaneous response to a thing as entering into another's (social) behaviour, and this upon both sides.[22] (emphasis added)

Intersubjectivity, described here by Dewey (and later in a more epistemological vein by Ziman) is the cornerstone of any "thought collective," as we saw in the discussion of the different perspectives of teachers and researchers in the previous section. In a memorable phrase Mary Douglas commented on how institutions think that "not any busload of people form a thought collective";[23] the individuals concerned need to be like-minded. This whole social way of thinking would be quite incomprehensible to any eighteenth century subjectivist. Within the scientific community the social consensus formed is very powerful, and indeed norms of scientific conduct have been put in place which, it is hoped, will prevent the risk of total mental gridlock. It is also the case that, in our modern times when the community practices of science have become so pronounced, the epistemological standing of its "constructed" knowledge has also been changed. Unfortunately, there are many scientists, philosophers, and lay people who have neither perceived this nor acknowledged the change. It is out of this misunderstanding and confusion that the Science Wars have broken out.

The Science Wars Raging Around Constructivism

This controversial aspect of constructivism had scarcely emerged in 1993; but in recent years in Britain the temperature of disagreement has risen rather than fallen. It has been argued in the previous section that as science became a communal rather than an individual activity its epistemology altered. Instead of the scientist being a solitary and heroic Galileo-type figure exploring the movements of terrestrial and heavenly bodies and constructing his own explanations for them against a background of persecution from those who wanted to suppress free investigation, the scientist had now become part of a strong and somewhat exclusive community. Naturally its members were proud of their achievements, and they put these successes down to their use of a superior way of thinking which they called "scientific method." By the 1940s and 50s a number of semi-popular books like C. H. Waddington's *The Scientific Attitude* and John Bernal's *Science as History*[24] had driven this point home, very much at the expense of ethics and of the new social sciences both of which, these authors appeared to believe, could be done much better by scientists. In Britain several of them gave the impression that all social science was a bit of a joke, and as late as 1990 the President of the Royal Society, no less, stated publicly that psychology was not a science at all. Where, he seemed to be saying, were the objective experiments and the logical thinking which defied human context and existed only in a rarified domain of abstract thought to be found in the social or human sciences?[25]

In recent years a kind of revenge has been exacted for this savaging of the social sciences. In 1994 a noisy and rather ill-natured exchange erupted between Harry Collins (an arch relativist) and Louis Wolpert (Fellow of the Royal Society and also, perhaps surprisingly, prominent in the field of the Public Understanding of Science) at a public meeting of the British Association for the Advancement of Science. Since then the Science Wars have raged on, gathering material from the debate about BSE (Mad Cow Disease) and problems about the environment. Mary Midgley based her commonsensical analysis of this contemporary confrontation on a comparison between polemical works from both camps. After one rather extreme quotation she wrote:

> Passages like this are written in the mythic mode. They accept the convention used by scientistic writers. . . . of treating science as a potent figure, a kind of demon. Anything written in this style has an extraordinarily strong and primitive appeal. In such sentences, deep speaks unto deep without the inconvenient interruption of serious thought. . . . An author who uses this kind of language, even for two or three sentences in the course of a book, can be sure that these are the sentences which will be remembered.[26]

Within her vision of embattled science Midgley describes a kind of constructivism which has taken up an extreme sociological position. Put

simply, the question at issue is whether scientific knowledge is really discovered and consolidated through the venerable processes of careful disinterested empirical or logical test—the "Legend" as Philip Kitcher[27]
nicely called it—or whether it is constructed through messy and incon-
clusive experiments whose conclusions might turn out to be directed as
much by the entrenched inclinations of the scientists, embodied in the
fallible instruments they design and use to trap the data, and the methods of interpretation that they most favor. This is an awkward conclusion for those who urge us to teach scientific method in the schools.

Controversies between philosophers frequently become somewhat
strident, but usually they are of little interest to anyone other than
those directly concerned. The same could have been said about the
debate between Thomas Kuhn and Karl Popper in the late 1960s but,
as I have argued, it was out of this that the first wave of constructivism
in the science classroom emerged. The very title of the early paper by
Driver and Easley, "Pupils and Paradigms," indicated this philosophical
strand in constructivist thinking.[28] The constructivist movement in science education enlisted the vocabulary and thinking of both Kuhn and
Popper[29] wherever it could. From Popper the constructivists chose the
notion of children's intuitions as a basis for subsequent test and selection, out of which a mental construction could develop. From Kuhn
they welcomed the idea of revolution and "paradigm shift," which later
became the more problematic idea of teaching for conceptual change.
The constructivists' treatment of Piagetian theory, which was then
required reading for every educator, was eclectic. Where Piaget had
written of children's "frameworks of existing judgments" his idea was
received as usefully child-centered. The phrase "Piagetian constructivism" was to be read far and wide in the literature, although largely
disconnected from the developmental logic which had been so essential
to Piagetian thinking. Where his schema might have trapped emerging
educational constructivism in a straitjacket of developmental stages,
constructivists ignored his views, except in the sense that both schools
of thought totally rejected the possibility of learning through the simple transmission of knowledge from teacher to student. This constituted an essential, skillful, and valuable mapping out of familiar pieces
of an older vocabulary upon which a new understanding could be built.

In the Science Wars between sociology and science no very valuable outcome has emerged. Modern sociologists have studied the institutions of science and its practices just as Durkheim and Weber had
studied prisons and asylums in their times. One branch of this movement holds that scientific knowledge, facts and all, are constructed by

scientists using their specialized instruments, rather than just being discovered or uncovered in the place where they had lain hidden awaiting wakening by disinterested researchers. Following the tradition of Kuhn much of this research was historical.

The second branch was sociological rather than historical, and put forward what was called "the Strong Program for the sociology of scientific knowledge (SSK)."[30] This tried to identify the social and cultural forces within society which would not only bring about the emergence of new scientific knowledge, but also explain the nature of scientific controversies. This was part of a larger ambitious movement based on a kind of sociological determinism which might examine and even predict the substance of all knowledge, behavior, and opinion. Not surprisingly, the adherents of this program also wrote of the authority of science as being a sociological artifact; they held that this authority was embedded in collective opinion and was thus relativist rather than objective. But if sociology was also embedded in the collective opinion, could there be objective determinism in sociology which would uncover relativism in science? Would not the pursuit of knowledge in both science *and* sociology be subject to the same constraints? In an early manifesto of the Strong Program Bloor argued that sociology would be an investigation of the same type as science and could no more be protected from being theory-driven than could empirical science:

> . . . the strong programme possesses a certain kind of moral neutrality, namely the same kind as we have learned to associate with all the other sciences. It also imposes upon itself the need for the same kind of generality as other sciences. It would be a betrayal of these values, of the approach of empirical science, to choose to adopt a teleological view . . . these points do make clear the ramifications of the choice and expose those values that are going to inform the approach to knowledge. From this . . . the sociology of knowledge can proceed.[31]

The third branch of warfare, if such it was, explored in detail how science is carried out today. It was strongly relativist in nature, seeing any scientist's claim to be using uniquely scientific methods for discovering the truth about the natural world as hopelessly naive and realist. They held that it was impossible to distinguish between cognitive outcomes and social influences. If "doing science"—one of their favorite terms—was a special social activity which included the use of specially constructed apparatus, special status and group-standing, and interpretations of data, then the outcomes would be bound to be irretrievably mixed up with the social practice which had generated them.

Their detailed investigations showed, they claimed, that scientists "invented" (a stronger and more pejorative term than "constructed") new particles like quarks and solar neutrinos. It would not be impossible to imagine other types of socioscientific approaches which would result in quite different "cognitive" constructions.

This relativist movement then turned upon the Strong Program of sociology of knowledge (SSK) with a total rejection of the idea that there were any overarching meta-studies which could explore knowledge systems—science, sociology or any other—to explain, justify, or even describe them. The critique from the works of Jurgen Habermas and Jean-Francois Lyotard[32] had already attacked several of these meta-systems which seem to have their being outside the domain of the factors that they set out to explain. The philosophers had Marxism, metaphysics, and science prominently in their sights. These relativist constructivists developed an outright cynicism about the procedures of both science and the sociology of knowledge. Not content with claiming that there were no special scientific methods and that scientists behaved and constructed their scientific theories just as anyone else might do in their own sphere, they also admitted that the methods of sociological research could not reliably reveal hidden sociological truths. These relativists set out to present and substantiate a view of the construction of all knowledge as being essentially beyond method.

This whole area of strong theoretical critique has been included here because not only was it the most challenging celebration of constructivism within science, but also because it impinged on science education during the last few years. The first strand, which has largely been experimental, may have influenced the work of Michael Nott and others on the ways in which teachers and student teachers admit and justify their "rigging" of experiments, so that pupils can more easily use the results in their own constructions of "sound" scientific knowledge.[33]

In the second place the Strong Program, with its emphasis on "moral neutrality" between one kind of science and another, finds echoes in the practical efforts of Glen Aikenhead and others to research and teach science in a multicultural setting.[34, 35] Teaching modern Western science to non-Western students can be seen as forcing them to undertake potentially dangerous crossings of the cultural boundaries. Such attempts at forced assimilation are not only of little value because they so rarely deliver proper understanding, they are also at odds with the goal of a tolerant and richly multicultural society which most modern nations claim for their education. Drawing on the work of Anita Rampal and Olugbemeiro Jegede concerning the teaching of Western science to children living within Indian and African cultures, Aiken-head recommends the teaching of cross-cultural Science Technology and Society (STS) courses. These, he argues, would be useful to all the students in the classroom, to those who come from the science cultures of other nations as well as to those who find it difficult to cross the less visible borders between science knowledge and life-world knowledge which lie within the national frontiers. Conversely, it would also enrich the perspectives of those who fit easily into the subculture of science and might fail to recognize the perspectives of other sciences. This takes us right back to the personal constructivist tradition, but without the pressure for conceptual change which can be very oppressive in the multicultural context. Traditional science educators may fulminate against this, but it is in sympathy with the Strong Program's mandate, and in addition it provides a far more realistic goal for school science education. Aikenhead writes:

> Rather than insist that students develop knowledge, values, and skills for assimilation into the subculture of science, a cross-cultural STS curriculum will help students enrich their own life-world subcultures by empowering them to draw upon the subculture of science in appropriate situations. . . . Situated cognition accounts for the fact that some students . . . can understand the subculture of science without integrating it into their life-world.[36]

As Andrew Furnham, Alan Irwin, and others have shown,[37] many (al-though not all) members of the adult public learn to carry out this kind of "bilingual" constructivism with considerable fluency when faced with modern technological risk. And within school classrooms, too, evidence for two co-existing domains of knowledge are not uncom-mon.[38]

The third strand of extreme relativism is also knocking on the door of science education. A direct challenge is to be found in the last sec-tion of the book by Harry Collins and Trevor Pinch, *The Golem*.[39] True to Mary Midgley's dictum that a few rather wild sentences in the course of any book are the very ones which will be remembered, we find a rather disproportionate interest from educationalists such as Helge Kragh, which is antagonistic, and Sandra Costa and colleagues, which is favorable,[40] to what might be called their "school relativist constructivism." The substance of this particular challenge is illus-trated by the final ten minutes of the messier of school science lessons when the teacher tries to knit together the sometimes wild variations in her pupils' results to a simple practical exercise like measuring the boil-ing point of water. This, assert Collins and Pinch, exactly mirrors the antics of real scientists and should be protected from the kind of excuses and class consensus-making which science teachers often use to defuse it.

> . . . that ten minutes illustrates better the tricks of professional frontier science than any university or commercial laboratory. . . . They all come up with wildly varying results. . . . In the end, however it is the scientific community who brings order to this chaos, transmitting the clumsy antics of the collective Golem Science into a neat and tidy scientific myth. There is nothing wrong with this: the only sin is not knowing that it is always thus.[41]

Most scientists would probably agree that experimental work is difficult and even messy and that the findings are never completely accurate. A moment's reflection also confirms that experiments have to be designed with some kind of expectation in mind in order to come into existence at all. However, as in the case of the long struggle to verify the existence of solar neutrinos which Collins and Pinch describe effectively, the chosen equipment gives a measurement of computable error, and woe betide the experimental results which lie significantly outside this. Then nothing can tidy up that story, as this chapter in *The Golem* so clearly shows. The construction of scientific knowledge, whether by filtration through a child's intuitive ideas or via the discipline of experiment, is never easy. The only remaining question is which of the possible constructions of the position held by Collins and Pinch will be picked up by the few science teachers who read the book.

The scientific adherents of the "legend" about the nature of science have not remained silent through this phase of the Science Wars. Britain—which has simultaneously been riven by more general Culture Wars between those who believe that all standards in art, literacy, and education were being "dumbed down" by wild progressives and those who seek more accessible knowledge for all—has suffered a resurgence of a crude form of defense of the "legend." Most of this was at the hands of the new super-confident breed of biologists like Steve Jones, Richard Dawkins, and Lewis Wolpert. The last of these authors, extrapolating from the difficulties that students experience in believing that the Earth goes round the Sun, or that the weighty substance of trees is formed from a minority gas in the air, has claimed that science is contrary to commonsense reasoning.[42] All students, Wolpert urges, should be taught that science is unnatural knowledge to which they, as mere students, can have nothing to contribute. While this might have constituted an all-out attack on the humanistic kind of educational constructivism practiced by Driver and her colleagues, in effect it has provoked rather more incredulity and irritation than consternation in the science education community.

Children's Selfhood and Creativity

The questioning of children about their ideas on why certain phenomena happen had been basic to constructivism from the very first. And although it might not have been a direct and economical way to teach orthodox science, there are some very sound reasons for valuing the activity. Education is deeply and centrally concerned with the development of the children's selfhood, and we might interpret this to mean that they must become conscious of their own ideas and able to express them:

> Knowledge has first of all to be made meaningful to students before it can be made critical. It never speaks for itself, but rather is constantly mediated through the ideological and cultural experiences that students bring to the classroom.[43]

This brief extract translates very readily into the familiar language of constructivism. It denies a transmission view of learning and a mind which is a *tabula rasa*. In addition, it seems to welcome multiculturalism and development of personal ideologies. Henry Giroux's voice may well be an authentic one of the new age of constructivism, and if it sounds both radical and postmodern, teachers need not feel uncomfortable. It will be argued in this final section that the new message about science education is that it should be used both to enhance students' feelings of selfhood and to develop a new kind of creativity.

In some areas of the ordinary public system of education there seems to be ample room for students to give voice to their ideas. Art, poetry, and music, for example, appear well placed to allow lots of self-expression, which the liberal educator has always prized. It is through self-expression that selfhood grows, precisely because we adults, as well as children, only know who we are and what we want to achieve by trying to frame an answer to those who ask us questions, or by our asking questions of those who show us new phenomena. Science has always been so enmeshed in the framework of accepted facts that the very notion of developing self-expression through its study might have seemed unlikely. Richard Rorty saw this as crucial to his study of what he called the contingency of selfhood:

The final victory of poetry in its ancient quarrel with philosophy—the final victory of metaphors of self creation over metaphors of discovery—would consist in our becoming reconciled to the thought that this is the only sort of power over the world which we can hope to have. For that would be the final abjuration of the notion that truth, and not just power and pain, is to be found "out there."[44]

This quotation is particularly apt since it contains, in its tail, a denial of that positivism which is the enemy to all constructivism. If these metaphors of self-creation are the substance of constructivism, as many teachers believe they are, this would explain why many of them became so delighted by the practice of talking about personal ideas in their science classrooms, instead of just rehearsing the exploits and discoveries of remote and often dead scientists. As teachers of the young, we have overwhelming reason to encourage the development of the students' sense of emerging personhood. Whether the subject they are learning is science or poetry, they need the opportunity of including topics in their studies which touch upon the things about which they hold personal views. If we consider the ambiance of any classroom, we can see that both social and personal forces are involved. For the students the daily peer interactions through which prestige is achieved are all important. When inspired constructivist teachers manage to infiltrate the substance of a science topic into these interactions, we can be sure that the forces of honor among peers and those of emerging personhood are yoked together to the benefit of science education.

Teachers, like doctors, practice in isolation where they often have to perform unpopular actions. What sustains and directs their actions is an inner feeling that Rom Harré usefully calls by the rather old-fashioned term "honor." This is not only deeply personal, it is also dependent on external social recognition: "people have a deep sense of their own dignity, and a craving for recognition as beings of worth in the opinion of others."[45] In a more recent book, Harré wrote in terms that constructivists would certainly recognize, despite his approach being linguistic and cultural and theirs being more individualistic and developmental. What he emphasizes throughout is the fusion of the individual with the social in a way that echoes our considerations of the different aspects of personal constructivism in the communal setting of science education. He begins by saying, "It is the acquisition of a point of view that is the matter of interest for the theorist of personhood, since that is one of the singularities of self, expressed in personal discourse."[46] When Harré writes about the social construction of this apparently singular concept, he shows that cultures, on both a large national scale and on a small family scale, interact to produce the diversity of opinions amongst the students whom we meet in the school classrooms.

Linking this with the work of Henry Giroux and others we may extract two principles. First, teachers prize their authority and social honor because they believe they have valuable knowledge to bring to the students. Second, they simultaneously try to loosen this armor of authority in order to give the students a voice in their education, both in order to monitor the success of their teaching and to support the emerging "science selfhood" of their students. Of these two principles it is clear that the second should be deeply receptive to the advent of constructivism in the classroom, while the first stresses the value of the professional knowledge the teachers have brought to the lesson. Any conflict between the two, as might happen during constructivist lessons when teachers are advised to withhold their knowledge for an uncomfortably long time while the majority of the class seem to be constructing incorrect views, makes teachers feel sidetracked and even dishonored. This is one of the chief reasons why first-wave constructivist teaching has largely been abandoned in British science classrooms. Initially it seemed very liberal and creative, but now for many it is just too painful to watch their young charges ignore the science knowledge which they had hoped to see them celebrating. How long, Pamela Wadsworth asks, should we wait before telling our students the right answer?[47]

At this late point in the chapter we seem to have encountered the old constructivist impasse once again. The easiest route to letting loose the children's creativity, by permitting them to talk together and construct their own scientific knowledge, does not seem to be viable. STS lessons, on the other hand, where the students may discuss the social issues by giving their own opinions about the operation of civic justice and community care, do allow a real measure of valuable creativity whatever the cultural background. Indeed, in this kind of discussion the pressure to arrive at a consensus is far less strong than it is in the endeavor of science itself. The principles of modern social justice, such as the theory put forward by John Rawls,[48] are dependent upon some level of understanding of a number of the different prevailing points of view and vulnerabilities. It may be that discussion of the interplay of socioscientific concerns takes us back to somewhere near the realms of poetry in its "final victory" of which Rorty wrote. Where children in our parents' age marveled at the "wonders of science" (as at a kind of poetry), their modern descendants busy themselves with ethical and social conjectures.

Practical work also seems to offer some measure of creativity. Dewey, as we have seen, believed that practical experience could promote a kind of natural education, and insofar as designing and making artifacts are concerned, he was undoubtedly right. This kind of technological endeavor thrives on the individual creativity of the engineer or the school student.[49] The environment of use provides a habitat where the made object can either succeed or fail and, quite unlike science lessons, all students finish with their own individual artifact. Variety and creativity are the lifeblood of this sort of education, just as Dewey had indicated.

Donald Campbell's learning theory, which he called "Blind Variation and Selective Retention," is a general method of gaining knowledge which can be compared to Darwinian evolution.[50] In biological examples one could speak of a kind of "learning" on the part of the organism which takes place by means of random variation through genetic mutation, followed by the brutal process of selective survival of some, or none, of the mutant individuals. This "learning" is thus imposed by the contingencies of the environment. This is similar to what might be called "the struggle of conjectures" to succeed. It is important to note that the earliest stage of this process, which is similar to the production of mutations, is a creative process, unlike blind trial and error. It is based on previous technological experiences and on new ideas which are added in a pragmatic way as the design seems to need them. The success or failure of the artifact depends crucially upon how it reacts during its practical evaluation. Darwinian theories are very popular at this time in many fields of study—economics, technology, culture, and even education—but they have little to offer when the teacher or textbook has predefined the limits of variation and of selective retention, as happens in most science education. Creativity in education implies that there is some stage in the learning where a variety of conjectures is welcomed.

Creative learning does take place occasionally in Interactive Science Centers if the exhibits are specifically designed to encourage this, but it is not very common for the reason given above. Indeed, some careful meta-research by Marcia Linn has shown that previous specific knowledge of science is almost, although not quite, a necessary condition for any successful student-generated explorations to take place.[51, 52]

The Last Loophole for Creative Constructivism?

Many of the problems with classroom constructivism arise precisely because educators tend to look for a high level of originality and creative self-expression in their pupils, at the same time as charging them with the correct learning of a body of pre-existing knowledge. In Rorty's terms we are looking for "metaphors of self-expression" at the same time as demanding "metaphors of discovery." If constructivists drop the fallacy of "discovery" in the context of old established knowledge, could we find a more realistic way of recognizing that creativity which is the hallmark of personal constructivism? This search will touch on a selection of exciting new literature within the general field of cognition.

Nearly twenty years ago there were already occasional papers from artificial intelligence and cognitive psychology, which suggested that what the mind did with experiences was not just to store them or to forget them. From David Rumelhart and Donald Norman we read that "information is not stored anywhere in particular. Rather it is stored everywhere."[53] From John Biggs, who had used his research into how students study in order to reinterpret the learning process, we began to see information as not just being encoded at some level in the mind, but also as being moved to new places—"elaborated," as Vygotsky might have written—by being linked with other ideas during the process of study and reflection. Biggs wrote memorably that "Studying is to elaboration as teaching is to encoding."[54] It seemed that ideas in the mind might be both more localized and yet also more mobile than had been expected, and that it was the students' reflection which made them mobile. Hence, it seemed, there might be a very strong connection between creativity, and hence constructivism, on the one hand, and the organization of mental processes on the other.

Recent investigations into the structure of the mind provide us more detailed routes to explore. Research into the mind's activity has exploded recently from the perspective of infant development in the work of Annette Karmiloff-Smith,[55] to prehistory and the emergence of homo sapiens in the work of Stephen Mithen,[56] and from artificial intelligence in the work of Margaret Boden[57] to the neurophysiology of the brain. In every case a picture is painted of a heavy load of general routine learning input, which brain scans exhibit by great swathes of light illuminating large areas at work, followed by contraction to a smaller region as the initial learning task is completed at a much greater speed. This is the activation of more specialized and localized "representations." It is common to speak in this context of "sub-routines" in a particular module of the brain, and of these connecting with other representations by parallel linking. Boden and Mithen both characterize this as "cognitive fluidity." Most theorists of the mind see these smaller and more mobile representations as capable of generating new combinations of ideas, which seem to be central to creative learning and to which most of these theorists are willing to give the term "creative." Mithen focuses on the flowering of early cave art and religion some fifty thousand years ago when representations from natural history knowledge became able to be linked with representations of technological knowledge and skills in stonework. Boden speaks from the study of artificial intelligence about the "transformation of style" in a program produced when a system becomes self-transforming by producing meta-representations of lower level skills. This makes for what she frequently calls "creative potential." And Karmiloff-Smith describes something very similar going on in the mind of a small child in the midst of imaginative play.

If, after the first chaotic input from experience, the mind can form specific conceptual representations which later, when appropriate, can be called upon to link up with quite other representations, then this may prove to be a new way of thinking about analogy. Vygotsky's term for this internal cognitive work which moves inputs from one place to another was "elaboration" (as it was also for Biggs). In science education theory these ideas are reminiscent of the work of David Ausubel in some respects and of research into analogy in others. Analogy is not a new study for those in either science or science education. The role of metaphorical redescription has long been recognized in the philosophy of science,[58] and also in students' learning of science although there are outstanding differences of opinion as to whether all analogy lies on a continuum of difficulty or not, and also how far the cognitive fluidity is content independent. Certainly, purely descriptive kinds of analogy are achieved earlier than the functional ones. Creative analogy is similar to, but not the same as, constructivist learning. It uses the students' mobile mental representations at a later stage, after the first teacher inputs, in order to link them up with each other so that this cognitive fluidity can lead to creative juxtaposition and so to analogy. This may even be a valuable way in which teachers can encourage their students to produce an individual point of view (see Harré's confirmation of selfhood mentioned above) not by constructing their own scientific ideas *ab initio*, but by making analogical links between new and previously learned representations.

It has been noted by Janet Burns and others that when advanced chemistry students talked about their learning they used phrases like "it fits together" or "it clicks," which seem similar to the idea of cognitive fluidity.[59] Research by Susan Carey and Elizabeth Spelke has used the mobility of domain-specific representations to explain the scientific "misconceptions" that secondary students hold.[60] They argue that these links can be broken and reformed by the process of conceptual change, but other researchers disagree to some extent. Cognitive change is certainly a difficult feat to produce once firm connections have been formed. However, it may be that more than one parallel link can be formed to a sub-routine in the mind, so that science knowledge and life-world knowledge may co-exist to be used as and when the context seems to demand it.

This chapter on constructivism has concluded with a reference to scholarship in a neighboring cognitive field rather than within the realm of science education. The hypothesis, and it is no more than that, is that, if we could take our students after the first rather heavy input of transmitted scientific knowledge and find ways to help them play with the sub-routines that they have begun to form in the mind so as to create their own analogies, then we might be leading them towards a new and valuable kind of constructivism. Karmiloff-Smith gives it as her opinion that neither chimpanzees nor any other primates can operate with this kind of mental fluidity. We may be getting near to the hard work that constructing meaning always is, for all of us:

. . . in the human, internal representations become objects of cognitive manipulation such that the mind extends well beyond its environment and is capable of creativity. . . . Let me go as far as to say that the process of re-description is one of the human instincts for inventiveness.[61]

NOTES

1. Joan Solomon, "The Rise and Fall of Constructivism," *Studies in Science Education* 23 (1994): 1-19.

2. George Kelly, *The Psychology of Personal Constructs* (New York: Norton, 1955).

3. Thomas Kuhn, *The Structure of Scientific Revolutions* (Chicago: University of Chicago Press, 1962).

4. Rosalind Driver and Valerie Oldham, "A constructivist approach to curriculum development in science," *Studies in Science Education* 13 (1986): 105-122.

5. Robin Millar, "Constructive Criticisms," *International Journal of Science Education* 11 (1989): 587-596.

6. Teresa Wightman, *The Construction of Meaning and Conceptual Change in Classroom Settings: Case Studies on the Particulate Nature of Matter* (Leeds: University of Leeds, 1986).

7. Patricia Harding and Leo Vining, "The impact of the knowledge explosion on science education," *Journal of Research in Science Teaching* 34 (1997): 969-975.

8. Andrew Boulton and Debra Panizzon, "The Knowledge Explosion in Science Education: Balancing Practical and Theoretical Knowledge," *Journal of Research in Science Teaching* 35 (1998): 475-481.

9. Rosalind Driver, "The Application of Science Education Theories: A Reply to Stephen Norris and Tone Kvernbekk," *Journal of Research in Science Teaching* 34, no. 10 (1997): 1015; see also, Stephen Norris and Tone Kvernbekk, "The Application of Science Education Theories" in the same journal issue.

10. Ludwig Fleck, *The Genesis and Development of a Scientific Fact* (Chicago: University of Chicago Press, 1935).

11. John Elliot and Clement Adelman, "Stranger in the Classroom," *The Ford Teaching Project* (Norwich: University of East Anglia, 1974).

12. David Hargreaves, *Teaching as a Research-Based Profession* (London: Teacher Training Agency, 1996).

13. Donald McIntyre, "The Profession of Educational Research," *British Educational Research Journal* 23, no. 2 (1997): 127-140.

14. Daniel Dennett, "True Believers: The Intentional Strategy and Why It Works," in *Scientific Explanation*, ed. A. F. Heath (Oxford: Clarendon Press, 1981), pp. 53-75; Karl Popper, *Objective Knowledge* (Oxford: Clarendon Press, 1972); John Ziman, *Reliable Knowledge* (Cambridge: Cambridge University Press, 1978).

15. Ernst von Glasersfeld, *Radical Constructivism: A Way of Knowing and Learning* (London: Falmer Press, 1995).

16. Steven Shapin, and Simon Schaffer, *Leviathan and the Air Pump: Hobbes, Boyle and the Experimental Life* (Princeton, NJ: Princeton University Press, 1985).

17. Kuhn, *The Structure of Scientific Revolutions.*

18. John Ziman, *Public Knowledge* (Cambridge: Cambridge University Press, 1968).

19. Robert Merton, "Science and Technology in a Democratic Order," *Journal of Legal and Political Science* 1 (1973): 115-126. Reprinted in Robert Merton, *The Sociology of Science* (Chicago: University of Chicago Press, 1942), pp. 267-278.

20. John Dewey, "Experience and Nature," in *John Dewey: The Middle Years*, ed. J. Boydson (Carbondale: Southern Illinois University Press, 1988).

21. John Dewey, *Democracy and Education* (New York: The Free Press, 1916), p. 141.

22. James Garrison, "An Alternative to von Glasersfeld's Subjectivism in Science Education: Deweyan Social Constructivism," *Science and Education* 6 (1997): 543-554.

23. Mary Douglas, *How Institutions Think* (London: Routledge & Kegan Paul, 1987).

24. John Bernal, *Science as History* (London: Watts, 1954); C. H. Waddington, *The Scientific Attitude* (West Drayton, UK: Penguin, 1941).

25. For a review of the ultra-defensive and super-triumphant views of science in this genre on both sides of the Atlantic see Felicity Mellor, "Scientists' Rhetoric in the Science Wars," *Public Understanding of Science* 8 (1999): 51-56.

26. Mary Midgley, "Visions of Embattled Science," in *Science Today. Problem or Crisis?*, eds. R. Levinson and J. Thomas (London and New York: Routledge, 1997), p. 40.

27. Philip Kitcher, *The Advancement of Science: Science Without Legend, Objectivity Without Illusions* (Oxford: Oxford University Press, 1993).

28. Rosalind Driver and John R. Easley, "Pupils and Paradigms: A Review of the Literature Related to Concept Development in Adolescent Science Students," *Studies in Science Education* 5 (1978): 61-84.

29. Karl Popper, *Objective Knowledge* (Oxford: Clarendon Press, 1972).

30. David Bloor, *Knowledge and Social Imagery* (London: Routledge & Kegan Paul, 1976).

31. Ibid., p. 10.

32. Jurgen Habermas, *Postmetaphysical Thinking* (Cambridge: Polity Press, 1992); Jean-Francois Lyotard, *The Postmodern Condition: A Report on Knowledge*, trans. Geoff Bennington and Brian Massumi (Manchester: Manchester University Press, 1984).

33. Michael Nott and R. Smith, "Talking Your Way Out of It, 'Rigging' and 'Conjuring': What Science Teachers Do When Practicals Go Wrong," *International Journal of Science Education* 17, no. 3 (1995): 339-410; see also Michael Nott and Jerry Wellington, "Producing the Evidence: Science Teachers' Initiation into Practical Work," *Research in Science Education* 27, no. 3 (1997): 395-409.

34. Michael Matthews, *Challenging New Zealand Science Education* (Palmerston North, NZ: Dunmore Press, 1996).

35. Glen Aikenhead, "Science Education: Border Crossing into the Subculture of Science," *Studies in Science Education* 27 (1996): 43; see also Olugbemeiro Jegede, "School Science and the Development of Scientific Culture: A Review of Contemporary Science Education in Africa," *International Journal of Science Education* 19, no. 1 (1997): 1-20; and Anita Rampal, "Innovative Science Teaching in Rural Schools in India: Questioning Social Beliefs and Superstition," in *STS Education: International Perspectives on Reform*, eds. Joan Solomon and Glen Aikenhead (New York: Teachers' College Press, 1994).

36. Aikenhead, "Science Education," p. 43.

37. Andrew Furnham, "Lay Understanding of Science: Young People and Adults' Ideas of Scientific Concepts," *Studies in Science Education* 20 (1992): 29-64; see also the general argument in Alan Irwin, *A Citizen Science: A Study of People, Expertise and Sustainable Development* (London: Routledge, 1995).

38. Joan Solomon, "Learning About Energy: How Children Think in Two Domains," *European Journal of Science Education* 59 (1983): 49-59.

39. Harry Collins and Trevor Pinch, *The Golem. What Everyone Should Know about Science* (Cambridge: Cambridge University Press, 1993).

40. Helge Kragh, "Social Constructivism and the Teaching of Physics," *Science and Education* 7, no. 3 (1998): 233-243; and Sandra Costa, Thomas B. Hughes, "Bringing It All Back Home: Some Implications of Recent Science and Technology Studies for the Classroom Science Teacher," *Research in Science Education* 28, no. 1 (1998): 9-21.

41. Collins and Pinch, *The Golem*, p. 151.

42. Lewis Wolpert, *The Unnatural Nature of Science* (London: Faber & Faber, 1993).

43. Henry Giroux, *Pedagogy and the Politics of Hope: Theory, Culture and Schooling* (Boulder, CO: WestView Press, 1997), p. 110.

44. Richard Rorty, *Contingency, Irony and Solidarity* (Cambridge: Cambridge University Press, 1989), p. 40.

45. Rom Harré, *Social Being* (Oxford: Basil Blackwell, 1979), p. 3.

46. Rom Harré, *The Singular Self* (London: Sage Publications, 1998), p. 13.

47. Pamela Wadsworth, "When Do I Tell Them the Right Answer?," *Primary Science Review* 49 (1997): 23-24.

48. John Rawls, *A Theory of Justice* (Harvard: Harvard University Press, 1971).

49. For an engineer's perspective see Walter Vincenti, *What Engineers Know and How They Know It* (Baltimore: Johns Hopkins Press, 1992); and for a collection of essays on this general theme, see John Ziman, *Technological Innovation as an Evolutionary Process* (Cambridge: Cambridge University Press, 1999).

50. Donald Campbell, "Blind Variation and Selective Retention in Creative Thought as in Other Knowledge Processes," *Psychological Review* 67 (1960): 380-400.

51. Heather Brooke and Joan Solomon, "From Playing to Exploring: Research in an Interactive Science Centre for Primary Pupils," *International Journal of Science Education* 20, no. 8 (1997): 959-971.

52. Marcia Linn, "Free-Choice Experiences: How Do They Help Children to Learn?" *Science Education* 64, no. 2 (1980): 237-248.

53. David Rumelhart and Donald Norman, "A Comparison of Models," in *Parallel Models of Associative Memory*, eds. G. Hinton and J. Anderson (Hillsdale, NJ: Lawrence Erlbaum Associates, 1981).

54. John Biggs, "Developmental Processes and Learning Outcomes," in *Cognition, Development and Instruction*, eds. John Biggs and John Kirby (New York: Academic Press, 1980), pp. 91-118.

55. Annette Karmiloff-Smith, *Beyond Modularity: A Developmental Perspective on Cognitive Science* (Cambridge, MA: MIT Press, 1992), p. 192.

56. Steven Mithen, *The Prehistory of the Mind* (London: Thames and Hudson, 1996).

57. Margaret Boden, "What Is Creativity?," in *Dimensions of Creativity*, ed. Margaret Boden (Cambridge, MA: MIT Press, 1994), pp. 75-118.

58. Mary Hesse, *Models and Analogies in Science* (Notre Dame, IN: Notre Dame University Press, 1966).

59. Janet Burns, John Clift, and James Duncan, "Understanding of Understanding: Implications for Learning and Teaching," *British Journal of Educational Psychology* 61 (1991): 276-289.

60. Susan Carey and Elizabeth Spelke, "Domain Specific Knowledge and Conceptual Change," in *Mapping the Mind: Domain Specificity in Cognition and Culture*, eds. Lawrence Hirschfeld and Susan Gelman (Cambridge: Cambridge University Press, 1994), pp. 169-200.

61. Karmiloff-Smith, *Beyond Modularity*, p. 192.

CHAPTER XI

Moving Beyond the Impasse

NICHOLAS C. BURBULES

In this chapter I offer a reexamination of the philosophical and pedagogical merits of this thing (these things) called "constructivism," in light of the discussions and criticisms offered by the authors in this collection. As they make clear, "constructivism" refers to many ideas, joined by the merest thread of family resemblance and often expressing quite contradictory views. Whenever a philosopher encounters a term used so variously, especially when it conjures powerful allegiances and opponents under one or another of its guises, one's conceptual warning lights start flashing. As a first question, an outsider to this dispute might observe: Where is all this passion coming from? What is at stake that so energizes—and polarizes—these debates? The very vehemence of these discussions frequently suggests that something deeper must be at stake than the relative merits of John Locke versus Jean Piaget, or Socrates versus Lev Vygotsky.

To me this seems one of those situations in which the apparent terms of an argument stand in for what people are actually disagreeing about. The terrain of "constructivism," partly because of the multiplicity of meanings people attach to the concept, has become a battleground for people to argue over larger issues like the objectivity of science, the perils of relativism, the spread of "postmodernist" ideas (another one of those multifarious terms), the transition from positivist to postpositivist philosophies of science, the emptiness of identity politics (in which race, gender, and so on are regarded as "mere constructions."[1]) People argue over constructivism at least in part because they see within it the potential, or the danger, of promulgating *other* ideas to which it becomes attached.

In response, I hope to suggest a few ways of moving beyond the impasse between the pro- and anti-constructivists. First, I want to point

Nicholas C. Burbules is Professor of Educational Policy Studies at the University of Illinois, Urbana/Champaign. He has published numerous articles and several books in philosophy of education, educational policy, and technology studies in education. He serves as editor of the journal of *Educational Theory*.

out some of the ways in which the *characterizations* of what constructivism is, pro and con, contribute to misunderstandings and unfruitful dichotomies. Second, I will try to reframe the epistemological and metaphysical disputes that advocates and critics seem to think divide them, when in fact they are often differing only in the relative weight they give to certain factors that most of them agree must be given some weight in assessments of what is true. This section will conclude with a set of five propositions that I believe most participants to this debate, whether pro- or anti-constructivism, can subscribe to. Third, I want to move past the philosophical disputes—which I am suggesting are often exaggerated and self-perpetuating—to the pedagogical merits of constructivism as a view of learning and as a view of teaching (two significantly different things), and conclude by building upon some of the important pedagogical conclusions offered by other chapters in this collection.

Misframing the Debate

As Denis Phillips, Eric Bredo, Michael Matthews and others demonstrate well, one ought to use the term "constructivism*s*" to represent this debate because of the variety of things meant by the term. Individual or social, wishy-washy or radical, realist or idealist, learning theory or epistemology (or the argument that a learning theory *is* an epistemology), constructivism comes in many flavors, and other philosophical assumptions or purposes often get attached to constructivism that may or may not be "constructivist" in origin. Let's pause to reexamine what is going on here.

Phillips notes that the term has "attained the status of political correctness," particularly in the field of education.[2] When broad (and multifarious) ideas do become widely accepted, there is a tremendous incentive to attach one's theoretical (and often political) agenda to that term. In seeking allies, one is halfway toward success because people already feel a passionate (if vague) commitment to the broader notion; and if one can assert persuasively that acceptance of that idea also commits one to other conclusions, many people will not scrutinize the logic that carries them from one thing to the other. Constructivism is hardly the only concept that has received such treatment, particularly in education: a similar analysis could be given of "choice," "democratic classrooms," "equal opportunity," "progressive education," and similar terms. As a result, fights over what "constructivism" *really* means (and commits one to) take on the vigor of a crusade because other important allegiances are at stake.

In the same way, opponents of what "constructivism" has come to stand for often attribute to it assumptions that mischaracterize or oversimplify what the view commits one to (although it must be said that they are aided in this by the exaggerated claims made by some of its proponents, as I will discuss later). So we encounter characterizations like that of David Hull, quoted by Phillips in Chapter I: "The most extreme constructivists seem to hold that all of us, scientists included, are helpless victims in the maws of our societies." Well, who would want to believe *that*? It sounds like being devoured by a giant creature in a monster movie.

And here I want to give a cautionary tip to readers: always watch for the word "mere" (or similar terms). Often constructivists are excoriated for holding that knowledge is "merely constructed," or that personal identity is a "mere social construction," and so on. Notice that these criticisms actually do acknowledge, tacitly, that such matters *are* in some sense constructed, but not *merely* so. Recognizing how "mere" operates to exaggerate and oversimplify the opposing view allows one to shift the issue to different and, I think, more productive questions: What elements of such beliefs are subject to construction and which ones are not? If knowledge (or identity, etc.) isn't *merely* constructed, how constructed is it? For example, there is certainly a sense in which categories of racial identity are a construction and not merely a consequence of skin color; yet it is also true that skin color is a relatively objective factor in this process. The idea of a "quark" is a construction, since we can never observe such things; yet it bears upon evidence that *can* be observed and given a fairly widespread consensual interpretation. The appellation "mere" gives the impression that constructivists think there is nothing to say beyond affirming whatever individuals or social groups—any individual or social group—might happen to come up with as an account of their social or natural environments. But only *some* constructivists say such things, and criticisms of such views are better leveled against those writers than against "constructivism" *per se*. Some authors in this yearbook are careful to make such distinctions; others are less so. Indeed, as amply demonstrated in these chapters, it is often other constructivists who argue most strongly against such extreme views.

The fight, by some advocates and critics alike, to identify *the* constructivism clearly flies in the face of the multiplicity of views actually associated with the term. I am a big fan of studies that try to understand and explore this sort of complexity, and do justice to it, rather than accepting a polarized characterization that, for some advocates, suggests that if one does not accept this particular version, one is not a

"real" constructivist; or, for some critics, sets up a particularly out-
landish set of beliefs to argue the dangers of the view generally. (Surprisingly, the work of Ernst von Glasersfeld seems to serve both sorts
of purposes simultaneously.)

Another aspect of the debate that has ill served a thoughtful consideration of these complexities is, as Matthews says in Chapter VI, that
"constructivism" is often treated as a package deal, by advocates and
critics alike, where commitment to a certain approach to learning automatically commits one to a theory of teaching, a view of epistemology, a
conception of reality, and so on. This can be seen as an expression of
the phenomenon described earlier, that subscribing to certain *isms* is
taken as an all-or-nothing affair. Yet, ironically, this is a very un-con-
structivist thing to claim. If one believes that theoretical understandings
are to some degree constructed, then a corollary is that these constructions will vary, and that different people or groups will account for matters in different ways—and this must pertain to alternative versions of
constructivist theory itself. The attempt to offer a *systematic* account of
constructivism, and what certain beliefs *necessarily* commit one to, seems
not only inconsistent, but suggests the desire to impose a set of views
rather than to engage the very processes of construction argued for
within the theory. This seems to be akin to arguments for relativism, or
pronouncements about the need for everyone to believe postmodernism: where do such arguments stand in relation to their own claims?

In addition, as Thomas Popkewitz shows, constructivism is a theory that has its own genealogy.[3] When viewed as a historically unfolding and changing theory, constructivism appears as much less obviously wedded to the liberating, open-ended forms of pedagogy that its
adherents tend to support. Without reviewing all of Popkewitz's argument here, the point of his analysis is to suggest that a constructivist
understanding of constructivism itself would have to regard its
premises and its implications much less as ahistorical, essential logical
connectives that stand or fall together, and more as socially mediated
associations that are formulated, expressed, and accepted for various
reasons by situated persons and groups, and that have identifiable consequences for larger patterns of social inclusion and exclusion.

At the start, then, I am suggesting that the debate over constructivism is often mischaracterized by both sides. On the one hand, the
discussion is not advanced by those critics who use exaggerated characterizations of what constructivism is to avoid having to acknowledge
the rather inescapable conclusion that all human knowledge *is* (in
some sense at least) constructed by sentient actors situated in concrete

circumstances of institutional identification, social relations of power, and personal interest. All the interesting questions follow from this acknowledgment: What are the constraints that limit just any belief from taking hold as true? What are the correctives built into social organizations of inquiry that question, test, and modify such beliefs? What are the conditions that allow for the comparison of beliefs, as a way of assessing alternative accounts of phenomena? My point, which I will develop below, is that there is no need to step outside a constructivist framework to give answers to such questions.

On the other hand, I have suggested, the discussion is also not advanced by advocates of constructivism who mischaracterize a broad range of opposing epistemological stances as all holding a naive "correspondence" view of truth, when the entire trend of postpositivist philosophies of science has been to concede a number of the specific claims of the constructivist account (for example, that one's theoretical commitments influence the ways in which phenomena are perceived), while denying that this leads to the more extreme relativist conclusions that some constructivists still seem to maintain. I have tried to point out here how utterly inconsistent such a relativistic stance is for anyone who argues that constructivism just *is* the way people learn, or *is* the way societies create and negotiate identities, or *is* the way in which "truth" (their quotation marks) gets made.

To commentators on both sides I want to say, "You aren't being constructivist *enough*."

Epistemological and Metaphysical Antinomies

The *epistemological* debate between constructivism and its critics seems to be primarily about whether there can be a *warrant* for knowledge that rests upon criteria that are not socially and culturally specific. The *metaphysical* debate between constructivism and its critics seems to be primarily about whether there is a reality that is external to our attempts to grasp it.

Both of these debates are, I want to suggest, misguided and—as framed here—irresolvable. They are instances of the problems that arise when the way in which an issue has been defined guarantees that the disputants will occupy positions that reinforce their stereotypes of one another and strengthen their resolve that the other view represents a narrow-minded and dangerous notion that must be resisted at all times.

On the issue of epistemology, constructivism is typically characterized as the view, as Kenneth Howe and Jason Berv put it in Chapter II, that there are "no criteria [of truth] outside of what people say and do," or as Luise McCarty and Thomas Schwandt put it in Chapter III, "no meanings or standards outside or alternative to those of the community to which community members can appeal." When the issue is characterized this way, constructivists come off (to their critics) as relativists. At the same time, the critics come off (to constructivists) as seeming to think that there are free-floating "criteria" out there that can always settle knowledge disputes in an objective, impartial manner; the constructivists wave their well-worn copies of Thomas Kuhn's *Structure of Scientific Revolutions*, and both sides of the dispute settle down into another round of that old familiar waltz around the issue of paradigms and incommensurability.

Please, let's move on.

The self-perpetuating character of this debate, in which the roles and arguments are so well known and rehearsed, reminds me of that story where the jokes told in a prison become so familiar that they are just identified by number—"14!" the inmate yelled, and all the others laughed. And as often happens when advocates "know" what their opponents are going to say, real listening and engagement cease to be possibilities.

I would like to suggest a different starting point and hence a different way of framing the question. It seems quite apparent to me that all endeavors of human thought and language are socially situated. That means that any criteria we could ever have will be socially formulated, negotiated, interpreted, and applied. Any assessments of warrant will be socially formulated, negotiated, interpreted, and applied. Any methods of inquiry will be socially formulated, negotiated, interpreted, and applied. Any description of an external world will be socially formulated, negotiated, interpreted, and applied. Thus, any knowledge claim will be socially formulated, negotiated, interpreted, and applied. For that matter, any account of epistemology will be socially formulated, negotiated, interpreted, and applied.

The new question I wish to pose is, "socially formulated, negotiated, interpreted, and applied *by whom?*" because the actual dispute that seems to be operating at the ground level here is that one group disagrees with the criteria, the assessments of warrant, the methods of inquiry, the descriptions of an external world, and so on, of another group (from here on, I will refer to this cluster of interrelated ideas as "criteria, etc."). The critics of constructivists worry that they are insufficiently respectful of a set of criteria, etc., that *they* (the critics) value; they see in the apparent relativism of constructivism an assault, not on the possibility of criteria, etc., generally (although this is how the criticism is typically stated), but on *their* criteria, etc. What most bothers the critics of constructivism, I think, is that constructivism seems to deprive them of the basis for claiming that their criteria, etc. are not just the ones that happen to be recognized by their own social group, but ones that should be held by everyone.

But this is where my reformulation is meant to be helpful, for the critics need to acknowledge that their criteria, etc., *are* the ones that happen to be held by their social group—it could not be otherwise—but that this does not disqualify them from *also* having a value and weight that could be recommended to others. It simply deprives them of the argument that the reason why they have such a value and weight is that they are the real or true criteria, etc., which *must* be binding on all groups whether they realize it or not. Instead, they have to do what they always had to do anyway, which is to seek to persuade others that their criteria, etc., *are* better accounts. If they succeed in this, everyone is happy. If they fail in this, then the only purpose served by the claim that these really are the proper criteria, etc., and that others are just foolishly (or stubbornly) failing to recognize them, is to grant legitimacy to social policies and institutions that impose such criteria, etc., on persons and groups who for whatever reason are resisting them. Reframing the matter in social terms, as this is, reveals how disturbing an option such an outcome would be.

Far better, then, to explore with greater care the dynamics by which criteria, etc., *come to be shared* across different persons and groups. Constructivism does not have to deny the possibility of their being shared, or discount its desirability. Conversely, critics of constructivism can be asked to "ante up" their confidence that the criteria, etc., which they favor really are the better, more rational, more fruitful ones. If my argument is successful at all, that little word "outside" in the quotations above from Howe and Berv and from McCarty and Schwandt has been transformed: there are never any criteria, etc., *outside* the holdings of a particular group unless and until another group comes to hold them also. If the critics of constructivism believe that there "really are" such criteria, etc., outside of their particular shared beliefs, the only way to instantiate that claim is by persuading others to come to hold them also. No part of this analysis steps outside the social (constructed) realm. The only alternative here is the rather widely discredited philosophical notion that these criteria, etc., drift abstractly, timelessly, above and apart from human affairs (whether we have discovered them yet or not) and that we need philosophers and other wise men and women to glimpse them and explain them to the rest of us. This is "outside" in the sense that Plato's prisoner had to go outside the Cave and then report back to the poor devils inside, arguing about "mere" shadows on the wall; and we all know that he was totally unsuccessful in changing *anyone's* view of things there.

When Peter Slezak argues that constructivists believe that "knowledge is *merely* consensus upon *arbitrary* convention" (italics added), we see a fairly typical example of how the issues are being misframed. A set of conventions (criteria, etc.) that come to be socially shared are in no way arbitrary, even if one thinks they are mistaken; for one thing, not just any set of conventions can come to be commonly shared. Unless a social group is totally delusional, their criteria, etc., must have *something* to be said for them, must have *some* value and efficacy, it seems to me. Challenging or changing them will require something more than calling them "arbitrary." For another thing, we again encounter that word "merely," as if social consensus were not inherently part of the processes by which any system of belief needs to be formulated, negotiated, interpreted, and applied. And if any constructivists are so foolish as to assert that "knowledge is merely consensus upon arbitrary convention," one need only reply that this position then gives no reason whatsoever to accept the constructivist account itself.

So, in the first instance, I have tried to change an apparent epistemological dispute about objectivism and relativism into a discussion of which social groups accept which criteria, assessments of warrant, methods of inquiry, etc., and how they might come to be shared across different groups. I have suggested that the only meaning of "outside" that does any worthwhile philosophical work here is one grounded in the idea of criteria, etc. that come to be shared through a process of engagement and persuasion; that if this process is in good faith there cannot be any presumption about *whose* criteria, etc. are destined to win over the other; that an assertion that some are the "real and true" criteria, etc. which others are compelled to accept is a rhetorical move, not a persuasive one; and that any other meaning of "outside" tends to impede such conversations by prejudging what the conclusion of the engagement must be, or imposing that outcome by philosophical fiat.

On the issue of metaphysics, we come to the timeless philosophical question about the independent existence of an external world. I have given long and careful thought to this problem, and I would like to propose a seriously considered response: *Who cares?*

The question of the existence of an external world is, I believe, one of those philosophical pseudo-questions that are not answerable in the terms given. It is a more sophisticated version of that sophomoric conundrum about trees falling in forests. It expresses an article of faith rather than a demonstrable philosophical postulate, and as with other articles of faith it is not interesting to ask whether it is true or not, but only *why* people believe it and *what effects* their belief has.

Constructivists err profoundly when they take on the metaphysical issue. As McCarty and Schwandt point out, both Kenneth Gergen and Ernst von Glasersfeld claim to be "agnostic" on this question, and yet neither one can apparently resist the temptation to weigh in on the subject. Too bad: agnosticism is the better road for any constructivist, I believe. By *denying* the existence of an external world, one takes on the same unredeemable burden of proof as those who assert it. But for the constructivist, this question cannot and does not need to be answered either way; the question needs to be reframed as, "What difference would it make to the processes of constructing an understanding based on experience?" The faith in the existence of an independent, unchanging external world has two important effects: it wants to guarantee (a) the consistency of experience and (b) the ultimate decidability of disputes over particular truth claims.

But on the first issue one must simply say, either our experience is consistent or it is not (consistent for the individual over time, and consistent across individuals). If it is, then why it is need not concern us; we go about the business of constructing a coherent account of things, given what we and others experience, and leave the rest as superfluous information. If it is not, then no coherent account of things is possible anyway, and embracing the postulate of an independent, unchanging external world will not make it any more so. All that we need in order for the pursuit of knowledge to go forward, individually and socially, is consistency of experience: under the same apparent circumstances the same experiences tend to be produced. This is often expressed as "the world is stubborn," for people who seem to think that one needs a referent—"the world" or "reality"—to stand behind and confirm what they believe to be true. But if the reasons and evidence for that belief are sufficient for it to be called "true," it adds nothing to say, ". . . and it really *is* true, too!" or ". . . it is true because the world really *is* that way."

Phillips falls into this error, I think, while discussing the change in belief from the earth being flat, to the belief that it was round. He says, "It is the shape itself, and not only political and social factors at work in discourse communities, that influences the knowledge that we generate about that shape."[4] But the knowledge that the earth "really is round" was an *outcome* of those changing beliefs. *It only makes sense to say that its actual shape drove the process of belief change after that belief change has already happened.* The problem is that tomorrow we might figure out that its shape is something else again (even widely held scientific beliefs sometimes turn out to be mistaken). If we say that "the shape itself" explains that new shift in belief, is this the *same* "shape itself" that explained the previous shift? Or was that previous "shape itself" mistaken (since it was the product of a theory which said that the shape was round)?

This is the problem that arises when people feel the need to supplement "we believe this is true" with "and that belief accords with reality." What the supplement comes to is really just a statement of strength of confidence; that a belief or hypothesis was previously based on certain partial experiences, and that later experiences were consistent with that belief and so tended to reinforce it (so that it increases the confidence that "reality" has been captured). In fact, the supplemental phrase cannot mean anything more than this, since anything that one might say about the relation of a belief to reality is either an expression of very strong confidence, based upon repeated, consistent experiences, or it is, as mentioned before, an expression of faith. Either way, it might turn out to be mistaken.

This expression of faith also has relevance to the second issue mentioned above: it tends to support a hope that multiple versions of the world will either converge, or that the best one will win out (because the stubborn world will adjudicate the dispute in favor of one or another). But this hope for decidability is primarily motivational; it does not have any persuasive force itself. Indeed, it can be counterproductive to promoting agreement when it expresses the attitude that "there is a way that the world is; we know it and you do not." Using allusions to "reality" in this way, as a trump, has the effect of blocking inquiries into the elements of social and cultural particularity in *any* understanding of the world, and of evading the responsibility to acknowledge that possibility and the limits of one's ability to see the limitations, interests, and biases built into one's version—limitations that can often only be seen by others who do not share it. If one only views this relation in terms of "we are right and you are wrong," or "this is the way the world is," a crucial opportunity for *reciprocal* enlightenment is missed.

In short, realists on this issue are more likely to think that knowledge can be objective, complete, and unchanging, and that knowledge disputes can be settled by allusions to "the way the world is." Constructivists and others who reject that premise are more likely to think that knowledge will be partial, provisional, and imperfect, and that knowledge disputes will be more intractable because strongly held beliefs are intertwined with other social and cultural elements that groups may be reluctant to give up or change. Who is right on this issue? I hope to have made it clear that the question cannot be answered at that level; *both* positions tend to prejudge what sorts of social agreement will or will not be possible, and they use claims about "reality" (one way or another) to undergird what are really premises about the likelihood of being able to settle certain types of disagreement. Rather than ask who is right, I have suggested that a more fruitful way of framing the matter is to ask what the *effects* of these competing beliefs might be; and I have suggested that for both the pro- and anti-constructivists, their presuppositions obscure and might actually inhibit the possibilities of pursuing and achieving actual understandings and agreements in the matters under dispute.

As I have said, many constructivists have no one but themselves to blame for mishandling such epistemological and metaphysical questions. Where they should be agnostic or silent, they cannot resist sticking a thumb in the eye of conventional philosophical views. Probably the most egregious example of this habit is the work of von Glasersfeld, whose more extreme and often philosophically confused claims (as is amply documented by the criticisms posed against him in this volume) are a kind of weight dragging down the credibility of constructivism generally. Von Glasersfeld has a persistent habit of "bait and switch" argument; using a term or concept one way in one context, then later using it in a very different way and for a very different purpose. For example, one of his primary analogies is that of "match" versus "fit" as two views of knowledge. The first view says that to be true a belief must match or correspond to an independent reality. On the second view, von Glasersfeld's preferred alternative, a belief must "fit" (like a key in a lock); it must do some work for us. Speculating on the nature of the lock is pointless, he believes; all we can know is whether our "key" (our constructed belief) is successful for our purposes. Matching reality has nothing to do with it.[5]

I do not think that von Glasersfeld realizes that this distinction misses the point he thinks he is establishing. The match-versus-fit views are not necessarily competing views about "reality"; the fit view posits an independent reality just as much as the match view does. We construct the key, but we do not (as I read von Glasersfeld here) construct whether it fits or not. Indeed, von Glasersfeld himself invokes the term "reality" in explaining this concept of fitness.[6] In this context, the match-versus-fit views are really just two alternative ways of *conceiving* what the relation between beliefs and reality is. Yet later in this same essay, von Glasersfeld says something very different: that it is the *object* of understanding that we construct that "fits."[7] This is a crucial and highly misleading conflation. That we construct an understanding of the world (that must "fit" reality) is not a particularly radical notion at all; that we construct the objects of our understanding, partly to fit our beliefs, is not only a different view but a diametrically opposed one. It seems that here von Glasersfeld draws readers into accepting a relatively straightforward and commonsensical account of what it means to "fit," then changes his use of it to suggest that this acceptance commits one to other claims that are much more extreme in their epistemological and metaphysical implications.

We see numerous examples of this same tendency in other quotations from von Glasersfeld, many of them cited in this book. Phillips's 1997 article quotes von Glasersfeld as saying that "'facts' are not elements of an observer's independent world but elements of an observer's experience."[8] This is misleading: a "fact" isn't an element in either place; it is an assessment of a *relation* between an experience and the world (a relation like, say, *fit*). Von Glasersfeld seems to be saying something provocative here, but he is only contesting a superficial and sloppy way in which people commonly use words like "fact," as if facts were scattered around the world like gemstones waiting to be collected. He is right: no serious thinker would say such a thing. But rejecting that view does not necessarily throw one over into von Glasersfeld's preferred alternative, that "facts" are just a certain category of experience. Phillips provides another good illustration of this tendency: in Chapter I he quotes von Glasersfeld as saying, "knowledge, no matter how it is defined, is in the heads of persons . . . the thinking subject has no alternative but to construct what he or she knows on the basis of . . . experience." This is put rather awkwardly, I think, but it is pretty easy to grasp. But the *consequence* of this belief, von Glasersfeld says immediately after, is that "all kinds of experience are basically subjective," and that knowledge claims can't be reliably compared between persons. Yet in another quotation, from Howe and Berv's chapter, von Glasersfeld says that "Where knowledge is concerned, the concepts, theories, beliefs, and other abstract structures which the individual subject has found to be viable, gain a higher degree of viability when successful predictions can be made by imputing the use of this knowledge to others. The additional viability can be interpreted as indicating intersubjectivity and constitutes the constructivist substitute for objectivity." Not only is the intersubjectivity account of viability in conflict with the "fit" account von Glasersfeld provided previously; it is inconsistent, as far as I can see, with his own claim in the second passage quoted by Phillips, above, about the subjectivity of experience, in which according to von Glasersfeld the most one can say is that "I may find reasons to believe that my experience may not be unlike yours." (Which, I must say, is some pretty slippery phraseology.) It certainly falls far short of an account of intersubjectivity (or, as he insists on putting it, what "can be interpreted as indicating intersubjectivity").

I have a special impatience with von Glasersfeld's style of argument, but these shortcomings are not unique to him. Even Gergen, an author I tend to have much more in common with, still insists on saying such things as: there are a "multiplicity of ways in which 'the world' is, and can be, constructed" (also quoted by Phillips in 1997). Taken in one sense, this is an unremarkable observation; we know that understandings of the world are in fact fascinatingly pluralistic. But the slippage here is in saying that this pluralism supports the conclusion that "*the world* is, and can be constructed," and it is less clear what that means or what it commits one to. Let me posit a few queries about what it might mean: Is this mountain here a construction? Is the experience of having walked up it a construction? Is the activity of measuring its height a construction? Is this sketch or photograph of it a construction? Is "Mt. Rainier" a construction? Is "the highest peak in Washington state" a construction? Is the white dot representing Mt. Rainier on this map a construction? Is the co-referentiality of these different versions of Mt. Rainier a construction? Our experience of the world, our labels for it, our representations and descriptions of it, and our inferences about the significance of those descriptions of it are indeed multiple, perhaps limitlessly so. But the applicability of a term like "construction" is quite different in these different contexts. When we recognize the differences between "construction" as a characterization of our *versions* or *understandings* and as a characterization of *the world*, we can begin to see that the latter meaning is *useless* to constructivists, as much as they may like to invoke it. It expresses a superfluous opinion about a matter that only inflames the sort of opposition we see in this book, and that interferes with the kinds of questions I am trying to foreground, those dealing with the ways in which and the degrees to which we can expect those multiple versions/understandings/constructions to engage one another in a process of comparative assessment that can (sometimes, at least) reliably adjudicate those differences.

And so, I am suggesting, constructivists have often been their own worst enemy in misframing issues, or taking on issues, that a more thoroughgoing constructivist account ought to approach in a very different way. It seems clear, for example, that even a construction is constructed out of *something* (let's call it "evidence"). One can then argue that evidence is constructed, but it must be constructed out of something (let's call it "experience" or "perception"). One can then argue that experience or perception is constructed, but this too must be constructed out of something. At some point you get to something that is not "constructed" in the sense that this term is meant. This is not necessarily the level of "reality," but it is an element in our experience that is not susceptible to construction, or at least not in the same way that these other interpretations are. (Notice that even the attribution of construction to these stages is an assertion about something that is "really happening" in our mental processes, and in everyone else's too.) Constructivists want to insist that individuals or groups construct different versions of the world, or make sense of the same information or experiences in different ways (and I think they are clearly correct in this); but many of them do not seem to realize that this very conclusion rests upon a presumption of potentially shared experiences that may or may not provide a basis for agreement—not only through "mere" social and political consensus, but because at some level they are referring to (what they come to recognize as) the "same" thing. Beyond this point, I am suggesting, it is an empty dispute to argue about whether that thing is caused by or corresponds to an external world. What matters here are *social* processes through and through: what are the grounds for establishing the generalizability of such knowledge claims; what are the grounds for testing them; and what are the grounds for adjudicating competing knowledge claims? I see no reasons why most constructivists and non-constructivists alike cannot address these sorts of questions and reach some agreement on them.

Five Propositions

As a way of advancing that conversation, I want to suggest five propositions, or basic ideas, that potentially cut across the pro- and anti-constructivist positions. They are not universally shared views within this debate, but I do believe that they identify points that any account must acknowledge and respond to, even if they would be given varying relative weights of significance by different accounts. As I said at the beginning, I think many debates in this area primarily come down to the strength of such relative weightings, not to fundamental disagreements.

1. *All understandings of the world partake of a social environment, even when they are formulated by individuals alone.* The very idea of a "construction" means invoking ways of making sense of experiences that are learned. With the possible exception of some innate quasi-Kantian categories, we construct understandings the same ways that we undertake any other complex human practice—under the guidance of others or drawing from examples of how to do it that we have learned from others. Von Glasersfeld's idea that construction comes first, and that even our social interactions, relations, and intersubjective agreements with others are merely apparent accounts of the world that we may or may not accept, is far too neat, and can give no account of why we commonly construct the world in certain ways rather than others. If construction in any interesting and rich sense is possible, it is *because* it is a social process. Yet at the same time, this social perspective commits one (though some constructivists do not seem to recognize this) to some implicit view of a shared reality, not only as an accidental artifact that we happen to come to share, but as a condition of sociality itself.

2. *Language provides the conditions for both understanding and misunderstanding.* Appropriations of ideas such as Ludwig Wittgenstein's notion of "language games" have led some theorists to the idea that such pockets of language use are by definition incommensurable (which is far from Wittgenstein's meaning, but that is another issue). A great deal is made, especially in some postmodern sources, that language can express such profound conceptual differences that the pursuit of intersubjective understanding is futile. (Jean-François Lyotard calls them "islands of meaning.") Other authors, such as Hans-Georg Gadamer or Jürgen Habermas, are much more optimistic about the possibilities of understanding or agreement. What is at stake here is the degree to which the processes of construction, which are expressed and negotiated through the available language(s), can be expected to reconcile radically different versions of the world. The pessimists and the optimists here both miss the point, I would suggest. The issue is not with the nature of the language, but with the *practice of communication*. The available language both facilitates and constrains the possibilities of communication (it is not a remarkable observation to say this); but whether communication can generate shared constructions is not determined by the available language itself so much as by the ways in which persons enact the communicative relation. In fact, the very language that makes understanding possible makes misunderstanding possible *and vice versa*.

In the present context, my point has been that questions such as "Is there an objective, commonly shared reality?" do not lead anywhere useful. Because differences in experiences and the ways in which we construct understandings of these experiences are almost always adjudicated in and through language, the more salient question is, "Does it help or hinder this process to make assertions like, 'This is the way the world is'?" I have suggested that in most cases it adds nothing constructive, and may inhibit a more substantial engagement of views.

3. *Our efforts at understanding the world always occur at a distinct time and place and under a set of circumstances that motivate and influence our choice of questions, methods, and reference groups for cross-checking our understandings.* Clearly some theorists seem to read off this premise a host of relativistic conclusions, since every person or group is by definition situated differently from every other. This is an entirely unnecessary conclusion. It seems clear to me that the *inevitability* of social and political influences on our attempts to construct workable understandings of the world does not mean that these conclusions are *merely* social and political. Denying such influences is one sort of mistake, I believe, but giving them determinative weight and force is another.

This discussion opens up another question addressed in several of the foregoing chapters: Is science different? Some writers seem willing to acknowledge that "social construction" is not a very remarkable thesis when applied to the phenomena of the social world, which seem directly susceptible to our efforts to define and describe them; but that the world of natural or physical science is different because it is about phenomena that have an independent existence, apart from our efforts to describe or characterize them. This is a mistake. The processes of constructing understanding, and the relation between our versions and the phenomena and regularities they are trying to account for, are not fundamentally different in these two realms, even if the two sides of that relation might be given different degrees of weight in the social and in the natural contexts (although even there I would say that the differences can be exaggerated).

What makes the physical or natural sciences different is primarily something else, not the nature of the phenomena they are dealing with. They have, for a variety of reasons, established a stronger set of common standards of practice, common vocabularies, and common techniques of inquiry. Together these sorts of factors have made the practice of science more orderly and overtly consensual, while other forms of inquiry appear less so. But this difference does not mean that one endeavor depends less on constructions than the other. The tendency to put certain sciences in a separate category, as if they were about the cleaner and more objective pursuit of truth, has made it a special point of emphasis among certain social constructivists to try to show how the same factors of peer approval, self-interest, winning over others to one's point of view, rivalry, avoiding group ridicule, seeking acclaim or financial reward, and so on, operate within these scientific communities of inquiry as they do in any other. This does not automatically make the practice of science corrupt, but it is difficult to imagine that they do not affect the practice of science, and how its theories get constructed and negotiated, in some very important ways.

4. *The underlying issue that divides the anti- and pro-constructivists is their attitudes toward difference and disagreement.* I mean this as a rather surprising claim. It seems clear to me that underneath the disputes over relativism, the existence of an external world, and so on, that are sketched in this book, what really divides the advocates of constructivism and its critics is that one side wants to maintain a broader scope for idiosyncrasy and pluralism in unreconciled (and perhaps irreconcilable) alternative accounts of the world, while the other expects, and wants to encourage, a resolution of differences in terms of criteria, etc., that can come to be commonly shared and applied. I have already argued that the latter desire is a matter to be demonstrated in practice, rather than asserted on *a priori* grounds: if these common standards do have some objective advantage, then bringing others to share them is the only way of actually establishing their generalizability. At the same time, the view favoring, or at least being willing to tolerate, a greater degree of idiosyncrasy and pluralism in competing accounts of the world regards the imposition of criteria, etc., that people do not in fact share as presumptuous at best and a kind of intellectual domination at worst. Constructivism in its contemporary form provides a rationale for the more pluralistic view: this is pretty clearly behind the social constructivist project, and it is even more apparent in the radically individualistic constructivism argued for by von Glasersfeld.

Certainly advocates for inquiry of all sorts generally favor the benefits of disagreement, even vigorous and fundamental disagreement, as part of the process that subjects beliefs to rigorous questioning and testing, and that generates alternative hypotheses and potential solutions to problems. But these disagreements remain disagreements within an implicit compact of values, assumptions, and procedures that are not questioned; hence, however vigorous the disagreement might be, it does not challenge the fundamental purpose and legitimacy of the endeavor itself. This view can be linked in some respects with the characteristics of what Kuhn calls "normal science." But the more extreme, and potentially irreconcilable, forms of disagreement—of alternative constructions, if you will—are not just differences against a background of shared values, assumptions, and procedures, but a questioning of these as well. They pose a very different sort of challenge to the attempt to foster understanding and agreement across these differences, and they face a much greater chance of failing to do so. Moreover, they often require ways of speaking and imagining across differences that do not fit within the conventional languages and methodologies of scientific practice. It is this threat, I have suggested, that drives the insistence that there *must* be a set of common criteria, etc. that can be relied upon to adjudicate such differences, and that there *must* be a common world against which to compare, and ultimately settle, these differences. I have also suggested that some constructivists have erred in the opposite direction by denying out of hand that such commonalities exist, or can be established.

Instead I have suggested a greater agnosticism; that the identification and justification of shared criteria, etc. is itself a form of inquiry, one that has to operate within and across the existing views, and differences, of the persons and groups involved, and one that has to proceed with few preconceptions about what the end result of that shared inquiry will generate.

5. *Constructivism operates within a problem-based framework, in which one potential problem is always the status of one's constructions themselves.* I have said that a fault that can be attributed to constructivists and their critics alike is in not being constructivist enough. On the constructivist side, this sometimes takes the form of stipulating what views constructivists can or cannot subscribe to, attempting to erect a superstructure of theory that is an account of "pure" constructivism, or leaping from a set of premises to a series of conclusions that are not particularly constructivist at all. If anything is constructed in our understandings, then everything must be, even the objects of our understanding themselves—which, as I have said, is not a very constructivist way of arguing.

On the other side, the critics of constructivism sometimes minimize the extent to which "constructions" (imagined, creative attempts to go beyond a set of given data to build meaningful and plausible accounts of the world) are an inevitable dimension of human inquiry, not a remarkable, or radical, or relativistic challenge to it. In this chapter I have suggested that this is not where the disputes between constructivists and their critics reside: it is in taking on, from both sides, a set of broader epistemological and metaphysical assertions that are neither necessary to the constructivist account nor, in my view, particularly helpful to it. What can provide a way beyond this impasse, I have suggested, is to bracket such disputes (which simply cannot be resolved, in the terms within which they are framed, and do not need to be), and to focus on trying to understand the practices and procedures by which constructions come to be created, adjudicated, and commonly shared. I have suggested, in fact, that the standard epistemological and metaphysical disputes have often served a counterproductive purpose; and that since these arguments cannot be resolved, the chief remaining question is how *holding* such beliefs, and arguing about them, itself affects the substantive processes of inquiry.

Is generalizability possible? Can our knowledge be objectively proven? Is there a reality that grounds and affirms our constructions of it? Instead of questions such as these, I have suggested a different set of issues, informed by these five propositions: What are the processes and practices through which the activities of generalizability, objectivity, intersubjectivity, testing, and adjudicating differences must proceed? How do they work? How do they affect, and how are they affected by, the social and institutional contexts in which they take place? What are the points over which they can break down? What are their reasonable end points? As I have said, this seems to me a more thoroughgoing constructivist approach, and nothing outside of a constructivist account needs to be added to it. Where disagreements, conflicts, errors, and failures do arise, there is nothing outside of these same processes that can redeem, reconcile, or correct them.

The Educational Benefits of Constructivism

In the area of pedagogy, I have less to add to the sensible and useful observations made in several of the preceding chapters. It does seem to me worth underlining, as Matthews, McCarty and Schwandt, and others say, that constructivist approaches to pedagogy would be generally better off if their advocates stayed out of the epistemological and metaphysical speculations that they seem unable to resist. First, these broader pronouncements are neither necessary for constructivist pedagogy, nor particularly helpful to it; they distract the discussion far afield from the concerns pedagogues actually need help with. Second, people who might have excellent contributions to make to the area of constructivist pedagogy may not have the background to appreciate the depth and complexity of the epistemological and metaphysical disputes they are taking on when they wade into those waters. The sorts of questions about *how* social construction takes place, I have suggested, offer a far better starting point for thinking about pedagogy since the way persons and social groups generally construct understandings may be a very good guide for how these processes take place in classrooms.

It seems to me almost a truism to say that all learning is constructed; understanding and evaluating new ideas and skills, even those of the most apparently rote character, requires reinterpreting them in light of one's existing understandings and abilities. A corollary of this assumption is that no two people ever learn the "same" material in precisely the same way. As is touched upon in some of the preceding chapters, some educational writers seem to think that there is a fundamental dispute between more didactic versus more discovery-oriented approaches to teaching. But the way material is taught may not be the determining factor in how it is learned; even ideas and skills presented in the most structured and directive manner will still need to go through a process of filtering and reinterpretation as they are being learned. There may be *other* reasons to avoid such general approaches to teaching; they may, for example, tend to promote a "hidden curriculum" of deference to authority, an attitude toward knowledge as something given, not subject to question, and so on. Even so, there may be instances where certain students, and certain subject matters, are taught best and most easily by adopting such an approach. One of the most important points made in this book, it seems to me, is echoed by Howe and Berv and by McCarty and Schwandt: that one of the most detrimental legacies of constructivism as a view of pedagogy is that this "ism," like so many others, has been promulgated as the One Best Way of teaching; and that with almost religious fervor the advocates of constructivist approaches believe that the entire system of education should be transformed around their principles. Admittedly, constructivism is by no means the first or the only approach to do this, and by and large its stance has been one of correcting or counterbalancing the overwhelming dominance in schools of more didactic, content-oriented, test-driven methods. Yet the only intelligent approach to teaching is one that recognizes that skilled teachers need many resources in their bags of tricks, and that different situations, different students, and different subject matters require the ability to adopt and adapt multiple approaches if they are going to be able to succeed as teachers in the face of many learning styles and degrees of motivation found among students. Constructivist approaches are valuable, but not the only resources they will need.

The other major lesson to be drawn from this discussion, also made clear by preceding chapters, is that a theory of teaching and a theory of learning are not logically locked together. The belief that they are remains a broadly held assumption in nearly every school of education, district or state office, and school in the country. Ironically, a constructivist view of learning should be especially aware that how new ideas or skills are presented does not determine how they will be learned. There may be *other* reasons why constructivist approaches to teaching have appeal, and there may be important ways in which they are more motivating or facilitative for students' learning. But a very "inquiry-oriented" lesson may still result in a student ending up with a rigid and inflexible belief; and a more didactic approach may actually trigger a very active and imaginative process of reflection in the learner. The error made here is a typical one in the field of education: adopting a means-ends attitude toward teaching, in the endless pursuit of the "methods" that will reliably yield the "results" sought. It may be especially ironic that constructivists turn out to be just as susceptible to this myth as have others. But it also should cause us to consider why it is that this aspiration has such a hold over educators, why it continually reappears with each new One Best Way of teaching, and why its hegemony is so powerful that it even absorbs into it views of teaching and learning that ought to be highly critical of it, as in the case of constructivism.

The principles of constructivist pedagogy—encouraging collaboration, promoting activity and exploration, respecting multiple points of view, emphasizing "authentic" problem-solving—have a number of benefits, and among these may be that these approaches do facilitate a more creative, synthetic attitude toward learning. But I have suggested here that the primary reasons why we might favor such an approach generally have less to do with driving a particular learning process and more to do with the ways in which this sort of classroom reflects *other* values we might hold, or the ways in which these types of activities and relationships tend to foster *other* lessons, apart from the subject matter itself, that we also value.

One example of this way of reframing the pedagogical issue concerns the ways in which science is taught. A constructivist approach to science teaching would tend to try to reproduce in the classroom the kinds of conditions that drive scientific exploration generally.[9, 10, 11] This is *not* necessarily because children learn science in the same ways that experts in the field establish new knowledge, but because learning how science is done is itself an important educational goal, apart from learning scientific content itself. First, the skills and dispositions of inquiry and collaboration may have relevance to all sorts of other activities in later life. Second, situating the content of science in the context of narratives about how science gets done (James Watson's *The Double*

Helix, for example), can be extremely motivating for students, regarding the process of scientific exploration more like a mystery, or a race, or a comedy of errors, than a desiccated, cold, impersonal endeavor. Third, this sort of understanding of science also tends to demystify the status of scientific knowledge, making it clear that beliefs change, that they don't come from "nowhere," and that the kinds of factors that influence human practices generally are not absent from the scientific domain either; this seems to be a crucial, underestimated educational goal in itself. Constructivist accounts of the scientific disciplines have provided a valuable perspective in looking behind the closed doors of laboratories, I believe, even when the broader epistemological and metaphysical conclusions of the sociology of scientific knowledge may have been overdrawn.

This discussion reveals another of those instances where reflection on an *educational* problem provides insight into rethinking a *philosophical* issue (although the line of influence is typically drawn in the other direction). Teaching and learning in a constructivist manner force us to narrow in on understanding the practices and procedures by which human actors in specific social contexts generate hypotheses, assess them, compare them with others, adjudicate disagreements or controversies over methods of inquiry, and so on. The irony is that debates over constructivist theory quickly lose sight of these factors and get embroiled in disputes that are almost entirely generated at an abstract level. As I have said, nothing could be less constructivist than that.

NOTES

1. Ian Hacking, "Are You a Social Constructionist?", *Lingua Franca* (May/June 1999): 65-72.

2. D. C. Phillips, "How, Why, What, When, and Where: Perspectives on Constructivism in Psychology and Education," *Issues in Education: Contributions from Educational Psychology* 3, no. 2 (1997): 151-194.

3. Thomas S. Popkewitz, "Dewey, Vygotsky, and the Social Administration of the Individual: Constructivist Pedagogy as Systems of Ideas in Historical Spaces," *American Educational Research Journal* 35, no. 4 (1998): 535-570.

4. Phillips, "How, Why, What, When, and Where," p. 189.

5. Ernst von Glasersfeld, "An Introduction to Radical Constructivism," in *The Invented Reality: How Do We Know What We Believe We Know? Contributions to Constructivism*, ed. Paul Watzlawick (New York: W .W. Norton, 1984): 17-40.

6. Ibid, p. 22.

7. Ibid, p. 36.

8. Phillips, "How, Why, What, When, and Where," p. 185.

9. Nicholas C. Burbules and Marcia C. Linn, "Science Education and Philosophy of Science: Congruence or Contradiction?", *International Journal of Science Education* 13, no. 3 (1991): 227-241.

10. Marcia C. Linn and Nicholas C. Burbules, "Construction of Knowledge and Group Learning" in *The Practice of Constructivism in Science Education*, ed. Kenneth Tobin (Washington, DC: American Association for the Advancement of Science, 1993): 91-119.

11. Marcia C. Linn, "The Role of the Laboratory in Science Learning," *Elementary School Journal* 97, no. 4 (1997): 401-417.

Name Index

N.B. The Notes at the end of each chapter have not been indexed.

Subject Index

RECENT PUBLICATIONS OF THE SOCIETY
1. The Yearbooks

99:1 (2000) *Constructivism in Education.* D. C. Phillips, editor. Cloth.

99:2 (2000) *American Education: Yesterday, Today, and Tomorrow.* Thomas L. Good, editor. Cloth.

98:1 (1999) *The Education of Teachers,* Gary A. Griffin, editor. Cloth.

98:2 (1999) *Issues in Curriculum,* Margaret J. Early and Kenneth J. Rehage, editors. Cloth.

97:1 (1998) *The Adolescent Years: Social Influences and Educational Challenges.* Kathryn Borman and Barbara Schneider, editors. Cloth.

97:2 (1998) *The Reading-Writing Connection.* Nancy Nelson and Robert C. Calfee, editors. Cloth.

96:1 (1997) *Service Learning.* Joan Schine, editor. Cloth.

96:2 (1997) *The Construction of Children's Character.* Alex Molnar, editor. Cloth.

95:1 (1996) *Performance-Based Student Assessment: Challenges and Possibilities.* Joan B. Baron and Dennie P. Wolf, editors. Cloth.

95:2 (1996) *Technology and the Future of Schooling.* Stephen T. Kerr, editor. Cloth.

94:1 (1995) *Creating New Educational Communities.* Jeannie Oakes and Karen Hunter Quartz, editors. Cloth.

94:2 (1995) *Changing Populations/Changing Schools.* Erwin Flaxman and A. Harry Passow, editors. Cloth.

93:1 (1994) *Teacher Research and Educational Reform.* Sandra Hollingsworth and Hugh Sockett, editors. Cloth.

93:2 (1994) *Bloom's Taxonomy: A Forty-year Retrospective.* Lorin W. Anderson and Lauren A. Sosniak, editors. Cloth.

92:1 (1993) *Gender and Education.* Sari Knopp Biklen and Diane Pollard, editors. Cloth.

92:2 (1993) *Bilingual Education: Politics, Practice, and Research.* M. Beatriz Arias and Ursula Casanova, editors. Cloth.

91:1 (1992) *The Changing Contexts of Teaching.* Ann Lieberman, editor. Cloth.

91:2 (1992) *The Arts, Education, and Aesthetic Knowing.* Bennett Reimer and Ralph A. Smith, editors. Cloth.

90:1 (1991) *The Care and Education of America's Young Children: Obstacles and Opportunities.* Sharon L. Kagan, editor. Cloth.

89:2 (1990) *Educational Leadership and Changing Contexts of Families, Communities, and Schools.* Brad Mitchell and Luvern L. Cunningham, editors. Paper.

88:1 (1989) *From Socrates to Software: The Teacher as Text and the Text as Teacher.* Philip W. Jackson and Sophie Haroutunian-Gordon, editors. Cloth.

88:2 (1989) *Schooling and Disability.* Douglas Biklen, Dianne Ferguson, and Alison Ford, editors. Cloth.

Order the above titles from the University of Chicago Press, 11030 S. Langley Ave., Chicago, IL 60628. For a list of earlier Yearbooks still available, write to the Secretary, NSSE, 5835 Kimbark Ave., Chicago, IL 60637.

2. The Series on Contemporary Educational Issues

This series has been discontinued.

The following volumes in the series may be ordered from the McCutchan Publishing Corporation, P.O. Box 774, Berkeley, CA 94702-0774. Phone: 510-841-8616; Fax: 510-841-7787.

Academic Work and Educational Excellence: Raising Student Productivity (1986). Edited by Tommy M. Tomlinson and Herbert J. Walberg.

Adapting Instruction to Student Differences (1985). Edited by Margaret C. Wang and Herbert J. Walberg.

Choice in Education (1990). Edited by William Lowe Boyd and Herbert J. Walberg.

Colleges of Education: Perspectives on Their Future (1985). Edited by Charles W. Case and William A. Matthes.

Contributing to Educational Change: Perspectives on Research and Practice (1988). Edited by Philip W. Jackson.

Educational Leadership and School Culture (1993). Edited by Marshall Sashkin and Herbert J. Walberg.

Effective Teaching: Current Research (1991). Edited by Hersholt C. Waxman and Herbert J. Walberg.

Improving Educational Standards and Productivity: The Research Basis for Policy (1982). Edited by Herbert J. Walberg.

Moral Development and Character Education (1989). Edited by Larry P. Nucci.

Motivating Students to Learn: Overcoming Barriers to High Achievement (1993). Edited by Tommy M. Tomlinson.

Radical Proposals for Educational Change (1994). Edited by Chester E. Finn, Jr. and Herbert J. Walberg.

Reaching Marginal Students: A Prime Concern for School Renewal (1987). Edited by Robert L. Sinclair and Ward Ghory.

Restructuring the Schools: Problems and Prospects (1992). Edited by John J. Lane and Edgar G. Epps.

Rethinking Policy for At-risk Students (1994). Edited by Kenneth K. Wong and Margaret C. Wang.

School Boards: Changing Local Control (1992). Edited by Patricia F. First and Herbert J. Walberg.

The two final volumes in this series were:

Improving Science Education (1995). Edited by Barry J. Fraser and Herbert J. Walberg.

Ferment in Education: A Look Abroad (1995). Edited by John J. Lane.

These two volumes may be ordered from the Book Order Department, University of Chicago Press, 11030 S. Langley Ave., Chicago, IL 60628. Phone: 312-669-2215; Fax: 312-660-2235.